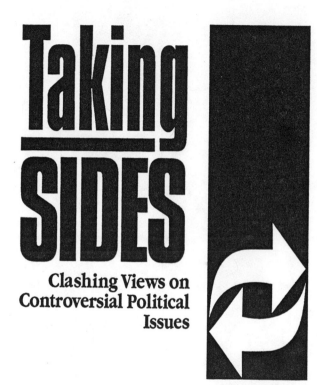

Taking SIDES

Clashing Views on Controversial Political Issues

Ninth Edition

Taking SIDES

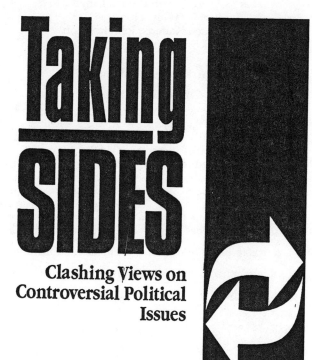

Clashing Views on Controversial Political Issues

Ninth Edition

Edited, Selected, and with Introductions by

George McKenna
City College, City University of New York

and

Stanley Feingold
Westchester Community College

The Dushkin Publishing Group, Inc.

In memory of Hillman M. Bishop and Samuel Hendel, masters of an art often neglected by college teachers: teaching.

Photo Acknowledgments

Part 1   New York Stock Exchange
Part 2   White House
Part 3   United Nations/John Robaton
Part 4   New York State Department of Commerce

Cover Art Acknowledgment

Charles Vitelli

Library of Congress Cataloging-in-Publication Data

Main entry under title:
    Taking sides: clashing views on controversial political issues/edited, selected, and with introductions by George McKenna and Stanley Feingold.—9th ed.
    Includes bibliographical references and index.
    1. Social conflict—United States. 2. Social problems. 3. United States—Social conditions—1980-. 4. United States—Social policy—1980-1993. I. McKenna, George, *comp*. II. Feingold, Stanley, *comp*.
    HN59.2.T35   303.6'0973—dc20
    1-56134-322-6   94-34809

The Dushkin Publishing Group, Inc.

PREFACE

Dialogue means two people talking to the same issue. This is not as easy as it sounds. Play back the next serious conversation you hear between zealots on opposing sides of a controversial issue; listen to them try to persuade one another of the truth, logic, and virtue of their own views and the falsity, irrationality, and downright evil of the others'.

What is likely to go wrong? At the outset, they are unlikely to make clear the nature of the issue, defining or describing it with enough clarity and specificity to make sure that they are both talking about the same area of controversy. As they proceed, they are likely to employ vague, emotion-laden terms without spelling out the uses to which the terms are put. When the heat is on, they may resort to shouting epithets at one another, and the hoped-for meeting of minds will give way to the scoring of political points and the reinforcement of existing prejudices. When, for example, the discussion of affirmative action comes down to both sides accusing the other of "racism," or when the controversy over abortion degenerates into taunts and name-calling, then no one really listens and learns from the other side.

It is our conviction that people *can* learn from the other side, no matter how sharply opposed it is to their own cherished viewpoint. Sometimes, after listening to others, we change our view entirely. But in most cases, we either incorporate some elements of the opposing view—thus making our own richer—or else learn how to answer the objections to our viewpoint. Either way, we gain from the experience. For these reasons we believe that encouraging dialogue between opposed positions is the most certain way of enhancing public understanding.

The purpose of this ninth edition of *Taking Sides* is to continue to work toward the revival of political dialogue in America. As we have done in the past eight editions, we examine leading issues in American politics from the perspective of sharply opposed points of view. We have tried to select authors who argue their points vigorously but in such a way as to enhance our understanding of the issue.

We hope that the reader who confronts lively and thoughtful statements on vital issues will be stimulated to ask some of the critical questions about American politics. What are the highest-priority issues with which government must deal today? What positions should be taken on these issues? What should be the attitude of Americans toward their government? To what extent, if any, does it need to be changed? How should it be organized in order to achieve the goals we set for it? What are these goals? Our conviction is that a healthy, stable democracy requires a citizenry that considers these questions and participates, however indirectly, in answering them. The alternative is apathy, passivity, and, sooner or later, the rule of tyrants.

i

Plan of the book   Each issue has an issue *introduction*, which sets the stage for the debate as it is argued in the YES and NO selections. Each issue concludes with a *postscript* that makes some final observations and points the way to other questions related to the issue. In reading the issue and forming your own opinions you should not feel confined to adopt one or the other of the positions presented. There are positions in between the given views or totally outside them, and the *suggestions for further reading* that appear in each issue postscript should help you find resources to continue your study of the subject. At the back of the book is a listing of all the *contributors to this volume*, which will give you information on the political scientists and commentators whose views are debated here.

Changes to this edition   Over the past 16 years we have put out eight editions of this book, each time revising and updating it extensively. For this ninth edition, we virtually stripped the book apart, top to bottom, and rebuilt it with new material.

Thirteen issues—well over half the book—are brand new in this edition. They include: *Do Political Campaigns Inform Voters?* (Issue 2); *Should There Be Term Limits for Members of Congress?* (Issue 5); *Do We Need a Strong Presidency?* (Issue 6); *Will Mandatory Sentencing Reduce Crime?* (Issue 9); *Do We Need Tougher Gun Control Laws?* (Issue 11); *Should Hate Speech Be Punished?* (Issue 13); *Should Welfare Recipients Be Put to Work?* (Issue 14); *Do We Need National Health Care Insurance?* (Issue 15); *Should Women Have a Right to Abortion?* (Issue 16); *Does the Religious Right Threaten American Freedoms?* (Issue 17); *Must America Be the World Leader?* (Issue 18); *Should the United States Pursue Economic Competitiveness?* (Issue 19); and *Should the United States Put More Restrictions on Immigration?* (Issue 20). In addition, we have changed five of the carry-over issues so completely that we feel we should count them as brand new. They include: *Is American Government Dominated by Big Business?* (Issue 1); *Does the News Media Have a Liberal Bias?* (Issue 4); *Does the Government Regulate Too Much?* (Issue 7); *Is Capital Punishment Justified?* (Issue 10); and *Is Affirmative Action Reverse Discrimination?* (Issue 12). Altogether there are 36 new selections in this edition. More than 85 percent of the book is new material.

We worked hard on this, and we hope you will be delighted with the result. Let us know what you think by dropping us a line in care of The Dushkin Publishing Group, Inc., Sluice Dock, Guilford, CT 06437. Suggestions for further improvement are always welcome.

A word to the instructor   An *Instructor's Manual With Test Questions* (multiple-choice and essay) is available through the publisher. A general guidebook, called *Using Taking Sides in the Classroom*, which discusses methods and techniques for integrating the pro/con approach into any classroom setting, is also available.

Acknowledgments We received many helpful comments and suggestions from our friends and readers across the United States and Canada. Their suggestions have markedly enhanced the quality of this edition of *Taking Sides* and are reflected in the totally new issues and the updated selections.

Our thanks go to those who responded with suggestions for the ninth edition:

Larry R. Beck
New Mexico State University

Robert L. Bock
Western New England
 College

Gene A. Brewer
Truett McConnell College

Gary Bryner
Brigham Young University

Larry Carps
Northwestern Michigan
 College

Kenneth N. Ciboski
Wichita State University

Lawrence Fleischer
City College, City University
 of New York

Terry Garrett
University of Central
 Oklahoma

Sharon E. Gramby
Rutgers University

Joe Green
Dixie College

Ruth M. Grubel
University of
 Wisconsin–Whitewater

Robert J. Kelly
Brooklyn College

John J. Kennedy
Kutztown University

Sherry Moore Malone
Truett McConnell College

Theodore R. Mosch
University of Tennessee

Harold W. Moses
Bethune-Cookman College

Roger Murphy
Indiana University,
 Bloomington

Timothy J. O'Neill
Southwestern University

Paul C. Phillips
University of Maryland

Jeffrey L. Prewitt
Appalachian State University

Robert H. Puckett
Indiana State University

James H. Read
St. John's University

Theodore Reller
Canada College

Todd M. Schaefer
Colorado College

Stewart P. Shapiro
Bentley College

Kathy Smith
Wake Forest University

Zachary Smith
Northern Arizona University

Stephen Sobieck   Robert M. Speel
Citrus College   Behrend College

We also appreciate the spontaneous letters from instructors and students who wrote to us with comments and observations. We wish to acknowledge the support given to this project by Rick Connelly, president of The Dushkin Publishing Group. We are grateful as well to Mimi Egan, publisher for the Taking Sides series, for her very able editorial supervision. Needless to say, the responsibility for any errors of fact or judgment rests with us.

George McKenna
City College, City University of New York

Stanley Feingold
Westchester Community College

CONTENTS IN BRIEF

CONTENTS

Political reporter Thomas Byrne Edsall argues that the increasing political sophistication of big business has given it more power in the government than ever before. Jeffrey M. Berry, a professor of political science, contends that public interest pressure groups have effectively challenged the political power of big business.

Professor of political science Samuel L. Popkin argues that presidential election campaigns inform and unify the American people. Political scientist Gil Troy maintains that modern campaigns alienate voters because the candidates tend to ignore the important issues.

Fred Wertheimer, the president of Common Cause, a citizen's lobbying organization, argues that PACs allow special interests to get the ear of elected officials at the expense of the national interest. Political analyst Herbert E. Alexander insists that PACs help enhance the political power of the individual.

Journalism professor H. Joachim Maitre argues that news reporters are liberals who allow their political views to seep into their reporting. Media critics Martin A. Lee and Norman Solomon argue that media bias in reporting is toward the conservative status quo.

Columnist George Will argues that term limits will bring fresh perspectives into Congress and restore the spirit of citizen politics. Associate professor of government Charles R. Kesler contends that term limits will deprive the nation of the wisdom gained by incumbents.

Political writer Terry Eastland argues that only a strong president can fulfill the requirements of modern government. Political scientist Donald L. Robinson maintains that shared power between the president and Congress will help prevent future abuses of executive authority.

Attorney Robert B. Charles argues that government regulation cripples the productivity of American industry. Professor of public administration Susan Tolchin and journalist Martin Tolchin contend that without vigorous regulation, businesses will endanger lives for the sake of profits.

Former judge Robert H. Bork argues that the "original intent" of the framers of the Constitution can and should be upheld by the federal courts of today. Professor of history Leonard W. Levy believes that the "original intent" of the framers cannot be applied in dealing with contemporary constitutional issues.

James Wootton, the president of Safe Streets Alliance in Washington, D.C., argues that mandatory sentencing sends a signal to would-be felons that they will pay heavily if they commit a crime. Judge Lois G. Forer contends that mandatory sentencing not only fails to deter crime, but it disrupts families, increases welfare costs, and hurts the poor and minorities.

Essayist Robert W. Lee argues that capital punishment is the only fair response to certain heinous crimes. Matthew L. Stephens, a prison chaplain, contends that the death penalty is motivated by revenge and is racist in its result.

Writer Carl Bogus argues that gun control laws will reduce the number of gun-related crimes. Professor of law Daniel D. Polsby contends that gun control laws may actually increase the incidence of robbery and other gun-related crimes.

Associate professor of English Shelby Steele argues that affirmative action programs demoralize both blacks and whites. Professor of law Stanley Fish asserts that affirmative action ultimately eliminates the advantages that whites have historically held over blacks.

Charles Lawrence III, a professor of law, believes that speech should be impermissible when it inflicts injury on its victims. Nadine Strossen, executive director of the American Civil Liberties Union, concludes that any limits on speech threatens the expression of all ideas.

Magazine editor Mickey Kaus believes that replacing welfare payments with jobs will restore family and community cohesion and reduce crime and poverty. Social scientists Richard A. Cloward and Francis Fox Piven maintain that workfare will greatly increase welfare costs without raising the living standards of the poor.

President Bill Clinton argues that a new health care system aimed at providing universal and affordable coverage for all Americans must be implemented. Irwin M. Stelzer, the director of Regulatory Policy Studies at the American Enterprise Institute, maintains that any radical changes in the American health care system will imperil the quality of medicine.

Philosopher Ronald Dworkin argues that women have a right to control their own bodies, including making the decision to have an abortion. Philosopher Francis J. Beckwith maintains that pro-choice arguments cannot withstand logical and moral analysis.

Anti-Defamation League analyst David Cantor warns that the "religious right" seeks to impose its moral views on American society. Republican U.S. representative Dick Armey (Texas) believes that traditional values are promoted by cultural and religious conservatives who oppose having values imposed upon them.

The late president Richard M. Nixon argues that America is the only responsible power with the ability to lead the world. Writer Jonathan Clarke says that the United States must stop trying to play the world's policeman.

Economist Lester Thurow believes that America must redirect its economy to compete more successfully in international markets. Economist Paul Krugman believes that an obsession with international competitiveness may be damaging to increased economic well-being.

Daniel James, an advisor to Carrying Capacity Network in Washington, D.C., wants a moratorium on immigration, which, he claims, is causing America much social and economic harm. Economist Stephen Moore insists that immigrants have greatly enriched the American economy and culture.

Foreign policy strategist Edward N. Luttwak contends that the United States
is declining in power because of the failure of its economic policies and social
programs. *Wall Street Journal* editor Robert L. Bartley asserts that America
will continue to play the role of world leader.

INTRODUCTION

Labels and Alignments in American Politics

George McKenna
Stanley Feingold

Liberalism, conservatism, radicalism, pluralism, left wing, right wing, moderate, extremist, radical—do these terms have any meaning? Or are they just descriptive words that are used to rally the faithful and batter the enemy? Are they, as Shakespeare would have said, full of sound and fury but signifying nothing, or do they contain some specific, core meanings? We think that they do have intelligible meanings; however, they must be used thoughtfully. Otherwise, the terms may end up obscuring or oversimplifying positions. Our purpose in this Introduction is to explore the basic, core meanings of these terms in order to make them useful to us as citizens.

LIBERALS VERSUS CONSERVATIVES: AN OVERVIEW

Let us examine, very briefly, the historical evolution of the terms *liberalism* and *conservatism*. By examining the roots of these terms, we can see how these philosophies have adapted themselves to changing times. In that way, we can avoid using the terms rigidly, without reference to the particular contexts in which liberalism and conservatism have operated over the past two centuries.

Classical Liberalism

The classical root of the term liberalism is the Latin word *libertas*, meaning "liberty" or "freedom." In the early nineteenth century, liberals dedicated themselves to freeing individuals from all unnecessary and oppressive obligations to authority—whether the authority came from the church or the state. They opposed the licensing and censorship of the press, the punishment of heresy, the establishment of religion, and any attempt to dictate orthodoxy in matters of opinion. In economics, liberals opposed state monopolies and other constraints upon competition between private businesses. At this point in its development, liberalism defined freedom primarily in terms of freedom *from*. It appropriated the French term *laissez-faire*, which literally means "leave to be." Leave people alone! That was the spirit of liberalism in its early days. It wanted government to stay out of people's lives and to play a modest role in general. Thomas Jefferson summed up this concept when he said, "I am no friend of energetic government. It is always oppressive."

Despite their suspicion of government, classical liberals invested high hopes in the political process. By and large, they were great believers in democracy. They believed in widening suffrage to include every white male, and some of them were prepared to enfranchise women and blacks as well. Although liberals occasionally worried about "the tyranny of the majority," they were more prepared to trust the masses than to trust a permanent, entrenched elite. Liberal social policy was dedicated to fulfilling human potential and was based on the assumption that this often-hidden potential is enormous. Human beings, liberals argued, were basically good and reasonable. Evil and irrationality were believed to be caused by "outside" influences; they were the result of a bad social environment. A liberal commonwealth, therefore, was one that would remove the hindrances to the full flowering of the human personality.

The basic vision of liberalism has not changed since the nineteenth century. What has changed is the way it is applied to modern society. In that respect, liberalism has changed dramatically. Today, instead of regarding government with suspicion, liberals welcome government as an instrument to serve the people. The change in philosophy began in the latter years of the nineteenth century, when businesses—once small, independent operations—began to grow into giant structures that overwhelmed individuals and sometimes even overshadowed the state in power and wealth. At that time, liberals began reconsidering their commitment to the *laissez-faire* philosophy. If the state can be an oppressor, asked liberals, can't big business also oppress people? By then, many were convinced that commercial and industrial monopolies were crushing the souls and bodies of the working classes. The state, formerly the villain, now was viewed by liberals as a potential savior. The concept of freedom was transformed into something more than a negative freedom *from*; the term began to take on a positive meaning. It meant "realizing one's full potential." Toward this end, liberals believed, the state could prove to be a valuable instrument. It could educate children, protect the health and safety of workers, help people through hard times, promote a healthy economy, and—when necessary—force business to act more humanely and responsibly. Thus was born the movement that culminated in New Deal liberalism.

New Deal Liberalism

In the United States, the argument in favor of state intervention did not win a truly popular constituency until after the Great Depression of the 1930s began to be felt deeply. The disastrous effects of a depression that left a quarter of the workforce unemployed opened the way to a new administration—and a promise. "I pledge you, I pledge myself," Franklin D. Roosevelt said when accepting the Democratic nomination in 1932, "to a new deal for the American people." Roosevelt's New Deal was an attempt to effect relief and recovery from the Depression; it employed a variety of means, including welfare programs, public works, and business regulation—most of which involved government intervention in the economy. The New Deal liberalism relied on government to liberate people from poverty, oppression, and economic exploitation. At the same time, the New Dealers claimed to be as zealous as the classical liberals in defending political and civil liberties.

The common element in *laissez-faire* liberalism and welfare-state liberalism is their dedication to the goal of realizing the full potential of each individual. Some still questioned whether this was best done by minimizing state involvement or whether it sometimes requires an activist state. The New Dealers took the latter view, though they prided themselves on being pragmatic and experimental about their activism. During the heyday of the New Deal, a wide variety of programs were tried and—if found wanting—abandoned. All decent means should be tried, they believed, even if it meant dilution of ideological purity. The Roosevelt administration, for example, denounced bankers and businessmen in campaign rhetoric but worked very closely with them while trying to extricate the nation from the Depression. This set a pattern of pragmatism that New Dealers from Harry Truman to Lyndon Johnson emulated.

Progressive Liberalism

Progressive liberalism emerged in the late 1960s and early 1970s as a more militant and uncompromising movement than the New Deal had ever been. Its roots go back to the New Left student movement of the early 1960s. New Left students went to the South to participate in civil rights demonstrations, and many of them were bloodied in confrontations with southern police; by the mid-1960s they were confronting the authorities in the North over issues like poverty and the Vietnam War. By the end of the decade, the New Left had fragmented into a variety of factions and had lost much of its vitality, but a somewhat more respectable version of it appeared as the New Politics movement. Many New Politics crusaders were former New Leftists who had traded their jeans for coats and ties; they tried to work within the system instead of always confronting it. Even so, they retained some of the spirit of the New Left. The civil rights slogan "Freedom Now" expressed the mood of the New Politics. The young university graduates who filled its ranks had come from an environment where "nonnegotiable" demands were issued to college deans by leaders of sit-in protests. There was more than youthful arrogance in the New Politics movement, however; there was a pervasive belief that America had lost, had compromised away, much of its idealism. The New Politics liberals sought to recover some of that spirit by linking up with an older tradition of militant reform, which went back to the time of the Revolution. These new liberals saw themselves as the authentic heirs of Thomas Paine and Henry David Thoreau, of the abolitionists, the radical populists, the suffragettes, and the great progressive reformers of the early twentieth century.

While New Deal liberals concentrated almost exclusively on bread-and-butter issues such as unemployment and poverty, the New Politics liberals introduced what came to be known as social issues into the political arena. These included: the repeal of laws against abortion, the liberalization of laws against homosexuality and pornography, the establishment of affirmative action programs to ensure increased hiring of minorities and women, and the passage of the Equal Rights Amendment. In foreign policy too, New Politics liberals departed from the New Deal agenda. Because they had keener memories of the unpopular and (for them) unjustified war in Vietnam than of World War II, they became doves, in contrast to the general hawkishness of the New Dealers. They were skeptical of any claim that the United States must be the leader of the free world or, indeed, that it had any special mission in the world; some were convinced that America was already in decline and must learn to adjust accordingly. The real danger, they argued, came not from the Soviet Union but from the mad pace of our arms race with the Soviets, which, as they saw it, could bankrupt the country, starve our social programs, and culminate in a nuclear Armageddon.

New Politics liberals were heavily represented at the 1972 Democratic national convention, which nominated South Dakota senator George McGovern for president. By the 1980s, the New Politics movement was no longer new, and many of its adherents preferred to be called progressives. By this time their critics had another name for them: radicals. The critics saw their positions as inimical to the interests of the United States, destructive of the family, and fundamentally at odds with the views of most Americans. The adversaries of the progressives were not only conservatives but many New Deal liberals, who openly scorned the McGovernites.

This split still exists within the Democratic party, though it is now more skillfully managed by party leaders. In 1988 the Democrats paired Michael Dukakis, whose Massachusetts supporters were generally on the progressive side of the party, with New Dealer Lloyd Bentsen as the presidential and vice-presidential candidates, respectively. In 1992 the Democrats won the presidency with Arkansas governor Bill Clinton, whose record as governor seemed to put him in the moderate-to-conservative camp, and Tennessee senator Albert Gore, whose position on environmental issues could probably be considered quite liberal but whose general image was middle-of-the-road. Both candidates had moved toward liberal positions on the issues of gay rights and abortion.

Conservatism
Like liberalism, conservatism has undergone historical transformation in America. Just as early liberals (represented by Thomas Jefferson) espoused less government, early conservatives (whose earliest leaders were Alexander Hamilton and John Adams) urged government support of economic enterprise and government intervention on behalf of privileged groups. By the time of the New Deal, and in reaction to the growth of the welfare state since that time, conservatives had argued strongly that more government means more unjustified interference in citizens' lives, more bureaucratic regulation of private conduct, more inhibiting control of economic enterprise, more material advantage for the less energetic and less able at the expense of those

who are prepared to work harder and better, and, of course, more taxes—taxes that will be taken from those who have earned money and given to those who have not.

Contemporary conservatives are not always opposed to state intervention. They may support larger military expenditures in order to protect society against foreign enemies. They may also allow for some intrusion into private life in order to protect society against internal subversion and would pursue criminal prosecution zealously in order to protect society against domestic violence. The fact is that few conservatives, and perhaps fewer liberals, are absolute with respect to their views about the power of the state. Both are quite prepared to use the state in order to further *their* purposes. It is true that activist presidents such as Franklin Roosevelt and John Kennedy were likely to be classified as liberals. However, Richard Nixon was also an activist, and, although he does not easily fit any classification, he was far closer to conservatism than to liberalism. It is too easy to identify liberalism with statism and conservatism with antistatism; it is important to remember that it was liberal Jefferson who counseled against "energetic government" and conservative Alexander Hamilton who designed bold powers for the new central government and wrote: "Energy in the executive is a leading character in the definition of good government."

Neoconservatism and the New Right

Two newer varieties of conservatism have arisen to challenge the dominant strain of conservatism that opposed the New Deal. Those who call themselves (or have finally allowed themselves to be called) neoconservatives are recent converts to conservatism. Many of them are former New Deal Democrats, and some like to argue that it is not they who have changed, it is the Democratic party, which has allowed itself to be taken over by advocates of progressive liberalism. They recognize, as did the New Dealers, the legitimacy of social reform, but now they warn against carrying it too far and creating an arrogant bureaucracy. They support equal opportunity, as they always did, but now they underscore the distinction between equal opportunity and equality of result, which they identify as the goal of affirmative action programs. Broadly speaking, neoconservatism shares with the older variety of conservatism a high respect for tradition and a view of human nature that some would call pessimistic. Neoconservatives, like all conservatives, are also deeply concerned about the communist threat to America. They advise shoring up America's defenses and resisting any movement that would lead the nation toward unilateral disarmament.

A more recent and more politically active variant of conservatism is called the New Right. Despite the semantic resemblance between the New Right and neoconservatism, the two differ in important ways. Neoconservatives are usually lapsed liberals, while New Rightists tend to be dyed-in-the-wool conservatives—though ones who are determined to appeal to wider constituencies than did the "old" Right. Neoconservatives tend to be academics, who appeal to other similar elites through books and articles in learned journals. The New Right aims at reaching grassroots voters through a variety of forums, from church groups to direct-mail solicitation. Neoconservatives customarily talk about political-economic structures and global strategies; New Rightists emphasize the concerns of ordinary Americans, what they call family issues—moral concerns such as abortion, prayer in public schools, pornography, and what they consider to be a general climate of moral breakdown in the nation. These family issues are very similar to the social issues introduced into the political arena by the advocates of progressive liberalism. This should not be surprising, since the rise of the New Right was a reaction to the previous success of the progressive movement in legitimizing its stands on social issues.

Spokesmen for progressive liberalism and the New Right stand as polar opposites: The former regard abortion as a woman's right; the latter see it as legalized murder. The former tend to regard homosexuality as a lifestyle that needs protection against discrimination; the latter are more likely to see it as a perversion. The former have made an issue of their support for the Equal Rights Amendment; the latter includes large numbers of women who fought against the amendment because they believed it threatened their role identity. The list of issues could go on. The New Right and the progressive liberals are like positive and negative photographs of America's moral landscape. Sociologist James Davison Hunter uses the term *culture wars* to characterize the struggles between these contrary visions of America. For all the differences between progressive liberalism and the New Right, however, their styles are very similar. They are heavily laced with moralistic prose; they tend to equate compromise with selling out; and they claim to represent the best, most authentic traditions of America. This is not to denigrate either movement, for the kinds of issues they address are indeed moral issues, which do not generally admit much compromise. These issues cannot simply be finessed or ignored, despite the efforts of conventional politicians to do so. They must be aired and fought over, which is why we include some of them, such as abortion (Issue 16) and church-state relations (Issue 17), in this volume.

RADICALS, REACTIONARIES, AND MODERATES

The label *reactionary* is almost an insult, and the label *radical* is worn with pride by only a few zealots on the banks of the political mainstream. A reactionary is not a conserver but a backward-mover, dedicated to turning the clock back to better times. Most people suspect that reactionaries would restore us to a time that never was, except in political myth. For many, the repeal of industrialism or universal education (or the entire twentieth century itself) is not a practical, let alone desirable, political program.

Radicalism (literally meaning "from the roots" or "going to the foundation") implies a fundamental reconstruction of the social order. Taken in that sense, it is possible to speak of right-wing radicalism as well as left-wing radicalism—radicalism that would restore or inaugurate a new hierarchical society as well as radicalism that calls for nothing less than an egalitarian society. The term is sometimes used in both of these senses, but most often the word *radicalism* is reserved to characterize more liberal change. While the liberal would effect change through conventional democratic processes, the radical is likely to be skeptical about the ability of the established machinery to bring about the needed change and might be prepared to sacrifice "a little" liberty to bring about a great deal more equality.

Moderate is a highly coveted label in America. Its meaning is not precise, but it carries the connotations of sensible, balanced, and practical. A moderate person is not without principles, but he or she does not allow principles to harden into dogma. The opposite of moderate is extremist, a label most American political leaders eschew. Yet, there have been notable exceptions. When Arizona senator Barry Goldwater, a conservative Republican, was nominated for president in 1964, he declared, "Extremism in defense of liberty is no vice! . . . Moderation in the pursuit of justice is no virtue!" This open embrace of extremism did not help his electoral chances; Goldwater was overwhelmingly defeated. At about the same time, however, another American political leader also embraced a kind of extremism, and with better results. In a famous letter written from a jail cell in Birmingham, Alabama, the Reverend Martin Luther King, Jr., replied to the charge that he was an extremist not by denying it but by distinguishing between different kinds of extremists. The question, he wrote, "is not whether we will be extremist but what kind of extremist will we be. Will we be extremists for hate, or will we be extremists for love?" King aligned himself with the love extremists, in which category he also placed Jesus, St. Paul, and Thomas Jefferson, among others. It was an adroit use of a label that is usually anathema in America.

PLURALISM

The principle of pluralism espouses diversity in a society containing many interest groups and in a government containing competing units of power. This implies the widest expression of competing ideas, and in this way, pluralism is in sympathy with an important element of liberalism. However, as James Madison and Alexander Hamilton pointed out when they analyzed the sources of pluralism in the *Federalist* commentaries on the Constitution, this philosophy springs from a profoundly pessimistic view of human nature, and in this respect it more closely resembles conservatism. Madison, possibly the single most influential member of the convention that wrote the Constitution, hoped that in a large and varied nation, no single interest group could control the government. Even if there were a majority interest, it would be unlikely to capture all of the national agencies of government—the House of Representatives, the Senate, the presidency and the federal judiciary —each of which was chosen in a different way by a different constituency for a different term of office. Moreover, to make certain that no one branch exercised excessive power, each was equipped with "checks and balances" that enabled any agency of national government to curb the powers of the others. The clearest statement of Madison's, and the Constitution's, theory can be found in the 51st paper of the *Federalist:*

> It may be a reflection on human nature that such devices should be necessary to control the abuses of government. But what is government itself, but the greatest of all reflections on human nature? If men were angels, no government would be necessary.

This pluralist position may be analyzed from different perspectives. It is conservative insofar as it rejects simple majority rule; yet it is liberal insofar as it rejects rule by a single elite. It is conservative in its pessimistic appraisal of human nature; yet pluralism's pessimism is also a kind of egalitarianism, holding as it does that no one can be trusted with power and that majority interests no less than minority interests will use power for selfish ends. It is possible to suggest that in America pluralism represents an alternative to both liberalism and conservatism. Pluralism is antimajoritarian and antielitist and combines some elements of both.

SOME APPLICATIONS

Despite our effort to define the principal alignments in American politics, some policy decisions do not neatly fit into these categories. Readers will reach their own conclusions, but we may suggest some alignments to be found here in order to demonstrate the variety of viewpoints.

The conflicts between liberalism and conservatism are expressed in the opposing approaches of Lois Forer and James Wootton to the question of how to deal with crime (Issue 9). Wootton's defense of mandatory sentencing proceeds from the conservative premise that the best way to fight crime is to get criminals off of the streets and to show would-be criminals that punishment for crime will be swift and certain. Forer, who believes that most violent crime is impulsive, adopts the liberal view that society should aim to rehabilitate rather than simply punish criminals. More difficult to classify is the issue of whether or not the government regulates too much (Issue 7). Susan Tolchin and Martin Tolchin's defense of government regulation is compatible with either New Deal or progressive liberalism, while Robert Charles's case against regulation is reminiscent of classical liberalism, or libertarianism.

Robert Lee's defense of the death penalty (Issue 10) is a classic conservative argument. Like other conservatives, Lee is skeptical of the possibilities of human perfection, and he therefore regards retribution—giving a murderer what he or she "deserves" instead of attempting some sort of "rehabilitation" —as a legitimate goal of punishment. Affirmative action, the topic of Issue 12, has become a litmus test of the newer brand of progressive liberalism. The progressives say that it is not enough for the laws of society to be color-blind or gender-blind; they must now reach out to remedy the ills caused by racism and sexism. New Deal liberals, along with conservatives and libertarians, generally oppose affirmative action, which they regard as racism in reverse. The welfare debate (Issue 14) also pits a New Deal viewpoint against a more leftist, progressive brand of liberalism. Mickey Kaus suggests ending welfare not simply by cutting it off—the conservative solution—but by putting poor people to work on government-sponsored projects like those of the Works Progress Administration (WPA) in the Roosevelt administration during the 1930s. Kaus thus fits the mold of New Deal liberalism. His view is opposed by Richard Cloward and Frances Fox Piven, who regard his solution as simply another means to keep wages down. They share the progressives' suspicion of any program that seeks to force poor people into work programs.

Former federal court of appeals judge Robert Bork's case (in Issue 8) for using "original intent" as the basis of constitutional interpretation is a classic conservative argument, seeking as it does to extract from the thought of the Constitution's founders some authentic guide for interpreting the Constitution today. Leonard Levy's criticism of this approach is liberal in its insistence that the Constitution's meaning must change with the times.

The argument over national health care insurance (Issue 15) also divides along liberal-conservative lines. Despite the distaste congressional liberals have for President Bill Clinton's health care proposals, liberals have long favored *some* form of national health insurance. Conservatives, however, tend to share the view expressed by Irwin Stelzer that there really is no health care "crisis" that requires a major new federal program. Another more or less predictable division between liberals and conservatives is on the issue of gun control (Issue 11). Liberals generally agree with Carl Bogus's view that stronger gun control laws than currently exist may reduce gun violence and at any rate are worth trying. Conservatives tend to agree with Daniel Polsby, who maintains that if gun control laws are tightened, criminals will be all the more tempted to use guns while committing crimes because they could then be reasonably sure that law-abiding citizens will not be carrying their own guns for self-defense. The arguments over bias in the news media (Issue 4) and the religious right (Issue 17) have conservatives on one side and different kinds of liberals on the other. Representative Dick Armey (R-Texas), who defends the religious right, is a self-proclaimed conservative; by contrast, David Cantor of the Anti-Defamation League criticizes the religious right from a traditional liberal perspective. H. Joachim Maitre, also taking a conservative perspective, argues that the news media have a liberal bias, while Martin Lee and Norman Solomon, who argue that the media are too conservative, seem more like progressive liberals.

This book contains a few arguments that are not easy to categorize. The issue on hate speech (Issue 13) is one. Liberals traditionally have opposed any curbs on free speech, but Charles Lawrence, who would certainly not call himself a conservative, believes that curbs on speech that abuses minorities may be necessary. Opposing him is Nadine Strossen of the American Civil Liberties Union, who takes the traditional liberal view that we must protect even the thoughts that we hate. Issue 16, on whether or not women have a right to abortion, also eludes easy classification with regard to liberal-conservative lines. The pro-choice position, as argued by Ronald Dworkin, is not a traditional liberal position. Less than a generation ago, liberals such as Senator Edward M. Kennedy (D-Massachusetts) and the Reverend Jesse Jackson opposed outright legalized abortion, and even today some liberals—such as Pennsylvania governor Robert Casey and columnist Nat Hentoff—continue to oppose it. Nevertheless, most liberals now adopt some version or another of Dworkin's pro-choice philosophy—although Francis Beckwith, who opposes Dworkin's view, does so in part on civil rights grounds, which sounds more liberal than conservative.

Issue 18, on America's role as a world leader, features former president Richard Nixon's argument that America must remain a world leader and Jonathan Clarke's argument that such views would simply freeze U.S. foreign policy into a "neo–cold war orthodoxy." Nixon was no reactionary in matters of foreign policy—he was the first to break the ice of the cold war with the Soviet Union and China—but his overall view of human nature and the human condition was conservative (he would likely call it "realistic"). Jonathan Clarke, on the other hand, deplores large amounts of defense spending, and he calls for a broadscale American disengagement from unilateral military commitments. Although a few conservatives might agree with Clarke, his position seems more in tune with post-Vietnam liberalism.

Obviously one's position on the issues in this book will be affected by circumstances. However, we would like to think that the essays in this book are durable enough to last through several seasons of events and controversies. We can be certain that the issues will survive. The search for coherence and consistency in the use of political labels underlines the options open to us and reveals their consequences. The result must be more mature judgments about what is best for America. That, of course, is the ultimate aim of public debate and decision making, and it transcends all labels and categories.

PART 1

Democracy and the American Political Process

Democracy *is derived from two Greek words,* dēmos *and* kratia, *and means "people's rule." The issue today is whether or not the political realities of America conform to the ideal of people's rule. Are the people really running the country? Some contend that big business runs the economy and controls the political agenda. Is that a fair charge, or is it based on simplistic premises? Political campaigns have come under fire in recent years for failing to give the voting population relevant information about the issues and candidates' positions on them. Is this true, or do campaigns provide a fair representation of candidates? Another issue generating controversy is the power of pressure groups, particularly that of political action committees (PACs). Do these groups undermine people's rule, or do they help to make democracy work? Finally, in this section, we address the issue of the news media's role in the governmental process.*

- Is American Government Dominated by Big Business?

- Do Political Campaigns Inform Voters?

- Do Political Action Committees Undermine Democracy?

- Does the News Media Have a Liberal Bias?

ISSUE 1

Is American Government Dominated by Big Business?

YES: Thomas Byrne Edsall, from *The New Politics of Inequality: How Political Power Shapes Economic Policy* (W. W. Norton, 1984)

NO: Jeffrey M. Berry, from "Citizen Groups and the Changing Nature of Interest Group Politics in America," *The Annals of the American Academy of Political and Social Science* (July 1993)

ISSUE SUMMARY

YES: Political reporter Thomas Byrne Edsall argues that the power of big business is stronger than ever because of the increasing political sophistication of big business coupled with the breakdown of political parties.

NO: Jeffrey M. Berry, a professor of political science, contends that public interest pressure groups that have entered the political arena since the end of the 1960s have effectively challenged the political power of big business.

Since the framing of the U.S. Constitution in 1787, there have been periodic charges that America is unduly influenced by wealthy financial interests. Richard Henry Lee, a signer of the Declaration of Independence, spoke for many Anti-Federalists (those who opposed ratification of the Constitution) when he warned that the proposed charter shifted power away from the people and into the hands of the "aristocrats" and "moneyites." Before the Civil War, Jacksonian Democrats denounced the eastern merchants and bankers who, they charged, were usurping the power of the people. After the Civil War, a number of radical parties and movements revived this theme of antielitism. The ferment—which was brought about by the rise of industrial monopolies, government corruption, and economic hardship for western farmers—culminated in the founding of the People's party at the beginning of the 1890s. The Populists, as they were more commonly called, wanted economic and political reforms aimed at transferring power away from the rich and back to "the plain people."

By the early 1900s the People's party had disintegrated, but many writers and activists have continued to echo the Populists' central thesis: that the U.S. democratic political system is in fact dominated by business elites. Yet the thesis has not gone unchallenged. During the 1950s and the early 1960s, many social scientists subscribed to the *pluralist* view of America. Pluralists argue that because there are many influential elites in America, each group has a tendency to counterbalance the power of the others. Labor groups are often opposed to business groups; conservative interests challenge liberal interests, and vice versa; organized civil libertarians sometimes fight with groups that seek government-imposed bans on pornography or groups that demand tougher criminal laws. No single group, the pluralists argue, can dominate the political system

Pluralists readily acknowledge that American government is not democratic in the full sense of the word; it is not driven by the majority. But neither, they insist, is it run by a conspiratorial "power elite." In the pluralist view, the closest description of the American form of government would be neither majority rule nor minority rule but *minorities* rule. (Note that in this context, "minorities" does not necessarily refer to racial or ethnic minorities but to any organized group of people with something in common—including race, religion, and social concerns—not constituting a majority of the population.) Each organized minority enjoys some degree of power in the making of public policy. In extreme cases, when a minority's back is to the wall, its power may take a purely negative form: the power to derail policy. When the majority—or, more accurately, a coalition of other minorities—attempts to pass some measure that threatens the vital interests of some organized minority, that group may use its power to disrupt the policy-making process. (Often cited in this connection is the use of the Senate filibuster, which is the practice of using tactics during the legislative process that cause extreme delays or prevent action, thus enabling a group to "talk to death" a bill that threatens its vital interests.) But in the pluralist view, these interests possess more than negative power: they often work together and reach consensus on certain issues, which results in new laws and policy initiatives that enjoy broad public support. Pluralism, then, does not have to produce gridlock. It may produce temporary gridlock when a group fears that it is about to be steamrolled by the majority, but ultimately it leads to compromise, consensus, and moderation.

Critics of pluralism argue that pluralism is an idealized, prettified depiction of a political system that is in the grip of powerful elite groups. Critics fault pluralist theory for what they consider to be its failure to acknowledge that big business dominates the policy-making process. They question the pluralist premise that interest groups contend with one another on a level playing field, believing instead that it is tilted in favor of big business. In the selections that follow, Thomas Byrne Edsall supports this view and argues that well-financed business groups, having learned from challengers to their power in the 1970s, now know how to more or less control the political process. Jeffrey M. Berry, in opposition, argues that thanks to new consumer, environmental, and other citizen groups, big business no longer enjoys the cozy relationship it once had with Washington policymakers.

YES

Thomas Byrne Edsall

THE NEW POLITICS OF INEQUALITY

In the United States in recent years there has been a significant erosion of the power of those on the bottom half of the economic spectrum, an erosion of the power not only of the poor but of those in the working and middle classes. At the same time, there has been a sharp increase in the power of economic elites, of those who fall in the top 15 percent of the income distribution.

This transfer of power has coincided with an economic crisis: productivity growth, which for the three decades following the Second World War had been the source of a continuing rise in the standard of living, slowed to zero by the end of the 1970s; the median family income, which had doubled in real, uninflated dollars from 1950 to 1973, declined during the next ten years, paralleling a decline in the average factory worker's weekly earnings; and inflation and unemployment, instead of acting as counterbalancing forces, rose simultaneously.

This mounting economic crisis provided an opportunity for newly ascendant representatives of the interests of the business community and of the affluent to win approval of a sea change in economic policy. For nearly fifty years, since the formation of the New Deal coalition in the 1930s, there had been a sustained base of support for both social spending programs and a tax system that modestly redistributed income and restricted the concentration of wealth in the hands of the few. These deeply rooted liberal traditions were abandoned during the late 1970s in favor of policies calling for a major reduction of the tax burden on income derived from capital, and for reductions in domestic spending programs directed toward the poor and the working poor. These shifts in tax and spending policies, in combination with inflation, have had enormous distributional consequences, resulting, for the period from 1980 through 1984, in losses for every income group except the very affluent.

Although the election of Ronald Reagan to the presidency has been the catalyst for much of this alteration of policy, its roots run far deeper. The delicate balance of power between elites and larger groups seeking representation in the political process has been changing in almost all quarters, including

From Thomas Byrne Edsall, *The New Politics of Inequality: How Political Power Shapes Economic Policy* (W. W. Norton, 1984). Copyright © 1984 by W. W. Norton and Company, Inc. Reprinted by permission. Notes omitted.

the Democratic party, the Republican party, the business lobbying community, organized labor, and the intellectual establishment. These changes have been both accelerated and exacerbated throughout the entire electorate by increasingly class-skewed voting patterns. In each of these areas, the changes are resulting in a diminution of the representation of the majority in the development of economic policy, and in the growing leverage of the well-to-do.

Underlying this shift in the balance of political power among economic groups is a changed economic environment that has forced fundamental revisions in political strategies for both political parties. The economic crisis of the past decade has cut to the heart of a tradition in American politics, particularly in Democratic politics, playing havoc with that party's tradition of capitalizing on a growing and thriving economy in order to finance a continuing expansion of benefits for those toward the bottom of the income distribution. Past economic growth had provided the federal government with a fiscal dividend in additional tax revenues with which to finance growth in such broad-based programs as Social Security and Medicare, while simultaneously maintaining popular support, as all wage earners benefited from rising real incomes.

Altered economic circumstances have turned politics into what Lester Thurow has termed a zero-sum process. The balance of power in the competition for the benefits of government has shifted increasingly in favor of those in the top third of the income distribution. In many respects these shifts have pushed the national debate well to the right of its locus ten or twenty years ago. In 1964, the Republican presidential nominee, Senator Barry Goldwater, was decisively defeated while advocating a major reduction in domestic federal spending and a sharp increase in military spending; sixteen years later, Ronald Reagan, one of Goldwater's most ardent supporters, was elected to the presidency on a platform remarkably similar to Goldwater's and succeeded in persuading Congress, including a Democratic House of Representatives, to act into law legislation that would have been politically inconceivable at any time during the previous fifty years.

The roots of this shift to the right are by now deeply imbedded in the political system, severely restricting the scope of choices available to either party particularly to the Democratic party. Just as the shift to the left in public policy in the early 1960s resulted from fundamental alterations in the balance of power—ranging from rapid postwar economic growth, to the cohesiveness of the liberal-labor coalition, to the political vitality of the civil rights movement—the shift to the right over the past decade has resulted from complex, systemic alterations in the terms of the political and economic debate and in the power of those participating in the debate.

... [C]onservative forces, ... are not only within the Republican party, the right-wing ideological groups, and the business community but within the Democratic party itself. Not only are these forces present in all major elements of the political system; even with economic recovery, lowered inflation, declining unemployment, and growth in the gross national product, the shape of economic and political pressures on the electorate at large would appear to preclude, for at least the near future, the emergence of a consensus in support of a revived liberal agenda. ...

During the 1970s, the political wing of the nation's corporate sector staged one of the most remarkable campaigns in the pursuit of political power in recent history. By the late 1970s and the early 1980s, business, and Washington's corporate lobbying community in particular, had gained a level of influence and leverage approaching that of the boom days of the 1920s. What made the acquisition of power in the 1970s remarkable was that business achieved its goals without any broad public-political mandate such as that of the 1920s, when probusiness values were affirmed in the elections of 1920, 1924, and 1928. Rather, business in the 1970s developed the ability to dominate the legislative process under adverse, if not hostile, circumstances. Corporate leaders had been closely associated with Watergate and its related scandals, and a reform-minded Democratic party with strong ties to the consumer and environmental movements had gained increasingly large majorities in Congress.

Despite these devastating odds, the political stature of business rose steadily from the early 1970s, one of its lowest points in the nation's history, until, by the end of the decade, the business community had achieved virtual dominance of the legislative process in Congress. The rise of the corporate sector is a case study in the ability of an economic elite to gain power by capitalizing on changes in the political system. In the case of the Democratic party, the shift in the balance of power toward the affluent, the erosion of the labor union movement, and the vastly increased importance of money in campaigns all combined to make Democratic politicians more vulnerable to pressures from the right. In the case of the Republican party, a de facto alliance has emerged between the GOP and much of the business community, a relationship paralleling the ties between the Democratic party and labor but lacking the inherent conflicts characteristic of that liaison. The political ascendancy of the business community, furthermore, has coincided with a sustained and largely successful attack upon organized labor, an attack conducted both in private-sector union representation fights and in legislative battles on Capitol Hill.

In 1978, in the midst of the corporate political revival, R. Heath Larry, president of the National Association of Manufacturers, contended that the single most important factor behind the resurgence of business was "the decline in the role of the party, yielding a new spirit of independence among congressmen—independent of each other, of the president, of the party caucus." Larry's perception of the role of the decline in political parties in the revival of the stature of business was accurate, but his contention that this decline produced increased independence is wrong. In fact, the collapse of political parties and of traditional political organizations, especially those at the local level that formerly had the power to assure or to deny reelection, has been a key factor in a network of forces and developments undermining the independence of politicians and augmenting the strength of the business community....

By the mid-1970s,... the decline of party loyalties, congressional reforms weakening the power of committee chairmen, and the diffusion of power to junior members of Congress forced a major alteration in lobbying strategies. "As long as you could go and get the cooperation of the committee chairman and the ranking members, and maybe a few others, you didn't have to have the vast network we are talking about now," [Ford Motor Company executive Wayne H.] Smithey noted. Smithey's reference to a "vast network" describes both the development of grass-roots lobbying as a legislative tactic and a much more pervasive effort to set the terms of the legislative debate in the nation's capital. Not only have the targets of lobbyists changed over the past generation, but the technology of public opinion molding has undergone changes of unprecedented magnitude, producing computerized direct-mail communications in which much of the nation's adult population has been broken down into demographic and "psychographic" profiles. A group or institution seeking to mobilize support or opposition on any issue can seek out ready-made lists of allies in the general public from computer specialists who can then communicate almost instantaneously with any selected constituency via letters produced on high-speed laser printers. If lobbying during the 1950s, in the words of one of the most eminent Washington lobbyists, Charles E. Walker, consisted of personal access to four natives of Texas—President Dwight Eisenhower, House Speaker Sam Rayburn, Senate Majority Leader Lyndon Baines Johnson, and Treasury Secretary Robert Anderson—it currently involves minimally the ability to recognize the interests of 535 members of the House and Senate, an acute sensitivity to potential malleability in public opinion, the cultivation of both print and electronic media, the use of sophisticated technologies both to create and to convey an impression of public sentiment, and the marshaling on Capitol Hill and across the country of legions of newly enlisted corporate personnel.

The effort on the part of the business community to shape the legisla-

tive debate has taken place on a number of fronts, one of the most important of which has been the politicization of employees and stockholders. Atlantic Richfield (Arco), for example, spends about $1 million annually on a program in which 15,000 employees are members of politically active local committees. In addition, the nearly 80,000 Arco stockholders, suppliers, and distributors are on a mailing list for company newsletters and publications focusing on political and public policy issues. W. Dean Cannon, Jr., executive vice-president of the California Savings and Loan League, suggested in 1978 to savings and loan firms that they give employees "specific assignments to work in politics" and that an employee's raises "might well be tied directly to his involvement in the political assignment you have given him." During the debate over the 1978 tax bill, officials of a single, mid-sized firm, the Barry Wright Corporation in Watertown, Mass, generated 3,800 letters from its stockholders to members of Congress in favor of a reduction in capital gains taxation.

The politicization of management-level employees is a critical element in achieving effective grass-roots lobbying: an employee who sees a direct economic interest in the outcome of legislative battles will be a far more effective and persistent advocate than an employee who is acting in response only to orders or implied orders from superiors. Stockholders, in turn, represent an ideal target for political mobilization. Only 15 percent of American citizens hold stock, according to liberal estimates by the Securities Industry Association, and those who do are, on average, in the upper-income brackets. They have little or no direct interest in the expansion or maintenance of domestic spending programs, although they have considerable interest in lowering tax rates. In this sense, the economic interests of affluent individuals and of corporations are sharply intertwined. Both stockholders and corporations, for example, share a direct interest in either lowering the capital gains rate or shortening the minimum holding period to qualify for the more favorable capital gains rate....

An equally, if not more, effective use of business money in altering the terms of the policy debate has been in the total or partial financing of such private institutions engaged in research and scholarship as the American Enterprise Institute; the Heritage Foundation; the Hoover Institution on War, Revolution and Peace; the National Bureau of Economic Research; the Center for the Study of American Business at Washington University in St. Louis, and the American Council for Capital Formation. In a decade during which economic stagnation contributed to the undermining of the intellectual basis of traditional Democratic economic and political strategies, these organizations, among others, have functioned to lay the scholarly and theoretical groundwork for a major shift in public policy favoring business and the higher-bracket taxpayers....

BUSINESS AND
ECONOMIC POLICY

The rising political power of business has been associated with the general increase in the number of political action committees [PACs] and with the growing volume of money channeled through them. This line of thinking, in turn, has given rise to charges that Congress, overwhelmed by the flow of cash from the PACs, has become the

puppet of special interests, a forum in which every organized group, from doctors to dairymen, can, in return for campaign contributions, receive special antitrust exemption from competition or from taxpayer-financed price supports, or special insulation from the federal regulatory process. The most vocal critic of the system has been Common Cause, the principal reform lobby. "Our system of representative government is under siege because of the destructive role that political action committees or PACs are now playing in our political process," Fred Wertheimer, president of Common Cause, declared in 1983....

These analyses, while both accurate and timely, fail to take into account a number of less frequently reported factors adding to the complexity and subtlety of the current political situation on Capitol Hill. For one, Common Cause and the press have become increasingly effective watchdogs over the legislative process, preventing many of the attempts by special-interest groups to slip through favorable legislation. More important, however, while these analyses, particularly [New Yorker correspondent Elizabeth] Drew's detailed description of the overwhelming concern with fundraising in Congress, accurately portray an essential element of the political process, neither recognizes what has been a major ideological shift in Congress. Business has played a key role in this shift, using not just PAC contributions but increasingly sophisticated grass-roots lobbying mechanisms, the financing of a sympathetic intellectual community, and the expenditure of somewhere in the neighborhood of $1 billion annually on institutional advertising.

This ideological shift in the nation's capital has been pervasive, alerting basic tax, spending, and regulatory policies and moving both political parties well to the right over the past decade. Of the various elites that have gained strength in recent years, business has been among the most effective. Not only has it gained from highly favorable tax treatment and from a major reduction in regulation, but government action has increased the bargaining leverage of management in its relations with organized labor. This increased leverage grows out of reductions in unemployment compensation and out of the elimination of the public service job programs, and through the appointment of promanagement officials at such key agencies as the Occupational Safety and Health Administration and at the National Labor Relations Board. The end result is a labor movement that has lost much of its clout at the negotiating table and in the polling booth....

THE WAGES OF INEQUALITY

In the late 1970s, a set of political and intellectual forces began to converge and to gain momentum, joining together in a direction that substantially altered economic policy in the United States. While the forces involved were by no means in agreement as to the specific goals to be achieved, they shared an interest in seeking to change the basic assumptions that have dominated taxation and spending policies in the United States. For nearly fifty years, since the administration of Franklin Delano Roosevelt, two dominant themes of taxation and spending policy have been equity and the moderate redistribution of income. The forces gaining ascendancy in the late 1970s sought to replace such liberal goals with a drive to slow the rate of growth in federal spending in order to increase the availability of

money for private capital formation; with a reduction of corporate and individual tax rates, particularly of those rates in the top brackets, in order to provide predicted incentives for work, savings, and investment; and with the paring down of government regulation to facilitate a more productive marketplace. In short, the goal became to influence government policy so as to supplant, in an economic sense, equity with efficiency.

The inherent contradictions between equity, efficiency, redistribution, and investment go to the heart of the conflict in developing economic policy in advanced capitalist democracies. The political resolution of such contradictions determines the balance between competing claims on government: that is, whether government is granted the authority to intervene in the private marketplace in order to correct or to modify inequities inherent in the market system, through a progressive tax rate schedule and through the payment of benefits to the poor; whether it is the role of government to subsidize, encourage, and direct marketplace forces with tax incentives and loan subsidies targeted toward specific industries; or whether government should reduce to a minimum its role in the economy, remaining as remote from and as disengaged as possible from the private sector.

The period from 1977 through the first months of 1982, however, marked a rare moment in American history, when the disparate forces supporting the conservative coalition on these basic economic questions all simultaneously became politically ascendant. Forces coalescing on the political right included a politically revitalized business community; increasing sophistication and centrality among leaders of the ideological new right; the sudden explosion of wealth in the domestic oil community following the 1973 OPEC embargo; the emergence within the academic community and within the major economic research institutions of proponents of tax cuts and of sharp reductions in the tax rate on capital income; a Republican party whose financial resources were exponentially increased by computerized direct-mail and other new political technologies, providing often decisive access to television, to polling, and to highly sophisticated voter targeting tactics; and the rise of politically conservative evangelical Christian organizations. The emergence of these forces coincided with a series of developments and trends giving conservatism new strength. The business and the new, or ideological, right-wing communities developed a shared interest in the candidates of the Republican party, as such organizations as the Chamber of Commerce and the National Conservative Political Action Committee became de facto arms of the GOP. Voting patterns increased the class bias of voter turnout, as the affluent became a stronger force both within the electorate as a whole and within the Republican party.

Conversely, the forces making up the liberal coalition, represented in large part by major segments of the Democratic party—organized labor, civil rights and civil liberties organizations, political reformers, environmental groups, and feminists—were experiencing increasing disunity. The power of organized labor, essential to any coalition of the left, had been steadily declining. Even more damaging was the emergence of growing inflation and unemployment, a continued decline in the rate of productivity growth, and a drop in the take-home pay of the average worker. This economic deterioration not only splintered the fragile coali-

tion of Democrats that had supported policies of equity and redistribution over the previous forty years but created a growing belief that the nation was caught in an economic crisis that the Democratic party could not resolve, a belief compounded by Democratic disarray.

It was this combination of trends, all favoring the right, that provided the opportunity for a major alteration in public policy. The election in 1980 of Ronald Reagan to the presidency and the takeover of the Senate by the Republican party created the political opportunity for this fundamental realignment, but the groundwork had already been carefully laid. This groundwork included an increasingly sophisticated political strategy capitalizing on the conflicts within the fragile Democratic majority, the careful nurturing and financing of intellectual support both in academia and within a growing network of think tanks financed by corporations and conservative foundations, and the advance preparation of specific legislative proposals, particularly of tax legislation....

The power shift that produced the fundamental policy realignment of the past decade did not result from a conservative or Republican realignment of the voters; nor did it produce such a realignment after the tax and spending legislation of 1981 was enacted. Rather, these policy changes have grown out of pervasive distortions in this country's democratic political process. These distortions have created a system of political decision making in which fundamental issues—the distribution of the tax burden, the degree to which the government sanctions the accumulation of wealth, the role of federal regulation, the level of publicly tolerated poverty, and the relative strength of labor and management—are resolved by an increasingly unrepresentative economic elite. To a large extent, these changes have turned the Republican party, in terms of the public policies it advocates, into a party of the elite. For the Democratic party, the political changes of the past decade have distorted the distribution of power and weakened the capacity of the party to represent the interests of its numerous less affluent constituents.... As long as the balance of political power remains so heavily weighted toward those with economic power, national economic policy will remain distorted, regardless of which party is in control of the federal government.

NO

Jeffrey M. Berry

CITIZEN GROUPS AND THE CHANGING NATURE OF INTEREST GROUP POLITICS IN AMERICA

Many protest movements have arisen in the course of American history, each affecting the political system in its own way. The social movements that took hold in the 1960s had their own unique set of roots but seemed to follow a conventional life span. The civil rights and antiwar groups that arose to protest the injustices they saw were classic social movements. Their views were eventually absorbed by one of the political parties, and, after achieving their immediate goals, their vitality was sapped. The antiwar movement disappeared, and black civil rights organizations declined in power. The most enduring and vital citizen groups born in this era of protest were never protest oriented. Consumer groups, environmental groups, and many other kinds of citizen lobbies have enjoyed unprecedented prosperity in the last 25 years. Never before have citizen groups been so prevalent in American politics, and never before have they been so firmly institutionalized into the policymaking process.

The rise of citizen groups has not only empowered many important constituencies, but it has altered the policymaking process as well. This article focuses on how citizen groups have affected interest group politics in general and how these organizations have contributed to the changing nature of public policymaking. A first step is to examine the initial success of liberal advocacy organizations as well as the conservative response to this challenge. Next, I will look at the impact of this growth of citizen group politics on the policymaking process. Then I will turn to how Congress and the executive branch have tried to cope with a dense population of citizen groups and the complex policymaking environment that now envelops government.

Finally, I will speculate as to how all of this has affected policymaking in terms of how democratic it is. The popular perception is that the rise of interest groups along with the decline of political parties has had a very negative impact on American politics. Analysis of the decline of parties will be left to others, but a central point here is that the growth in the numbers of citizen

From Jeffrey M. Berry, "Citizen Groups and the Changing Nature of Interest Group Politics in America," *The Annals of the American Academy of Political and Social Science*, vol. 528 (July 1993). Copyright © 1993 by The American Academy of Political and Social Science. Reprinted by permission of Sage Publications, Inc. Notes omitted.

groups and of other lobbying organizations has not endangered the political system. There are some unfortunate developments, such as the increasing role of political action committees in campaign financing, but the rise of citizen groups in particular has had a beneficial impact on the way policy is formulated. The overall argument may be stated succinctly: the rise of liberal citizen groups was largely responsible for catalyzing an explosion in the growth of all types of interest groups. Efforts to limit the impact of liberal citizen groups failed, and the policymaking process became more open and more participatory. Expanded access and the growth in the numbers of competing interest groups created the potential for gridlock, if not chaos. The government responded, in turn, with institutional changes that have helped to rationalize policymaking in environments with a large number of independent actors.

THE RISE OF CITIZEN GROUPS

The lobbying organizations that emerged out of the era of protest in the 1960s are tied to the civil rights and antiwar movements in two basic ways. First, activism was stimulated by the same broad ideological dissatisfaction with government and the two-party system. There was the same feeling that government was unresponsive, that it was unconcerned about important issues, and that business was far too dominant a force in policymaking. Second, the rise of liberal citizen groups was facilitated by success of the civil rights and antiwar movements. More specifically, future organizers learned from these social movements. They learned that aggressive behavior could get results, and they saw

that government could be influenced by liberal advocacy organizations. Some activists who later led Washington-based citizen lobbies cut their teeth as volunteers in these earlier movements.

For liberal consumer and environmental groups, an important lesson of this era was that they should not follow the protest-oriented behavior of the civil rights and antiwar movements. There was a collective realization that lasting influence would come from more conventional lobbying inside the political system. For consumer and environmental organizers, "power to the people" was rejected in favor of staff-run organizations that placed little emphasis on participatory democracy. This is not to say that these new organizations were simply copies of business lobbies; leaders of these groups like Ralph Nader and John Gardner placed themselves above politics-as-usual with their moralistic rhetoric and their attacks against the established political order.

While there was significant support for these groups from middle-class liberals, a major impetus behind their success was financial backing from large philanthropic foundations. The foundations wanted to support social change during a time of political upheaval, but at the same time they wanted responsible activism. This early support, most notably from the Ford Foundation's program in public interest law, was largely directed at supporting groups relying on litigation and administrative lobbying. The seed money for these organizations enabled them to flourish and provided them with time to establish a track record so that they could appeal to individual donors when the foundation money ran out. Other groups emerged without the help of foundations, drawing on a combination of large donors, dues-paying memberships, and government grants. Citizen lobbies proved remarkably effective at raising money and at shifting funding strategies as the times warranted.

Citizen groups emerged in a variety of areas. In addition to consumer and environmental groups, there were organizations interested in hunger and poverty, governmental reform, corporate responsibility, and many other issues. A number of new women's organizations soon followed in the wake of the success of the first wave of citizen groups, and new civil rights groups arose to defend other groups such as Hispanics and gays. As has been well documented, the rise of citizen groups was the beginning of an era of explosive growth in interest groups in national politics. No precise baseline exists, so exact measurement of this growth is impossible. Yet the mobilization of interests is unmistakable. One analysis of organizations represented in Washington in 1980 found that 40 percent of the groups had been started since 1960, and 25 percent had begun after 1970.

The liberal citizen groups that were established in the 1960s and 1970s were not simply the first ripples of a new wave of interest groups; rather, they played a primary role in catalyzing the formation of many of the groups that followed. New business groups, which were by far the most numerous of all the groups started since 1960, were directly stimulated to organize by the success of consumer and environmental groups. There were other reasons why business mobilized, but much of their hostility toward the expanded regulatory state was directed at agencies strongly supported by liberal citizen groups. These organizations had seemingly seized control of the political agenda, and the new social regulation demanded increased business mobilization. New conservative citizen lobbies, many focusing on family issues such as abortion and the Equal Rights Amendment, were also begun to counter the perceived success of the liberal groups.

The swing of the ideological pendulum that led to a conservative takeover of the White House in 1980 led subsequently to efforts to limit the impact of liberal citizen groups. The Reagan administration believed that the election of 1980 was a mandate to eliminate impediments to economic growth. Environmental and consumer groups were seen as organizations that cared little about the faltering American economy; President Reagan referred to liberal public interest lawyers as "a bunch of ideological ambulance chasers." Wherever possible, liberal citizen groups were to be removed from the governmental process....

The Reagan administration certainly succeeded in reducing the liberal groups' access to the executive branch. On a broader level, however, the conservative counterattack against the liberal groups was a failure. The reasons go far beyond the more accommodating stance of the Bush administration or the attitude of any conservative administrations that may follow. These organizations have proved to be remarkably resilient, and they are a strong and stable force in American politics. Most fundamentally, though, the Reagan attempt failed because the transformation of interest group politics led to large-scale structural changes in the public policymaking process.

CONSEQUENCES

The rise of citizen groups and the rapid expansion of interest group advocacy in general have had many important long-term consequences for the way policy is formulated by the national government. Most important, policymaking moved away from closed subgovernments, each involving a relatively stable and restricted group of lobbyists and key government officials, to much broader policymaking communities. Policymaking in earlier years is typically described as the product of consensual negotiations between a small number of back-scratching participants.

Policymaking is now best described as taking place within issue networks rather than in subgovernments. An issue network is a set of organizations that share expertise in a policy area and interact with each other over time as relevant issues are debated. As sociologist Barry Wellman states, "The world is composed of networks, not groups." This is certainly descriptive of Washington policymaking. Policy formulation cannot be portrayed in terms of what a particular group wanted and how officials responded to those demands. The coalitions within networks, often involving scores of groups, define the divisions over issues and drive the policymaking process forward. Alliances are composed of both old friends and strange bedfellows; relationships are built on immediate need as well as on familiarity and trust. Organizations that do not normally work in a particular issue network can easily move into a policymaking community to work on a single issue. The only thing constant in issue networks is the changing nature of the coalitions.

The result of issue network politics is that policymaking has become more open, more conflictual, and more broadly participatory. What is crucial about the role of citizen groups is that they were instrumental in breaking down the barriers to participation in subgovernments. Building upon their own constituency support and working with allies in Congress, citizen groups made themselves players. They have not been outsiders, left to protest policies and a system that excluded them. Rather, they built opposition right into the policymaking communities that had previously operated with some commonality of interest. Even conservative administrators who would prefer to exclude these liberal advocacy groups have recognized that they have to deal with their opponents in one arena or another. The Nuclear Regulatory Commission, the epitome of an agency hostile to liberal advocacy groups, cannot get away with ignoring groups like the Union of Concerned Scientists. The consensus over nuclear power has long been broken. Critics and advocacy groups like the Union of Concerned Scientists have the technical expertise to involve themselves in agency proceedings, and they have the political know-how to get themselves heard on Capitol Hill and in the news media.

Issue networks are not simply divided between citizen groups on one side and business groups on another. Organizations representing business usually encompass a variety of interests, many of which are opposed to each other. As various business markets have undergone rapid change and become increasingly competitive, issue networks have found themselves divided by efforts of one sector of groups to use the policymaking process to try to gain market share from another sector of the network. Citizen groups, rather than simply being the enemy of business, are potential coalition partners for different business sectors. A characteristic of the culture of interest group politics in Washington is that there are no permanent allies and no permanent enemies.

Citizen groups are especially attractive as coalition partners because they have such a high level of credibility with the public and the news media. All groups claim to represent the public interest because they sincerely believe that the course of action they are advocating would be the most beneficial to the country. Since they do not represent any vocational or business interest, citizen groups may be perceived by some to be less biased—though certainly not unbiased—in their approach to public policy problems. This credibility is also built around the high-quality research that many citizen groups produce and distribute to journalists and policymakers in Washington. Reports from advocacy organizations such as Citizens for Tax Justice or the Center for Budget and Policy Priorities are quickly picked up by the media and disseminated across the country. Most business groups would love to have the respect that these citizen groups command in the press. For all the financial strength at the disposal of oil lobbyists, no representative of the oil industry has as much credibility with the public as a lobbyist for the Natural Resources Defense Council.

Despite the growth and stability of citizen groups in national politics, their reach does not extend into every significant policymaking domain. In the broad area of financial services, for example, citizen groups have played a minor role at best. There are some consumer groups that have been marginally active when specific issues involving banks, insurance companies, and securities firms arise, but they have demonstrated little influence or staying power. There is, however, a vital consumer interest at stake

as public policymakers grapple with the crumbling walls that have traditionally divided different segments of the financial services market. Defense policy is another area where citizen groups have been relatively minor actors. But if citizen groups are conspicuous by their absence in some important areas, their overall reach is surprisingly broad. They have become major actors in policy areas where they previously had no presence at all. In negotiations over a free trade agreement with Mexico, for example, environmental groups became central players in the bargaining. These groups were concerned that increased U.S. investment in Mexico would result in increased pollution there from unregulated manufacturing, depleted groundwater supplies, and other forms of environmental degradation. To its dismay, the Bush White House found that the only practical course was to negotiate with the groups.

The increasing prominence of citizen groups and the expanding size of issue networks change our conception of the policymaking process. The basic structural attribute of a subgovernment was that it was relatively bounded with a stable set of participants. Even if there was some conflict in that subgovernment, there were predictable divisions and relatively clear expectations of what kind of conciliation between interest groups was possible. In contrast, issue networks seem like free-for-alls. In the health care field alone, 741 organizations have offices in Washington or employ a representative there. Where subgovernments suggested control over public policy by a limited number of participants, issue networks suggest no control whatsoever. Citizen groups make policymaking all the more difficult because they frequently sharpen the ideological debate; they have different organizational incentive systems from those of the corporations and trade groups with which they are often in conflict; and they place little emphasis on the need for economic growth, an assumption shared by most other actors.

This picture of contemporary interest group politics may make it seem impossible to accomplish anything in Washington. Indeed, it is a popular perception that Congress has become unproductive and that we are subject to some sort of national gridlock. Yet the policymaking system is adaptable, and the relationship between citizen groups and other actors in issue networks suggests that there are a number of productive paths for resolving complicated policy issues.

COMPLEX POLICYMAKING

The growth of issue networks is not, of course, the only reason why the policymaking process has become more complex. The increasingly technical nature of policy problems has obviously put an ever higher premium on expertise. Structural changes are critical, too. The decentralization of the House of Representatives that took place in the mid-1970s dispersed power and reduced the autonomy of leaders. Today, in the House, jurisdictions between committees frequently overlap and multiple referrals of bills are common. When an omnibus trade bill passed by both houses in 1987 was sent to conference, the House and the Senate appointed 200 conferees, who broke up into 17 subconferences. The growth of the executive branch has produced a similar problem of overlapping jurisdictions. In recent deliberations on proposed changes in wetlands policy, executive branch participants included the Soil Conservation Service in the Agriculture Department,

the Fish and Wildlife Service in Interior, the Army Corps of Engineers, the Environmental Protection Agency (EPA), the Office of Management and Budget, the Council on Competitiveness, and the President's Domestic Policy Council.

Nevertheless, even though the roots of complex policymaking are multifaceted, the rise of citizen groups has been a critical factor in forcing the Congress and the executive branch to focus more closely on developing procedures to negotiate settlements of policy disputes. The quiet bargaining of traditional subgovernment politics was not an adequate mechanism for handling negotiations between scores of interest groups, congressional committees, and executive branch agencies.

Citizen groups have been particularly important in prompting more structured negotiations for a number of reasons. First, in many policy areas, citizen groups upset long-standing working arrangements between policymakers and other interest groups. Citizen groups were often the reason subgovernments crumbled; under pressure from congressional allies and public opinion, they were included in the bargaining and negotiating at some stage in the policymaking process.

Second, citizen groups could not be easily accommodated in basic negotiating patterns. It was not a matter of simply placing a few more chairs at the table. These groups' entrance into a policymaking community usually created a new dividing line between participants. The basic ideological cleavage that exists between consumer and environmental interests and business is not easy to bridge, and, consequently, considerable effort has been expended to devise ways of getting mutual antagonists to negotiate over an extended period. As argued above, once accepted at the bargaining table, citizen groups could be attractive coalition partners for business organizations.

Third, ... citizen groups typically have a great deal of credibility with the press. Thus, in negotiating, they often have had more to gain by going public to gain leverage with other bargainers. This adds increased uncertainty and instability to the structure of negotiations.

Fourth, citizen groups are often more unified than their business adversaries. The business interests in an issue network may consist of large producers, small producers, foreign producers, and companies from other industries trying to expand into new markets. All these business interests may be fiercely divided as each tries to defend or encroach upon established market patterns. The environmentalists in the same network, while each may have its own niche in terms of issue specialization, are likely to present a united front on major policy disputes. In a perverse way, then, the position of citizen groups has been aided by the proliferation of business groups. (Even without the intrusion of citizen lobbies, this sharp rise in the number of business groups would have irretrievably changed the nature of subgovernments.) ...

CONCLUSION

Citizen groups have changed the policymaking process in valuable an enduring ways. Most important, they have broadened representation in our political system. Many previously unrepresented or underrepresented constituencies now have a powerful voice in Washington politics. The expanding numbers of liberal citizen groups and their apparent success helped to stimulate a broad mobilization

on the part of business. The skyrocketing increase in the numbers of interest groups worked to break down subgovernments and led to the rise of issue networks.

Issue networks are more fragmented, less predictable policymaking environments. Both Congress and the executive branch have taken steps to bring about greater centralized control and coherence to policymaking. Some of these institutional changes seem aimed directly at citizen groups. Negotiated regulations, for example, are seen as a way of getting around the impasse that often develops between liberal citizen groups and business organizations. Centralized regulatory review has been used by Republican administrations as a means of ensuring that business interests are given primacy; regulators are seen as too sympathetic to the citizen groups that are clients of their agencies.

Although government has established these and other institutional mechanisms for coping with complex policymaking environments, the American public does not seem to feel that the government copes very well at all. Congress has been portrayed as unproductive and spineless, unwilling to tackle the tough problems that require discipline or sacrifice. At the core of this criticism is that interest groups are the culprit. Washington lobbies, representing every conceivable interest and showering legislators with the political action committee donations they crave, are said to be responsible for this country's inability to solve its problems.

Although it is counterintuitive, it may be that the increasing number of interest groups coupled with the rise of citizen groups has actually improved the policymaking system in some important ways. More specifically, our policymaking process may be more democratic today because of these developments. Expanded interest group participation has helped to make the policymaking process more open and visible. The closed nature of subgovernment politics meant not only that participation was restricted but that public scrutiny was minimal. The proliferation of interest groups, Washington media that are more aggressive, and the willingness and ability of citizen groups in particular to go public as part of their advocacy strategy have worked to open up policymaking to the public eye.

The end result of expanded citizen group advocacy is policy communities that are highly participatory and more broadly representative of the public. One can argue that this more democratic policymaking process is also one that is less capable of concerted action; yet there is no reliable evidence that American government is any more or less responsive to pressing policy problems than it has ever been. There are, of course, difficult problems that remain unresolved, but that is surely true of every era. Democracy requires adequate representation of interests as well as institutions capable of addressing difficult policy problems. For policymakers who must balance the demand for representation with the need for results, the key is thinking creatively about how to build coalitions and structure negotiations between large groups of actors.

POSTSCRIPT

Is American Government Dominated by Big Business?

Berry argues that the rise of new, "citizen" pressure groups (civil rights, consumer, and environmental groups) have given pluralist politics a new lease on life. According to Berry, the "policy-making process [has become] more open and more participatory." But this raises questions: Don't some groups have more money and power than others? And won't these groups be more successful than weaker, less well financed groups in getting their way in Washington? In short, the new "openness" and accessibility of the U.S. policy-making process may magnify the effects of existing inequalities in America.

Social science literature contains a number of works that discuss the issues of pluralism and corporate power. Charles E. Lindblom was one of those early pluralists who made the journey all the way over to elite theory. His earlier book, written with political scientist Robert A. Dahl, is *Politics, Economics, and Welfare* (Harper, 1953). His repudiation of pluralism was complete by the time he published *Politics and Markets: The World's Political-Economic Systems* (Basic Books, 1977). Lindblom may have been influenced by some of the critiques of pluralism that appeared in the 1960s, including Peter Bachrach, *The Theory of Democratic Elitism* (Little, Brown, 1967), and Theodore Lowi, *The End of Liberalism* (W. W. Norton, 1969). Recent works arguing that corporate elites possess inordinate power in American society include Michael Schwartz, ed., *The Structure of Power in America* (Holmes & Meier, 1987), and G. William Domhoff, *The Power Elite and the State* (Aldine de Gruyter, 1990).

One way of evaluating the pluralist and elitist perspectives on who rules America would be to study them in terms of concrete examples. We might ask, for example, what significant events have occurred in America over the past 20 years. The list might include the civil rights revolution, the women's movement, the establishment of stricter environmental laws, the withdrawal of U.S. forces from Vietnam, the legalization of abortion, the Camp David (Middle East peace) accords, the Panama Canal treaties, the deregulation of the airline industry, the savings and loan crisis, the soaring budget deficits, the Persian Gulf War, and the new, friendly relationship between the United States and the former Soviet Union. Were all these the work of one elite "establishment" or did they result from an interaction of groups in the political arena?

ISSUE 2

Do Political Campaigns Inform Voters?

YES: Samuel L. Popkin, from *The Reasoning Voter: Communication and Persuasion in Presidential Campaigns* (University of Chicago Press, 1991)

NO: Gil Troy, from *See How They Ran: The Changing Role of the Presidential Candidate* (Free Press, 1991)

ISSUE SUMMARY

YES: Professor of political science Samuel L. Popkin argues that presidential election campaigns perform a unique and essential service in informing and unifying the American people.

NO: Political scientist Gil Troy maintains that modern campaigns alienate voters because the candidates tend to make emotional appeals to voters and ignore the important issues.

Political campaigns in the United States run longer and are more expensive than those in any other democratic country; yet, a smaller proportion of American voters participates in elections than in other democracies. In a country in which the constitutional right to vote is a cherished freedom to most people, how can this be?

Perhaps as much as $100 million was spent on the 1992 presidential campaign. But despite the cost, length, and breadth of the campaign, only 55 percent of the electorate turned out to vote. Although that figure is up from 1988's all-time low of just 50 percent, it remains the lowest turnout for a modern election for all the major democracies in the world.

A president seeking reelection is, in one sense, always campaigning. That is, the president is always in the public eye and is therefore constantly being evaluated by the public. Rivals for the other major party's nomination must organize their campaigns at least one year before the election in order to compete in the state primaries, which choose the delegates who nominate the candidate.

Television has changed the nature of presidential campaigns in part because it is no longer necessary for voters to come out to rallies to see the candidates—they can be seen close up at televised rallies and in the presidential debates, as well as in informal conversation with news anchors and talk show hosts. The major candidates for the 1992 election, for example, were seen variously on "Larry King Live," "Today," and "The Arsenio Hall Show." The importance of television to a campaign became clear when Ross

Perot launched his independent candidacy on television; he attracted such an enthusiastic response that first Governor Bill Clinton and then President George Bush began to appear more frequently on camera.

The impact of presidential campaigns is influenced by the declining importance of parties, which once organized the door-to-door solicitation of voters and local rallies. The national party convention used to be where delegates determined who would be the party's nominee. Now the nominee is chosen by qualified voters in the primaries, making the convention nothing more than the beginning of the actual campaign.

Critics of current political campaigns argue that one difference between old-style campaigns and electronic (televised or radio broadcast) campaigns is the depth and length of exposure to the candidate. In the days before television, candidates delivered 30-minute speeches in person, in which they spoke of issues, indicated sentiments, and made promises. Today, candidates are most often presented in 60-second commercials or in even shorter sound bites (brief, recorded statements) on the evening news. Critics argues that the candidate is put into a contrived setting, portrayed as an image, and often reduced to a slogan. Furthermore, critics say, the sound bites rarely consist of issues; more often they either try to reinforce the candidate's virtue or implicitly undermine his or her opponent.

Another criticism is that there is too much negative campaigning, that the candidates spend too much of their campaigns trying to show their opponents in as bad a light as possible. Recent campaigns have involved mudslinging, character bashing, and the criticism of political records, which has often entailed blatant misrepresentation of candidates' records. Negative campaigning, however, is not a new development, and it was often harsher in the past. But television's graphic depictions have increased the impact of negative campaigning.

The unique nature of American campaigns derives in large part from political characteristics that distinguish the United States from most other democracies. Unlike nations in which all power is in the national government, America has a federal system that places more power in the states than other countries place in their local units. The U.S. national government is based on a separation of political powers between the executive power of the president and the legislative power of the Congress. Both federalism and the separation of powers mean that many more officers must be elected and many more elections must be held. Finally, in large part because of these features, America's major political parties do not stand for clear and opposed principles. Some representatives, even when they seem to be united with their party, will desert their party leadership.

In the selections that follow, Samuel L. Popkin maintains that campaigns serve the purpose of bringing together a diverse population and that voters need to see more campaigning and fuller coverage, not less. Gil Troy disagrees, asserting that campaigns fail to educate the public and that many Americans are turned off by modern presidential campaigns.

YES

Samuel L. Popkin

THE REASONING VOTER

I believe that voter turnout has declined because campaign stimulation, from the media and from personal interaction, is also low and declining, and there is less interaction between the media and the grass-roots, person-to-person aspects of voter mobilization. The lack of campaign stimulation, I suggest, is also responsible for the large turnout gap in this country between educated and uneducated voters.

The social science research shows clear relations between the turnout and social stimulation. Married people of all ages vote more than people of the same age who live alone. And much of the increase in turnout seen over one's life cycle is due to increases in church attendance and community involvement. I believe that in this age of electronic communities, when more people are living alone and fewer people are involved in churches, PTA's, and other local groups, interpersonal social stimulation must be increased if turnout is to increase. . . .

Political parties used to spend a large portion of their resources bringing people to rallies. By promoting the use of political ideas to bridge the gap between the individual "I" and the party "we," they encouraged people to believe that they were "links in the chain" and that the election outcome would depend on what people like themselves chose to do. Today, less money and fewer resources are available for rallies as a part of national campaigns. And parties cannot compensate for this loss with more door-to-door canvassing; in the neighborhoods where it would be safe to walk door-to-door, no one would be home.

Some of the social stimulation that campaigns used to provide in rallies and door-to-door canvassing can still be provided by extensive canvassing. This is still done in Iowa and New Hampshire. These are the first primary states, and candidates have the time and resources to do extensive personal campaigning, and to use campaign organizations to telephone people and discuss the campaigns. In research reported elsewhere, I have analyzed the effect of the social stimulation that occurs in these states. People contacted by one political candidate pay more attention to all the candidates and to the campaign events reported on television and in the papers. As they watch the campaign they become more aware of differences between the candidates. And as they become more aware of the differences, they become more likely to vote.

This suggests a surprising conclusion: The best single way to compensate for the declining use of the party as a cue to voting, and for the declining social stimulation to vote at all, might be to increase our spending on campaign activities that stimulate voter involvement. There are daily complaints about the cost of American elections, and certainly the corrosive effects of corporate fund-raising cannot be denied; but it is not true that American elections are costly by comparison with those in other countries. Comparisons are difficult, especially since most countries have parliamentary systems, but it is worth noting that reelection campaigns to the Japanese Diet—the equivalent of the U.S. House of Representatives—cost over $1.5 million per seat. That would be equivalent to $3.5 million per congressional reelection campaign, instead of the current U.S. average of about $400,000 (given the fact that Japan has one-half the U.S. population and 512 legislators instead of 435). Although the differences in election systems and rules limit the value of such comparisons, it is food for thought that a country with a self-image so different from America's spends so much more on campaigning.

I believe that voters should be given more to "read" from campaigns and television, and that they need more interpersonal reinforcement of what they "read." Considering the good evidence that campaigns work, I believe that the main trouble lies not with American politicians but in the fact that American campaigns are not effective enough to overcome the increasing lack of social stimulation we find in a country of electronic as well as residential communities. This confronts us with some troubling questions. What kinds of electronic and/or social stimulation are possible today? To what extent can newspaper and television coverage provide the kinds of information citizens need to connect their own concerns with the basic party differences that campaigns try to make paramount? Is there a limit to what electronic and print stimulation can accomplish, so that parties must find a way to restore canvassing and rallies, or can electronic rallies suffice? Does watching a rally on television have the same effect as attending a rally? Could a return to bumper stickers and buttons, which have become far less prominent since campaigns began pouring their limited resources into the media, make a difference by reinforcing commitments and encouraging political discussions?

The problem may also be not simply a *lack* of social stimulation, but the growing *diversity* of social stimulation, and a resulting decline in reinforcement. In 1948, Columbia sociologists collected data about the social milieu of each voter and related the effects of the mass media on the voter to the political influences of family, friends, church, etc. They found that a voter's strength of conviction was related to the political homogeneity of the voter's associates. At that time, most voters belonged to politically homogeneous social groups; the social gulf between the parties was so wide that most voters had no close friends or associates voting differently from them. A decline in the political homogeneity of primary groups would lead to less social reinforcement; since the political cleavage patterns which exist today cut more across social groups, voters are in less homogeneous family, church, and work settings and are getting less uniform reinforcement. Whether there is less overall social stimulation today, or whether there is simply less uniformity of social stimulation, the demands on campaigns to pull segments together and create coalitions are vastly greater today than in the past.

What Television Gives Us

Television is giving us less and less direct communication from our leaders and their political campaigns. Daniel Hallin, examining changes in network news coverage of presidents from 1968 to 1988, has found that the average length of the actual quote from a president on the news has gone from forty-five seconds in 1968 to nine seconds today. Instead of a short introduction from a reporter and a long look at the president, we are given a short introduction from the president and a long look at the reporter.

In the opinion of Peggy Noonan, one of the most distinguished speech-writers of recent years, who wrote many of President Reagan's and President Bush's best speeches, the change from long quotes to sound bites has taken much of the content out of campaigning: "It's a media problem. The young people who do speeches for major politicians, they've heard the whole buzz about sound bites. And now instead of writing... a serious text with serious arguments, they just write sound bite after sound bite." With less serious argument in the news, there is less material for secondary elites and analysts to digest, and less need for candidates to think through their policies.

We also receive less background information about the campaign and less coverage of the day-to-day pageantry—the stump speeches, rallies, and crowds.

Moreover, as Paul Weaver has shown, the reporter's analysis concentrates on the horse-race aspect of the campaign and thus downplays the policy stakes involved. To a network reporter, "politics is essentially a game played by individual politicians for personal advancement... the game takes place against a backdrop of governmental institutions, public problems, policy debates, and the like, but these are noteworthy only insofar as they affect, or are used by, players in pursuit of the game's rewards."

As a result of this supposedly critical stance, people are losing the kinds of signals they have always used to read politicians. We see fewer of the kinds of personalized political interactions, including the fun and the pageantry, that help people decide whose side they are on and that help potential leaders assemble coalitions for governing.

Gerald Ford went to a fiesta in San Antonio because he wanted Hispanic voters to see his willingness to visit them on their own ground, and to demonstrate that some of their leaders supported him. He also wanted to remind them of his willingness to deal respectfully with the sovereignty issues raised by the Panama Canal question. But when he bit into an unshucked tamale, these concerns were buried in an avalanche of trivial commentary. Reporters joked that the president was going after the "klutz" vote and talked about "Bozo the Clown." From that moment on, Ford was pictured in the media as laughably uncoordinated. Reporters brought up Lyndon Johnson's contemptuous jibe that Ford "was so dumb he couldn't walk and chew gum at the same time." Jokes circulated that he had played too much football without his helmet. For the rest of the campaign, his every slip was noted on the evening news. Yet the news photos supposedly documenting the president's clumsiness reveal a man of remarkably good balance and body control, given the physical circumstances—not surprising for a man who had been an all-American football player in college and was still, in his sixties, an active downhill skier.

Similarly, during the 1980 campaign, Ronald Reagan visited Dallas and said, in response to a question, that there were "great flaws" in the theory of evolution and that it might be a good idea if the schools taught "creationism" as well. This statement was characterized in the media as the sort of verbal pratfall to be expected from Reagan, and much of the coverage related such gaffes *entirely* to questions about his intellectual capacity, not to the meaning of his appearance or the implications of the appearance for the coalition he was building.

What difference would it have made if press and television reporters had considered these actions by Ford and Reagan as clear and open avowals of sympathy for political causes dear to their hearts? What if Ford's political record on issues dear to Hispanics had been discussed, or if the guest list for the fiesta had been discussed to see which prominent Hispanics were, in fact, endorsing him? The nature of the gathering Reagan attended was noted at the time, but it was never referred to again. It was not until 1984 that Americans uninvolved in religious fundamentalism understood enough about what the Moral Majority stood for to read anything from a politician's embrace of Jerry Falwell, its president, or a religious roundtable such as the one Reagan attended in 1980. By 1988, as more people on the other side of the fundamentalism debates learned what the Moral Majority

stood for, the group was disbanded as a political liability.

Television, in other words, is not giving people enough to read about the substance of political coalition building because it ignores many important campaign signals. That rallies and other campaign events are "staged" does not diminish their importance and the legitimate information they can convey to voters. When Richard Nixon met Mao Tse Tung in 1972, the meeting was no less important because it was staged. And when Jesse Jackson praised Lloyd Bentsen by noting the speed with which he could go from biscuits to tacos to caviar, he was acknowledging another fact of great importance: in building coalitions, a candidate must consider the trade-off between offering symbols and making promises.

If politicians cannot show familiarity with people's concerns by properly husking tamales or eating knishes in the right place with the right people, they will have to promise them something. As Jackson noted, the tamales may be better than promises, because promises made to one segment of voters, or one issue public, will offend other groups and therefore tie the politician's hands in the future policy-making process.

Is it more meaningful when a governor of Georgia hangs a picture of Martin Luther King Jr., in the statehouse, or when a senator or congressman votes for a bill promising full employment? Is it better for a politician to eat a kosher hot dog or to promise never to compromise Israel's borders? When voters are deprived of one shortcut—obvious symbols, for example—obvious promises, for example —instead of turning to more subtle and complicated forms of information.

How good a substitute are electronic tamales for the real thing? Does watching a fiesta provide any of the stimulation to identification and turnout that attendance at a fiesta provides? How long does it take to bring us together, at least in recognizable coalitions? We need not have answers to these questions to see that they speak to the central issue of stimulating turnout and participation in elections in an age of electronic communities. The media *could* provide more of the kinds of information people use to assess candidates and parties. However, I do not know if electronic tamales provide the social stimulation of interacting with others, or the reinforcement of acting with others who agree, and I do not know how much more potent are ideas brought clearly to mind through using them with others. The demands placed on television are greater than the demands ever placed on radio or newspapers because the world is more diverse today and there are more segments which need to be reunited in campaigns.

OBJECTIONS AND ANSWERS

Two notable objections can be made to my suggestions for increasing campaigning and campaign spending. The first is the "spinmaster" objection: contemporary political campaigns are beyond redemption because campaign strategists have become so adept at manipulation that voters can no longer learn what the candidates really stand for or really intend to do. Significantly, this conclusion is supported by two opposing arguments about voter behavior. One objection is that voters are staying home because they have been turned off by fatuous claims and irrelevant advertising. A variant of this is that voters are being manipulated with great success by unscrupulous campaign advertising, so that their votes reflect more concern with Willie Horton* or school prayer or flag burning than with widespread poverty, the banking crisis, or global warming. The second objection is that popular concern with candidates and with government in general has been trivialized, so that candidates fiddle while America burns. In the various versions of this hypothesis, voter turnout is down because today's political contests are waged over small differences on trivial issues. While Eastern Europe plans a future of freedom under eloquent spokesmen like Vaclav Havel, and while Mikhail Gorbachev declares an end to the cold war, releases Eastern Europe from Soviet control, and tries to free his countrymen from the yoke of doctrinaire communism, in America Tweedledum and Tweedledee argue about who loves the flag more while Japan buys Rockefeller Center, banks collapse, and the deficit grows.

Both of these critiques of the contemporary system argue that campaigns themselves are trivial and irrelevant, that campaign advertising and even the candidates' speeches are nothing but self-serving puffery and distortion. This general argument has an aesthetic appeal, especially to better-educated voters and the power elite; campaign commercials remind no one of the Lincoln-Douglas debates, and today's bumper stickers and posters have none of the resonance of the Goddess of Democracy in Tiananmen Square. But elite aesthetics is not the test of this argument; the test is what voters learn from campaigns.

*[Willie Horton, a convicted murderer, escaped a prison furlough approved by then-governor of Massachusetts Michael Dukakis and committed a violent crime. George Bush exploited the incident in his campaign against Dukakis during the 1988 presidential race.—Eds.]

There is ample evidence that voters *do* learn from campaigns. Of course, each campaign tries hard to make its side look better and the other side worse. Despite that, voter perceptions about the candidates and their positions are more accurate. Furthermore, ... there is no evidence that people learn less from campaigns today than they did in past years. This is a finding to keep in mind at all times, for many of the criticisms of campaigns simplistically assume that because politicians and campaign strategists have manipulative intentions, campaigns necessarily mislead the voter. This assumption is not borne out by the evidence; voters know how to read the media and the politicians better than most media critics acknowledge.

... Voters remember past campaigns and presidents, and past failures of performance to match promises. They have a sense of who is with them and who is against them; they make judgments about unfavorable new editorials and advertisements from hostile sources, ignoring some of what is favorable to those they oppose and some of what is unfavorable to those they support. In managing their personal affairs and making decisions about their work, they collect information that they can use as a reality test for campaign claims and media stories. They notice the difference between behavior that has real consequences, on one hand, and mere talk, on the other.

... The ability of television news to manipulate voters has been vastly overstated, as one extended example will suggest. In television reporting—but not in the academic literature—it was always assumed before 1984 that winning debates and gaining votes are virtually one and the same. But on Sunday, October 7, 1984, in the first debate between Walter Mondale and Ronald Reagan, this assumption was shown to be flawed. Mondale, generally a dry speaker, was unexpectedly relaxed and articulate, and Reagan, known for his genial and relaxed style, was unexpectedly tense and hesitant. Mondale even threw Reagan off guard by using "There you go again," the jibe Reagan had made famous in his 1980 debate with Jimmy Carter. Immediately after the debate, the CBS News/*New York Times* pollsters phoned a sample of registered voters they had interviewed before the debate, to ask which candidate they were going to vote for and which they thought had done a better job in the debate. Mondale was considered to have "done the best job" by 42 percent to 36 percent, and had gained 3 points in the polls. As a result of similar polls in the next twenty-four hours by other networks and news organizations, the media's main story the rest of the week was of Mondale's upset victory over the president in the debate. Two days later, when another CBS News/*New York Times* poll asked voters about the debate and about their intended vote, Mondale was considered to have "done the best job" not by 42 percent to 36 percent margin of Sunday, but by 65 percent to 17 percent. Media reports, then, claimed that millions of voters had changed their minds about what they themselves had just seen days earlier. Yet in the three days during which millions changed their minds about who had won the debate, the same poll reported, few if any, changed their minds about how they would vote.

This example emphasizes just how complex the effects of television can be. Voters now have opinions about opinions. When asked who won the debate, they may say not what they think personally, but what they have heard that the majority of Americans think. It is easier to change their opinions about what their neighbors think than to change their own opinions. And most important of all, it is clear that they understand the difference between a debater and a president, and that they don't easily change their political views about who they want to run the country simply on the basis of debating skills.

Critics of campaign spinmasters and of television in general are fond of noting that campaigners and politicians intend to manipulate and deceive, but they wrongly credit them with more success than they deserve. As Michael Schudson has noted, in the television age, whenever a president's popularity has been high, it has been attributed to unusual talents for using television to sell his image. He notes, for example, that in 1977 the television critic of the *New York Times* called President Carter "a master of controlled images," and that during the 1976 primaries David Halberstam wrote that Carter "more than any other candidate this year has sensed and adapted to modern communications and national mood.... Watching him again and again on television I was impressed by his sense of pacing, his sense of control, very low key, soft." A few years later this master of images still had the same soft, low-key voice, but now it was interpreted as indicating not quiet strength but weakness and indecision. Gerald Rafshoon, the media man for this "master of television," concluded after the 1980 campaign that all the television time bought for Carter wasn't as useful as three more helicopters (and a successful desert rescue) would have been.

As these examples suggest, media critics are generally guilty of using one of the laziest and easiest information shortcuts of all. Assuming that a popular politician is a good manipulator of the media or that a winner won because of his media style is not different from what voters do when they evaluate presidents by reasoning backward from known results. The media need reform, but so do the media critics. One cannot infer, without astonishing hubris, that the American people have been successfully deceived simply because a politician wanted them to believe his or her version of events. But the media critics who analyze political texts without any reference to the actual impact of the messages do just that.

Negativism and Triviality

Campaigns are often condemned as trivial—as sideshows in which voters amuse themselves by learning about irrelevant differences between candidates who fiddle over minor issues while the country stagnates and inner cities burn—and many assume that the negativism and pettiness of the attacks that candidates make on each other encourage an "a pox on all your houses" attitude. This suggests a plausible hypothesis, which can be given a clean test in a simple experiment. This experiment can be thought of as a "stop and think" experiment because it is a test of what happens if people stop and think about what they know of the candidates and issues in an election and tell someone what they know. First, take a random sample of people across the country and interview them. Ask the people selected what they consider to be the most important issues facing the country, and then ask them where the various candidates stand on these issues. Then ask them to state their likes and dislikes about the candidates' personal qualities and issue stands, and about the state of the country. Second, after the election, find out whether these interviewees were more or less likely to vote than people who were not asked to talk about the campaign. If the people interviewed voted less often than people not interviewed, then there is clear support for the charge that triviality, negativism, and irrelevancy are turning off the American people and suppressing turnout.

In fact, the National Election Studies done by the University of Michigan's Survey Research Center, now the Center for Political Studies, are exactly such an experiment. In every election since 1952, people have been asked what they care about, what the candidates care about, and that they know about the campaign. After the election people have been reinterviewed and asked whether they voted; then the actual voting records have been checked to see whether the respondents did indeed vote.

The results convincingly demolish the triviality and negativism hypothesis. In every election, people who have been interviewed are more likely to vote than other Americans. Indeed, the reason the expensive and difficult procedure of verifying turnout against the voting records was begun in the first place was that the scholars were suspicious because the turnout reported by respondents was so much higher than either the actual turnout of all Americans or the turnout in surveys conducted after the election. So respondents in the national election studies, after seventy minutes of thinking about the candidates, the issues, and the campaign, were both more likely than other people to vote and more likely to try to hide the fact that they did not vote! Further, if people are reinterviewed in later elections, their turnout continues to rise. Still further, while an interview cuts nonvoting in a presidential election by up to 20 percent, an interview in a local primary may cut nonvoting by as much as half.

The rise in no-shows on voting day and the rise of negative campaigning both follow from the rise of candidate-centered elections. When voters do not have information about future policies they extrapolate, or project, from the information they have. As campaigns become more centered on candidates, there is more projection, and hence more negative campaigning. Negative campaigning is designed to provide information that causes voters to stop projecting and to change their beliefs about a candidate's stand on the issues. "Willie Horton... was a legitimate issue because it speaks to styles and ways of governance. In that case Dukakis's."

As Noonan has also noted of the 1988 campaign, "There should have been more name-calling, mud slinging and fun. It should have been rock-'em-sock-'em the way great campaigns have been in the past. It was tedious." Campaigns cannot deal with anything substantive if they cannot get the electorate's attention and interest people in listening to their music. Campaigns need to make noise. The tradition of genteel populism in America, and the predictable use of sanitary metaphors to condemn politicians and their modes of communication, says more about the distaste of the people who use the sanitary metaphors for American society than it does about the failing politicians.

The challenge to the future of American campaigns, and hence to American democracy, is how to bring back the excitement and the music in an age of electronic campaigning. Today's campaigns have more to do because an educated, media-centered society is a broadened and segmented electorate which is harder to rally, while today's campaigns have less money and troops with which to fight their battles.

*   *   *

When I first began to work in presidential campaigns I had very different ideas about how to change campaigns and their coverage than I have today. Coverage of rallies and fiestas, I used to think, belonged in the back of the paper along with stories about parties, celebrity fundraisers, and fad diets. Let the society editor cover banquets and rubber chickens, I thought; the reporters in Washington could analyze the speeches and discuss the policy implications of competing proposals.

I still wish that candidates' proposals and speeches were actually analyzed for their content and implications for our future. I still wish that television told us more about how elites evaluate presidential initiatives than what my neighbors said about them in the next day's polls. However, I now appreciate the intimate relationships between the rallies and governance which escaped me in the past. I now appreciate how hard it is to bring a country together, to gather all the many concerns and interests into a single coalition and hold it together in order to govern.

Campaigns are essential in any society, particularly in a society that is culturally, economically, and socially diverse. If voters look for information about candidates under streetlights, then that is where candidates must campaign, and the only way to improve elections is to add streetlights. Reforms can only make sense if they are consistent with the gut rationality of voters. Ask not for more sobriety and piety from citizens, for they are voters, not judges; offer them instead cues and signals which connect their world with the world of politics.

NO

Gil Troy

THE SEARCH FOR VIRTUE IN THE PRESIDENTIAL CAMPAIGN

By 1988, Americans had evolved an elaborate campaign ritual, with the candidate at the center. A dozen candidates chased nearly thirty-five million votes in thirty-eight state primaries for almost two years before George Bush and Michael Dukakis emerged as the presidential nominees. Even after their respective party conventions the two candidates continued their cross-country blitz of preening, parading, glad-handing, backslapping, baby-kissing, and debating. By November 8 the candidates were exhausted and the nation demoralized. Barely half of those eligible had bothered to vote. Two-thirds of those surveyed considered the campaign unduly negative and the candidates undesirable. . . .

Clearly, stumping during the primary helped a winner emerge. But after the conventions, the impact was less clear. It was much easier to reach the people via TV than through whistle-stops and prop-stops. In seeking to explain why candidates still stumped, political scientists retreated into double negatives. "[No] one is absolutely certain that whistle-stop methods produce no useful result," Nelson W. Polsby and Aaron Wildavsky concluded in their oft-reprinted textbook on presidential campaigning.

With voter turnout so low and frustration with the campaign so high, stumping did not even help legitimize the people's choice. Campaigns fostered cynicism, not pride. More and more Americans considered campaign appearances mere pseudo-events, melodramas staged for the nightly news. In 1988 the crowds seemed smaller and less enthusiastic than ever before. If these exercises demeaned the candidates and American politics, why not change tactics?

Still, the candidates hit the campaign trail, fourteen-hour day after fourteen-hour day. Again and again, contradictory expectations clouded their efforts. For example, by 1988 Americans' appetite for personal information about their candidates seemed endless. Even before any primary votes were cast, the character question sank two Democratic candidacies. In May 1987, former Senator Gary Hart withdrew when word leaked of his *Monkey Business* with a Miami model. That fall, Senator Joseph Biden quit amid reports that he

Excerpted with permission of The Free Press, a division of Macmillan, Inc., from *See How They Ran: The Changing Role of the Presidential Candidate*, by Gil Troy. Copyright © 1991 by Gil Troy. Notes omitted.

had plagiarized in law school and had lifted rhetoric from other politicians. At countless dinner tables throughout the land, Americans debated whether they preferred a morally flawed nominee with whom they agreed, or a Mister Clean whose views they disliked. Strict democrats deemed the character issue irrelevant. They simply wanted to know where their candidate stood. But individual peccadillos often illuminated more serious flaws. Thus Hart's extracurricular adventures confirmed doubts about "his judgment and credibility," *Newsweek* wrote, while Biden's rhetorical larceny substantiated fears that he was shallow.

Unsure of which course to chart, both Bush and Dukakis wavered. In accepting the nomination, Dukakis made an appeal based on character rather than issues: "This election is not about ideology; it's about competence," he declared at the Democratic convention in Atlanta, presenting himself as solid and trustworthy. Yet, as his campaign progressed (or, as some said, degenerated), Dukakis became known as a "policy nerd" more interested in technicalities than personalities. When he embraced specific policies, advocating for example guaranteed college loans for all, Bruce Morton of CBS branded the issue complicated and boring. Even Dukakis's professed distaste for negative campaigning appeared to be a sign of weakness, not of virtue. In a "photo opportunity" aimed at broadening his appeal, Dukakis donned a helmet and climbed into the Army's much-vaunted M-1 tank. He ended up looking more like Snoopy fighting the Red Baron than General Patton defending freedom. This ridiculous image epitomized Dukakis's ineffectual campaign and his inability to choose between em-phasizing his character or the issues, between pandering and educating.

On the other hand, Bush began with issues and retreated into personalities. In his "final" instructions to the speechwriter working on his acceptance, Peggy Noonan, Bush insisted: "No personal attack on Dukakis.... Just the issues." Yet Bush's campaign featured a visit to an American flag factory, attacks on Dukakis for granting prison furloughs to murderers, and a refusal to say the "L-word," thereby treating his rival's liberal beliefs as a schoolboy would treat a girl with cooties. So despite his stated preference, Bush became known as the campaign's mudslinger. Simultaneously, he was dogged by what he, out of frustration, called "the vision thing," the demand for the bold rhetoric that Ronald Reagan loved—and that so many Reagan critics hated.

These contradictory and changing strategies obscured fundamental policy differences. The tumult of the 1960s and 1970s had made many voters more passionate about certain issues, and most candidates had responded in kind. With the divisions persisting into the eighties, Michael Dukakis and George Bush disagreed about social issues, defense, and the best way to reduce the budget deficit. They released reams of position papers on issues ranging from abortion and air pollution to Zimbabwe and Zaire. With the explosion of news coverage that began in the 1960s and seemed overwhelming by 1988, reporters generated more stories about issues, even if the overall percentage of substantive coverage decreased. Nevertheless, few voters were satisfied that the candidates had highlighted these differences in the campaign. By the end of October, even George Bush yearned for substance: "I want to get back to the issues, and quit talking about *him*," Bush told his consultant, Roger Ailes. "We plan to do that November 9," the day *after* the election, Ailes replied.

* * *

Viewing the elections in historical perspective reveals that many of the dilemmas that faced the Founding Fathers persist; lines linking the traditional republican ideology with more contemporary concerns continue to emerge. Foremost among these concerns is the continuing obsession with virtue. In a world of marathon campaigns and "spin-doctors," politics still seem distasteful....

American politicians were still trying to transcend their demeaning profession. Whenever presidents "stood" for reelection they acted as if campaigning somehow diminished both the office and the man. In 1984, Ronald Reagan's campaign chairman called the incumbent President, two-time Governor, and four-time presidential aspirant "nonpolitical." The "Rose Garden" strategy of both Gerald Ford and Jimmy Carter reflected this republican sense that governing was worthy of a President, campaigning was not. These charades further undermined the legitimacy of campaigning and fostered increased cynicism.

... [A]mbivalence about ambition and success goes beyond politics. As the 1990s began, many Americans felt that after a decade of rampant ambition, they now had to pay the piper. Authors celebrated the end of the "Predators' Ball" on Wall Street as judges sent financiers like Michael Milken to jail. Milken and his pals became the latest characters in the American morality play warning against ambition that stretched from Henry Clay through Jay Gould to Richard Nixon in history, and from Captain Ahab

through Jay Gatsby to Sherman McCoy in literature. While still valuing Horatio Alger, Americans feared that ambition debauched otherwise good men.

Ambitious but virtuous politicians were hard to find. Thus, even though Americans in the 1980s were less moralistic than their ancestors, they scrutinized candidates more carefully, assuming that everything counted—that the smallest of incidents, no matter how inconsequential, could reveal the man. This emphasis on personality was considered to be the least dignified aspect of the modern campaign. Yet, in many ways, it marked a return to the Founding Fathers' republican notion that good character was the most important requirement for a good president.

But how could "character" be measured? Originally, Americans believed that such assessments could be made only by gentlemen who knew the candidates intimately. Two centuries later, television was supposed to have allowed the entire American public to "X-ray" the candidates' personality. Instead, many feared, television had become the most potent weapon in the modern demagogue's arsenal of artifice. Attacks against the "electronic election" complained that candidates were no longer authentic, that they were invented by their handlers. The contributions of ghost-writers and consultants were routinely acknowledged, as observers matter-of-factly referred to "Peggy Noonan's acceptance speech, which Bush recited at the Republican convention." Still, each candidate claimed that his rival was held hostage by handlers. The Democrats even produced a series of television commercials about the handlers cynically plotting Republican strategy. "The Vice President seems willing to do anything they say," Democratic campaign manager Susan Estrich charged. I want a "real person," one voter grumbled.

Handlers were the modern-day "adversaries of republican government," seducing the people with images and sound bites instead of intrigues and rhetoric. A direct line could be drawn from Alexander Hamilton's warning in *Federalist 68* against demagoguery and cabals, through William Henry Harrison's attack on ambitious politicians acting like "auctioneers," and continuing through William Randolph Hearst's characterization of Franklin D. Roosevelt as a "chanter or a crooner," to the *Boston Globe's* speculation in 1988 about the "mischief" a "devious" candidate could make "with a quiver of finely honed commercials and 15-second sound bites." The "body of the people" remained in danger of "corruption" from unscrupulous candidates or manipulative cabals.

Television had become the republican bogeyman, realizing traditional fears through modern means. "Politics is a more simplistic, less subtle, less thoughtful pursuit today" than it was a generation ago, Richard Nixon lamented in 1990. "The reason for the change is television." *Time's* essayist Lance Morrow blamed TV for making the issues "as weightless as clouds of electrons," and the candidates "mere actors in commercials." Walter Cronkite's 1952 warning that ugly politicians were doomed became a cliché; most assumed that in the television age the homely Abraham Lincoln would have lost to a good-looking rival.

These laments overlooked television's democratic benefits, especially its ability to introduce the candidates to millions of people. TV was neither as influential nor as revolutionary as its critics assumed.

Yet again a new technology, after failing to save the campaign, bore the blame for its decline. And once again the traditional dilemmas underlying the continuing frustrations were ignored. Sound bites about "No New Taxes" were, in fact, more substantitive than Harrisonesque slogans about "Log Cabins and Hard Cider." These tirades betrayed contempt for a democratic medium which brought politics to the masses, as well as a continuing nostalgia for good old days that never really existed.

The republican distrust of the people lingered in what was supposed to be the world's greatest democracy. Most voters, Nelson Polsby and Aaron Wildavsky wrote, "are not interested in most public issues most of the time." The Bush victory showed that "If something is correctly packaged, virtually anything can be sold," one TV reporter sneered. Increasingly, scholars, reporters, consultants, and candidates treated the people as idiots. Even the people condemned themselves—or their neighbors, at least. In one 1988 poll, 35 percent of those surveyed felt that voters did not make a strong enough effort "to find out about the candidates." Modern American politics not only kept alive the Founder's initial distrust of democracy, but seemingly proved it.

Many of the jeremiads found the sins of modern America in the sins of the candidates. "It was a pretty empty campaign," James K. Glassman wrote in *The New Republic* in 1988, "but face it, we're a pretty empty country these days." The tendency in these attacks to sugarcoat the past, be it the Lincoln–Douglas or Kennedy–Nixon debates, also reflected the republican fear of national decline. "1988, you're no 1960," *Time* magazine pronounced, with no hint of irony and little memory of the frustrations of 1960. Americans continually looked back to a mythic golden era. "We used to have marvelous presidential elections," John Chancellor of NBC sighed. As they longed for those good old days, Americans forgot that Arcadia could always be found twenty years earlier —that Americans had always believed previous elections to be better than the present ones.

* * *

Ironically, these republican complaints helped keep alive the essentially democratic practice of stumping. Stumping was no longer a novelty, but a tradition. The metaphors used to justify stumping revealed its importance—and the distance traveled in 150 years. John F. Kennedy compared campaigning to a lawyer addressing a jury; others compared it to a job applicant interviewing with his employer. These metaphors testified to the businesslike rhetoric of modern Americans; few contemporaries would compare candidates to Coriolanus or Caesar, as their ancestors had done. The metaphors also acknowledged the democratic nature of this exchange: It was in the end the people who determined whether a candidacy would live or die.

Candidates came to believe that stumping was the only way to campaign. "If we put him in front of cameras all day, he wouldn't think he had campaigned," Hubert Humphrey's director of scheduling noted during the 1972 primaries. "Only by meeting and talking to people in person can a [candidate] get the feel of what the voters are really interested in," Richard Nixon preached. With the rise of primaries having obliterated many traditional distinctions between the nominating campaign and the general election,

candidates simply kept their winning formulas. Dukakis, for example, won state after state with a no-nonsense but platitudinous approach that promised "good jobs at good wages." But this strategy did not translate effectively into the general campaign. "It took us a while to understand" that the nomination was a gateway to a "different world," Dukakis would confess to the talk-show host Larry King in late October.

Even if candidates did not want to campaign, they often felt they had no choice. Until the voters finally spoke on that first Tuesday after the first Monday in November, the campaign mostly took place on America's front pages and television screens. To a great extent, campaigns became prolonged fights for positive media exposure. Candidates had to vie for attention daily, not only with each other but with the myriad distractions of an entertainment-drenched society. Politicians became fluent in the language and mores of media—slogans became sound bites; visits to politically important locales became exposure in regional media markets.

Recent political history also fed the belief that stumping indeed counted. On the campaign planes every underdog was a "Harry Truman," every frontrunner a "Tom Dewey" or "Richard Nixon in 1960." During the last week of the campaign, *both* Dukakis *and* Bush invoked Truman's name daily. Candidates also aspired to be John F. Kennedy, and, by 1988, Ronald Reagan. When the Democratic vice-presidential candidate Lloyd Bentsen chided his Republican rival, Dan Quayle, "You're no Jack Kennedy," the smooth-talking elderly Senator appeared Reaganesque. Even in the modern scientific age the political myths of Truman, Kennedy, and Reagan were more potent than the skeptical empirical studies of political scientists.

Many candidates admitted that, to a large extent, they were playing a confidence game. By going out and greeting crowds of screaming partisans, they "reinforce[ed] previous convictions"—the one outcome academics since the 1940s were sure that campaigning accomplished. And, even if staged, these enthusiastic displays helped make the candidate appear more presidential, the campaign more winnable. Ironically, most losing efforts ended with a burst of such campaigning, one final attempt to captivate the nation. Michael Dukakis's campaign ended with what he called a last-minute "surge." Crowds increased in size and intensity. Dukakis displayed a vigor he previously had lacked. "It's doable," John Sasso of the Dukakis campaign exclaimed, making the eventual loss all the more devastating.

Stumping expressed confidence in oneself, as well as in the outcome. Modest men did not win a major party nomination. After months of stumping for votes in the primaries, and often years of stumping in local elections, candidates came to believe in their own powers of persuasion.

There were other, more tangible outcomes to stumping as well. As candidates moved from one media market to another, they fortified their coalitions and acknowledged that, under the Electoral College system, the presidential campaign remained fifty-one separate elections. The decline of political parties and the proliferation of interest groups made these activities especially important. Even in an era of mobile phones and faxes, the personal touch and local pride remained important.

While candidates wooed distinct regions and interest groups, they also kept their eye on the national audience. To the extent that governing had become a "permanent campaign," with a constant need to rally the people, stumping tested an essential presidential skill. Campaigns functioned as elaborate auditions for the rhetorical themes and central policies that would shape the coming presidency. Two years after the campaign, George Bush's clunky but straightforward cry—"Read my lips: No new taxes"—would still resonate, complicating the budget process.

Nevertheless, if American politics had evolved in an orderly fashion, by the mid-twentieth century stumping would have gone the way of the human tail, webbed feet, and other outmoded adaptations. But the modern campaign grew haphazardly, shaped by the changing institutional and technological environment, a divided political ideology, and the constant calculation of candidates and their advisers. Vast changes over two centuries in communications, transportation, the party system, and the presidency itself created the necessary conditions for change. These developments expanded the horizons, making it possible, even desirable, to stump and to debate—but they were not enough. The surprising persistence of the republican remnant offset the otherwise "natural" democratic evolution of the presidential campaign. Throughout the nineteenth century, this atavistic obsession with virtue kept candidates off the stump long after technological developments, party needs, and the growth of the presidency demanded precisely such participation. Once candidates entered the campaign, republicanism left a lingering taint, a sense that most campaigning was unseemly and undignified.

For all their importance, neither the republican remnant nor its liberal-democratic counter functioned as independent historical agents. Rather, these impulses, attitudes, and prejudices were filtered through a system much like the one that engineers call a "feedback loop." Politicians interested in their own advancement sensed the public mood, most often as articulated in the popular press. These readings of the popular pulse in turn determined the candidates' actions, thereby shaping future public attitudes. Campaign tactics did not evolve rationally under the controlled conditions of a laboratory, but were forged on the streets and in smoke-filled, now smokeless, rooms.

Amid new environs, stumping's symbolic meaning changed. Initially, stumping demonstrated the candidate's commitment to party ideals, his willingness to peddle the party's policies. It also demonstrated respect for the people. By the 1980s it was a declaration of the candidate's authenticity and independence, proof that the voters would be electing a "real person." As skepticism about the campaign grew, stumping became all the more important, calming many republican fears. The same ideological impulse that initially inhibited stumping now perpetuated it. On the stump the candidate faced the people, emerging from behind the blue smoke and mirrors of the modern campaign.

Countering republican fears of artificiality and demagoguery, candidates "in the flesh" and "pressing the flesh" broke down television's mythical "fourth wall" between performers and viewers. Even with elaborately staged pseudo-events, by meeting citizens at factory gates and beauty shops, at baseball stadiums and barbecues, candidates emerged from behind their makeup and their studios, their consultants and their advertising budgets, and revealed themselves to the people. The impromptu and intimate nature of many of the exchanges humanized both the campaign and the candidates. When candidates plunged into crowds their Secret Service agents tensed and their handlers worried, but many citizens cheered. By taking to the stump, whether such contact won votes or not, candidates forged a direct and human link with the voters.

Nominees, then, were stumping on the fault line of American politics, on the divide between liberal democracy and republicanism. In keeping with the growing demands of American democracy, the presidential nominee emerged from the periphery to move to the center of the campaign. Stumping focused attention on the individual—his personality and his character. While speaking about the issues, a candidate confronted a series of obstacles which tested his moral fiber and psychological makeup. Trading in the accepted democratic currency, which is to say issues, candidates could be judged by traditional republican standards, which is to say character. Candidates could showcase their policy positions and their personalities at the same time. Thus could the dueling gods of liberal democracy and republicanism be pleased—to a degree.

* * *

Such is the modern American presidential campaign. It is, on the one hand, a remarkably sophisticated endeavor, reliant on the latest technology to transmit sights and sounds to almost 250 million citizens. On the other hand, the ritual is strikingly primitive, as Americans continue to struggle with the fundamental political question that vexed their ancestors: "Who shall lead us?" Americans are still looking for a leader to advance political positions, to embody the hopes of the nation, to be greater than themselves, and to make themselves feel good.

The modern presidential campaign reflects its mixed ancestry and haphazard growth. A monument to liberal democracy, it is the most inclusive leadership selection process in the world. From Eastern Europe to South America, aspiring democrats look to the United States for inspiration in establishing free elections. Never before have so many American voters participated in so many stages of the process. At long last, women and blacks gained the franchise; discriminatory poll taxes and literacy tests were outlawed. Today, primaries involve millions in what had been the nominating prerogatives of a handful of party bosses. Never before have voters enjoyed so much access to the nominees. And never before have voters been exposed to so much information about each nominee's personal life and policy views. By the end of the presidential campaign, few biographical facts now remain unearthed, few political issues unaddressed.

At the same time, the presidential campaign has disillusioned millions with its nonsense and manipulation. As a result, more citizens choose not to exercise their right to vote in the United States than anywhere else in the world. Primaries seem endless, pointless, and unnecessarily weighted in favor of showmen rather than statesmen. The cynicism is so deep that even when candidates act nobly their motives are questioned, and when they have substantive differences the disagreements are ignored. Increasingly, policy positions themselves have verged on becoming mere poses, simply

the currency used to showcase personalities. And the stumping pentathlon, forcing candidates to drudge through snow, flip flapjacks, munch kielbasas, and drive tanks, steers many qualified people from even considering a run for the presidency. Washington columnist David Broder suggests that anyone willing to undergo the indignities of the current type of campaign thereby reveals that "He is too loony to be trusted with office."

In some ways, modern American politics is afflicted by the worst of both the democratic and republican legacies. In the nineteenth century the rise of liberal democracy countered the elitist and overly dignified republican campaign. Stumping made the candidates more accessible and forced them to address the issues. But the late-twentieth-century amalgam in which hyperactive candidates expose themselves from coast to coast lacks both substance and dignity. If George Washington's stiff silence was the republican thesis, and William Jennings Bryan's bombastic crusades were the liberal-democratic antithesis, Jimmy Carter's *Playboy* interview makes for a most unappealing synthesis. Trying to be all things to all people, too many modern candidates end up being of little use to anyone.

These conflicting traditions have created a political schizophrenia of sorts. Today, each candidate claims that whereas he addresses issues, his rivals devise tactics; he is virtuous, "they" are corrupt. As a result, American politics enjoys a renewable virginity, a sense each time that *this* campaign will be different, more honorable, more substantive. Yet, inevitably, the campaign soon becomes the "worst ever," as partisanship intensifies and disappointments of previous years are forgotten. Finally, on Election Day, Americans celebrate the greatest democracy on earth and the "sacred ballot box" that once again solves America's conflicts peacefully. This republican morality play undermines Americans' faith in themselves, then renews it.

The simultaneous triumphs and humiliations of the presidential contest illustrate why the campaign will not be repaired so easily. Welcome advances have often spawned unfortunate consequences. For example, primaries democratized the process but disillusioned millions. Television brought the candidates to the people even while creating a new artificial distance. Polling articulated—then subverted—the opinions of the masses. The interest in character has come at the cost of a commitment to policy debates. The ever-expanding demands on active candidates, as well as the increasing scrutiny of their entire lives, have produced greater openness at the cost of the individual's dignity and the institution's majesty.

The problem of the presidential campaign is not a matter of mechanics. If engineers tried to invent the ideal democratic process, many would design a system as inclusive and comprehensive as the one that evolved. Over the years the American drift toward liberal democracy has short-circuited the least democratic aspects of electoral politics, including the Electoral College, the republican taboo, and the boss-centered party nominating system. Rather than tinkering with the primaries or with federal funding or with anything else, reformers need to inject civility, substance, openness, and dignity into the present system—commodities that cannot be produced on demand.

America needs a campaign which can accommodate both Walter Mondale who does not relish a two-year merry-go-round of Holiday Inns, and a George Bush able to stick to "the facts" as closely as he claims he had hoped to. Today, any candidate who takes it easy, or takes such a high road, will be dismissed as either a poseur or a loser. But before changing the electoral system, Americans have to determine just how their ideal candidate can be dignified yet accessible, issue-oriented yet intimate, acceptable to lofty editorialists yet electric on the streets, as "sensible" as Adlai Stevenson and as charming as Ronald Reagan.

These dilemmas bring us back to the fundamental conflicts that the Founding Fathers failed to resolve: Shall the president be a king or a prime minister, the most virtuous man or the most representative one? Should the people —or their betters—decide? Should the decision be one based on careful calculation or tempered emotion? Characteristically, the Founders tried to finesse the problems, and in so doing created a contradictory system which operates today in ways very different from those they imagined. No wonder that, two hundred years later, Americans remain miffed.

"Democracy begins in conversation," the Progressive philosopher and educator John Dewey declared on his ninetieth birthday. Until presidential candidates broke the republican code of silence and began conversing with the people, American elections could not be considered "democratic." Candidates had to face the people, reveal themselves, and commit themselves publicly. The dialogue with the people was both a mark of respect and a sign of a dynamic democracy. It also was an essential tool of leadership, helping to solidify the president's role at the center of the American political universe.

Now, only a few decades after the candidates entered the conversation, the opposite problem looms—candidates say so much that they appear to be saying nothing. And much of what they say is dismissed as calculating. Candidates need occasionally to trust to silence, to think; but there is no time for that on the three-media-market-a-day campaign trail. They end up speaking *at* the people, not *to* them. While this verbosity appears to be a gain for liberal democracy at the expense of republicanism, it merely follows the form, not the essence, of democracy. The solution, however, is neither to stop the conversation nor to impose artificial limits on it by restraining either campaigns or candidates. Rather, Americans finally have to acknowledge their contradictory expectations for both the candidates and the campaign, and then, harder than ever, continue to seek a balance between inspiration and education, between openness and dignity, between the man and the message, and—still with us from our earliest days—between liberal democracy and republican virtue.

POSTSCRIPT

Do Political Campaigns Inform Voters?

The right of people to choose who governs them is the very essence of democracy. Why, then, are people in America often so unhappy about the process? Reforms adopted for the 1972 presidential nominations (with small revisions in every presidential election since) led to the apportionment of delegate votes in accordance with the support each candidate received in the caucus or primary at which the delegates were chosen.

Two significant results are that the local party organizations no longer handpick delegates, and the national convention ratifies the choice of the delegates without any real deliberation. This increases the importance of voters in choosing the candidates. Ideally, voters should be motivated and informed during the primary campaign before the candidates are chosen as well as during the general election campaign. Are they?

Troy believes that candidates spend too much money, give voters too little information regarding the issues, and provide too little insight into their proposals. Popkin believes that political campaigns work well and that they would work better if they ran longer. What do you think?

A classic text on this subject is Nelson W. Polsby and Aaron Wildavsky, *Presidential Elections: Contemporary Strategies of American Electoral Politics*, 8th ed. (Free Press, 1991). An analysis of campaign strategy and tactics, media, finance, and other elements of the 1988 election campaign can be found in Stephen J. Wayne, *The Road to the White House 1992: The Politics of Presidential Elections* (St. Martin's Press, 1992).

A different perspective on the 1988 presidential election can be found in Richard Ben Cramer, *What It Takes: The Way to the White House* (Random House, 1992), which explores why people seek power, specifically why George Bush, Michael Dukakis, and four other would-be candidates sought nomination. Thomas E. Patterson, *Out of Order* (Alfred A. Knopf, 1933) is a sharp criticism of the decline of political parties and the increasing importance of the media in presidential elections.

ISSUE 3

Do Political Action Committees Undermine Democracy?

YES: Fred Wertheimer, from "Campaign Finance Reform: The Unfinished Agenda," *The Annals of the American Academy of Political and Social Science* (July 1986)

NO: Herbert E. Alexander, from "The Case for PACs," A Public Affairs Council Monograph (1983)

ISSUE SUMMARY

YES: Fred Wertheimer, the president of Common Cause, a citizen's lobbying organization, argues that PACs exert too much influence over the electoral process, allowing special interests to get the ear of elected officials at the expense of the national interest.

NO: Political analyst Herbert E. Alexander insists that PACs make significant contributions to the American political system and help enhance the political power of the individual.

American folk humorist Will Rogers once observed that it took a lot of money even to *lose* an election. What would Will Rogers say if he were alive today?

The cost of television as a medium of communication and persuasion has greatly increased the expenditures in election campaigns. The cost of campaigning for Congress is rising dramatically. Campaign spending on House and Senate races totaled $678 million in 1991–1992, up almost $200 million from 1987–1988. Money, said a prominent California politician, is the "mother's milk of politics."

More controversial than the amount of money spent in politics is its source. Political action committees, groups that are formed to raise and contribute money to the candidates who are most likely to advance the group's interests, have become a major factor in financing American election campaigns. PACs (as they are called) have proliferated in recent years, with more than 100 new special-interest groups being founded each year. It is estimated that there are now more than 4,000 PACs, representing almost every conceivable political interest.

By raising money from political sympathizers, association members, and public solicitations, PACs have provided the funds with which candidates reach the public. PACs spent more than $180 million on congressional campaigns in 1991–1992, most of it going to Democrats. In the Senate, Democratic candidates received $28.8 million from PACs, while Republicans got $22.2 million. The difference was much greater in races for the House of Representatives, which has a larger percentage of Democrats. Democratic House candidates got more than $85 million in PAC money, while Republicans received only $41.6 million. The top 10 richest PACs in 1991–1992 included those connected to professional organizations like the American Medical Association, to labor and business groups like the United Auto Workers and the Realtor's Association, and to feminist and abortion-rights groups like Emily's List and the National Abortion Rights Action League.

Some PACs are explicitly liberal or conservative, but most are not concerned with ideology. Business PACs, for example, are just as likely to contribute to liberal Democrats as they are to conservative Republicans, who, historically, have been the most pro-business members of Congress. Business PACs prefer to back winners, regardless of party or ideology, and that usually means backing incumbents. Representative Robert Dornan (R-California) put it rather bluntly: "Corporate managers . . . don't care who's in office, what party or what they stand for. They're just out to buy you."

Legislators are divided on the influence of PACs. Representative Barney Frank (D-Massachusetts) has said, "You can't take thousands of dollars from a group and not have it affect you." But Representative Henry J. Hyde (R-Illinois) offers a different perspective. "The more PACs proliferate," he says, "the less influence any individual PAC has. . . . Their influence is diminished by their proliferation."

Critics argue that PAC money in recent years probably influenced congressional votes on bills to maintain high dairy price supports and to defeat legislation that would have required warranties on used cars. On the other hand, defenders of PACs maintain that they are less interested in influencing members of Congress who are opposed to their points of view than in electing new members who are sympathetic.

PACs are not a new phenomenon. Pressure groups, or factions, as founding father James Madison called them, have always been part of the political process. To eliminate them would be to destroy liberty itself. What Madison hoped for was the broadest participation of interest groups, so that compromises among them would result in an approximation of the national interest.

Has this happened? In the following selections, Fred Wertheimer, president of Common Cause, a self-styled citizens' lobby, argues that the opposite has occurred. In his view, the proliferation of PACs has given special interests the power to override the national interest. Herbert E. Alexander contests this view and identifies a number of significant contributions that PACs have made to the American political system.

YES   Fred Wertheimer

CAMPAIGN FINANCE REFORM: THE UNFINISHED AGENDA

Our democracy is founded on the concept of representation. Citizens elect leaders who are given responsibility to weigh all the competing and conflicting interests that reflect our diversity and to decide what, in their judgment, will best advance the interests of the citizenry.

It is obviously a rough system. It often does not measure up to the ideal we might hope to attain. But we continue to place our trust in this system because we believe our best chance at governing ourselves lies in obtaining the best judgment of elected representatives.

Unfortunately, that is not happening today. We are not obtaining the best judgment of our elected representatives in Congress because they are not free to give it to us. As a result of our present congressional campaign financing system—and the increasing role of political action committee (PAC) campaign contributions—members of Congress are rapidly losing their ability to represent the constituencies that have elected them.

We have long struggled to prevent money from being used to influence government decisions. We have not always succeeded, but we have never lost sight of the goal. Buying influence violates our most fundamental democratic values. We have long recognized that the ability to make large campaign contributions does, in fact, make some more equal than others....

CONGRESSIONAL CAMPAIGN FINANCING

The last decade of congressional campaign financing has been marked by an exponential increase in the number of PACs formed by corporations, labor unions, trade associations, and other groups. In 1974 there were 608 PACs. Today there are more than 4000.

This explosion in PACs can be traced to congressional action—and inaction—in 1974. Ironically, at the very time when members of Congress were acting to clean up presidential elections, they opened the door for PACs to enter the congressional arena in an unprecedented way. The key to the PAC explosion was a provision attached to the 1974 law by labor and business groups, over the opposition of Common Cause and other reform advocates, that authorized government contractors to establish PACs. In addition, by creating public financing for presidential campaigns, but not for congressional races, the 1974 amendments focused the attention and interest of PACs and other private campaign donors on Congress.

The resulting growth in PACs was no accident, and it certainly was not a reform. The growth of PACs, moreover, is certainly no unintended consequence of the 1974 law—the provision was included to protect and enhance the role of PACs in financing campaigns, and it has.

This tremendous increase in the number of PACs has not resulted in balanced representation in Washington. As Senator Gary Hart, Democrat of Colorado, has told the Senate:

> It seems the only group without a well-heeled PAC is the average citizen—the voter who has no special interest beyond low taxes, an efficient government, an honorable Congress, and a humane society. Those are the demands we should be heeding—but those are the demands the PACs have drowned out.

In fact, the increasing number of PACs has largely served to increase the ability of single interests to bring pressure to bear on a congressional candidate or a member of Congress. There are more than 100 insurance company PACs, more than 100 PACs sponsored by electric utilities, and more than 300 sponsored by labor unions. Representative David Obey, Democrat of Wisconsin, has observed that frequently in Washington:

> an issue affects an entire industry and all of the companies and labor unions in that industry.... When that occurs,

[and] a large number of groups which have made substantial contributions to members are all lobbying on the same side of an issue, the pressure generated from those aggregate contributions is enormous and warps the process. It is as if they had made a single, extremely large contribution.

The increase in the number of PACs, not surprisingly, has also produced a tremendous increase in PAC contributions to congressional candidates. In 1974, PACs gave $12.5 million to congressional candidates. By the 1984 elections, their contributions had exceeded $100 million, an eightfold increase in ten years.

PAC money also represents a far more important part of the average candidate's campaign funds than it did ten or so years ago. In 1974, 15.7 percent of congressional candidates' campaign money came from PACs; by the 1984 election, that proportion had increased to 30 percent.

Yet these numbers only begin to tell the story. The increased dependence on PAC contributions has been greatest for winners, those individuals who serve in Congress and who cast votes that shape our daily lives. In the Ninety-ninth Congress (1985–86), over 150 House members received 50 percent or more of their campaign funds from PACs, including 20 of the 27 committee chairs and party leaders. House winners in the 1984 election received an average of 41 percent of their campaign dollars from PACs. Of all winning House candidates in the 1974 election, only 28 percent received one-third or more of their campaign funds from PACs. By 1984, that figure had grown to 78 percent.

For senators, PAC contributions are also becoming a more important source of campaign dollars. Senators elected in 1976 received a total of $3.1 million from PACs; Senate winners in the 1984 election raised $20 million from OACs. In the 1984 elections, 23 winning Senate candidates raised more than $500,000 each from PACs.

Some have suggested that the growth in PACs is an important new form of citizen involvement in the political process. Yet PAC participation is often likely to be more of an involvement in the corporate process or the union process or the trade association process than it is in the political process. University of Minnesota professor Frank J. Sorauf has noted:

> To understand political participation through PACs, we need also to note the nature of the participation. Some of it is not even political activity; buying a ticket in a raffle, the proceeds of which go to a PAC, a party, or a candidate, does not qualify as a political act by most standards. Even the contributory act of writing a check or giving cash to a PAC is a somewhat limited form of participation that requires little time or immediate involvement; in a sense it buys political mercenaries who free the contributor from the need to be personally active in the campaign. It is one of the least active forms of political activity, well suited to the very busy or to those who find politics strange, boring, or distasteful.

In fact, the growth of PACs and the increased importance of PAC money have had a negative effect on two different parts of the political process —congressional elections and congressional decision making. First, PAC money tends to make congressional campaigns less competitive because of the overwhelming advantage enjoyed by incumbents in PAC fund-raising. The ratio of PAC contributions to incumbents over challengers in 1984 House races was 4.6 to 1.0; in the Senate, incumbents in 1984 enjoyed a 3.0 to 1.0 advantage in PAC receipts. On the average, 1984 House incumbents raised $100,000 more from PACs than did challengers. This $100,000 advantage was true even in the most highly competitive House races, those in which the incumbent received 55 percent or less of the vote. In these races, incumbents received an average of over $230,000 from PACs; their challengers received less than $110,000. The advantage enjoyed by incumbents is true for all kinds of PAC giving—for contributions by labor groups, corporate PACs, and trade and membership PACs.

Second, there is a growing awareness that PAC money makes a difference in the legislative process, a difference that is inimical to our democracy. PAC dollars are given by special interest groups to gain special access and special influence in Washington. Most often PAC contributions are made with a legislative purpose in mind. The late Justin Dart, former chairman of Dart Industries, once noted that dialogue with politicians "is a fine thing, but with a little money they hear you better." Senator Charles Mathias, Republican of Maryland, has stated:

> An official may not change his or her vote solely to accommodate the views of such contributors, but often officials, including myself, will agree to meet with an individual who made a large contribution so the official can hear the contributor's concerns and make the contributor aware these concerns have been considered.... Since an elected official has only so much time available, the inevitable result of such special treatment for the large contributor is that

other citizens are denied the opportunity they otherwise would have to confer with the elected official.

Common Cause and others have produced a number of studies that show a relationship between PAC contributions and legislative behavior. The examples run the gamut of legislative decisions, including hospital cost containment, the Clean Air Act, domestic content legislation, dairy price programs, gun control, maritime policies, and regulation by the Federal Trade Commission of professional groups or of used-car sales.

PAC gifts do not guarantee votes or support. PACs do not always win. But PAC contributions do provide donors with critical access and influence; they do affect legislative decisions and are increasingly dominating and paralyzing the legislative process.

In the last few years, something very important and fundamental has happened in this country—and that is the development of a growing awareness and recognition of the fact that the PAC system is a rotten system that must be changed. We know that concern is growing when Irving Shapiro, former chairman and chief executive officer of duPont and the former chairman of the Business Roundtable, describes the current system of financing congressional campaigns as "an invidious thing, it's corrupting, it does pollute the system." . . .

CONCLUSION

In the spring of 1973, Common Cause chairman John Gardner told the Senate Commerce Committee that "there is nothing in our political system today that creates more mischief, more corruption, and more alienation and distrust on the part of the public than does our system of financing elections. Despite major progress in improving the presidential campaign-financing system, that observation remains true today with regard to the congressional campaign-financing system. As former Watergate special prosecutor and current Common Cause chairman Archibald Cox has observed, inaction has resulted in "a Congress still more deeply trapped in the stranglehold of special interests which threatens to paralyze the process of democratic government." Congress needs to complete the reforms begun in the wake of Watergate by fundamentally transforming its own campaign-financing system and by making other adjustments needed to preserve the integrity of presidential public financing, campaign reporting requirements, and limitations on contributions by individuals and PACs.

A consensus has been reached in this country that PACs are inimical to our system of representative government. The question now remaining is whether that public consensus can be translated into congressional action.

No solution that may be adopted will be final and perfect. We will always need to reevaluate and adjust any campaign finance system. The presidential public financing system demonstrates the need for periodic adjustments. But more important, the experience of presidential public financing shows us that fundamental improvement in our campaign finance laws is indeed attainable.

We can and must have a better system for financing congressional campaigns. Representative government is at stake.

NO   Herbert E. Alexander

THE CASE FOR PACs

Seen in historical perspective, political action committees represent a functional system for political fund raising that developed, albeit unintentionally, from efforts to reform the political process. PACs represent an expression of an issue politics that resulted from attempts to remedy a sometimes unresponsive political system. And they represent an institutionalization of the campaign fund solicitation process that developed from the enactment of reform legislation intended to increase the number of small contributors.

Despite the unforeseen character of their development, PACs have made significant contributions to the political system:

1. PACs increased participation in the political process.   The reform efforts that spawned PACs were designed to allow more voices to be heard in determining who will become our nation's elected officials. Thanks in part to PACs, that goal has been achieved.

Although it is difficult to determine how many individuals now participate in the political process through voluntarily contributing to political action committees, some useful information is available. The survey of company PACs by Civic Service, Inc., found that in the 1979–1980 election cycle more than 100,000 individuals contributed to the 275 PACs responding to the survey, and that the average number of donors to those PACS was 388. By extrapolation, it appears that all corporate PACs active in the 1979–1980 cycle received contributions from at least 210,000 individuals.

The largest conservative ideological group PACs, which rely on direct mail solicitations, received about 1.3 million contributions in 1979–1980, though individuals may well have contributed to more than one of those groups. It is difficult to estimate the total number of persons who gave to professional and membership association PACs, though information about specific groups is available. For example, an official of the National Association of Realtors PAC estimated that his group had 80,000 contributors in 1979, 87,000 in 1980, 92,000 in 1981 and about 95,000 in 1982. It is more difficult still to estimate the number of contributors to labor PACs, although here, too, information is available regarding specific groups. According to a National Education

Association official, for example, the NEA PAC received donations from about 600,000 persons in the 1979–1980 election cycle.

Surveys taken between 1952 and 1976 indicate that from 8 to 12 percent of the total adult population contributed to politics at some level in presidential election years, with the figure standing at 9 percent in 1976. According to a survey by the Center for Political Studies at the University of Michigan, however, 13.4 percent of the adult population—about 17.1 million persons—gave to candidates and causes during the 1979–1980 election cycle. Survey data suggest that the increase registered in 1980 is due to the increased number of persons giving to interest groups. Of those surveyed, 6.8 percent gave to candidates, 3.8 percent gave to parties, and 6.8 percent gave to interest groups. Since those figures add up to well over 13.4 percent, it is obvious that a significant number of persons contributed in two or all three categories.

2. *PACs allow individuals to increase the impact of their political activity.* PACs and their interest group sponsors not only encourage individual citizens to participate in the electoral process, they provide them with a sense of achievement or effectiveness that accompanies taking part in political activity with like-minded persons rather than merely acting alone.

3. *PACs are a popular mechanism for political fund raising because they respect the manner in which society is structured.* Occupational and interest groups have replaced the neighborhood as the center of activities and source of values and the ideologically ambiguous political parties as a source of political action. Individuals seem less willing to commit themselves to the broad agenda of the parties; they are interested mainly in single issues or clusters of issues. PACs, organized on the basis of specific occupational or socioeconomic or issue groupings, allow individuals to join with others who share their values and interests and to undertake action to achieve the political goals they perceive as most important to them.

4. *PACs and the interest groups they represent serve as a safeguard against undue influence by the government or by the media.* By energetically promoting their competing claims and views, such groups prevent the development of either a single, official viewpoint or a media bias. They demonstrate the lively pluralism so highly valued and forcefully guaranteed by the framers of the Constitution.

5. *PACs have made more money available for political campaigns.* By helping candidates pay the rising costs of conducting election campaigns, PACs help to assure the communication of the candidates' views and positions and thus to clarify campaign issues. They also encourage individuals without wealth to run for office.

6. *PACs have contributed to greater accountability in election campaign financing.* Corporations are legitimately concerned about public policy, but prior to the FECA they were uncertain about the legality of providing financial support to candidates who would voice their concerns. That many corporations resorted to subterfuges to circumvent the law is common knowledge. By sanctioning the use of PACs by corporations, the law has replaced the undisclosed and often questionable form of business participation in politics with the public and accountable form practiced by corporate and other business-related PACs today. However much money now is derived from corporate PACs, it is not clear that corporate PAC money today is greater proportion-

ally than was business-derived money when there were no effective limits on giving and when disclosure was less comprehensive.

HOW PACs CAN RESPOND

PACs enjoy a growing constituency, but, in view of current anti-PAC publicity and endeavors, PAC supporters must engage in a concerted educational effort regarding their methods and goals if PACs are to avoid being restricted in their ability to participate in the political process. That effort should include, certainly, responding with specific and accurate information to criticisms made of PACs and making plain the many values PACs bring to the political process.

Educational efforts also might include using the methods of PAC opponents to the advantage of the PAC movement. For example, PAC opponents frequently correlate PAC contributions and legislative outcomes and conclude that the contributions resulted in specific legislative decisions. PAC critics publicized widely the fact that maritime unions contributed heavily to some members of the House Merchant Marine Committee who favored a cargo preference bill introduced in 1977 and supported by the unions. They implied the committee members were influenced by the contributions to report out a favorable bill. PAC supporters did little to discover and publicize the committee members' other sources of funds. The American Medical Association Political Action Committee, for example, contributed to every incumbent on the House Committee, yet AMPAC and the medical practitioners who support it had no vested interest in the cargo preference bill or in other legislation considered by the committee. Nor

was much publicity given to the fact that the two committee members who received the greatest financial support from the unions represented districts in which there is a significant amount of port activity and that consequently they would understandably be responsive to maritime interests.

When critics use simplistic correlations to demonstrate undue PAC influence on the decisions of legislators, PAC supporters should endeavor to present the whole campaign finance picture: What percentage of the legislators' campaign funds came from the interest group or groups in question? Did those groups also contribute to other legislators whose committee assignments gave them no formative role in legislation of particular interest to the groups? Did groups with no special interest in the legislation in question contribute to the legislators dealing with it at the committee or subcommittee level? What factors in the legislators' home districts or states might have influenced the legislators' decisions? What non-monetary pressures were brought to bear on the legislators?

It also might be useful for PAC supporters to publicize "negative correlations," which would demonstrate that PAC contributions often do not correlate with specific legislative decisions.

PAC supporters also should question the unarticulated assumptions at the basis of much of the anti-PAC criticism.

- Money is not simply a necessary evil in the political process. By itself money is neutral; in politics as in other areas its uses and purposes determine its meaning.

- There is nothing inherently immoral or corrupting about corporate or labor contributions of money, any more than any other private contribution of funds.

- All campaign contributions are not attempts to gain special favors; rather, contributing political money is an important form of participation in a democracy.
- Money is not the sole, and often not even the most important, political resource. Many other factors affect electoral and legislative outcomes. (At the close of the 97th Congress, for example, an immigration reform bill that reportedly had widespread support in the House and the Senate died because of the effective lobbying efforts of employees, labor unions and minorities who believed they would be adversely affected by it; few, if any, campaign contributions were involved in the effort to forestall the legislation.)
- Curbing interest group contributions will not free legislators of the dilemma of choosing between electoral necessity and legislative duty. Even if PACs were eliminated, legislators would still be confronted with the sometimes conflicting demands between doing what will help them remain in office and serving what they perceive as the public good.
- A direct dialogue between candidates and individual voters without interest group influence is not possible in a representative democracy. Politics is about people, their ideas, interests and aspirations. Since people seek political fulfillment partly through groups, a politics in which supportive groups are shut out or seriously impaired is difficult to conceive.

There is danger, clearly, in our pluralistic society if groups are overly restricted in their political activity. It is useful to recall that five of the most significant movements of the last two decades—the civil rights movement, the Vietnam peace movement, the political reform movement, the women's rights movement, and the movement toward fiscal restraint—originated in the private sector, where the need for action was perceived and where needed interest organizations were established to carry it out. *These movements would not have taken place if like-minded citizens had not been permitted to combine forces and thereby enhance their political power.*

One hundred and fifty years ago, de Tocqueville recognized that in America "the liberty of association [had] become a necessary guarantee against the tyranny of the majority." The freedom to join in common cause with other citizens remains indispensable to our democratic system. The pursuit of self-interest is, as Irving Kristol has pointed out, a condition, not a problem.

POSTSCRIPT

Do Political Action Committees Undermine Democracy?

Interestingly, both Alexander and Wertheimer couch their arguments in terms of democratic values: open government, fairness to all, and popular participation. Alexander claims that PACs bring a wide variety of groups into the political process, give new groups a chance to be heard, and let corporations contribute funds openly instead of resorting to back-channel routes. Wertheimer pins much of his argument on the need for equality in the democratic process, and he worries that PACs make some voters "more equal" than others.

Edward Roeder has edited a useful directory of PACs that supplies information about their sources, their funds, and whom they support. See his *PACs Americana: The Directory of Political Action Committees and Their Interests*, 2d ed. (Sunshine Service, 1986). Larry Sabato's *PAC Power* (W. W. Norton, 1984) is a comprehensive overview of PACs: what they are, how they operate, and their impact. Frank J. Sorauf's *What Price PACs?* (Priority Press, 1985) studies PAC financing and its implications. For an excellent general study of interest groups, including PACs, see Graham K. Wilson's *Interest Groups in the United States* (Clarendon Press, 1981). Dan Clawson et al., in *Money Talks: Corporate PACs and Political Influence* (Basic Books, 1992), examine the influence of corporate PACs and argue that "business exercises power on many fronts, [and] that power must be opposed on every front."

Other countries succeed in setting strict limits on campaign spending. Can America do it without inhibiting political expression? Should PAC contributions be replaced by public financing of congressional elections? Or should PACs be accepted as a vigorous expression of political freedom? In short, do PACs undermine or do they underline democracy?

ISSUE 4

Does the News Media Have a Liberal Bias?

YES: H. Joachim Maitre, from "The Tilt to the News: How American Journalism Has Swerved from the Ideal of Objectivity," *The World and I* (December 1993)

NO: Martin A. Lee and Norman Solomon, from *Unreliable Sources: A Guide to Detecting Bias in News Media* (Carol Publishing Group, 1992)

ISSUE SUMMARY

YES: Journalism professor H. Joachim Maitre argues that news reporters are liberals who allow their political views to seep into their reporting.

NO: Media critics Martin A. Lee and Norman Solomon argue that the media are owned and operated by men and women whose bias in reporting is toward the conservative status quo.

"A small group of men, numbering perhaps no more than a dozen 'anchormen,' commentators and executive producers... decide what forty to fifty million Americans will learn of the day's events in the nation and the world." The speaker was Spiro Agnew, vice president of the United States during the Nixon administration. The thesis of Agnew's speech, delivered to an audience of midwestern Republicans in 1969, was that the television news media are controlled by a small group of liberals who foist their liberal opinions on viewers under the guise of "news." The upshot of this control, said Agnew, "is that a narrow and distorted picture of America often emerges from the televised news." Many Americans, even many of those who were later shocked by revelations that Agnew took bribes while serving in public office, agreed with Agnew's critique of the "liberal media."

Politicians' complaints about unfair news coverage go back much further than Agnew and the Nixon administration. The third president of the United States, Thomas Jefferson, was an eloquent champion of the press, but after six years as president, he could hardly contain his bitterness. "The man who never looks into a newspaper," he wrote, "is better informed than he who reads them, inasmuch as he who knows nothing is nearer to truth than he whose mind is filled with falsehoods and errors."

The press today is much different than it was in Jefferson's day. Newspapers then were pressed in hand-operated frames in many little printing shops around the country; everything was local and decentralized, and each paper averaged a few hundred subscribers. Today, newspaper chains have taken over most of the once-independent local newspapers. The remaining independents rely heavily on national and international wire services. Almost all major magazines have national circulations; some newspapers, like *USA Today* and the *Wall Street Journal*, do too. Other newspapers, like the *New York Times* and the *Washington Post*, enjoy nationwide prestige and help set the nation's news agenda. Geographical centralization is even more obvious in the case of television. About 70 percent of the national news on television comes from three networks whose programming originates in New York City.

A second important difference between the media of the eighteenth century and the media today has to do with the ideal of "objectivity." In past eras, newspapers were frankly partisan sheets, full of nasty barbs at the politicians and parties the editors did not like; they made no distinction between "news" and "editorials." The ideal of objective journalism is a relatively recent development. It traces back to the early years of the twentieth century. Disgusted with the sensationalist "yellow journalism" of the time, intellectual leaders urged that newspapers cultivate a core of professionals who would concentrate on accurate reporting and who would leave their opinions to the editorial page. Journalism schools cropped up around the country, helping to promote the ideal of objectivity. Although some journalists now openly scoff at it, the ideal still commands the respect—in theory, if not always in practice—of working reporters.

These two historical developments, news centralization and news professionalism, play off against one another in the current debate over news "bias." The question of bias was irrelevant when the press was a scatter of little independent newspapers. If you did not like the bias of one paper, you picked another one—or you started your own, which could be done with modest capital outlay. Bias started to become an important question when newspapers became dominated by chains and airwaves by networks, and when a few national press leaders like the *New York Times* and the *Washington Post* began to emerge. Although these "mainstream" news outlets have been challenged in recent years by opinions expressed in a variety of alternative media—such as cable television, talk radio, newsletters, and computer mail—they still remain powerful conveyers of news.

Is media news reporting biased? Those who present the news usually contend that "bias is in the eyes of the beholder," that people simply read into the news what they *think* is its bias—and they always seem to think that it is biased against their point of view. Media critics insist that the bias is not an illusion but a reality. The critics, however, often disagree about whether such bias is liberal or conservative, as is the case with this issue. In the following selections, H. Joachim Maitre argues that the news media tilt to the left, while Martin A. Lee and Norman Solomon contend that the slant of the news media supports a conservative status quo.

YES

H. Joachim Maitre

THE TILT TO THE NEWS: HOW AMERICAN JOURNALISM HAS SWERVED FROM THE IDEAL OF OBJECTIVITY

"Mr. President," said the nation's second-ranked television news anchorman on May 27 [1993] and via satellite, "if we could be one-hundredth as great as you and Hillary Rodham Clinton have been in the White House, we would take it right now and walk away winners.... Thank you very much, and tell Mrs. Clinton we respect her and we are pulling for her."

Dan Rather's declaration of adoration and active support for the presidential couple was not meant for public viewing but—recorded through a technical glitch—caused yet another puncture in the perforated armor of American journalism. In professionally purer times, Rather's indiscretion would have destroyed what was left of his credibility as an honest news broker. He had shown his tilt.

Finally, after years of heated public debates and often tedious scholarly discourse over alleged institutional liberal bias in the American news media, there is no argument on the basics any longer. "Everyone knows," said political scientist James Q. Wilson in the June 21, 1993, edition of the *New Republic*, "that the members of the national media are well to the left of the average voter."

For those skeptics still demanding statistical evidence that journalists tend to hold liberal political views, numbers were provided in a summer 1992 survey of fourteen hundred journalists, reported in *The American Journalist in the 1990s*, published by the New York–based Freedom Forum Media Studies Center. It concluded that 44.1 percent of those polled consider themselves Democrats and only 16.3 percent Republicans. The gap had grown since 1982, when a similar survey was done, and is now far larger than among the general population.

BIAS CREEPS INTO REPORTING

These figures as such would be of limited interest if they did not strengthen the suspicion that the journalist's personal political and philosophical preferences, his system of beliefs, his world-view would—unavoidably—seep into his reporting and that the stated imbalance between liberal and conservative leanings and loyalties already is gravely affecting the ways and worth of news reporting in this country. Slant is becoming ever more visible, nowhere more so than on television "news."

Examples of liberal bias and resulting slant abound. President Clinton had been in office less than a month when megastar Dan Rather offered his helping hand: Clinton's program "will include money to put people back to work repairing this country's infrastructure, roads, bridges, and other public works" (CBS, February 17). Rather's unspoken message: The Clinton administration will rebuild the America run down through years of neglect by Clinton's Republican predecessors in the White House. Bill Clinton will create the employment lost in previous years. News, or partisan propaganda?

Soon, Dan Rather's new coanchor, Connie Chung, another Clinton fan, identified Clinton's adversary: "The Senate Republicans are threatening to block the president's $16 billion job creation program" (CBS, April 1). Or: "Held up in the Senate is President Clinton's $16 billion plan to bring unemployment down" (CBS, April 2). And: "President Clinton says the $16 billion is crucial to boosting the economy" (CBS, April 6).

But what was the opposition's line of argumentation? Neither Rather nor Chung ever addressed the conceptual base for Republican resistance to Clinton's ambitious employment program and to "Clintonomics" in general, to wit: In free societies, the creation of jobs is a central task for private enterprise, not for the government and its various bureau-cracies. This concept in its implementation resulted in the creation of millions of jobs in the 1980s, but that had been under President Reagan—anathema for the liberal mind-set.

The rule of liberal media bias starts with terminology. The term *liberal* is generally used in a positive sense in America. "Liberal social policies" are good by implication; "restrictive social policies" are bad. To be "liberal" suggests generosity and open-mindedness; to be "conservative" implies selfishness and closed-mindedness. Derived from the Latin word *liber* (free), *liberal* once stood for persons and ideas that favored freedom. In many European countries, that original meaning still prevails. Not so in America, where—in particular when applied to public policy—*liberal* has come to mean favoring government intervention and control to secure economic and social justice.

Thus, the expansion of government activities and the growth of government itself are favored by today's liberals, while liberating commerce (through deregulation) and the economy from government intervention and control has become a conservative ideal. Classic liberal spokesmen for a free economy such as Friedrich von Hayek and Milton Friedman (both recipients of the Nobel Prize in economics) have been relegated to conservative status by the liberal class dominant in the media and in politics. At the same time, contemporary America's most successful advocate of government intervention in commerce and the economy, Sen. Edward Kennedy, is also America's best-known "liberal"—or socialist, in reality.

Television news coverage of American economic affairs has been the subject of an in-depth report by Ted Smith of Virginia Commonwealth University.

The study, titled *The Vanishing Economy: Television Coverage of Economic Affairs, 1982–87*, involved systematic analysis of three full years of coverage during the Reagan presidency and found a highly consistent pattern of emphasis and omission. Smith demonstrates that network news journalists have chosen not only to stress problems and failures but to limit or eliminate coverage of gains and success. In some instances, Smith says, "those restrictions have been so extreme that it would be difficult or impossible for a person who relied exclusively on television evening news for his knowledge of the world to form an accurate understanding of the world." He concludes: "To be blunt, systematic suppression of positive information, economic or otherwise, is nothing less than systematic censorship. As such, it strikes at the foundations of the democratic process."

THE MEDIA AND THE DEMOCRATS: SUPPRESSING NEGATIVE INFORMATION

With Clinton's election and the return of the Democrats to majority rule in Congress, television's coverage of economic affairs faces the challenge of liberal economic policies and their implementation. Chances are that the "systematic suppression of positive information," as found by Smith, will be replaced by systematic suppression of negative information. Liberal policies and plans will be granted the benefit of the doubt. During the budget debates of the past summer, criticism of Reagan policies far outweighed serious analysis of Clinton's campaign platform and his economic package, advertised as seeking a "deficit reduction."

The purpose of the phrase *deficit reduction* was to avoid the more candid term *tax increase* and, at the same time, to mislead Americans into thinking "that the change has something to do with reducing the federal budget," says Tom Bethell, one of the country's few nonconforming journalists, in an article in the September 1993 issue of the *American Spectator*. Bethell reveals numbers and trends that easily could have been published in prestigious newspapers (but were not) or made public on television news programs (but were not thought newsworthy) and concludes:

The Clinton economic plan has all along been an exercise in deception, with the news media acting as collaborators or dupes.... On April 8, the Office of Management and Budget [OMB] published the 1994 federal budget. The next day, major newspapers published full-page stories on the budget, but all failed to give the outlay and revenue totals. It has become a convention among journalists that only the deficit, or "difference," should be published. The difference between what and what? We are rarely told. The failure to publish the totals, of course, disguises the extent to which they continue to rise. An uncritical Washington press corps has permitted Clinton to talk of "spending cuts" without publishing the numbers on which his claim is based.

Many ordinary citizens agree with this assessment of today's media. One man, Douglas Losordo, chastised the *Boston Globe* in a letter printed on September 7, 1993, for repeatedly referring to "spending reductions" in the Clinton budget "when in fact the only proposed real decreases in spending are in the defense budget."

Losordo cited OMB figures to the effect that outlays (spending) will increase from $1.468 trillion [in 1993] to $1.781 trillion in 1998, while defense spending will drop from $277 billion to $239 billion over the same period. "How is this a spending cut?" Losordo asks, charging that the *Globe* is "simply repeating the distortions of fact presented by our politicians."

[In 1986] social scientists Robert Lichter, Stanley Rothman, and Linda Lichter published *The Media Elite*, a ground-breaking study of political leanings and perspectives among the nation's leading journalists and how those preferences affected their work. They concluded:

> The media elite are a homogeneous and cosmopolitan group, who were raised at some distance from the social and cultural traditions of small-town middle America. Drawn mainly from big cities in the Northeast and North Central states, their parents tended to be well-off, highly educated members of the middle class. Most have moved away from any religious heritage, and very few are regular churchgoers. In short, the typical leading journalist is the very model of the modern Eastern urbanite. The dominant perspective of this group is equally apparent. Today's leading journalists are politically liberal and alienated from traditional norms and institutions. Most place themselves to the left of center and regularly vote the Democratic ticket. Yet theirs is not the New Deal liberalism of the underprivileged, but the contemporary social liberalism of the urban sophisticate. They favor a strong welfare state within a capitalist framework. They differ most from the general public, however, on the divisive social issues that have emerged since the 1960s—abortion, gay rights, affirmative action, et cetera. Many are alienated from the "system" and quite critical of America's world role. They would like

to strip traditional powerbrokers of their influence and empower black leaders, consumer groups, intellectuals, and... the media.

These findings were complemented by an article in the summer 1986 edition of *Policy Review* magazine by Dinesh D'Souza, who analyzed television network conformism:

> No matter where he comes from... the aspiring TV journalist typically adopts a left-liberal worldview as he picks up the tools of his trade. There is nothing conspiratorial in this. To get their stories on the air, TV journalists have to embrace the culture of network news, either consciously or unconsciously.... And since the culture of television journalism is liberal, it is hardly surprising that reporters get their idea of what is news— ultimately the most ideological question in journalism—from a whole range of left-liberal assumptions, inclinations, and expectations.

THE EDITOR AS IDEOLOGICAL GATEKEEPER

In television as well as newspaper journalism, the reporter's role in the running of the newsroom and production of the final copy is subservient to that of the desk editor; it is certainly secondary or insignificant when measured against the power of managing editors and executive editors and of their television news counterparts. The reporter and the editor are both "journalists." It is the editor, however, in his function as gatekeeper, who determines which story will be covered, what news is "fit to print," and who gets hired and fired.

Take the *New York Times*, the nation's ranking and undisputedly liberal newspaper. Max Frankel, its executive editor, is not known for having hired any openly conservative reporter or editor during his seven-year tenure. Moreover, "one of the first things I did was stop the hiring of nonblacks and set up an unofficial little quota system," Frankel boasted in an interview with Ken Auletta.

Auletta, writing in the June 18, 1992, issue of the *New Yorker*, added: "The new publisher [Arthur Ochs Sulzberger, Jr.] applauded Frankel's hiring policies and also the newsroom's more extensive coverage of women and gays, despite grumbling by some members of the staff that the *Times* was becoming politically correct."

Grumbling over hiring practices and program content seems to be no longer an issue at the partly tax-supported National Public Radio (NPR), which is liberal to the core. (Think of Nina Totenberg, NPR's correspondent at the Supreme Court, and her stubborn effort to prevent Clarence Thomas from being confirmed as a justice of the Court.) A rare insight into the inner workings of NPR was offered in the Washington, D.C., weekly *City Paper* by Glenn Garvin, who conducted intensive research on the radio station:

It's not that the network's editorial brain trust meets each morning to plot the day's campaign to rid America of Republican taint. It's that the newsroom is composed almost entirely of like-minded people who share one another's major philosophical precepts.... Their thinking is apparent both in what they report and their approach to it. They believe that government is the fundamental agent of change, that government can and should solve most problems. They believe most of those solutions involve spending large sums of money. They believe that taxes are not only an appropriate way of raising money, but an impor-

tant social responsibility. They believe that, although individuals cannot always be trusted to make correct choices, bureaucrats usually can. In short, NPR reporters are the kind of people who voted for Michael Dukakis and Bill Clinton, not as the lesser evils, but enthusiastically, in the firm belief that what the world needs is better social engineering.

Like-minded people who share one another's major philosophical precepts and operate under unofficial but nonetheless binding rules of political correctness are not journalists. They are today's Media, less a profession than a culture and secular religion, attempting to reform society according to their left-radical agenda. The guiding motto of the *New York Times* —"All the news that's fit to print"—has been turned into a tool of self-censorship. Especially on feminism, the homosexual rights campaign, and pop culture, the *Times* "has in recent years become crassly partisan in an essentially frivolous way," writes critic Richard Neuhaus in the June/July edition of *First Things* magazine. "There is an absence of *gravitas*... it has become a generally vulgar and strident paper that is hostile to nuance and, it seems, editorially incapable of self-doubt or a modicum of intellectual curiosity."

The *Times* is still held to be the flagship of American journalism, but its traditional in-depth coverage of national and international events has been weakened by trendy treatment, obviously caused by imitating television coverage. Peter Steinfels, who writes the *Times'* Beliefs section, claims that journalists themselves know the problem: "The news media are sometimes less adept in telling truly new stories than in retelling old stories in new ways."

Steinfels, writing in the August 21, 1993, edition of the *Times*, offers a telling example of a tilt threatening to turn institutional: the coverage of Pope John Paul II's voyage to Colorado [summer 1993]. Steinfels observes:

> For the better part of a mid-August week some of the nation's most prized air time, from morning shows to evening newscasts, was devoted to Pope John Paul II's visit.... So were front-page stories in most newspapers.... No one can dispute that this reporting and commentary conveyed some powerful images of a charismatic religious leader and exuberant teenagers.... Nonetheless, fair questions can be raised about how much this impressive effort advanced the public's knowledge and understanding about the Pope, about the current state of Catholicism, about young people and about the moral issues that Pope John Paul II highlighted.

What was reported instead, in print and on the screen? "Journalists recounted," Steinfels wrote, "in some cases a bit breathlessly, the fact that many American Catholics disagree with their church's official teachings on birth control, ordaining women to the priesthood, and other questions about sex and roles for women." While the pope "repeatedly lamented the loss of belief in objective truth and in universally valid principles of morality," reporters wallowed in stereotypes: "Their estimates should have reflected the fact that the Pope's language might escape the ideological grid of American politics and the American news media."

The belief in objective truth and in universally valid principles, so central to Western culture, runs counter to the "anything goes" relativism of the counterculture, where truth is subject to debate and negotiation.

"Why do journalists tend to be liberals?" asks Michael Kinsley in a short, instructive essay tellingly titled "Bias and Baloney" in the December 14, 1992, edition of the *New Republic*. Conceding that the general liberal inclination of many journalists would be hard to deny, the much-in-demand liberal talk show host and columnist for the *Washington Post* and the *New Republic* states, only partly tongue-in-cheek:

> My own political views are more or less liberal. They were not genetically implanted, and I hold them under no form of compulsion except that of reason. It seems to me they are the sort of views a reasonable, intelligent person would hold. Since most journalists I meet are reasonable, intelligent people, the mystery to me is not why journalists tend to be liberals but why so many other reasonable, intelligent people are not.

Kinsley's smugness typifies the conviction of intellectual and moral superiority apparently shared by many contemporary liberal journalists. He rejects all conspiracy theories: "People freely choose their politics and freely choose their careers. No one is forcing journalists to hold liberal political views, and no one is preventing or even discouraging conservatives from becoming journalists. If it just happens to work out that way, so what?"

Kinsley also rejects the suspicion that a journalist's personal political worldview might taint his professional product through bias, claiming that "a political preference is not itself a 'bias.'"

THE DEATH OF PROFESSIONAL DETACHMENT AND OBJECTIVITY

Why, then, do political liberal preferences show so frequently, often blatantly, on network news programs, the average American's favored information watering holes? Why are the leading anchormen—Peter Jennings, Dan Rather, Tom Brokaw—known everywhere as liberal in their views and liberal in their presence on the screen? And why is there no conservative news anchor on network television? Is it because the medium of television, by its very nature, is hostile to balanced news presentation? That still would leave open the question of domination by liberals, a fact that had been documented and analyzed in John Corry's ground-breaking 1986 study *TV News and the Dominant Culture.*

Kinsley's flippant observation that "no one is preventing or even discouraging conservatives from becoming journalists" begs the larger question, which has nothing to do with personal political views or convictions: What happened to professional detachment, to objectivity?

Television news has long ceased to strive for objectivity, that forlorn ideal of yesteryear. Television news delivers "infotainment" instead, where whirl is king, tilt is trendy, and slant rules supreme. Likewise, objectivity has been driven from the pages of the nation's weekly newsmagazines. They also have surrendered to the lure of entertainment, allegedly expected or demanded by the viewing public, bored by print.

And commentary, the legitimate exercise of subjective opinion, once restricted to editorial and op-ed pages, is advancing glacierlike into the news pages of the *New York Times* and *Washington Post,* the nation's "prestige papers."

Driven by commercial television's soft assault, journalism attempts to adjust through imitation, thus betraying its mission and professional standards.

A new force is born: The Media. Or is it only show business with a mask?

NO

Martin A. Lee and
Norman Solomon

POLITICIANS AND THE PRESS

More than 20 years after Vice President Spiro Agnew's famous attack on the American press, the myth of the "liberal media" endures.

Agnew decried "the trend toward the monopolization of the great public information vehicles and the concentration of more and more power over public opinion in fewer and fewer hands." True enough, but his oratory targeted only the *Washington Post* and other major media outlets lacking enthusiasm for the Nixon administration. "Agnew was hypocritical in his attack on press monopolies," a critic later remarked. "Giant chains like Newhouse and Hearst—among the good guys in Agnew's press lord pantheon—escaped his ire."

Likewise, conservative owners of magazines with huge circulations, like *Reader's Digest* and *Parade,* received no brickbats from the White House. An outspoken Federal Communications Commissioner, Nicholas Johnson, observed at the time that Agnew was simply going public with "what corporate and government officials have been doing for years in the privacy of their luncheon clubs and paneled offices. They cajoled and threatened publishers and broadcasters in an effort to manage news and mold images."

Agnew's rhetorical barrage in November 1969 was to reverberate into the century's last decade. However deceptive, it struck a populist chord of resentment against media conglomerates. Rather than challenge the "liberal media" myth, right-leaning owners have encouraged it—and media under their control have popularized it.

The Vice President conveniently neglected to mention that a year earlier the majority of endorsing newspaper editorials backed the Nixon-Agnew ticket. And three years later, running for reelection, the same Republican duo received a whopping 93 percent of the country's newspaper endorsements. (Since 1932 every Republican presidential nominee except Barry Goldwater has received the majority of endorsements from U.S. daily newspapers. Ronald Reagan got 77 percent in 1980, and 86 percent in 1984; George Bush got 70 percent in 1988.) Before resigning in disgrace from the vice presidency, Agnew never explained why the "liberal" media so consistently favored conservative presidential candidates.

From Martin A. Lee and Norman Solomon, *Unreliable Sources: A Guide to Detecting Bias in News Media* (Carol Publishing Group, 1992). Copyright © 1992 by Martin A. Lee and Norman Solomon. Reprinted by permission of Carol Publishing Group. A Lyle Stuart Book.

Reporters' "liberalism" has been exaggerated quite a bit, as Duke University scholar Robert Entman found when he examined the study most commonly cited by purveyors of the cliché. Entman discovered that the study relied on "a non-random sample that vastly overrepresented perhaps the most liberal segment of journalism"—employees of public TV stations in Boston, New York and Washington. These journalists were much more heavily surveyed about their political attitudes than the personnel putting together the far more weighty *New York Times* and national CBS television news.

The much-ballyhooed conclusion that journalists are of a predominantly leftish bent failed to square with data compiled by researchers without a strongly conservative agenda. A Brookings Institution study, for instance, found that 58 percent of Washington journalists identified themselves as either "conservative or middle of the road."

A 1985 *Los Angeles Times* survey, comparing 3,000 journalists to 3,000 members of the general public, found that journalists were more conservative when asked if the government should act to reduce the gap between rich and poor. Fifty-five percent of the general public supported such measures, compared to only 50 percent of the "news staff" and 37 percent of the editors.

But all the heated number-crunching may be much ado about little. The private opinions of media workers are much less important than the end products. Mark Hertsgaard has astutely pinpointed "the deeper flaw in the liberal-press thesis" —"it completely ignored those whom journalists worked for. Reporters could be as liberal as they wished and it would not change what news they were allowed

to report or how they could report it. America's major news organizations were owned and controlled by some of the largest and richest corporations in the United States. These firms were in turn owned and managed by individuals whose politics were, in general, anything but liberal. Why would they employ journalists who consistently covered the news in ways they did not like?"

If there's a political tilt to news coverage, it derives principally from mass media owners and managers, not beat reporters. "Admittedly," said sociologist Herbert Gans, "some journalists have strong personal beliefs and also the position or power to express them in news stories, but they are most often editors; and editors, like producers in television, have been shown to be more conservative than their news staffs." To the extent that personal opinions influence news content, Gans added, "they are most often the beliefs of the President of the United States and other high federal, state and local officials, since they dominate the news."

However baseless, accusations by conservatives that the media lean left have made many journalists compensate by tilting in the other direction. In this sense, the liberal media canard has been effective as a pre-emptive club, brandished to encourage self-censorship on the part of reporters who "bend over backwards not to seem at all critical of Republicans," commented Mark Crispin Miller. "Eager to evince his 'objectivity,' the edgy liberal reporter ends up just as useful to the right as any ultra-rightist hack."

And there are plenty of those, dominating America's highest-profile forums for political commentary on television and newspaper editorial pages. "In terms of the syndicated columnists, if there is an ideological bias, it's more and more to the right," President Reagan's media point man David Gergen declared in a 1981 interview. As the decade wore on, the imbalance grew more extreme.

The syndicated likes of George Will, Patrick Buchanan, Robert Novak, William F. Buckley and John McLaughlin achieved monotonous visibility on national TV, thanks to producers casting nets wide for right-wing pundits. As a tedious ritual they were paired with bland centrists, so that supposed "debates" often amounted to center-right discussions —on PBS's *MacNeil/Lehrer NewsHour*, Gergen with the *Washington Post*'s charmingly mild Mark Shields; on ABC's *This Week With David Brinkley*, Will with the network's stylized but politically tepid Sam Donaldson; on CNN's *Crossfire*, Buchanan or Novak with somnolent ex-CIA-exec Tom Braden. (In late 1989, Braden yielded his seat "on the left" to Michael Kinsley of the *New Republic* magazine, but this didn't make the show any less unbalanced. "Buchanan is much further to the right than I am to the left," Kinsley acknowledged. As Howard Rosenberg wrote in the *Los Angeles Times*, "*Crossfire* should at least get the labeling right: Pat Buchanan from the far right and Michael Kinsley from slightly left of center.")

In early 1989, columnist Jack Newfield counted eight popular political opinion talk shows on national television. "These shows all have certifiably right-wing hosts and moderators," wrote Newfield. "This is not balance. This is ideological imbalance that approaches a conservative monopoly... Buchanan, who calls AIDS a punishment from God for sin, and campaigns against the prosecution of Nazi war criminals hiding in America, is about as far right as you can get."

A fixture on CNN, and often made welcome on the biggest TV networks, Buchanan has flaunted his admiration for prominent fascists past and present, like the Spanish dictator Francisco Franco (who came to power allied with Hitler) and Chile's bloody ruler Augusto Pinochet. "A soldier-patriot like Franco, General Pinochet saved his country from an elected Marxist who was steering Chile into Castroism," Buchanan effused in a September 1989 column, going on to defend the apartheid regime in South Africa: "The Boer Republic is the only viable economy in Africa. Why are Americans collaborating in a U.N. conspiracy with sanctions?"

Sharing much of the remaining op-ed space are others from the hard right, including former U.N. ambassador Jeane Kirkpatrick; William Safire (like Buchanan, an ex-speechwriter for the Nixon-Agnew team); erstwhile segregationist James J. Kilpatrick; Charles Krauthammer; former NBC News correspondent and Moral Majority vice president Cal Thomas; neo-conservative prophet Norman Podhoretz, and Ray Price (yet another Nixon speechwriter). Aside from a handful of left-leaning liberals, most of the other op-ed mainstays are establishment-tied middle-roaders such as Flora Lewis, David Broder, Jeff Greenfield, Georgie Anne Geyer, and Meg Greenfield.

The more honest conservatives readily admit to an asymmetry in their favor. Blunt acknowledgement has come from Adam Meyerson, editor of *Policy Review* magazine at the Heritage Foundation, the Washington think tank that drew up much of the Reaganite agenda. "Journalism today is very different from what it was 10 to 20 years ago," he said in 1988. "Today, op-ed pages are dominated by conservatives." The media market's oversupply of right-wingers was not without a drawback: "If Bill Buckley were to come out of Yale today, nobody would pay much attention to him... [His] ideas would not be exceptional at all, because there are probably hundreds of people with those ideas already there, and they have already got syndicated columns..." As for becoming an editorial writer, Meyerson could not be encouraging. "There are still a few good jobs here and there, but there's a glut of opinions, especially conservative opinions."

Factor in the proliferation of televangelists and far-right religious broadcasters, and the complaints about the "liberal media" ring even more hollow. By 1987, religious broadcasting had become a $2 billion a year industry, with more than 200 full-time Christian TV stations and 1,000 full-time Christian radio stations. This means that evangelical Christians control about 14 percent of the television stations operating in the U.S. and 10 percent of the radio stations, which bombard the American public with a conservative theo-political message. TV ministries continue to thrive, despite the widely-publicized preacher sex and money scandals of the late 1980s.

Some journalists may reject the mythology about liberal prejudice, but when addressing what *is* going on they're prone to denial. Instead of identifying the thumbs on news-media scales, the preference is to call the whole contraption neutral. "Everybody talks about media biases to the right or the left," syndicated columnist Ellen Goodman pooh-poohed in 1989. "The real media bias is against complexity, which is usually terminated with the words: 'I'm sorry, we're out of time.'" Of course, electronic news media are surface-skimming operations. Views that

seriously challenge the status quo, however, have few occasions to be interrupted, since they're so rarely heard at all.

As he celebrated Thanksgiving in 1989, Spiro Agnew had reason to be pleased on the twentieth anniversary of his bombast. Agnew's polemical legacy hadn't stopped refracting the light under which journalists in Washington furrowed their brows. Tagged as "liberal" despite the evidence, mass media continued to shy away from tough, independent reporting.

OFFICIAL SCANDALS: FROM WATERGATE TO CONTRAGATE

Although big media are an integral part of the American power structure, it doesn't mean that reporters never challenge a President or other members of the governing class. A number of Presidents have gotten into nasty spats with the press, which has been credited with exposing the Watergate scandal that drove Richard Nixon from the vestibules of authority.

While the orthodox view of Watergate depicts it as the ultimate triumph of a free and independent press, there is a contrary view held by award-winning investigative journalist Seymour Hersh. "Far from rooting Nixon out in Watergate, I would say the press made Watergate inevitable," Hersh told us.

Hersh's thesis is simple. During his first term, Nixon conducted several illegal and unconstitutional policies with hardly a whimper from the mainstream media: the secret bombing of Cambodia, subversive operations that toppled Chile's democratically-elected government, CIA domestic spying against antiwar dissenters, wholesale wiretapping of

American officials and other citizens. "If the press had been able to break any one of these stories in 1971," Hersh reflected, "we might have been able to save the President from himself. He might have been afraid to do some of the things he did in 1972, and this would have changed the course of history. But the press failed utterly to do anything during Nixon's first term, thereby making it easy for Nixon to walk into his own trap in Watergate."

Having gotten away with so much for so long, Nixon didn't think twice about launching a covert assault against leaders of the other established political party. When Nixon's private spies— the plumbers—were caught red-handed in the headquarters of the Democratic National Committee in June 1972, most media accepted White House claims that it was just a two-bit burglary. The pundits said there was no story there; *Washington Post* reporters Bob Woodward and Carl Bernstein were dismissed as a couple of precocious upstarts out to make trouble for the President.

Nearly all media were slow to delve into what proved to be a monumental political scandal. As Bernstein told an audience at Harvard University in 1989, "At the time of Watergate, there were some 2,000 full-time reporters in Washington, working for major news organizations. In the first six months after the break-in ... 14 of those reporters were assigned by their news organizations to cover the Watergate story on a full-time basis, and of these 14, half-a-dozen on what you might call an investigative basis." Bernstein added: "The press has been engaged in a kind of orgy of self-congratulations about our performance in Watergate and about our performance in covering the

news since. And it seems to me no attitude could be more unjustified."

"We realize that we did a lousy job on Watergate," said United Press International's Helen Thomas of the White House press corps. "We just sat there and took what they said at face value." Television was even slower than print media. As author Donna Woolfolk Cross wrote, "TV news did not pursue the story until it was already a well-established matter of discussion in the press and among politicians. During the times when Americans might have profited most from a full exploration of the scandal—before a national election—TV news was still presenting the story as the administration billed it: a 'second-rate burglary.' "

When the Iran-contra scandal broke in November 1986, comparisons with Watergate quickly came into vogue. Once again there were tales of a crusading press corps—journalistic Davids slaying White House Goliaths. But the wrong analogy was being drawn. A more accurate appraisal of the two scandals would not have been very flattering to the U.S. media. For if members of the press corps snoozed through Nixon's first term, they also winked and nodded off during almost six years of the Reagan presidency. Small wonder there were those in the Reagan administration who felt they could get away with escapades even more outlandish than Watergate.

Nixon, of course, was eventually forced to resign from office. Reagan managed to elude such a fate, in part because his aides pursued a more sophisticated media strategy. Whereas Nixon's people were often overtly hostile to the press, waging both a public and private war against journalists, the Reagan White House eschewed brass-knuckle tactics in favor of a more amicable relationship. When the *Washington Post* persisted in publishing detrimental Watergate revelations, Nixon threatened to revoke the broadcasting license of the *Post's* parent company. The Reagan administration tried a more enticing approach, expanding the number of lucrative broadcast affiliates that media corporations could own.

Reagan also benefited from the fact that the media's ideological pendulum had swung rightward since Nixon's final days—largely in reaction to Watergate. Media executives felt that perhaps they had gone too far when Nixon resigned. Roger Wilkins, who wrote *Washington Post* editorials about Watergate, later remarked that the press sought to prove "in the wake of Watergate that they were not irresponsible, that they did have a real sense of the national interest, that they had wandered out of this corporate club... But that essentially they were members in good standing of the club and they wanted to demonstrate that."

Nixon's fall from grace in 1974 came during a period of intense conflict within America's governing circles about the Vietnam War, economic policy and other matters. Nixon loyalists believe, probably correctly, that Woodward and Bernstein were used by unnamed U.S. intelligence sources—including their main source, nicknamed "Deep Throat"—to derail the Nixon presidency. This is not to detract from their accomplishments, but Woodward and Bernstein clearly had help from powerful, well-placed sources.

Shadowboxing in Washington

When Reagan became President in 1981, there was a high degree of consensus within America's corporate and political elites about domestic and foreign policy.

Abdicating the role of a real opposition party, Democratic leaders in Congress were more eager to put on a show than put up a fight. Sometimes the media used the passivity of the Democrats to justify their own. Either way, as Walter Karp put it, "the private story behind every major non-story during the Reagan administration was the Democrats' tacit alliance with Reagan."

It was a convenient arrangement for each of the three principals. The Reagan administration got credit for superb political smarts, and—after its nadir, the unraveling of the Iran-contra scandal—admirable resiliency. ("Howard Baker restored order to the White House," etc.) The Democrats scored points for slugging it out with the Reaganites. And the media reported the shadowboxing as a brawl instead of a contest that kept being thrown before it ever got bloody.

"For eight years the Democratic opposition had shielded from the public a feckless, lawless President with an appalling appetite for private power," Karp wrote. "That was *the* story of the Reagan years, and Washington journalists evidently knew it. Yet they never turned the collusive politics of the Democratic party into news. Slavishly in thrall to the powerful, incapable of enlightening the ruled without the consent of the rulers, the working press, the 'star' reporters, the pundits, the sages, the columnists passed on to us, instead, the Democrats' mendacious drivel about the President's 'Teflon shield.' For eight years, we saw the effects of a bipartisan political class in action, but the press did not show us that political class acting, exercising its collective power, making things happen, contriving the appearances that were reported as news.

One of the chronically contrived appearances was President Reagan's great popularity—phenomenal only in that it was a distortion. In April 1989, the *New York Times* reminded readers that Reagan was "one of the most popular Presidents in American history." Authoritative, but false—as University of Massachusetts political science professor Thomas Ferguson promptly documented for the umpteenth time. "It is tiresome," he wrote in *The Nation* magazine, "always to be pointing out that this ever-popular and seemingly indestructible refrain monumentally distorts the truth. But it does." The past half-century of polling data from Gallup Report showed Reagan's average public approval rating while in office (52 percent) to be lower than Presidents Johnson (54 percent), Kennedy (70 percent), Eisenhower (66 percent), and Roosevelt (68 percent). What's more, Reagan barely bested his three immediate predecessors —Carter (47 percent), Ford (46 percent) and Nixon (48 percent). Of the last nine Presidents, Reagan's approval ranking was a mediocre fifth.

POSTSCRIPT

Does the News Media Have a Liberal Bias?

As the opposing arguments in this issue indicate, we can find critics on both the Left and the Right who agree that the media are biased. What divides such critics is the question of whether the bias is left-wing or right-wing. Defenders of the news media may seize upon this disagreement to bolster their own claim that "bias is in the eye of the beholder." But the case may be that the news media are unfair to both sides. If that were true, however, it would seem to take some of the force out of the argument that the news media have a distinct ideological tilt at all.

Edward Jay Epstein's *News from Nowhere* (Random House, 1973) remains one of the great studies of the factors that influence television news shows. A study by S. Robert Lichter et al., *The Media Elite* (Adler & Adler, 1986), tends to support Maitre's contention that the media slant leftward, as does William Rusher's *The Coming Battle for the Media* (William Morrow, 1988), whereas Ben Bagdikian's *The Media Monopoly* (Beacon Press, 1983) and Mark Hertsgaard's *On Bended Knee: The Press and the Reagan Presidency* (Schocken, 1989) lend support to Lee and Solomon's view. A more recent S. Robert Lichter book, coauthored with Linda Lichter and Stanley Rothman, is *Watching America* (Prentice Hall, 1991), which surveys the political and social messages contained in television "entertainment" programs. Lichter has also written a media textbook with Thomas Dye and Harmon Ziegler entitled *American Politics in the Media Age*, 4th ed. (Brooks-Cole, 1992). David Halberstam's *The Powers That Be* (Alfred A. Knopf, 1979), a historical study of CBS, the *Washington Post*, *Time* magazine, and the *Los Angeles Times*, describes some of the political and ideological struggles that have taken place within major media organizations.

Edward Jay Epstein's book, previously cited, uses as an epigraph the following statement by Richard Salant, president of CBS News in the 1970s: "Our reporters do not cover stories from *their* point of view. They are presenting them from *nobody's* point of view." Most probably, Salant had not intended to be facetious or ironic, but the statement so amused Epstein that he parodied it in the title of his book: *News from Nowhere*.

PART 2

The Institutions of Government

The Constitution provides for three governing bodies: the president, Congress, and the Supreme Court. Over the years, the American government has generated another organ with a life of its own: the bureaucracy. In this section, we examine issues that concern all the branches of government (executive, legislative, and judicial). Many of these debates are contemporary manifestations of issues that have been argued since the country was founded.

■ Should There Be Term Limits for Members of Congress?

■ Do We Need a Strong Presidency?

■ Does the Government Regulate Too Much?

■ Should the Federal Courts Be Bound by the "Original Intent" of the Framers?

ISSUE 5

Should There Be Term Limits for Members of Congress?

YES: George Will, from *Restoration: Congress, Term Limits and the Recovery of Deliberative Democracy* (Free Press, 1992)

NO: Charles R. Kesler, from "Bad Housekeeping: The Case Against Congressional Term Limitations," *Policy Review* (Summer 1990)

ISSUE SUMMARY

YES: Columnist George Will argues that term limits will bring fresh perspectives into Congress and restore the spirit of citizen politics.

NO: Associate professor of government Charles R. Kesler contends that term limits will make members of Congress highly dependent upon their staffs, which will grow more powerful, and will deprive the nation of the wisdom gained by incumbents.

In America's early years, members of Congress were only part-time legislators. Congress met for only a few months of the year, and the rest of the time its members worked back in their home states and districts as farmers, lawyers, businessmen, or in some other private pursuit. Congressional pay was low, and it was not anticipated that members would serve many years in Congress. The ideal, much touted in the eighteenth and early nineteenth centuries, was of citizen lawmakers serving their nation in Congress for a few years before returning to local affairs and private employment. The expectation was that there would be frequent rotation in office and that nobody would think of congressional service as a full-time career.

For more than a century, actual practice approximated this model. The turnover of congressional seats was high, averaging 40 to 50 percent in each election; typically, members of Congress served a few terms, then moved out of Washington. In this century, however, particularly since World War II, Washington has become a city of career politicians: bureaucrats, lobbyists, congressional staffers—and members of Congress. Except for a few brief recesses, Congress meets year-round, and members spend most of their lives in Washington. Turnover in Congress is now very low; even 10 percent is a rare event in any election year. For most of its members today, Congress remains the center of their lives and the chief source of their income.

How do voters react to this state of affairs? Their attitude is unclear, even contradictory. On the one hand, voters are responsible for the low turnover in Congress. They are the ones who keep reelecting their representatives, and voter loyalty is remarkable: even legislators caught up in scandals often survive electoral challenges by appealing to constituents' attachment to "their congressman." On the other hand, voters in several states have indicated in unmistakable terms their unhappiness with the status quo. In 1992, 14 states had ballot initiatives calling for mandated term limits (most of them specifying a maximum of 12 years) for U.S. senators and representatives. Not only did all of these initiatives pass, in 13 of the 14 states they passed by huge margins. (Florida's and Wyoming's, for example, passed by a margin of 77–23.) The results of these initiatives are being challenged in the courts and may be overturned as unconstitutional. Nevertheless, they are strong indicators of grassroots opinion, and they could culminate in a new constitutional amendment. Such an amendment, of course, could not be overturned by any court.

Beyond the constitutional questions are the moral and political issues. What right have the voters to limit the number of terms for which a person can run for office? Aren't those who demand term limits not only hurting their representative but also hurting *themselves* by denying themselves, at some point, the freedom to reelect a worthy public servant? Supporters of term limits reply by pointing to the enormous resources available to congressional incumbents: name recognition, free mailings, rewards that can be reaped by doing favors for constituents, access to the media, and the ability to raise large sums of money from wealthy interests. Term limits, the argument goes, are the only way of countering these advantages and preventing the indefinite reelection of incumbents.

But what is wrong with reelecting incumbents? Proponents of term limits contend that Washington needs an infusion of fresh blood and a restoration of the old spirit of citizen politics; term limits, they believe, will help to realize these goals. Opponents of term limits insist that in today's world we need experienced men and women to represent us in Congress and that term limits will remove legislators just when they start to become most useful to their constituents. In general terms, these are the respective positions of George Will and Charles R. Kesler in the following selections.

YES

George Will

RESTORATION

A strong, and itself sufficient, reason for term limits is that they would restore to the legislative branch the preeminence and luster that it rightly should have. There is a kind of scorched-earth, pillage-and-burn conservatism that is always at a rolling boil, and which boils down to a brute animus against government. Those who subscribe to this vigorous but unsubtle faith have had jolly fun in the early 1990s as public esteem for government, and especially for Congress, has plummeted. However, that is not my kind of conservatism. I do not fathom how any American who loves the nation can relish the spectacle of the central institutions of American democracy being degraded and despised. Patriotism properly understood simply is not compatible with contempt for the institutions that put American democracy on display.

Congressional supremacy is a traditional tenet of American conservatism. It had better be, because it also is a basic constitutional fact. The Constitution begins with a brisk fifty-two-word preamble about why we, the people, are constituting ourselves. Then the Constitution buckles down to business, the first item of which—Article I—defines the composition, duties and powers of the legislative branch.

It is altogether appropriate that the home of this branch, the Capitol, is the noblest public building in daily use anywhere in the world. And it is fitting that this building sits at the conjunction of the four quadrants of the Federal City. That setting symbolizes the fact that Congress is and ought to be the epicenter of the political expression of the nation's collective life. But in modern America, and in the context of today's Leviathan-like federal government, Congress can be entrusted with that centrality only if it is reformed by term limits. This is so because only term limits can break the nexus between legislative careerists and the capacity of the modern state to be bent to the service of their careerism.

This nexus, degrading to Congress and demoralizing to the country, is one reason why government performs so poorly and is therefore so disdained. Contemporary evidence confirms what reason suggests: A permanent class of career legislators is inherently inimical to limited government—government that is discriminating in its ends and modest in its methods. Interest in term limits has risen as government's record of practical achievements has become steadily less impressive.

Furthermore, any attempt to understand the waning of respect for government in general, and for the Congress in particular, should begin with this fact: As government has become more solicitous, it has not become more loved or respected. As government has become more determinedly ameliorative, it has fallen in the esteem of the public whose condition it toils to improve. There is a perverse correlation between the increasing role of compassion in the rhetoric of governance and the decreasing regard for government on the part of the compassionated public. And there is a causal relation between many of the government's failures and the motives, attitudes and actions of legislative careerists. So to begin the argument for term limits, let us turn to the behavior of Congress that has imparted such momentum to the term limits movement....

"LIKE A STRONG WIND"

... [H]ow probable is it that a Congress operating under term limits will do worse than the Congress that has collaborated with the production of $400 billion deficits, the savings and loan debacle, and many other policy wrecks, and has driven away in despair many of its best members?

Consider a baseball analogy. In 1988 the Baltimore Orioles (on whose board of directors I sit) were dreadful. They were somewhat like today's Congress—expensive and incompetent. They lost their first twenty-one games, a record, and went on to lose a total of 107. After the season the Orioles' management had a thought: Hey, we can lose 107 games with

inexpensive rookies. The 1989 Orioles were major league baseball's youngest team and had the smallest payroll and came within a few October pitches in Toronto of winning the American League East.

Increasingly, the principal argument against term limits turns out to be a somewhat serpentine assertion. It is that limits would be both harmful and redundant—harmful because rotation depletes the reservoir of wisdom, and redundant because there already is a healthily high amount of rotation. Tom Foley, the Speaker of the House of Representatives, arrived on Capitol Hill (actually arrived there for a second time; he had previously been an aide to Senator Henry Jackson) in 1965. He was part of the bumper crop of new congressmen produced by the anti-Goldwater tide. By 1992 Foley was fond—rather too fond—of noting that 93 percent of the members of the House had arrived since he did, that 81 percent had arrived since the thunderous post-Watergate election of 1974, and that 55 percent had come since Reagan rode into town in 1981. However, a more pertinent number is this: Of the 1,692 congressmen who have sat since 1955, when Democratic control of the House began, 35.7 percent of the members, or 604 congressmen, have served seven terms or more. Of the current members of the 102d Congress (1991–92), 37.5 percent are already in at least their seventh term. In the last four elections (1984–90) the turnover in the House due to death, retirement or—much the least important cause—defeat averaged about 10 percent per election.

Much of the turnover comes not from the defeat of incumbents in competitive elections but from the voluntary departure of members who despair of enjoying useful service in a Congress geared to the service of careerism. The leadership of Congress—the ruling class that runs the committees and subcommittees that are the primary instruments for self-promotion—has not been changed nearly as much as Foley's numbers lead people to believe. Systematic changing by term limits would make serious service possible more quickly than it now is. Hence term limits would make Congress more attractive to serious people. In 1991 the economists W. Robert Reed of the University of Oklahoma and D. Eric Schansberg of Indiana University at New Albany argued that term limitations, while eliminating the possibility of long careers, would increase access to leadership positions. Representatives would be eligible for leadership positions much sooner than at present. "Currently," they said, "it takes sixteen years to reach the 80th percentile of seniority." On the basis of certain assumptions about how many members serving under term limitations will choose to serve the maximum permissible number of terms, and how many will die or be defeated, Reed and Schansberg calculated that under a six-term limit the time required to reach the 80th percentile would be cut in half, to eight years.

Some opponents of term limits say that limits are a recipe for institutionalizing ignorance. They say that if all congressional careers are short, no one will have time to master the subtleties and mysteries of the government's vast and increasing penetration of society, a penetration carried out by subsidies, taxation and regulation. But that argument tends to turn around and bite its authors, as follows: If government now is so omnipresent (because it strives to be omniprovident) and so arcane that it makes a permanent legislative class indispensable, that is less an argument in favor of such a class than it is an argument against that kind of government. It is an argument for pruning the government's claims to omnicompetence. It is an argument for curtailing government's intrusiveness at least enough so that the supervision of the government can be entrusted to the oversight of intelligent lay people. Or amateurs. Sometimes called citizens.

Critics of term limitation worry that compulsory rotation of offices will mean that a substantial number of representatives and senators will always be looking ahead to their next employment. This, say the critics, means, at best, that these legislators will be distracted from the public business, and it may mean that they will be corrupted by the temptation to use their last years in power to ingratiate themselves with potential employers. Both of these possibilities are, well, possible. But the critics must confront a question: Would such corruption be worse—morally more reprehensible, and more injurious to the public weal—than legislative careerism has proved to be? Careerism, after all, is the legislator's constant surrender—with an easy conscience—to the temptation to use every year in power to ingratiate himself with all the factions useful to his permanent incumbency.

Also, people who would come to Congress under term limits would be less susceptible than cynics think to the temptation to misuse their congressional service to court future employers. After all, people who will choose to spend a necessarily limited span of time in Congress are apt to come from serious careers and will want to return to them. Furthermore, the political incentive for private interests to hire politically influential people from the ranks of ex-congressmen will be radically reduced by the term limits that will swell those ranks. Think about it. One reason ex-legislators are hired by private interests today is to take advantage of their relationships with ex-colleagues who remain in Congress. But term limits will guarantee that those relationships are short-lived. Those ex-colleagues will soon be ex-congressmen.

Would term limits deplete the pool of talent from which we draw presidents? History, which is all we have to go by, says otherwise. Presidents are rarely launched from long legislative careers. How many people have become president after serving twelve or more consecutive years in the House or the Senate? Just three, and two became president by accident. The three are James Polk, Lyndon Johnson and Gerald Ford.

Unquestionably term limits would substantially increase the number of competitive congressional races. It is highly probable that this would lead to increased rates of voting. People are apt to vote at the end of campaigns that they have been talking and arguing about. They are more apt to talk and argue about campaigns when the outcomes are in doubt. Every four years the presidency provides the electorate with an election to argue about. Congress could be a much more prolific producer of wholesome arguments. Every four years Congress offers voters 936 elections —two elections of the 435 members of the House and elections of two-thirds of the one hundred senators. Term limits, by reducing the number of incumbents running, would increase the number of competitive races and would thereby enliven the nation's civic conversation....

* * *

In the famous first paragraph of the first of the Federalist Papers, Alexander Hamilton said that Americans, "by their conduct and example," will decide whether government by "reflection and choice" shall supplant government by "accident and force." Since that was written the world has turned many times, and many democracies have been born. America's sense of uniqueness, and hence of mission, has been somewhat diminished by this multiplication of democracies.

It has been diminished, but not extinguished. Ours is the oldest democracy and remains much the most important. Buy virtue of our relative antiquity, our example carries special saliency. And because of the material power we possess, which we have from time to time been called upon to deploy in defense of democracy, we feel, and are, more implicated than any other nation in the world's political evolution. Therefore how we do at the day-to-day business of democracy matters. It matters mostly to us, but not only to us. The world is watching.

NO
Charles R. Kesler

BAD HOUSEKEEPING: THE CASE AGAINST CONGRESSIONAL TERM LIMITATIONS

Everyone complains about Congress, but nobody does anything about it. Frustration with our national legislature, which is by almost every measure widespread among the American public, is about to be exploited by a national movement to throw the rascals out—the rascals, in this case, being incumbent congressmen and senators who have so mastered the art of reelection as to be thought unremovable by conventional means. The most widely touted solution to the problem is the extreme one of adding an amendment to the Constitution limiting the number of terms that members of the House and Senate can serve.

This notion appears to have been first circulated by the same informal network of radio talk-show hosts who were instrumental in rallying public opposition to last year's congressional pay raise. The idea has found support in public opinion polls and is being pressed by a new organization, Americans to Limit Congressional Terms (ALCT), that operates out of the offices of Republican political consultant Eddie Mahe and whose board includes both prominent Democrats and Republicans.

It is the latter party that stands to benefit most from limiting the years a congressman can serve, inasmuch as it is the Republicans who suffer under the rule of a more or less permanent Democratic majority in the House and Senate. In fact, term limitations were endorsed in the 1988 Republican platform. . . .

98-PERCENT PARADOX

This movement builds on the public's mounting dissatisfaction with a Congress that is seen not only as unresponsive but also as incompetent and corrupt. Indeed, in light of the chronically unbalanced federal budget, Congress's reluctance to perform even its minimal duty of passing a budget (balanced or not) without resort to omnibus continuing resolutions and reconciliation acts, the 51 percent salary increase for its members that it tried to brazen through without a rollcall vote, the generous privileges it extends to its members (large staffs, multiple offices, free travel allowances, frequent mailings at public expense, liberal pensions), the corruption-tinged resignations of former House Speaker Jim Wright and former Democratic Whip Tony Coelho, the metastasizing scandal of the Keating Five —in light of all these things, it is a wonder that congressmen get reelected at all.

And yet that is the paradox. Despite a deep dissatisfaction with Congress as an institution, the American people are reelecting their congressmen (that is, members of the House) at the highest rates in history.... By now we have all heard the jokes about there being more turnover in the British House of Lords or in the [former] Soviet Politburo than in the U.S. House of Representatives. The interesting question is, Why? What has happened to transform what the Framers of the Constitution envisioned as the most democratic, turbulent, changeable branch of the national government into the least changeable, most stable of the elective branches? And to come around to the question of the moment, will limiting the number of terms a congressman or senator can serve do anything to remedy the problem?

ANTI-FEDERALISTS: "VIRTUE WILL SLUMBER"

This is not the first time in American history that a limit on the reeligibility of elected federal officials has been proposed. At the Constitutional Convention in 1787, whether the president ought to be eligible for reelection was extensively debated, although always in close connec-

tion with the related questions of his term of office and mode of election. With the invention of the electoral college and with his term fixed at four years, it was thought to be productive of good effects and consistent with his independence from the legislature to allow the president to be eligible for reelection indefinitely; and so it remained until the 22nd Amendment was added to the Constitution. But what is less well known is that the Constitutional Convention also considered limitations on the reeligibility of the lower house of the legislature. The so-called Virginia Plan, introduced by [prominent Revolutionary War statesman] Edmund Randolph, would have rendered members of the House ineligible for reelection for an unspecified period after their term's end. The period was never specified because the Convention expunged the limitation less than a month after it had been proposed.

Nevertheless, the question of limiting congressional terms lived on. It was taken up vigorously by the Anti-Federalists, the opponents of the new Constitution, who urged that "rotation in office" be imposed not so much on House members as on senators, whose small numbers, long term of office, and multifaceted powers made them suspiciously undemocratic. The Anti-Federalists built upon the legacy of the Articles of Confederation, which had required that members of Congress rotate out after serving three one-year terms within any five-year period. Quite a few critics of the Constitution attacked the unlimited reeligibility of the president, too, but the brunt of their criticism fell upon the Senate. In their view, it was a fatal mistake to neglect "rotation, that noble prerogative of liberty." As "An Officer of the Late Continental Army" called it in a Philadelphia newspaper, rotation was the "nobel prerogative" by which liberty secured itself, even as the Tudor and Stuart kings had ignobly wielded their "prerogative power" in defense of tyranny.

The current appeal for limits on congressional office-holding echoes the major themes of the Anti-Federalists 200 years ago. One of the most rigorous of the Constitution's critics, the writer who styled himself "The Federal Farmer," put it this way: "[I]n a government consisting of but a few members, elected for long periods, and far removed from the observation of the people, but few changes in the ordinary course of elections take place among the members; they become in some measure a fixed body, and often inattentive to the public good, callous, selfish, and the fountain of corruption." After serving several years in office, he continued, it will be expedient for a man "to return home, mix with the people, and reside some time with them; this will tend to reinstate him in the interests, feelings, and views similar to theirs, and thereby confirm in him the essential qualifications of a legislator." Were the people watchful, they could recall him on their own and substitute a new representative at their discretion. But they are not sufficiently vigilant. As Patrick Henry warned at the Virginia ratifying convention, "Virtue will slumber. The wicked will be continually watching: Consequently you will be undone."

FEDERALISTS: THE PEOPLE ARE NOT FOOLS

The Anti-Federalist arguments were rejected by the advocates of the new Constitution. However it is only for the presidency that the authors of the most authoritative defense of the Constitution, *The Federalist*, give a detailed refutation of the scheme of rotation in office. In *The Federalist*'s view, there is "an excess of refinement" in the notion of preventing the people from returning to office men who had proved worthy of their confidence. The people are not fools, at least not all of the time, and they can be trusted to keep a reasonably sharp eye on their representatives. So far as history can confirm such a proposition, it seems to pronounce in favor of *The Federalist*. Throughout the 19th and most of the 20th centuries, American politics was not characterized by a professional class of legislators insulated from the fluctuations, much less the deliberate changes, of public opinion. In the 19th century, it was not unusual for a majority of the membership of Congress to serve only one term; congressional turnover consistently averaged 40 to 50 percent every election. Occasionally it reached 60 or 70 percent.

The young Abraham Lincoln, for example, served only one term in the House of Representatives, in keeping with an informal rotation agreement he had negotiated with two Whig Party rivals in his district. Such agreements were not uncommon, and betokened a vigorous intraparty political life as well as keen competition between the parties: no party wanted its officeholders to betray an unrepublican ambition. But ambition was controlled informally by rotation within a party's bank of candidates so that the party and the country enjoyed the best of both worlds—a circulation of capable and experienced men through public office, with the possibility of keeping truly exceptional ones in office if circumstances demanded it.

Accordingly, even the most distinguished congressmen and senators of the 19th century pursued what by today's standards would be frenetic and irregular political careers. Henry Clay, famous as "the Great Compromiser," was sent thrice to the Senate to serve out someone else's term (the first time despite his being less than 30 years old); served two years in the Kentucky assembly, the second as its speaker; was elected seven times (not consecutively) to the House and three times was chosen speaker, although he often resigned in midterm to take up a diplomatic post or run (unsuccessfully, three times) for president; and was elected twice to the Senate in his own right. Daniel Webster was elected to five terms in the House (not consecutively) and four terms in the Senate, in addition to running once (fruitlessly) for president and serving more than four nonconsecutive years as Secretary of State under three presidents. John C. Calhoun was elected to four terms in the House, served seven years as Secretary of War, was elected twice to the vice presidency, and then served two years of Robert Hayne's . . . Senate term, two Senate terms in his own right, one year as Secretary of State, and four more years in the Senate.

By the way, the ALCT's proposed constitutional amendment, which would limit members of Congress to 12 consecutive years in office (six terms for representatives, two for senators), would have had no impact on Clay's nor Calhoun's career but would have disabled Webster, who was elected three times in a row to the Senate.

THE SWING ERA ENDS

But the larger and more important point is that today's entrenched Congress is a product of the great changes in American politics that have occurred since the late 19th century, particularly the weak-ening of political parties and the great increase in the size and scope of the federal government. Serving in Congress has become a profession over the past 100 years. The average (continuous) career of congressmen hovered around five years at the turn of the century, already up significantly from its earlier levels; today, the figure has doubled again, with the average member of the House serving about 10 years. In the century after 1860, the proportion of freshmen in the House plummeted from nearly 60 percent to around 10 percent, about where it remains today. This gradual professionalization of Congress owes something to the gradual increase of power in Washington, which made it more attractive to hold office; and still more to the seniority system, introduced in the House after the famous revolt against the power of the Speaker around 1910. With the seniority system in place, districts had great incentives to keep their representatives serving continuously. But the contemporary problems of incumbency are something else again. Since 1971, when House Democrats voted in their caucus to elect committee chairmen by secret ballot rather than follow the rule of committee seniority, the perquisites of seniority have declined, in part. Yet congressional reelection rates have risen. If it is not the advantages of seniority that account for today's almost invulnerable incumbents, then what is it?

Since the Second World War, reelection rates have been very high, averaging more than 90 percent; they have risen even further recently, approaching 100 percent in the last few elections. The political scientist David Mayhew identified the key to the incumbency problem as "the vanishing marginals," that is, the decline over the past 40 years in the number of marginal or competitive House districts. (A victory margin of 50 to 55 percent makes a district marginal, that is, capable of being won by a challenger.) In 1948 most incumbents won narrowly, getting less than 55 percent of their district's vote. Twenty years later, three-fourths of the incumbents received 60 percent or more of their district's vote, making these essentially safe seats for the winning congressmen. So, not only are more incumbents than ever winning, they are winning by bigger margins than ever before.

Explanations for the decline in marginal districts have not been scarce. First, there is the effect of gerrymandered congressional districts, which tend to be drawn in such a fashion as to lock in incumbents of both parties. Researchers have shown, however, that marginal districts declined just as sharply in the 1960s in states that did *not* redistrict as in those that did; so gerrymandering cannot be the principal culprit. Then there is the effect of incumbency itself—the franking privilege, free publicity stemming from benefits delivered to the district, prodigious sums of money contributed by political action committees, all of which make possible the greater name recognition that is supposed to discourage unknown and underfunded challengers. As the rates of incumbent reelection have climbed, therefore, one would expect an increase in incumbents' name recognition. But, as John Ferejohn and other analysts have shown, the data do not bear this out: incumbents are no better known now than they were before the marginal districts started vanishing. For all of the incumbents' advantages in name recognition, this factor cannot be the crucial one in explaining the decline in competitive House districts.

FACELESS BUREAUCRACY'S FRIENDLY FACE

In his arresting book *Congress: Keystone of the Washington Establishment*, the political scientist Morris Fiorina puts his finger on the nub of the problem. During the 1960s, congressmen began to put an unprecedented emphasis on casework or constituent service and pork-barrel activities as a way to ensure their reelection. The new emphasis was made possible precisely by "big government," the federal government's expansion of authority over state and local affairs that began dramatically with the New Deal and accelerated during the Great Society. As the federal bureaucracy expanded, more and more citizens found themselves dealing directly with federal agencies —the Social Security Administration, the Veterans Administration, the Equal Employment Opportunity Commission, the Environmental Protection Agency, and so on. To penetrate the mysteries of the administrative state, to find a friendly face amid the "faceless" bureaucrats and a helping hand among so many seemingly determined to do injustice in particular cases, citizens began increasingly to turn to their congressman for succor.

And they were encouraged to do so, particularly by the younger and more vulnerable congressmen who had come into office in the great Democratic waves of 1964 and 1974. Eventually, however, almost all congressmen caught on to the "new deal" made possible and necessary by the increased reach of Washington. The beauty of the new politics was that the same congressmen who were applauded for creating new federal agencies to tackle social problems also got credit for helping their constituents through the labyrinths of these impersonal bureaucracies. In Fiorina's words: "Congressmen take credit coming and going. They are the alpha and the omega." The more ambitious of them exploit the paradox shamelessly: the more bureaucracy they create, the more indispensable they are to their constituents. To which one must add: the longer they've been around Washington, the more plausible is their claim to know precisely how to aid their constituents with the bureaucracy.

It is clear that knowledge of these bureaucratic folkways is more important to voters than ever before. But it requires only a very small number of swing voters, perhaps only 5 percent or so, to transform a district from being marginal or competitive into being safe (thus increasing the incumbent's vote from, say, 53 to 58 percent). To explain the disappearing marginal districts it is therefore necessary only for a very small sector of the electorate to have been won over to the incumbent by the constituent service and pork-barrel opportunities opened up by an activist federal government. To this group of voters in particular, perhaps to most voters to one degree or another, the congressman's job is now thought to be as much administrative as political. The spirit of nonpartisan, expert administration—central to modern liberalism as it was conceived in the Progressive Era—is gradually coloring the public's view of the House of Representatives, transforming it from the most popular branch of the legislature into the highest branch of the civil service.

If this is true, the congressman's expertise is a peculiar sort, involving as it does interceding with civil servants (and appointed officials) in the spirit of personal, particularistic relations, not the spirit of impersonal rule following associated with the civil service. Nonetheless, he is expected to keep benefits and services issuing to the district, just as a nonpartisan city manager is expected to keep the streets clean and the sewers flowing. And to the extent that ombudsmanship is a corollary of bureaucracy (as it seems to be, at least in democratic governments), his casework partakes of the spirit of administration rather than of political representation.

HAMILTON'S "SORDID VIEWS"

Given the origins and nature of the problem with Congress (really with the House of Representatives, inasmuch as Senate incumbents remain beatable), it is apparent that limiting congressional terms to 12 years will do little or nothing to remedy the situation. Any new faces that are brought to Washington as the result of such an amendment will find themselves up against the same old incentives. They will still be eligible for reelection five times. How will they ensure their continued political prosperity without seeing to constituents' administrative needs? If anything, these new congressmen will find themselves confronting bureaucrats rendered more powerful by the representatives' own ignorance of the bureaucracy; for in the administrative state, knowledge is power. It is likely, therefore, that the new congressmen will initially be at a disadvantage relative to the agencies. To counter this they will seek staff members and advisers who are veterans of the Hill, and perhaps larger and more district-oriented staffs to help ward off challengers who would try to take advantage of their inexperience. Is it wise to increase the already expansive power of bureaucrats and congressional staff for the sake of a new congressman in the district every half-generation or so?

The proposed limitation on congressional terms would also have most of the disadvantages of the old schemes of rotation in office that were criticized by the Federalists. Consider these points made by Alexander Hamilton in *Federalist* No. 72 (concerning rotation in the presidency, but still relevant to rotation in Congress). In the first place, setting a limit on officeholding "would be a diminution of the inducements to good behavior." By allowing indefinite reeligibility, political men will be encouraged to make their interest coincide with their duty, and to undertake "extensive and arduous enterprises for the public benefit" because they will be around to reap the consequences. Second, term limits would be a temptation to "sordid views" and "peculation." As Gouverneur Morris put it at the Constitutional Convention, term limits say to the official, "make hay while the sun shines." Nor does a long term of eligibility (12 years in this case) remove the difficulty. No one will know better than the present incumbent how difficult it will be to defeat the future incumbent. So the limits of his career will always be visible to him, as will the temptation to "make hay" as early as possible.

A third disadvantage of term limits is that they could deprive the country of the experience and wisdom gained by an incumbent, perhaps just when that experience is needed most. This is particularly true for senators, whose terms would be limited even though Senate races are frequently quite competitive (recall 1980 and 1986) and that the Senate was precisely the branch of the legislature in which the Framers sought stability, the child of long service.

DISTRACTION FOR GOP

For conservatives and Republicans, the pursuit of a constitutional amendment to limit congressional terms would act as a colossal distraction from the serious work of politics that needs to be done.

The worst effect of the incumbents' advantage in the House is to have saddled America with divided government since 1968 (excepting Jimmy Carter's administration, which was bad for other reasons). Professor Fiorina estimates that if marginal districts had not declined, the Republicans would have taken control of the House five times in the past quarter-century—in 1966, 1968, 1972, 1980, and 1984 (he did not evaluate the 1988 results). Because the marginals did decline, the Democrats, trading on the power of their incumbent members, retained control of the House throughout this period, despite the succession of Republican presidents who were elected.

It would be unfair, of course, to blame the Democrats' popularity wholly on the decline in marginal districts. The GOP has not done well enough in open-seat elections to rely on the incumbency effect as the all-purpose excuse for its inability to take the House. But it is a fair conjecture that the ethos of administrative politics works to the Republicans' disadvantage even in those districts lacking a Democratic incumbent. Which is not to say that Republican incumbents don't look out for themselves; they do. But the spirit of casework and pork-barrel cuts against the grain of conservative Republican principles, and so it is hard for Republican candidates to sound like Republicans when they are preaching the gospel according to FDR and LBJ. More to the point, it is difficult for the Republican Party to articulate why people ought to consider themselves Republicans and ought to vote a straight GOP ticket under these circumstances.

The attempt to limit congressional terms would do nothing to relieve Republicans of these tactical disadvantages. What is needed is not a gimmick to stir up political competition, but the prudence and courage to take on the strategic political questions dividing conservative Republicans and liberal Democrats. By (among other things) reconsidering the scope and power of the federal government, by opposing the extension of centralized administration over more and more of American life, Republicans could inaugurate robust political competition. President Reagan and the Republican Party were successful at this in 1980, when the GOP gained 33 seats in the House and took control of the Senate. But they seem to have neglected those lessons in succeeding elections.

... If the American people want to vote all incumbents out of office, or just those particular incumbents known as liberal Democrats, they can do so with but the flick of a lever. All they need is a good reason.

POSTSCRIPT

Should There Be Term Limits for Members of Congress?

Will contends that "a permanent class of career legislators is inherently inimical to limited government." But Kesler, who shares Will's philosophy of limited government, suggests that career legislators are precisely what are necessary to check the power of other Washington careerists. Without experienced legislators, he says, there will be an increase in "the already expansive power of bureaucrats and congressional staff."

In addition to Will's book, James K. Coyne and John H. Fund's *Cleaning House: America's Campaign for Term Limits* (Regnery Gateway, 1992) also makes a conservative case for term limits; the authors argue that such limits would result in the downsizing of government. Political scientist Nelson W. Polsby, in an article entitled "Congress-Bashing for Beginners," *The Public Interest* (Summer 1990), argues that term limits would "limit the effectiveness of the one set of actors most accessible to the people." Paul S. Herrnson, *Congressional Elections* (Congressional Quarterly Press, 1995) is an account of the campaign process which, among other things, indicates how difficult it is for newcomers to defeat incumbents.

Would term limits be more beneficial to Democrats than to Republicans, to liberals more than to conservatives? On one hand, term limits would end the careers of many long-term members, and most incumbents are Democrats. On the other hand, it would make it more possible for newcomers to enter Congress, and many of these newcomers are likely to be African Americans, Latinos, and other minorities, who in turn are likely to be Democrats. Yet, shorter terms would mean less time for members of Congress to create new social programs, which would probably make conservatives happy. But the promise of fresh blood and new thinking—one of the chief selling points of term limits—seems more in keeping with the liberal ethos.

ISSUE 6

Do We Need a Strong Presidency?

YES: Terry Eastland, from *Energy in the Executive: The Case for the Strong Presidency* (Free Press, 1992)

NO: Donald L. Robinson, from "The Presidency and the Future of Constitutional Government," in Martin L. Fausold and Alan Shank, eds., *The Constitution and the American Presidency* (State University of New York Press, 1991)

ISSUE SUMMARY

YES: Political writer Terry Eastland argues that only a strong president can fulfill the intentions of the framers of the Constitution and the requirements of modern government.

NO: Political scientist Donald L. Robinson maintains that the shared power of the Constitution must be restored to avoid future abuses of executive authority.

The founders of America set up Congress and the presidency in such a way as to invite conflict. The two branches are elected by different constituencies and for different terms of office. This would not necessarily lead to conflict if the president and Congress were tending to different tasks. But oftentimes they are dealing with the same matter, though approaching it from different perspectives. As political scientist Richard Neustadt once remarked, what the founders gave us was not separation of power but "a government of separated institutions *sharing* power." Both Congress and the president are involved in the legislative process, both make foreign policy decisions, and both are responsible for appointments to the federal judiciary. Seldom can either branch act effectively without the other, yet they are often in conflict.

Most modern democratic governments are structured differently. In parliamentary systems the chief executive, usually called a premier or prime minister, is elected by the majority in parliament and is the leader of the party that controls the parliament. The executive and legislative branches thus share common political interests, and the executive is virtually assured that any major piece of legislation he or she submits to parliament will be passed. There is no need for an executive veto because the parliament would never pass a bill opposed by the executive. This system seems to work fairly well in most democratic countries. Why did the United States not adopt it?

James Madison, often called "the father of the Constitution," insisted that the American system of government was deliberately and carefully crafted to produce tension between the branches of government; the idea was to prevent any single branch—legislative, executive, or judicial—from assuming all power. That, Madison said in the *Federalist Papers,* would be "the very definition of tyranny." The great safeguard against that eventuality was to give each branch both the means and the will to prevent encroachments by the other branches. "Ambition," Madison said, "must be made to counteract ambition." Such devices as the president's veto and the Senate's power to reject appointments and treaties are among the many checks by which each branch can reject the encroachments of the other.

The other principal author of the *Federalist Papers,* Alexander Hamilton, recognized that many of the states forming the Union were fearful of too great a concentration of power. At the same time, he believed that the success of the new government depended upon the concentration of power in a single executive. Hamilton argued, "Energy in the executive is a leading character in the definition of good government. It is essential to protection of the community against foreign attacks: It is not less essential to the steady administration of laws, to the protection of property... to the security of liberty." Only a single executive, he concluded, could possess the qualities of "decision, activity, secrecy, and dispatch."

When Franklin D. Roosevelt took office in 1933, the United States was in the depths of the Great Depression, and Congress was all too eager to surrender legislative initiative to him. World War II, the cold war, and hot wars in Korea and Vietnam required presidential initiatives in shaping foreign policy and conducting war as commander in chief. Television has provided the president with a platform far greater than the "bully pulpit" that Theodore Roosevelt so effectively used. The exposure that television provides may explain why the Americans tend to identify decision making and decisiveness more with the president than with Congress.

For the past two decades, most Americans have expressed unhappiness with the conflict that exists between the two political branches. After 12 years of gridlock in which Republican presidents Ronald Reagan and George Bush confronted Democratic majorities in the House of Representatives, some people were hopeful when Democratic Bill Clinton was elected president in 1992. However, the Clinton administration is still experiencing friction and stalemate with a Democratic congressional majority.

In the following selections, Terry Eastland and Donald L. Robinson both express disapproval with the way in which the U.S. government works. But where Eastland believes that the solution lies in the assertion of more stronger presidential leadership, Robinson believes that the excessive and arbitrary exercise of presidential power has resulted in grave abuses of power and an absence of cooperation between the president and Congress.

YES   Terry Eastland

THE STRONG PRESIDENCY AND PRESIDENTIAL LEADERSHIP

What, then, *is* a strong presidency? We may begin the answer by considering that the President needs the help of others to meet his constitutional duties. The President personally will select only a few of his aides, so he must have the assistance of a carefully staffed personnel office if the several thousand political positions within the executive branch are to be well appointed. Every candidate for a political position in the executive branch—and it makes no difference whether the position is appointed by the President or one of his subordinates (or one of their aides)—must be measured in terms of personal integrity and belief in public service, competence (for the position at issue), teamwork, toughness, commitment to change, and—last but not least—political compatibility with the President and dedication to his principles. The strong President will not waste appointments—or at least he will waste as few as possible—by naming or allowing the naming of people of unknown or unremarkable political views. Whatever the task—devising a legislative recommendation, drafting a State of the Union or veto message, enforcing a law, selecting a judge, negotiating a treaty, mapping a foreign policy—those who execute it must share the President's political premises. Personnel *is* policy. But policy is not just personnel. The energetic executive will establish and authorize White House systems to develop his policies and superintend their implementation through political appointees in the departments and agencies. Such mechanisms have critical roles to play in not only the administration of law but also the formulation of legislative measures.

Nothing can more quickly dissipate executive energy than charges of malfeasance, and actually wrongdoing itself, on the part of presidential subordinates—or the President, for that matter; think of President Nixon and Watergate, and think what might have happened to President Kennedy had his reckless liaisons with women and mobsters, which his most recent biographer, Thomas C. Reeves, has called "irresponsible, dangerous, and demeaning to the office of the chief executive," been reported while he was President. Self-interest as well as the office itself should motivate Presidents to act above suspicion. And the "new ethics era" as well as the Constitution, which requires the President to take care that the laws are faithfully executed, should lead every President, as soon as he is inaugurated, to take steps designed to prevent "ethics" problems or—human nature being what it is—reduce their number. President Reagan did not do that, but President Bush, in a demonstration of the strong presidency, did. One difference in the two administrations lies in the greater loss of energy Reagan suffered on the ethics front, best indicated by the number of months the effectiveness of [then–attorney general] Edwin Meese III was reduced on account of the two independent counsel investigations of alleged criminal misconduct on his part. Effective strategies against ethics problems will insist on law-abiding behavior, of course, but emphasize prudence. For whatever else Washington may be good at today, it is very good, thanks to new laws, new attitudes, and more journalists, at generating executive-branch scandals, many of which could have been prevented by good judgment. (Was it really necessary for John Sununu, Bush's first Chief of Staff, to have his government chauffeur drive him to New York for a stamp collection exhibition?) The strong President will work throughout his tenure to prevent ethics problems and thereby preserve his administration's political strength. He will remember Alexander Hamilton's wisdom, in *Federalist No. 70*: "A feeble executive is but another phrase for a bad execution; and a government ill-executed, whatever it may be in theory, must be, in practice, a bad government."

Ethics problems, as defined by the ethics laws, are not the only threat to executive energy. Aides who act as David Stockman did in 1981 in talking publicly against his administration's economic program also can enfeeble the presidency. Reagan should have discharged Stockman. Bush did not make that mistake in September 1990, when he relieved his Air Force Chief of Staff, not for talking against an administration program but for talking publicly about the possible military strategy against Saddam Hussein. The presidency is not well served by such behaviors as Stockman's or the Air Force Chief's. Presidential subordinates must remember that they work for the President, and that it is the President alone in whom the executive power is vested. If an appointee cannot in good conscience implement the President's policies, he should attempt to persuade the President of the merits of his views. Failing in that, he should resign. There is honor in that course of action, both moral and constitutional.

The strong presidency, then, is organized and staffed and managed in ways designed to ensure its energy in behalf of the President's policies, whether they are pursued legislatively, administratively, or in both ways at once.

In recommending legislation to Congress, the strong President will speak publicly in its behalf. Today he has no choice but to do that if he is to meet his constitutional duty—he cannot be silent in the manner of nineteenth century Presidents. (On the other hand, the strong presidency most emphatically is not found in the Wilsonian notion that presidential leadership depends not upon the President's place within the constitutional order but upon his contingent personal traits, especially his ability to read the thoughts of the American people and stir them to action through rhetoric.) The President may and should make his case to the American people. But he must conceive and execute his rhetorical strategies not with "winning" only in mind; he must speak in ways that at least do not undermine deliberative democracy. He will not ask his speechwriters for yet another "war" metaphor, nor otherwise seek to induce some false crisis. He will not speak in one idiom to the people and a different one (a more nuanced one) to Congress. And he will not prefer words to action. Reagan's 1988 State of the Union message might have been a satisfying television event, but it was not good governance; if Reagan did not like the continuing resolution presented to him the previous fall, he should have vetoed it. Thus he could have forced through his action greater attention to how much federal spending we should tolerate.

Rhetoric can be ill-used and underused. In 1980 Bush cut a profile in weakness when he opted for a budget summit behind closed doors with congressional leaders, thus declining to use his office to frame a badly needed public debate over how much government we need and are willing to pay for, tongue-tied for so long, Bush tried to save his negotiated budget accord with a last-minute, televised address to the nation, as though this were how to use the bully pulpit. The public did not rally to Bush's side but against him. Bush did not understand that rhetoric must be part of a comprehensive governing strategy. Ideally—as Reagan used it in behalf of tax reform—rhetoric is employed over time in a public effort that includes speeches, press conferences, and the like—all of which are aimed at arguing, not merely asserting, or sound-biting, the President's legislative case.

Reagan generally understood, as Bush in his budget summitry performance did not, that a modern President cannot "bargain" his way to consensus with legislators from both parties. Bush's approach —the style of leadership endorsed by Richard E. Neustadt in 1960—assumed a consensus in the electorate itself that was missing. Today a President must make a public legislative case. In doing that—through good arguments—he will build coalitions. With an electorate conflicted over major domestic policy questions, this is a demand of presidential leadership.

The energetic executive will argue his legislative case publicly and well, but he will also use his veto power, which unlike a speech can force Congress to pay attention to what the President thinks. The use of the veto includes not only its casting but its threatening. The more effective the threat, the less likely the veto will be cast. Effective veto threats are meant, and the only way they are known by Congress to be meant is through their casting when legislation has not been revised to satisfy the President. While, through early 1992, Bush did not "return" a bill on grounds of excessive or wrongheaded spending, he was, within the limited range of his veto presidency, a credible veto executive. With only one or two possible exceptions, he had followed through with vetoes of bills that did not measure up to his announced standards. By contrast, Reagan lost credibility as a veto executive because he often signed bills he had threatened to return.

The strong President will have a complete veto strategy. He will use his veto to block a bill he absolutely disagrees with or to shape one he can accept. He will use the power for policy reasons or constitutional reasons or, against the same bill, for both reasons. He will not accept the nonsense that it is somehow unconstitutional for a President to use the policy veto often, that frequent policy vetoes amount to "systematic policy control over" Congress, as Charles L. Black, among others, has argued. Prudence may limit the number of policy vetoes cast, but neither the Constitution nor constitutional policy does. The veto power is the President's, and he will use it whenever he cannot accept the policy served up to him by Congress. Policy vetoes can raise for public debate issues that have sorely needed it; the veto is a means, or at least a possible means, toward the end of greater deliberation. President Bush's 1990 veto of the civil rights bill on grounds that it promoted quotas did encourage a somewhat greater measure of thought over the degree to which race and ethnicity should be a basis for the allocation of benefits and opportunities in our society—an issue that had suffered from lack of legislative debate, having been dealt with primarily by the bureaucracy and the courts for twenty years.

The energetic President also will bear in mind the original reason the framers accorded the President the veto: constitutional self-defense (and in that a means of preserving a government of separated powers.) Twice did Reagan— a weak president in this ongoing battle with Congress—fail to veto legislation reauthorizing the independent counsel statute, which usurps what Hamilton called "the constitutional rights of the executive." By contrast, Bush... consistently acted in self-defense, casting his veto against presidentially offensive legislation.

A legislative tool and weapon, the veto is cast after measures having passed *both* houses of Congress (one constitutional requirement for a law) are *presented* to

the President (the second). The President who vetoes is under a constitutional obligation to explain himself, to give reasons, for the sake of deliberative democracy. That is why Presidents should take great care with what they say when they veto—just as they should when they recommend legislation and make popular appeals for it. The strong President will also go beyond what the Constitution requires when bills are presented to him. Article I, Section 7 discusses how a bill becomes law (and doesn't become law). The President may approve or veto a bill —or do nothing. Any bill not returned by the President within ten days becomes a law, just as surely as if the President had signed it. There is a qualification, however: if Congress passes a bill but then adjourns during the ten-day period, thus preventing the President from casting a veto, it "shall not be a law." From this provision has come the so-called "pocket veto," which President Madison was the first President to execute, in 1812. Note carefully: The constitutional text does not require the President to give reasons for what the Constitution suggests would have been a veto. But the energetic and responsible President, in cases of important legislation, will do that anyway, and Presidents from Madison through Andrew Johnson did so, the practice lapsing from Grant through Hoover before it was recovered by Franklin Roosevelt.

On this point, Bush provides a model. In the wake of Iran-contra [the controversial affair involving arms sales to Iran, the profits of which were secretly diverted to contra rebels, who were fighting the Sandanista government of Nicaragua], members of Congress wished to ensure that never again would a President wait as long as Reagan did to notify Congress about a special intelligence activity; a majority in the Senate formed as early as 1988 in favor of requiring the executive to notify Congress in advance of every single intelligence activity. (The relevant bill did not reach the House floor.) When the issue arose in 1989, as part of the intelligence reauthorization act, President Bush wrote the chairman and vice-chairman of the Senate Intelligence Committee, advising that while he intended to provide "prior notice" in "almost all instances," there would be "rare instances" in which notice could not be provided in advance but "within a few days." Bush explained: "Any withholding beyond this period would be based upon my assertion of the authorities granted this office by the Constitution." Bush thus stated his views for the record, and he threatened a veto. In 1990, Congress passed an intelligence authorization bill that included provisions encroaching on presidential authority, and then adjourned. Bush pocketvetoed the bill. But he did not do so silently. He wrote a memorandum of disapproval and made it public. This way he let his reasons be publicly known, and there could be no confusion about where he stood—either within the administration or on Capitol Hill (or in the press).

When approving legislation, the strong President will append statements to the most important bills, and in this way speak to Congress (although it is under no obligation to listen) and the executive branch (which is). Laws must be interpreted before they can be enforced. Signing statements thus become for a President vehicles—formal, public ones—for communicating to his "instruments of execution" how a new law should be implemented. Here again the President must take great care in what he says. President Bush junked a proposed signing statement for the Civil

Rights Act of 1991 when it appeared to commit him to interpretations of the new law that would have eliminated some forms of affirmative action he apparently approved.

Administering the laws of Congress forms the great bulk of the work of the executive branch. The strong President will seek an "administrative presidency" in the departments and agencies. Within a given department, the status quo can be changed. The means of change (not counting personnel) are a threesome: altering procedures, reorganizing offices, and coordinating activities. Any change must be done prudently, for good reasons, and consistent with the law and the Constitution. And whatever is done must have the President's influence and approval. Thus the need for strong White House systems, which will not simply monitor or coordinate what the agencies propose; working under the President's direction and with political appointees in the agencies, they will actively shape policy for the executive branch and oversee its implementation....

It is in the courts, of course, that the President's lawyers present their arguments. And it is in the exercise of his constitutional power to nominate and appoint judges that the strong President will seek a jurisprudential legacy, written in the thousands of opinions his judges will write. Presidents must choose their nominees with judicial philosophy centrally in mind, but to do that well they need help. The Justice Department and the White House Counsel's office are the places in which the energetic President will establish a reliable system for screening judicial candidates for the Supreme Court as well as the lower judiciary. The process by which the Reagan administration selected Antonin Scalia provides a worthy model for choosing a Supreme Court Justice; the system was established well in advance of any vacancy, and those who managed it focused intensively on the substantive views of potential nominees. The strong President will seek to avoid compromises on judicial philosophy especially in his Supreme Court choices; he should consider compromise only when a political situation clearly forces him to do so. This arguably occurred when Thurgood Marshall, the nation's first black Justice, stepped down, but plainly did not when, in filling the Potter Stewart vacancy in 1981, Reagan chose mainly on the basis of gender by naming Sandra Day O'Connor.

Of critical importance since the watershed battle over the [Robert H.] Bork nomination is the need for the President's engagement in getting his nominee confirmed. No President can afford to sit passively, as Reagan did while Bork's opponents waged political war against him. Presidential rhetoric may be necessary in confirmation battles—rhetoric that backs the nominee while seeking to elevate the public discourse. The memory of what happened to Bork should not lead Presidents to make confirmability the central criterion of selection, as unfortunately clearly did happen when President Bush chose David Souter for the Court in 1990. Finally, the truly energetic executive will be constant in his attention to lower court nominations, there being so many, so often. He will fight for his powers to select judges, and he will select with judicial philosophy in mind, aware that he is creating a minor league of sorts from which he—and his party successors —may have the opportunity to promote to the big league of the Supreme Court. Scalia, [Anthony M.] Kennedy, Souter,

and [Clarence] Thomas all put in time on benches below. ...

* * *

The strategic governance of the strong President... will take into account what may be achieved through the administrative presidency and what may need to be done through a legislative presidency, just as it will attend to what lawfully may be accomplished administratively in the implementation of new legislation. Not only the President but also his subordinates, in the White House and the departments and agencies, must think both administratively and legislatively. And so must the White House systems the President established to help him govern. ...

Thinking both administratively and legislatively, one cannot leave the subject without noting the opportunity and even the duty the strong President has in the extraordinary circumstance of a possible war. Alexander Hamilton saw clearly how the President, in exercising his constitutional powers, might create "an antecedent state of things" that might influence the legislative decision to authorize war. Bush, the strong President in this regard, exercised his powers— freezing assets, deploying troops, negotiating through the United Nations and around the world—and in so doing created the circumstance in which Congress, on January 12, 1991, voted to support the war effort that commenced four days later. In embarking upon the plainly "arduous" and "extensive" enterprises of extracting [Iraqi leader] Saddam Hussein from Kuwait, Bush was indeed the energetic executive, providing the leadership that could only have come, in our system of government, from the office he held.

The leadership of the constitutional officer who is the strong President thus has many definitions: in legislative contexts, in administrative ones, and in both, and in the selection and appointment of judges. His leadership not only will pursue substantive political goals, even "extensive and arduous enterprises" for the public good, but also seek to defend the office from which such pursuits—whether by him or his successors—are uniquely possible.

* * *

In 1861, after the attack at Fort Sumter, South Carolina, President Lincoln, among other actions extending executive power beyond their traditional limits, suspended the writ of habeas corpus. Against the charge that he had exercised a power that the Constitution appears to give Congress, Lincoln said that if he had done that (he would not concede that he had), his act would have been justified both by his constitutional duty to faithfully execute the laws, including the supreme law of the constitution, and also by his oath to preserve the government. When a President takes emergency action as Lincoln did, we may be taught something important about the inherent limits of law—namely, that it is incapable of fully realizing the public good. Only a Constitution large enough to allow actions against the law for the public good is, ironically, law adequate to democratic government; as Lincoln understood, the Constitution "is different *in its application* in cases of Rebellion or Invasion, involving the Public Safety, from what it is in times of profound peace and public security. Moreover, the genius of the Constitution is that such power as Lincoln exercised does not exist apart from the constitutional order, which provides means for checking exercises of the power. While the judgments of others

typically come after the fact of presidential action, when its consequences can be most accurately assessed, the Constitution facilitates those judgments; the presidency, after all, is part of a government of separated powers, and it is an elected office. Thus, Congress can hold hearings and even commence impeachment proceedings. Courts can disagree with Presidents, as occurred in Lincoln's case.... Public opinion, influenced by the press, has an informal but not inconsiderable role to play, and on Election Day, of course, the people can make their voices heard at a ballot box. These are not the only constraints. The very structure of the presidential office is such as to encourage energy *and* responsibility. A President who knows that he exists within a constitutional order designed to hold him accountable has an incentive to act more responsibly.

The strong President will know the Lincoln example and endeavor to rise to the occasion in such an extraordinary circumstance as Lincoln faced. He will not try, as Richard Nixon did, to lay claim to the Lincoln tradition of acting in the national interest as a defense for actions that may be deemed illegal. Suffice to say, Nixon did not face a clearly discernible crisis, as Lincoln manifestly had.

... To judge by certain pieces of legislation in recent years... Congress likes to force the President to concern himself with the merits of particular policies at the expense of his own powers. One way out of this bind might be for the President, early in his presidency, to state the political principles that will guide him and shape his policies in office. At the same time he would indicate in clear terms his determination to oppose encroachments by Congress upon the power of the office he holds. The reason for stating such intentions well in advance of their presence in any bill is that otherwise the President will not have laid down a marker to which he can refer once the legislation begins to move through Congress and toward his desk; the merits of what is in the legislation—or other political considerations—will dominate public discussion, and the President will more easily be forced to weigh policies that may not reflect his ideas against institutional power. It is very early on, for example, that the President could state clearly his intention to veto any legislation that contains a rider on some unrelated subject, any reauthorization of the independent counsel law, and any bill containing a legislative veto. It should go without saying that a President who takes such an unambiguous, institutional position should not himself undermine it by seeking legislation that proposes to compromise his authority. Whatever the political pressures might be, the strong president will resist, for the sake of his powers and therefore the cause of good government.

NO
Donald L. Robinson

THE PRESIDENCY AND THE FUTURE OF CONSTITUTIONAL GOVERNMENT

Thinking about the future is a little like thinking about the past. One looks both for continuities and for breaks in the pattern of events. The difference, of course, is that one's thoughts about the future are not pinned to facts. One is dealing in the realm of probabilities, of hopes and fears. There is a powerful urge to assume that the future will be merely an extension to the present, that constitutional government, having survived for two centuries, will muddle through future difficulties as well.

As citizens of a republic, however, it is especially important that we be aware of other possibilities, ranging from collapse to creative renewal. The health of a republic depends ultimately on the commitment of believing, caring men and women. We need to consider whether our constitutional system may now be imperiled after its two hundred years of development and by changes in its environment.

Rather than attempt to maintain suspense, let me state right at the outset the perspective on constitutional form that has emerged from my own studies and analysis. I believe that the presidency, as it has evolved since the middle of the twentieth century, poses a dire threat to constitutional government in this country. Unless we come to grips with these changes and make adjustments to compensate for them, we shall meanly lose the hope that has borne America through two turbulent centuries.

The summer of the bicentennial of the Constitution was a time of testing for the American political system. In November 1986, it came to light almost by accident that our government for over a year had been secretly engaged in selling weapons to a terrorist government in the Middle East. When the president asked the attorney general to look into the situation, it further developed that the profits from this wretched scheme were being used to support guerrilla movement in Central America, in violation of several laws. A series of investigations—by a presidentially appointed board headed by former Senator John Tower (R-Tex.); by a special prosecutor, Lawrence Walsh, appointed by a panel of federal judges at the request of the attorney general; and by a joint congressional committee co-chaired by Senator Daniel

From Donald L. Robinson, "The Presidency and the Future of Constitutional Government," in Martin L. Fausold and Alan Shank, eds., *The Constitution and the American Presidency* (State University of New York Press, 1991). Copyright © 1991 by State University of New York Press. Reprinted by permission. Notes omitted.

Inouye (D-Hawaii) and Representative Lee Hamilton (D-Ind.)—exposed an appalling set of operations, running "outside the constitutional fence."

It was dismaying to confront these revelations during the bicentennial summer. It presented a spectacle of abuse in high places that had few precedents in American history. It left our Middle East policy in a shambles, and the intelligence services of other nations were reluctant to cooperate with a government that managed its own affairs so badly.

Yet the affair was not without its redeeming features. Wrongdoers were exposed and punished; in that sense at least, the system could be said to be "working." Several key officials, including George Schultz, secretary of state, and Caspar Weinberger, secretary of defense, as well as several lawmakers—besides Hamilton and Inouye, Senators Warren Rudman (R-N.H.), Sam Nunn (D-Ga.), George Mitchell (D-Me.), and William Cohen (R-Me.), and Representatives Louis Stokes (D-Ohio), Richard Cheney (R-Wyo.) and Tom Foley (D-Wash.) —inspired new confidence in the system. And the nation got a much needed civics lesson.

There was a tendency, as the Iran-Contra investigations wound down, to breathe a sigh of relief. No "smoking gun" had been found in the president's hand, and it would not be necessary to endure the ordeal of an impeachment proceeding. James Reston, writing his last regular editorials in a distinguished career at the *New York Times,* took the view that it would "probably be a long time before the CIA and the NSC... run wild over or around the President and Congress, and a long time before the Constitution is violated in the name of conservative principles." He acknowledged

that the secretary of state in his testimony had told "an alarming story of corruption at the top of the government," that "unelected, unconfirmed and virtually unknown staff officers in the White House" had been making major foreign policy decisions on their own, lying to Congress and apparently not even obtaining the President's informed approval for some of their initiatives. Nevertheless, he drew comfort from what he saw as evidence that "this system of separate and equal powers can be manipulated only so far before it rallies under stress.

In constitutional terms, the Tower Board reached a similarly comforting conclusion: that the Iran-Contra fiasco was "a policy blunder caused, not by institutions, but by individuals." It took, as the epigraph of its report, the rhetorical question propounded by the Roman poet, Juvenal: "Who shall guard the guardians?" Presumably, by the Tower Commission's lights, this question was virtually unanswerable. Commissioner Edmund Muskie, a former senator and secretary of state, remarked as the report was being issued that it was up to the president to make the system work. It was made for his use, and "by actions, by his leadership, [he] determines the quality of its performance." It seemed almost a counsel of despair.

When Reston wrote that it would be "a long time" before any future president's men would be tempted to perpetrate a similar fiasco, it brought to mind the Watergate scandal and how quickly the impression of that episode had lost its monitory effect. Why were Reston and the Tower Board so loath to see a pattern in these recurrent crises? Why were they so reluctant to see implications for reform?

The answer is rooted in the prevailing conception of the role of the chief executive in constitutional government. At the beginning of its section entitled "Recommendations," the Tower Board indicated its disposition by citing the opinion of Justice George Sutherland in the famous case of *United States v. Curtiss-Wright Export Corporation*. This opinion has become the charter of presidential power in foreign affairs. It is built on the theory that the power to conduct foreign relations is inherent in a nation's sovereignty and is by nature an executive power. It therefore exists, as an executive power, from the moment the nation asserts its sovereignty. It is in that sense extra- or pre-constitutional, in a way even more fundamental than the Constitution itself. (Contrast James Madison's observation made in 1792: "In Europe, charters of liberty have been granted by power. America has set the example... of charters of power granted by liberty.")

All that a constitution can do, according to Justice Sutherland's theory, is to indicate certain exceptions to the general principle that the nation's power of foreign relations, vested in the executive, is plenary. Thus, the Constitution of the United States provides that the Senate must ratify treaties and confirm the appointment of the president's ambassadors and that Congress must declare war and raise and maintain armed forces. With these specific exceptions noted, however, the rest of the foreign policy power must be assumed to be the province of the executive. So, at any rate, runs the doctrine that Sutherland presents in *U.S. v. Curtiss-Wright*.

The Tower Board took this theory as its authority in considering what lessons to draw from the Iran-Contra Affair. In fact, it embellished it. Quoting Sutherland's view that "the President alone has the power to speak and listen as a representative of the nation," the Board added that, "whereas the ultimate power to formulate domestic policy resides in the Congress, the primary responsibility for the formulation and implementation of national security policy falls on the President."

Not surprisingly, given this point of departure, former Senator Tower and his associates came up empty, as far as institutional reforms are concerned. Not only should the president remain untrammeled by legislative interference, they concluded; so should his staff. The purpose of the NSC [National Security Council] and its staff is to advise the president and coordinate the activity of the department in service of the president's policies. "As a general matter," the NSC ought not to "engage in the implementation of policy or the conduct of operations." At the same time, however, "the inflexibility of a legislative restriction should be avoided," because a "legislative proscription might preclude some future president from making a very constructive use of the NSC staff."

To assess this conclusion, we must return to the sources of the American constitutional tradition. We should do so modestly, for, as Justice Robert Jackson warned in assessing President Truman's seizure of the steel mills in 1952, "Just what our forefathers did envision, or would have envisioned had they foreseen modern conditions, must be divined from materials almost as enigmatic as the dreams Joseph was called upon to interpret for the Pharaoh." This is particularly true for the executive, since the Framers had so little experience themselves with that part of the constitutional structure and their phrasing of Article II was so spare. Nevertheless, a candid consultation of the Framer's pronouncements on this subject does yield a few important clues about their intentions.

There was no executive at the national level under the Articles of Confederation. Congress administered its own affairs through ad hoc boards, and it had only a very limited bureaucracy to assist with administrative tasks. Thus Article II of the Constitution of 1787 established something new, and its Framers, whose experience with "the executive power" had been confined to state governments, had only a sketchy idea of the power they were vesting in the president.

By analogy with the state governments, the powers of the federal chief executive centered on the enforcement and implementation of the laws, including the appointment of officers to help him carry out these functions. In addition they included such responsibilities as giving information to the Congress on the state of the Union, granting reprieves and pardons, and vetoing legislation.

Beyond these powers which the president received by analogy with the state executives, however, the president was given responsibility for foreign relations. With the consent of two-thirds of the Senate, he could "make" treaties and, with the Senate majority's consent, appoint ambassadors; and he was directed to "receive ambassadors." He was also, of course, made commander in chief of the armed forces. (Some of the governors at that time were commanders in chief of state militia, but the new president's powers in the field were obviously more awesome.)

In sum, though the text of the Constitution does not say so explicitly, John Marshall was drawing a fair inference when he declared that "the president is the sole organ of the nation in its external relations and its sole representative with foreign nations." Sometimes, however, this oft-quoted sentence is made the basis for assertions that go far beyond Marshall's meaning. He was not arguing that presidents were free to make their own foreign policy, much less that they were free to ignore laws by which Congress sought to direct their actions in foreign relations. In fact, in the same speech, he commented that Congress was constitutionally free to "prescribe the mode" by which the laws, including treaties, might be carried out, was free in fact to "devolve on others [beside the president] the whole execution of the contract," but that "til this be done," it was the duty of the executive department to carry out the treaty "by any means he possesses."

It seems clear that the principal intention of the system of separated and checked powers established by the Constitution is to force the executive and legislative branches to cooperate. The sharing of power keeps the branches in contact and often brings them into conflict. That is indeed the Framers' most fundamental intent.

Note also that the Framers did not distribute the shares of power randomly. To Congress they gave the making of policy. To the executive they gave enforcement and administration. The assignments were not pure, of course. Each branch had a hand in the other's affairs, to keep a check on it. The executive could recommend measures, and he or she could veto enactments of which he or she disapproved and thereby require that only special majorities could enact them over his objections. Congress also had a hand in administration, by its power of the purse and authority to structure departments through legislation and set their assignments, and by the Senate's power to confirm the appointment of all major administrative officers.

Despite this mixing, however, the centers of gravity were clear. Congress, representing the various regions, occupations, and classes in the Union, would by its deliberations ascertain and establish the nation's will. The president, a single individual, would decisively and vigorously carry that will into execution.

So far there is no distinction between foreign and domestic affairs. With Senate consent, the executive makes treaties, which is a kind of lawmaking. But once made, the executive has the same obligation toward treaties as toward any other form of law: the obligation to "take care" that they are "faithfully" executed.

In assigning these roles, the Framers paid careful attention to the differing relationship of the two branches in the operation of "factions." Factions were unavoidable in republican political life. That is the point of Madison's argument in *Federalist Paper*, Number 10. Factions were groups of people ("men," in those days) who came together to promote their own interests. According to the Framers' doctrine of man, if people were free to form such combinations, they would always do so. Many theorists thought this tendency was fatal to republican government. Madison thought not. He believed that in a large republic there would be enough variety that no single group could form a majority by itself. So long as majorities ruled, no single "faction"—at any rate none based on economic interests—could gain control, certainly not for long.

Thus, it was safe, in legislative assemblies, to give free rein to factions. They would check one another.

Note, however, that Madison's famous theory does not apply to the executive. In the legislature many factions could be represented, but there was to be just one chief executive. Both the process by which he was selected and his mode of operation in office were thus utterly different from those pertaining to Congress. His election was rigged so as to minimize the likelihood that any single group of "designing men" could manipulate the process for partisan ends. Furthermore, according to Alexander Hamilton, his unique responsibilities required him to be capable of decisiveness and secrecy. Also, the electorate had to be able to focus accountability on him personally for the vigorous enforcement of the law.

Hamilton was perfectly clear on this point. He agreed with Madison that factions would inevitably arise in republican politics, but he insisted that their operation be confined to the legislature. It was imperative to keep their "baneful" effects out of the executive branch.

Hamilton spelled this position out in *Federalist Paper*, Number 70. Wherever two or more people were involved in a political enterprise, there was always the danger of bitter dissensions and animosity. "Whenever these happen," he wrote, "they lessen the respectability, weaken authority, and distract the plans and operations of those whom they divide." Such "inconveniences" were unavoidable in the legislature; in fact, "differences of opinion and the jarring of parties" in the legislature "often promote deliberation and circumspection, and serve to check the excesses of the majority" in the legislative arena. But it was far different where "the supreme executive magistracy of a country" was concerned. Here the disadvantages of dissension were "pure and unmixed." They constantly counteracted those qualities which were most unnecessary to the effective performance of the executive function, vigor and expedition, and without any counterbalancing good. Hamilton just gave one example of this operation: "In the conduct of war, in which the energy of the executive is the bulwark of the national security, everything would be apprehended from its plurality [that is, from vesting the executive power in the hands of a council, rather than a single individual]." On the basis of this understanding, the Framers vested the executive power in a single individual and designed an electoral process to enable presidents to come to office without mortgaging their authority to factions.

Thus, the Framers' reasons for preferring "unity" in the executive is clear. So also, unfortunately, is their failure to consider the two leading threats to the perpetuation of a "republican executive": the difference between domestic and foreign affairs, and the impact that a maturing bureaucracy would have on the balance of the branches. . . .

THE ENLARGEMENT OF THE EXECUTIVE BRANCH

Most constitutional traditions (Great Britain's, France's, Japan's) begin with an effort to put boundaries on the power of the administrative apparatus of the government. In America's case, the constitutional tradition begins with a need and desire to *create* a national government.

By 1987, the nation had been independent for a decade, but its administrative bureaucracy was still extremely primitive. There were few officials serving in its ranks, and neither the government as a whole nor any of its component boards had independent standing. Administrative capabilities were created more or less ad hoc, to serve the congressional sense of need. . . .

Beginning in the late nineteenth century, however, growth in the complexity of organization and in sheer numbers of federal employees began to gain momentum. In 1901 there were 239,476 civilian employees of the federal government. Fifty years later the number had increased tenfold. The executive branch grew during the twentieth century not only in size and complexity, but in its powers of initiation and in the exercise of "delegated powers." For example, it was not until Franklin Roosevelt's administration that the practice developed of drafting major pieces of legislation at the White House or in administrative bureaus. By President Nixon's time, a Congress controlled by the Democrats was willing to delegate far-reaching powers over wages and prices to a Republican president.

With these developments, the transformation of the Framers' system was complete. Whereas the Framers had expected Congress, the legislative assembly, to declare the regime's will through laws, primacy now lay in both domestic and foreign relations with the solitary executive and people who served at his pleasure. The president had become not only the initiator of policy ideas and the articulator of an integrated outlook on the nation's affairs (roles foreseen by the Constitution), but, by the exercise of delegated powers, the "chief legislator" and, by prerogative, the maker of the nation's foreign policy. Congress remained the most independent and in some ways the most powerful legislature in the world, but it had lost the centrality which led Woodrow

Wilson as late as 1885 to assert that ours was a "congressional government."

As Hamilton's analysis makes clear, the president's constitutional position and the electoral foundations of his office are entirely unsuited to these new responsibilities. It is incompatible with a republican form of government for one person, who is elected once every four years and whose tenure is invulnerable to political discipline, to exercise such extensive discretion. The rule of law cannot restrain him; its prescripts have of necessity become too broad to guide him in the application of principles to specific circumstances, and they are in any case inapplicable to vast areas of his discretion, particularly in the field of foreign policy.

Nor can the regime's "checks" bring him decisively to account, so long as he avoids conviction for "treason, bribery, or other high crimes and misdemeanors." Virulent opposition in the press and in Congress can cripple him, render him contemptible and politically impotent, but it cannot dislodge him without traversing the impeachment process. And even if a move for impeachment should produce a conviction (which it has not yet done for an American president), the office would devolve upon his hand-picked successor, the vice president. While contemplating these wretched alternatives, his critics are confronted with the choice of emasculating "the only president we've got" or finding some basis for cooperating with him....

In these circumstances—unless... we are prepared to forgo the values of constitutionalism—we need to do two things. The first is to clarify our thinking. We have to recognize that checks and balances, rather than the rule of law, are the principal reliance in our system for holding power accountable and that the Constitution's checks need to be adjusted to the new realities of American national governance....

In [President Reagan's] eyes, discretion in interpreting the laws' requirements remained with him. He promised that "maximum consultation and notification is and will be the firm policy of this administration," but he could not speak for future administrations. Even in his own case, we were left finally to trust him, rather than depend on countervailing institutions to restrain the abuse of power.

Clearly this was inadequate. If modern governance is to reflect the Framers' commitment to shared power, there had to be fundamental alterations....

[T]he second need [is] a change in the system of incentives set up by the Constitution to govern interactions between the president and Congress. The dynamic now favors confrontation. It thus leads to an excess of political posturing, governing by mutual finger-pointing, rather than responsible, coordinated action by legislators and executives on such problem as deficit reduction. Ominously, it leads responsible people in the executive branch to acts of evasion when the law imposes unwanted constraints or burdens or responsibilities. The present system also prevents the electorate from holding anyone accountable for these failures.

Rather than confrontation, our system needs to encourage cooperation, and when the existing elected officials cannot find a basis for cooperation, it ought to give the nation a chance to resolve the disagreement through elections. Elections in a large republic are primarily about the personnel of government, rather than its policies. Nevertheless, in choosing leaders voters sometimes make a statement about policy, too, as in 1860, 1896, 1932, and 1980. In those instances, deadlocks were resolved by putting new leadership in place. The elections were not a referendum on policy; they were a repudiation of failed leadership and a declaration of willingness to empower a new team.

When the government disgraces itself or falls into stalemate, there needs to be an opportunity for renewal. Such crises do not occur regularly, every two or four years. Nor is the impeachment process an adequate remedy for failed leadership. When policy is failing or the branches are deadlocked, it is beside the point to inquire whether one individual has committed "high crimes and misdemeanors." And even if a conviction can be gained (none has, during our first two centuries), it results only in the removal of the president and his replacement by a person of his own choosing. What the nation needs in those instances is renewal, not the purging of one individual.

In another place, I have spelled out a plan for dissolution and special elections when the political branches are deadlocked or when the government is weakened by scandal or demonstrated incapacity. I will not repeat that argument here, except to say that a carefully regulated system of special elections would not weaken one branch at the expense of the other. It would not disturb the existing balances. It would give point and purpose to disagreements between them and provide a mechanism for resolving them, if the people so determined.

Woodrow Wilson pointed out that, between presidential elections, the public often ignores political debates because they have no climax, no decisive result. In a parliamentary system, on the other hand, the attentive public pays heed, because catastrophe may befall any unwary government at any moment. Wilson's point may be overdrawn as applied to parliamentary systems today, but it nevertheless suggests an important feature of a system where, when a serious crisis develops, the public has reason to hope for a timely resolution, via elections.

We need not adopt a parliamentary system in order to enjoy the benefits that would come from borrowing one of its features. Indeed, there is great merit for us in a system of separated powers, if we can rid ourselves of the difficulties that arise from the extreme form it takes in our system. We have occasionally been saved from serious problems by the operation of independently elected branches that are able to check each other's excesses.

There is a difference, however, between salutary checks and persistent deadlock. It may be difficult to draw that line in the turmoil of everyday politics, and there is some risk that the government might resort to dissolution too often. But there is risk, too, in a system that cannot move for renewal under any circumstances, save on a regular, four-year cycle. The very regularity of that provision tends to undermine its usefulness as an occasion for genuine renewal. Candidates prepare for it years in advance, without knowing what qualifications or what sort of person will be needed when election day finally arrives. Also, renewal is short-lived, because the system tends to settle back into deadlock soon after the elections, as everyone begins to feel the system's incentives for confrontation and recalls that it will be four long years before there is another chance for a fresh start.

The best way to honor the Framers is to follow their example. That means being willing to take a hard look at the situation in which we find ourselves, courageously and carefully measuring our performance against the standard of our ideals. It also means overcoming inertia, summoning up the effort to think and act creatively, taking pains to adapt the shared ideals of the American political tradition to human and political realities. Because of the Framers' good work and (as Justice Thurgood Marshall has reminded us) the determination and sacrifices of those who were left out of the original design, we do not need to invent first principles of self-government. We do need to think afresh about how to realize those principles under modern conditions. Thinking about how to bring the presidency within the ambit of constitutional restraint is the right place to start.

POSTSCRIPT

Do We Need a Strong Presidency?

Americans today know more about the personalities, character, and nonpublic behavior of their presidents than they could ever have known in the past, and citizens do not always like what they learn. Moreover, public respect has declined as a result of scandals and allegations that have tarnished reputations and even drove one president—Richard Nixon, who resigned after the Watergate scandal—from office.

If the disintegration of the Soviet Union and the end of the cold war have reduced the urgency of the president's initiatives in some foreign policy areas, it is apparent that, even in domestic policy areas, the president retains a power to raise issues, if not to command assent. Without President Ronald Reagan's initiatives, Congress would not have adopted its far-reaching tax cuts in 1981. Without President Bill Clinton's initiatives, Congress would not have considered health care reform in 1994.

The relationship between the president and Congress is often stormy, each jealous of its prerogatives and fearful of being dominated by the other. But this arranged marriage (neither chose the other) can only be dissolved at the next election and without any assurance that the next match will be a happier one.

Lance T. LeLoup and Steven A. Shull, in *Congress and the President: The Policy Connection* (Wadsworth, 1993), examine how the president and Congress work together and against each other on a wide variety of domestic and foreign policy issues. Lyn Ragsdale, in *Presidential Politics* (Houghton Mifflin, 1993), traces how presidential power has grown at the expense of congressional power. Ragsdale argues that, despite the effective image of the single president, the growth of power and complexity have made the presidency a plural institution in which many participate in decision making. A thoughtful and provocative examination of the evolution of the presidency is Forrest McDonald, *The American Presidency: An Intellectual History* (University Press of Kansas, 1994). McDonald concludes that, on balance, the presidency "has been responsible for less harm and more good than perhaps any other secular institution in history."

A unique insight into the presidential office is in *The Haldeman Diaries: Inside the Nixon White House*, the posthumously published diaries of H. R. Haldeman, President Nixon's chief of staff. This intimate account explains the corruption of power and the decline in presidential prestige that followed Nixon's resignation. Also see Lou Cannon, *President Reagan: The Role of a Lifetime* (Simon & Schuster, 1991), which is considered by many to be the best political biography of a recent president.

ISSUE 7

Does the Government Regulate Too Much?

YES: Robert B. Charles, from "From Democracy to Regulocracy?" *The World & I* (July 1994)

NO: Susan Tolchin and Martin Tolchin, from *Dismantling America* (Houghton Mifflin, 1983)

ISSUE SUMMARY

YES: Attorney Robert B. Charles argues that the costs of government regulation are crippling the productivity of American industry.

NO: Professor of public administration Susan Tolchin and journalist Martin Tolchin contend that without vigorous regulation, businesses will destroy the environment and endanger lives for the sake of profits.

Government regulation of economic decision making is as old as the Interstate Commerce Commission, which was established in 1887 to regulate railroad rates. The Sherman and Clayton Antitrust Acts of 1890 and 1914, respectively, as well as the law establishing the Federal Trade Commission in 1914, were also designed to outlaw unfair methods of business competition.

Congress later established regulatory agencies to set standards for natural (or socially useful) monopolies, such as electric power companies and radio and television stations. Between 1920 and 1940, Congress set up the Federal Power Commission, the Federal Communications Commission, and the Civil Aeronautics Board. The national government also created the Federal Reserve System in 1913 and the Securities and Exchange Commission in 1934 (after the stock market crash) to regulate the investment of capital in industry and general banking practices.

Although governmental regulation of commerce on behalf of the public interest was introduced as early as the Pure Food and Drug Act of 1906 (now administered by the Department of Health and Human Services), most activity within this area is relatively recent. The Equal Employment Opportunity Commission was established in 1965. The Environmental Protection Agency, the Occupational Safety and Health Administration, and the National Highway Traffic Safety Administration were all created in 1970. The Consumer Product Safety Commission was set up in 1973, and the Office of Surface Mining Reclamation and Enforcement (within the Department of the Interior) came into being in 1977. With these and other newly established agencies, the federal government assumed wide-ranging responsibility to protect all persons against certain hazards that unrestrained private economic enterprise might otherwise create.

The rules written by these regulatory bodies have changed Americans' lives in many ways, altering the food we eat, the cars we drive, and even the air we breathe. Defenders of these agencies have applauded the protection that has been provided against profit-motivated predators who would otherwise adulterate food, threaten public safety, and pollute the environment in order to maximize profits.

On the other hand, many investigators have joined businessmen in condemning government's movement into these areas. Critics make the following arguments: (1) Regulation inhibits production by suppressing innovation and discouraging risk taking, which results in declining employment. (2) Regulation invariably overregulates by setting standards for every aspect of manufacturing when it could set overall objectives that businesses could meet in whatever ways they devise. Some economists maintain that government would accomplish more by assessing fees or taxes to discourage certain activities rather than fixing rigid standards. (3) Regulation costs to businesses are passed on to the consumer and increase government payrolls. Also, if government regulation drives a company out of business, the standard of living for those affected will go down. That is to say, the costs outweigh the benefits.

Different values will result in different assessments of the consequences of regulation or deregulation. The regulation of lumbering and mining to protect the environment, for example, pits those who place a higher value on environmental preservation, and who therefore tend to support regulation, against those who put economic well-being first, who tend to oppose regulation.

But sometimes deregulation can lead to results that cost a great deal of money. Deregulating the savings and loan (S&L) industry tempted many S&L banks into making high-profit but risky investments, and when the borrowers defaulted, the federal government stepped in to pick up the tab at a total cost of roughly half a trillion dollars. Seen from a different standpoint, however, S&L bailout was not the result of deregulation but of incomplete deregulation: the federal government stopped supervising the banks but continued to insure them.

In the following selections, attorney Robert Charles argues that regulation is crippling American industry and productivity. Professor Susan Tolchin and journalist Martin Tolchin, in opposition, insist that regulation is necessary to protect America against industries' reckless pursuit of profit at the expense of public safety and health and of the natural environment.

YES

Robert B. Charles

FROM DEMOCRACY TO REGULOCRACY?

America may rapidly be drifting from "wise and frugal" government into a tumbling current of regulatory whitewater. Today, mangroves of environmental regulation overlap, intertwine, and grow off the pages of the *Federal Register*.

The president introduces laws, Congress enacts them, and both are accountable. Regulators, on the other hand, are not. Federal regulators are powerful, unelected, essentially unaccountable, and often preoccupied, not with public policy questions that generate big legislation, but with making and enforcing the narrowest of rules.

A recent study by the American Enterprise Institute (AEI) and Harvard showed that "neither the House of Representatives nor the Senate is a key player in defining the details of many environmental policies." The study concluded that "a striking feature of many federal environmental policies is the extent to which program staff within the EPA [Environmental Protection Agency] play a central role in developing and advancing options."

Theoretically, the president has oversight. And it is true that Ronald Reagan took control of the regulatory process and reformed it, for a time. After a miniboom between 1990 and 1991, George Bush also imposed a moratorium on new statutes in January 1992. In his first year in office, Bill Clinton by contrast has hired more federal regulators than any president in history.

While Candidate Clinton declared, "I am going to stop handing down mandates to you and regulating you to death," President Clinton sits athwart, and actively promotes, the regulocracy. In fact, his administration is setting regulatory records.

COSTS TO BUSINESS

The best place to begin looking at America's regulation woes are unfunded federal mandates. In U.S. history before 1988, only 40 unfunded mandates were forced on the states. Between 1988 and 1991, more than three times that number were enacted. Since Clinton's arrival, the number has continued to increase. In fact, despite 20-odd bills floating around Congress to limit unfunded mandates, they are accelerating....

Nationwide, a full 12 percent of municipal revenues are now devoted to meeting unfunded federal mandates, an unprecedented development. In Atlanta, the mayor will issue $400 million in new debt instruments during 1994 and 1995 to comply with new unfunded mandates. In other cities, one hears similar sighs.

Consider, too, the burgeoning regulocracy's impact on small businesses. Economist Lawrence Kudlow estimates that most of 19 million jobs created during the 1980s, and at least two of every three created today, come from small business. Yet small businesses are increasingly regulators' prime target.

The Americans with Disabilities Act (ADA) will apply after July 26, 1994, to America's smallest companies, including those with 15 or more employees. Chicago economist Robert Genetski calculates that mandated physical modification of hospitals and other buildings alone comes to $65 billion.

Not included in Genetski's figures are the other ADA mandates for restaurants, hotels, trains, buses, rental cars, and planes. Airlines will soon, under new regulations, need to widen all aisles for the length of the plane, to accommodate wheelchairs at any seat.

New mandates from the Occupational Safety and Health Administration (OSHA) are even more frightening to small business. Consider the dry-cleaning industry. According to the National Federation of Independent Businesses, almost 100 forms and government manuals will soon be required to open a small dry-cleaning business. A different 1992 study concluded: "Environmental regulations [have] added as much as $138,700 to the direct costs of starting a new dry-cleaning establishment."

Every dry cleaner must now adopt the prescribed OSHA "energy control procedure" for machinery repair. Failure to do so results in stiff penalties. The procedure, known as "lock out," involves installing locks on all electrical plugs. OSHA estimates the risk of mortality without its lock-out procedure at four deaths per million. Meeting the regulation will cost dry cleaners roughly $70.9 million per theoretically averted death, according to the Office of Management and Budget.

Bread is another example. Anne Giesecke of the American Bakers Association (ABA) explained, in an interview for this article, that the EPA now considers the aroma of baking bread, in particular the nontoxic ethanol created by mixing flour, water, and yeast, to be a "volatile organic compound," or VOC. Thus, by late 1995 bakeries across the country will have to curtail their "emissions." The smell fits the definition of a VOC under regulations defining the Clean Air Act of 1990 (CAA) and therefore harms the ozone and must be eliminated.

What about the cost of retooling America's bakeries? The EPA is unconcerned; it just offers estimates. However, Giesecke explains, "the EPA compliance cost estimates are turning out to be too low. Where the EPA at first estimated a cost of $2,000 to $3,000 per ton for control of ethanol, our experience is now leading to the view that these costs are closer to $5,000 to $8,000 per ton." Why the difference? "The catalytic oxidizers [proposed by the EPA] do not work well on bakery ovens," according to Giesecke.

In search of solutions, the ABA is actually trying to convince the EPA to accept conversion of its 120,000 bakery trucks to cleaner-burning natural gas and propane—a substitute measure. A recent *Wall Street Journal* article suggested that bakers might win the right not to "muzzle their ovens," though they will stay on guard for what some call the EPA's "yeast police."

Beyond the unfunded mandates, there are other costs imposed by regulocracy. Litigation, for one. A 1992 Rand Institute study calculated that "business will spend a minimum of $31 billion on non-cleanup Superfund activities, primarily legal fees, over the next 30 years."

Economist Thomas Hopkins of the Rochester Institute of Technology released a study in 1992 of the nation's annual regulatory costs. In 1991 dollars, he found that regulatory costs topped $540 billion in 1977, fell to $473 billion in 1988, and rose to $542 billion in 1991. By the end of 1994, however, they are expected to exceed $588 billion.

Other studies are less convincing than Hopkins' assessment. In 1978, the Center for American Business sponsored a study by Murray Weidenbaum (later Reagan's chairman of the Council of Economic Advisors) that found regulation costs to be roughly $63 billion in 1976 (or $137 billion in 1988 dollars). A 1983 Yale study put private sector costs at $67–177 billion in 1977 (in constant 1988 dollars). An AEI study placed annual direct regulatory costs between $123 billion and $154 billion in 1988. Finally; a 1993 survey of existing economic literature put the cost somewhere between $364 billion and $538 billion (only slightly below the Hopkins estimate for 1991). Put differently, the cost is roughly $3,500 per American household.

THE CLEAN AIR ACT

The 1990 CAA legislation is the most comprehensive environmental law in 13 years. In theory, the CAA was supposed to reduce acid rain and clean up America's smoggy cities in a way that everyone—that is, manufacturers, consumers, state administrators, and environmentalists—could live with.

In practice, it is not turning out that way. Under the act, the EPA is charged with issuing dozens of new rules. States are required to develop regulations for VOCs and "hazardous air pollutant emissions," as well as "major source operating permits."

These will start to go into effect in 1995. As one industry expert explained, "the result is that the CAA tempo will pick up greatly over the next five years, as permits are issued in 1995 and billions of dollars are spent on air pollution control equipment to be installed in 1996, 1997, and 1998."

Meanwhile, Clinton's EPA is churning out more restrictive and more costly regulations than anyone anticipated and more than most thought possible. From toxic air pollution to fuel additives and reformulations, from source review standards to identifying and regulating substances that presumably deplete ozone, regulators are creating rules with unprecedented sweep. Overall, more than 120 new CAA regulations will be issued by 1995.

Only two months ago, the EPA declared that it will begin regulating gas-powered lawn mowers, chain saws, and even golf carts. To follow is regulation of small spark-ignition engines, including snowmobiles, motorcycles, motor boats, wood chippers, weed whackers, and model airplanes, among others.

Estimated compliance costs for the CAA now average around $24 billion, although they range from $104 billion down to $14 billion. Additionally, there is growing concern that at least one secondary effect will be a drop in America's gross domestic product by 2005 (the year of full CAA implementation).

Will regulators clean the air? Possibly, but pollution abatement, and environmental regulations in general, have a spotty performance record. Already pollution abatement mandates are negatively affecting U.S. employment, productivity, and international competitiveness. According to a November 1993 study by the Department of Commerce, there has long been an assumption that every dollar spent on pollution abatement only reduces productivity by one dollar (since the dollar is reallocated), but 1994 data from 107 oil refineries, 120 pulp and paper mills, and 60 steel mills indicate that "productivity was reduced by the equivalent of three to four dollars per dollar of pollution abatement costs."

Similarly, a 1994 survey of 2,000 manufacturing executives by the National Association of Manufacturers found:

- 64.3 percent have delayed hiring specifically due to government mandates and regulations;
- 86.1 percent rely more on overtime and temporary help than five years ago due to mandates and regulations;
- 84.6 percent of smaller companies are staying below 50 employees (i.e., not growing) to avoid mandates on those with over 50 employees; and
- paperwork requirements inhibit exporting for 50 percent of those companies that export.

To make matters worse, the EPA's cost estimates for pollution abatement, as the bread controls illustrate, are notoriously low. Dorothy Kellogg of the Chemical Manufacturers Association, when interviewed for this article, called them a "total joke" and offered this example. The EPA recently ordered chemical companies to "make an affirmative demonstration that waste [used in the manufacture of acrylic] was... non-hazardous."...

SUPERFUND'S SUPER LOSSES

Shifting gears, consider the Comprehensive Environmental Response, Compensation and Liability Act (CERCLA)—the Superfund toxic waste cleanup scheme—perhaps one of the greatest regulatory boondoggles ever. Although toxic waste sites have needed cleaning, Superfund has cost taxpayers plenty. Initially, a $10.1 billion trust fund was established on the public nickel (to be replenished). Then a private liability scheme was dreamed up. The scheme was based on the idea that a "deep pocket"—someone who can pay for every cleanup—exists.

Superfund's transaction costs alone are exceptional. On average, the EPA takes 43 months to proceed from locating a site to putting the site on its priority cleanup list. Then potentially responsible parties (PRPs), sometimes hundreds, are notified that the EPA has tagged them and that they may be on the hook for the full multimillion-dollar cleanup.

Naturally, the PRPs get lawyers. Fees begin to mount. Insurers are notified. More lawyers, more fees. Litigation lasts years. Negotiation is difficult, not only between the accused and the EPA, but between those accused. The reason? Superfund liability is a zero-sum game. Like musical chairs, regardless of fairness, someone will always lose—and it is often the party that did not get a lawyer to jump....

The EPA now estimates that it will take $30 billion to set things right, not counting transaction costs to industry. Regulators estimate that under current identification procedures the number of Superfund sites will grow from 1,200 to 2,100 by the year 2000.

At the same time, environmental proclamations continue fanning out from the Endangered Species Act of 1973 (costs include protection of the snail darter, spotted owl, California gnat-catcher, winter-run chinook salmon, and furbish lousewort); the 1974 Safe Drinking Water Act (costs to small towns, such as Lewiston, Maine, reached as much as $92 million; this year, the act will cost major cities more than $500 million); and the Clean Water and Wetlands Act of 1972 (major cities will be required to spend a total of $3.6 billion this year in this area)....

THE ROAD AHEAD

... America must get out of this regulatory whitewater and back into the clear water of "wise and frugal government." Here are concrete measures that would go far toward that end:

- Fund all unfunded mandates, and enact no more.
- Unabashedly make a national priority of stopping rule by regulocracy.

- Make the White House (or the Office of Information Resource Management) conduct a comprehensive review of all existing regulations, identifying significant rules and consolidating, rewriting, or rescinding every rule that poses excess transaction costs with unproven benefit.

- Support existing initiatives to restore flexibility to the regulatory process, such as the Regulatory Flexibility Act and Paperwork Reduction Act Amendments.

- Specifically concerning environmental regulation, offer incentives for pollution abatement, performance standards (instead of command and control), and greater cooperation with business on phase-in periods and cost estimates; and prioritize the environmental harms that must be addressed by business.

Benefits obviously derive from limited, well-crafted, and prudently enforced regulation. Regulation of interstate commerce, for example, facilitated everything from flood control and baseball leagues to civil rights, antitrust, and maritime safety. But America is at a crossroads. The next several years will determine whether the new regulocracy can be reined in. Otherwise, the consequences could be more than anyone bargained for.

NO   Susan Tolchin and Martin Tolchin

SILENT PARTNER:
THE POLITICS OF DEREGULATION

I don't know anybody who believes in dirty air or dirty water.

—Irving Shapiro, former chairman of the board
of the Du Pont Company

Regulation is the key to civilized society.

—The late Jerry Wurf, president of the American
Federation of State, County, and Municipal Employees

Century-old Anaconda, Montana, in the foothills of the well-named Bitter-root Range of the Rocky Mountains, became an instant ghost town on a crisp September morning in 1980. With little warning to its fifteen hundred employees, some of whose fathers and grandfathers had worked for the company, the Anaconda Copper Company closed the smelter that was as old as the town itself, and its reason for existence. The smelter had processed the copper ore mined in Butte, twenty-eight miles southeast, and the smelted copper was then sent by rail to a refinery in nearby Great Falls. The refinery was also closed soon afterward.

The company announced that because of the high cost of complying with government regulations, it would henceforth ship its copper to Japan, where it would be refined and smelted before being returned to the United States, a round trip of about fourteen thousand miles. Anaconda had recently been acquired by the ARCO Oil Company, which claimed that compliance with federal and state standards would cost between $300 and $400 million. At a press conference called to announce the closing, the president of the company explained that the decision was reached after "exhausting every option available" to bring the smelter into compliance with environmental, health, and work place regulations, but the costs of compliance were "prohibitive."

It was part of a pattern in which overregulation was blamed for reducing the United States to an underdeveloped nation, whose minerals were taken by industrialized nations that in turn sent back finished products.

This was a reversal of the industrial imperialism that had sent America and other industrial powers roaming the world for natural resources, exploiting their less-developed neighbors and intervening in their internal political and fiscal affairs. The emergence of a potent Japanese lobbying effort in the nation's capital, and its influence on legislation and regulation, is testimony that the United States is considered by some ripe for the picking, and on the verge of joining the industrial have-nots. Like the closing of the steel mills in Youngstown, Ohio, Anaconda highlighted a new trend that has disturbing implications for the national defense, as well as an estimated total nationwide cost of $125 billion in lost production and more than two million jobs.

Skeptics, and there were many, contended that the closing was really triggered by a costly labor dispute preceded by decades of poor management, when technological improvements were shunned in favor of the pursuit of profits. These skeptics cited a short-term approach, in which managers were encouraged to regard their positions as stepping stones to more prestigious and lucrative appointments, rather than developing long-term loyalties to institutions and rejecting immediate profits in favor of capital investments and long-term growth. As early as 1972, *Forbes* magazine observed that "Anaconda's problems seem to have stemmed directly from its corporate style of life; its patrician stance, its attitude of affluence." A major corporate blunder had been the company's failure to foresee the nationalization of its extensive copper mines in Chile by the government of Salvador Allende, which marked the beginning of a steady decline in Anaconda's fiscal fortunes. "The company was making so much money in Chile that they let

their domestic operations go a little flat," said L. R. Mecham, vice president of Anaconda.

Mecham added that labor troubles were a major factor in the closings. The plant had been idle since July, due to a nationwide strike against the copper industry. "Montana was notorious for having some of the worst labor practices in the country," he said.

The ranks of the skeptics also included government regulators, who argued not only that the costs of complying with regulations were far lower than the company's figures, but that they were willing to negotiate flexible timetables for meeting those standards. Challenging Anaconda's figures, the federal Environmental Protection Agency (EPA) put the price tag at about $140 million; the Occupational Safety and Health Administration (OSHA) added another $3 million to the estimate. Roger Williams, a regional administrator of EPA, said the finality of the decision came as a "complete surprise" to him because of Anaconda's earlier commitment to retrofit its existing facilities to meet air pollution requirements. "The company's past failure to investigate options with EPA," he wrote, "coupled with the company's ability to quickly secure profitable contracts with foreign industry piques my interest, and I'm sure the public's, in knowing the reasons behind the company's decision."

The real reasons, that is. For regulation had become the national whipping boy, and it was easier to lay the blame at the feet of faceless bureaucrats in Washington than on mismanagement, the greed of organized labor, the worldwide decline of the copper industry, or the fact that copper smelting's most valuable by-product—sulfuric acid—had become virtually unmarketable in the United

States. "They have used the closing as a political tool, to send a message to Congress about the Clean Air Act," said Steve Rovig, an aide to Senator Max Baucus, Democrat of Montana....

Similarly, the American automobile industry blamed its precipitous decline, not on its high prices, oversized cars, or shoddy products, but on the raft of government regulations intended to improve the safety and fuel efficiency of the vehicles and perhaps make them more marketable. No matter that Japan overcame its long standing reputation for shoddy production by applying rigorous standards of quality control, standards that were abandoned during the same period by Detroit. And how do the steel, copper, and auto industries reconcile their tendency to make regulations the scapegoat with the cold fact that their foreign competitors, most notably Japan, also live with stiff regulations, particularly in the environmental field?

By the late 1970s, complaints of excessive regulation had become management's all-purpose cop-out. Were profits too low? Blame regulation. Were prices too high? Blame regulation. Were inadequate funds and manpower earmarked for research and development? Blame regulation for sapping both funds and manpower. Was American industry unable to compete with foreign competitors? Blame regulation.

In a highly technological society such as ours, the need for increased regulation is manifest. It is inconceivable to think of "lessening the regulatory burden," as some put it, at a time when private industry has the power to alter our genes, invade our privacy, and destroy our environment. A single industrial accident in the 1980s is capable of taking a huge toll in human life and suffering. Only the government has the power to create and enforce the social regulations that protect citizens from the awesome consequences of technology run amuck. Only the government has the ability to raise the national debate above the "balance sheet" perspective of American industry. This is not to dismiss the many socially conscious businessmen who are concerned with the public interest, but, unfortunately, they do not represent the political leadership of the business community. After all, the "bottom line" for business is making a profit, not improving the quality of the environment or the work place. Its primary obligation is to its shareholders, not to the community at large.

Complaints against regulation have become a standard lament of American business, not without some justification. Horror stories abound. Federal bureaucrats were designing everything from toilet seats to university buildings. Small companies complained that they were drowning in paperwork and were being "regulated out of business." Douglas Costle, a former administrator of the Environmental Protection Agency in the Carter administration, estimated that his agency's regulations alone increased the Consumer Price Index by four-tenths of one percent each year, while estimates of the total cost of regulation exceeded $100 billion a year.

The complaints focused on what are known as social regulations, regulations not geared to a specific industry but to the general public. Regulations falling into this category included those whose benefits were designed to provide clean air and water, safety in the work place, product safety, pure food and drugs, and protection for the consumer in the marketplace. Their goals were ambitious, but expensive to implement....

TAKING CHARGE OF REGULATION

The long simmering battle against regulation finally found a champion during the 1980 presidential campaign. Ronald Reagan, en route to the White House, needed little prodding. Once a television host and lecturer for the General Electric Company, he had made a political career of championing the virtues of free enterprise, and had vowed during the campaign to "get the government off the backs of the people." Responding to this deeply bipartisan antiregulatory mandate, the new President initiated a crusade against government regulation and quickly laid the groundwork for the direction of regulation in the 1980s. To Reagan and his allies, the future lay in deregulation, or the removal of regulations from the books whenever possible in order to allow market forces to operate in their stead. Barely a week after his election, Ronald Reagan promised to dismantle existing regulations, and to freeze all new rules for at least a year after his inauguration. In living up to the spirit of his campaign promises, Reagan gave the American people a chance to see for themselves what life would be like without the onerous hand of big government....

The new President was so successful in capitalizing on his public relations victory over regulation that the system virtually reeled from its impact. Environmental protection became a thing of the past, as the EPA studiously ignored the laws and regulations dealing with clean air and water, as well as hazardous waste. Mine deaths shot up as regulations governing the safety of the mines were slowly dismantled through budget cuts and lack of enforcement. Through a program of consistent neglect, worker safety followed a similar path, victim of a more relaxed OSHA. No area of social protection was left untouched by White House efforts to unravel the regulations, the agencies, and the process. Even the nuclear regulators were encouraged to speed up the permit-granting process for nuclear plants by "streamlining" safety regulations....

It soon became apparent that in dismantling regulation, the President was dismantling America. Regulation is the connective tissue, the price we pay for an industrialized society. It is our major protection against the excesses of technology, whose rapid advances threaten man's genes, privacy, air, water, bloodstream, lifestyle, and virtual existence. It is a guard against the callous entrepreneur, who would have his workers breathe coal dust and cotton dust, who would send children into the mines and factories, who would offer jobs in exchange for health and safety, and leave the victims as public charges in hospitals and on welfare lines. "The child labor laws or the abolition of slavery would never have passed a cost-benefit test," said Mark Green, a public interest advocate, referring to the theory that now dominates regulatory decision making.

Regulations provide protection against the avarice of the marketplace, against shoddy products and unscrupulous marketing practices from Wall Street to Main Street. They protect legitimate businessmen from being driven out of business by unscrupulous competitors, and consumers from being victimized by unscrupulous businessmen. "Regulation is the key to civilized society," said the late Jerry Wurf, president of the American

Federation of State, County, and Municipal Employees. The extent to which we take regulations for granted in our daily lives is reflected by the confidence with which we drink our water, eat our food, take our medication, drive our cars, and perform hundreds of other tasks without thought of peril. This provides a striking contrast to the situation in many Third World nations, devoid of regulations, where those tasks can be performed only with extreme care. (Indeed, there is evidence that some of those countries adhere to United States regulations in the absence of their own government protections. The Squibb representative in Egypt, for example, said in 1979 that he could not market his company's drugs in that country unless they had been cleared by the United States Food and Drug Administration.)

In responding so agreeably to the critics of regulation, the politicians so quick to deregulate forgot that it was the very same process that prevented thalidomide—a tranquilizer prescribed to pregnant women that caused birth defects—from reaching the United States marketplace. A conscientious FDA medical officer, Frances Kelsey, spotted the drug and held it up, unimpressed with the fact that it had already been approved by the West German regulators. Critics also forgot that regulations have helped to restore the Great Lakes, which ten years ago were on their way to a polluted oblivion, and have brought the nation more breathable air by reducing sulfur emmissions by 17 percent since 1972. And although the Anaconda Copper Company complained bitterly about EPA regulations, lung disease in Western Montana declined significantly after the copper company took its first steps toward compliance with air quality standards.

When social regulation works, its benefits are invisible. It is hardly newsworthy, or even noticeable, that the nation's air and water have become considerably cleaner over the last decade, a regulatory development that could be viewed as a stunning success. So could the Consumer Product Safety Commission's regulations that changed the design of cribs and significantly reduced the number of crib deaths by strangulation.

The problem is that those who breathe and those whose lives were saved by a safer crib have no trade association to applaud the unseen and unheralded benefits of the regulatory process—when it is working well. They have no Political Action Committee to reward politicians who support the regulatory system, or to punish those who attack it. Indeed, most people are unaware that regulations play any role in their well-being. No constituency with significant power has developed over the years to bolster, promote, reinforce, and expand these "public goods." Yet this is another reason the regulatory process was created in the first place: to protect those public goods and those who benefit from them. Indeed, ever since the first United States Congress gave the President the power to make rules for trading with the Indians, regulation has grown geometrically, often with the enthusiastic support of Congress and the President, because it represented a system that held the promise of protecting the public against the incursions of more narrowly focused interests. "We created the regulatory agencies to do what we don't have time to do," said the late Sam Rayburn, when he was Speaker of the House.…

The social regulatory agencies have become the government's orphans, attacked by both management and labor.

Management contends that the cost of compliance will erode profits, while labor fears that it could cost jobs and lead to the destruction of entire industries. In an increasing number of cases, management and labor have joined forces to fight the regulatory agencies, producing formidable alliances. In one successful effort, the grain millers union fought side by side with management against the FTC's antitrust efforts to break up the giant cereal companies. In cases like this, who is left to provide the support network and the constituency so necessary to an agency's effective survival?

In this harsh political climate, it is no wonder that leadership on all fronts is in short supply. When President Carter claimed credit for returning salmon to the Columbia River, few applauded his efforts in cleaning up that once polluted waterway. When he attempted to intervene to cut the cost of environmental regulation, he was quickly branded an "enemy of the environment" by an army of critics. Nor did he find many friends among members of the business community, who faulted him for not moving fast enough to dismantle the regulatory process. . . .

Congress regards its interventions as part of its legitimate oversight function to monitor the regulatory agencies. This has more than a grain of truth to it. A closer look reveals, however, that Congress bears considerable responsibility for the current state of siege that confronts the agencies, as well as for the volatility of regulatory politics in general. With its ambiguous mandates, increasingly detailed legislation, vulnerability to special interests, and increased involvement in the budget process, Congress has reinforced the uncertainty surrounding regulation and done little to improve its troubled future.

What few citizens realize is that all regulation stems from a statutory base. Agencies do not regulate on the basis of whim. OSHA did not initiate the guarantee of a safe work place for every worker; Congress wrote the enabling legislation that created the agency and gave it that far-reaching mandate. It was also Congress that set the goals for air quality standards, not the EPA, although both Reagan and Congress eleven years later threatened to reduce the EPA's power during the renewal of the Clean Air Act—essentially penalizing the agency for doing its job.

Under the guise of responding to pressures, Congress is acting out a charade. The members bask in the applause when they are credited with giving the nation clean air and a safe work place, but recoil from the anger of those who must bear the brunt of the high cost of regulation. . . .

WHO BENEFITS AND WHO LOSES?

The most serious consequence of the trend to deregulate is the dismantling of the social regulations, which provide a connective tissue between the needs of the public and private sectors. Private industry is entitled to make a profit, but its employees are entitled to their health and safety, their consumers are entitled to safe and well-made products, and the public is entitled to have its air, water, and quality of life safeguarded.

The rapid pace of technological advances has given industry awesome tools with which to alter our genes, invade our privacy, and even destroy our lives. It is difficult, therefore, to regard the current dismantling of regulation as anything but an aberration, a trend that will soon be reversed. One can thus expect increased pressures on government for protection against forces over which individuals have less and less control. And one would certainly expect those forces to be resisted by the affected industries. That conflict will be resolved in the political arena, which will be the ultimate arbiter in the current attempt at dismantling America.

POSTSCRIPT

Does the Government Regulate Too Much?

Any consideration of social regulation by government must assess both costs and benefits. Society must ask how much it is willing to pay to avoid a given risk, just as workers will demand increased wages for taking greater risks. Most people are likely to agree that there are some benefits that merit the cost and some costs that outweigh the benefits. But that agreement is theoretical; in practice, people differ both in their values and their assessments of needs. Ardent environmentalists believe that industry cannot be allowed to do irremediable harm to the air, water, other species, and the Earth's atmosphere, while their critics believe with equal conviction that the dangers are exaggerated and that a possible loss to the environment must be weighed against the loss of jobs and living standards that would result from curbed economic activity.

Focusing on the Environmental Protection Agency and the Federal Trade Commission, Richard A. Harris and Sidney M. Milkus, in *The Politics of Regulatory Change: A Tale of Two Agencies* (Oxford University Press, 1989), provide an illuminating study of how the regulatory process works. Looking at the efforts by Presidents Ronald Reagan and George Bush to deregulate, they speculate: "Deregulation may be so difficult to accomplish not because regulatory policy is so fragmented, but because it is so coherent." Thomas Gale Moore's essay "Regulation, Reregulation, or Deregulation," in Annelise Anderson and Dennis L. Bark, eds., *Thinking About America: The United States in the 1990s* (Hoover Institution Press, 1988), takes a position similar to that of Charles, while David Bollier and Joan Claybrook, writing in *The Washington Monthly* in April 1986, defend what they call "Regulations That Work." Ian Ayres and John Braithwaite stake out a middle ground in the debate over free markets versus government regulation. In *Responsive Regulation: Transcending the Deregulation Debate* (Oxford University Press, 1992), they argue that the appropriate degree of regulation should depend upon the particular characteristics of firms, including their motivations, goals, and responsiveness to rules and regulations.

The world is a dangerous place. The supporters of government regulation believe that in the absence of such controls, the public will face greater hazards, and more dangers will be loosed upon the world by unscrupulous entrepreneurs. The opponents hold that industries and consumers alike will more surely be strangled by red tape and impoverished by the regulatory costs that make prices higher—if they do not actually make production unprofitable. It is tempting to counsel moderation between the extreme principles, but it is difficult to apply moderation in practice. Take, as an example, the debate on the development of nuclear energy for nonmilitary uses. Neither side would be happy with a compromise that means limited utilization of atomic power. Such a policy would not fulfill the hopes of those who see nuclear energy as a solution for the energy crisis, and it would not allay the fears of those who see it as a threat to the lives of millions of people living near nuclear plants. Yet it is possible that, in this area as in others, the give and take of politics will dictate solutions that are unsatisfactory to all concerned and thus keep the issue of regulation alive.

ISSUE 8

Should the Federal Courts Be Bound by the "Original Intent" of the Framers?

YES: Robert H. Bork, from "The Case Against Political Judging," *National Review* (December 8, 1989)

NO: Leonard W. Levy, from *Original Intent and the Framers' Constitution* (Macmillan, 1988)

ISSUE SUMMARY

YES: Educator and former judge Robert H. Bork argues that the "original intent" of the framers of the Constitution can and should be upheld by the federal courts, because not to do so is to have judges perform a political role they were not given.

NO: Professor of history Leonard W. Levy believes that the "original intent" of the framers cannot be found and that, even if it could, given these changing times, it could not be applied in dealing with contemporary constitutional issues.

Although the Supreme Court has declared fewer than 100 acts of Congress unconstitutional, judicial review (the power to exercise this judgment) is a critical feature of American government. It extends to all law—not simply federal law—and includes not only statutes but the actions of all agents of governmental power.

The power of judicial review consists not only of a negative power to invalidate acts contrary to the Constitution but also (and far more frequently) of a positive power to give meaning and substance to constitutional clauses and the laws enacted in accordance with constitutional power. Finally, individual cases have impact and reverberation, which may profoundly influence the future direction of law and behavior. To take a prominent example, when the Supreme Court reinterpreted the equal protection clause of the Constitution's Fourteenth Amendment in 1954, it changed forever the legal and social patterns of race relations in the United States.

Some limitations on judicial review are self-imposed, such as the Court's refusal to consider "political questions"—that is, questions better decided by the elective branches rather than the courts. But it is the Supreme Court that decides which questions are political. The Supreme Court has been notably reluctant to curb a president's extraordinary use of emergency power in wartime and has done so rarely.

Still other limitations on judicial review derive from the judicial process, such as the requirement that the party bringing a case to court (any court) must have sufficient "standing" as an aggrieved party to be heard. Some laws do not appear to give any contesting party the basis for bringing a suit. Other laws rarely present themselves in an appropriate form for judicial decision, such as the ordinary exercise of presidential power in foreign relations. These exceptions qualify, yet do not really negate, the spirit of French statesman Alexis de Tocqueville's observation of nearly a century and a half ago that "scarcely any political question arises in the United States that is not resolved, sooner or later, into a judicial question."

Judicial review is exercised by state courts and lower federal courts as well as by the U.S. Supreme Court, but the last word is reserved for the latter. Because its power is so vast and is exercised in controversial areas, the judiciary is subject to considerable criticism. Critics have argued that the framers of the Constitution did not intend for so great a power to be possessed by so unrepresentative (unelected) an organ of government.

The Court has been chided for going too far, too fast (for example, law enforcement agencies protest measures dealing with the rights of accused persons) and for not going far enough, fast enough (for example, by civil rights activists working for racial equality). In the 1930s liberals castigated the "nine old men" for retarding social progress by invalidating New Deal measures. In the 1950s conservatives pasted "Impeach Earl Warren" (then chief justice) stickers on their car bumpers, and they bemoaned the Court's so-called coddling of communists and criminals.

More recently, liberal critics have viewed the Supreme Court headed by chief justices Warren E. Burger (who served until 1986) and William H. Rehnquist as being less sympathetic to enforced integration, women's rights, the defense of accused persons, and the protection of socially disapproved expression.

The Supreme Court professes to decide these issues on the basis of constitutional principles. One view, argued in the following selection by Robert H. Bork, is that the Court should uphold the "original intent" of the framers as it is found in the Constitution and its amendments. To do otherwise is to engage in political decision making, which is not the Court's business.

The other view, argued by Leonard W. Levy, is that we cannot find the "original intent" of the framers because the framers (and ratifiers) differed among themselves, and, even if we could find it, we could not be bound by it in finding new solutions to new problems.

YES

Robert H. Bork

THE CASE AGAINST POLITICAL JUDGING

What was once the dominant view of constitutional law—that a judge is to apply the Constitution according to the principles intended by those who ratified the document—is now very much out of favor among the theorists of the field. In the legal academies in particular, the philosophy of original understanding is usually viewed as thoroughly passé, probably reactionary, and certainly—the most dreaded indictment of all—"outside the mainstream." That fact says more about the lamentable state of the intellectual life of the law, however, than it does about the merits of the theory.

In truth, only the approach of original understanding meets the criteria that any theory of constitutional adjudication must meet in order to possess democratic legitimacy. Only that approach is consonant with the design of the American Republic.

When we speak of "law," we ordinarily refer to a rule that we have no right to change except through prescribed procedures. That statement assumes that the rule has a meaning independent of our own desires. Otherwise there would be no need to agree on procedures for changing the rule. Statutes, we agree, may be changed by amendment or repeal. The Constitution may be changed by amendment pursuant to the procedures set out in Article V. It is a necessary implication of the prescribed procedures that neither statute nor Constitution should be changed by judges. Though that has been done often enough, it is in no sense proper.

What is the "meaning" of a law, that essence that judges should not change? It is the meaning understood at the time of the law's enactment. What the Constitution's ratifiers understood themselves to be enacting must be taken to be what the public of that time would have understood the words to mean. It is important to be clear about this, because the search is not for a subjective intention. If, for instance, Congress enacted a statute outlawing the sale of automatic rifles and did so in the Senate by a vote of 51 to 49, no court would overturn a conviction under the law because two senators in the majority later testified that they had really intended only to prohibit the *use* of such rifles. They said "sale" and "sale" it is. Thus, the common objection to the philosophy of original understanding—that Madison kept his notes of the convention at Philadelphia secret for many years—is off the mark. He knew that what mattered was public understanding, not subjective intentions.

Law is a public act. Secret reservations or intentions count for nothing. The original understanding is thus manifested in the words used and in secondary materials, such as debates at the conventions, public discussion, newspaper articles, dictionaries in use at the time, and the like.

* * *

The search for the intent of the lawmaker is the everyday procedure of lawyers and judges when they apply a statute, a contract, a will, or the opinion of a court. To be sure, there are differences in the way we deal with different legal materials, which was the point of John Marshall's observation in *McCulloch v. Maryland* that "we must never forget, that it is a *constitution* we are expounding." By that he meant narrow, legalistic reasoning was not to be applied to the document's broad provisions, a document that could not, by its nature and uses, "partake of the prolixity of a legal code." But in that same opinion he also wrote that a provision must receive a "far and just interpretation," which means that the judge is to interpret what is in the text and not something else. And, it will be recalled, in *Marbury v. Madison* Marshall based the judicial power to invalidate a legislative act upon the fact that a judge was applying the words of a written document. Thus, questions of breadth of approach or of room for play in the joints aside, lawyers and judges should seek in the Constitution what they seek in other legal texts: the original meaning of the words.

We would at once criticize a judge who undertook to rewrite a statute or the opinion of a superior court; and yet such judicial rewriting is often correctable by legislatures or superior courts, whereas the Supreme Court's rewriting of the Constitution is not correctable. At first glance, it seems distinctly peculiar that there should be a great many academic theorists who explicitly defend departures from the understanding of those who ratified the Constitution while agreeing, at least in principle, that there should be no departure from the understanding of those who enacted a statute or joined a majority opinion. A moment's reflection suggests, however, that Supreme Court departures from the original meaning of the Constitution are advocated *precisely because* those departures are not correctable democratically. The point of the academic exercise is to be free of democracy in order to impose the values of an elite upon the rest of us.

It is here that the concept of neutral principles, which Herbert Wechsler has said are essential if the Supreme Court is not to be a naked power organ, comes into play. Wechsler, in expressing his difficulties with the decision in *Brown v. Board of Education,* said the courts must choose principles which they are willing to apply neutrally; to apply, that is, to all cases that may fairly be said to fall within them. This is a safeguard against political judging. No judge will say openly that any particular group or political position is always entitled to win. He will announce a principle that decides the case at hand, and Wechsler has no difficulty with that if the judge is willing to apply the same principle in the next case, even when it means a group favored by the first decision is disfavored by the second.

When a judge finds his principle in the Constitution as originally understood, the problem of the neutral derivation of principle is solved. The judge accepts the ratifiers' definition of the appropriate ranges of majority and minority freedom. The "Madisonian dilemma" (essentially, the conflict of majority rule with minority rights) is resolved in the way that the Founders resolved it, and the judge accepts the fact that he is bound by that resolution as law. He need not, and must not, make unguided value judgments of his own.

This means, of course, that a judge, no matter on what court he sits, may never create new constitutional rights or destroy old ones. Any time he does so, he violates the limits of his own authority and, for that reason, also violates the rights of the legislature and the people. When a judge is given a set of constitutional provisions, then, as to anything not covered by those provisions, he is, quite properly, powerless. In the absence of law, a judge is a functionary without a function.

This is not to say, of course, that majorities may not add to minority freedoms by statute, and indeed a great deal of the legislation that comes out of Congress and the state legislatures does just that. The only thing majorities may not do is invade the liberties the Constitution specifies. In this sense, the concept of original understanding builds in a bias toward individual freedom. Thus, the Supreme Court properly decided in *Brown* that the equal protection clause of the Fourteenth Amendment forbids racial segregation or discrimination by any arm of government, but, because the Constitution addressed only governmental action, the Court could not address the question of private discrimination. Congress did address it in the Civil Rights Act of 1964 and in subsequent legislation, enlarging minority freedoms beyond those mandated by the Constitution.

* * *

The neutral definition of the principle derived from the historic Constitution is also crucial. The Constitution states its principles in majestic generalities that we know cannot be taken as sweepingly as the words alone might suggest. The First Amendment states that "Congress shall make no law ... abridging the freedom of speech," but no one has ever supposed that Congress could not make some speech unlawful or that it could not make all speech illegal in certain places, at certain times, and under certain circumstances. Justices Hugo Black and William O. Douglas often claimed to be First Amendment absolutists, but even they would permit the punishment of speech if they thought it too closely "brigaded" with illegal action. From the beginning of the Republic to this day, no one has ever thought Congress could not forbid the preaching of mutiny at sea or disruptive proclamations in a courtroom. One may not cry "Fire!" in a crowded theater.

But the question of neutral definition remains and is obviously closely related to neutral application. Neutral application can be gained by defining a principle so narrowly that it will fit only a few cases. Thus, once a principle is derived from the Constitution, its breadth or the level of generality at which it is stated becomes of crucial importance. The judge must not state the principle with so much generality that he transforms it. The difficulty in finding the proper level of generality has led some critics to claim that the application of the original understanding is actually impossible. That sounds fairly abstract, but an example will make clear both the point and the answer to it.

In speaking of my view that the Fourteenth Amendment's equal protection clause requires black equality, Dean Paul Brest said:

> The very adoption of such a principle, however, demands an arbitrary choice among levels of abstraction. Just what *is* "the general principle of equality that applies to all cases"? Is it the "core idea of *black* equality" that Bork finds in the original understanding (in which case Allan Bakke [a white who sued because a state medical school gave preference in admissions to other races] did not state a constitutionally cognizable claim), or a broader principle of *"racial* equality" (so that, depending on the precise content of the principle, Bakke might have a case after all), or is it a still broader principle of equality that encompasses discrimination on the basis of gender (or sexual orientation) as well?
>
> ... The fact is that all adjudication requires making choices among the levels of generality on which to articulate principles, and all such choices are inherently non-neutral. No form of constitutional decision-making can be salvaged if its legitimacy depends on satisfying Bork's requirements that principles be "neutrally derived, defined, and applied."

If Brest's point about the impossibility of choosing the level of generality upon neutral criteria is correct, we must either resign ourselves to a Court that *is* a "naked power organ" or require the Court to stop making "constitutional" decisions. But Brest's argument seem to me wrong, and I think a judge committed to original understanding can do what Brest says he cannot. We may use Brest's example to demonstrate the point.

The role of a judge committed to the philosophy of original understanding is not to *"choose* a level of abstraction." Rather, it is to find the meaning of a text—a process which includes finding its degree of generality, which is part of its meaning—and to apply that text to a particular situation, which may be difficult if its meaning is unclear. With many if not most textual provisions, the level of generality which is part of their meaning is readily apparent. The problem is most difficult when dealing with the broadly stated provisions of the Bill of Rights. It is to the latter that we confine discussion here. In dealing with such provisions, a judge should state the principle at the level of generality that the text and historical evidence warrant. The equal-protection clause was adopted in order to protect freed slaves, but its language, being general, applies to all persons. As we might expect, the evidence of what the drafters, the Congress that proposed the clause, and the ratifiers understood themselves to be requiring is clearest in the case of race relations. It is there that we may begin in looking for evidence of the level of generality intended. Without meaning to suggest what the historical evidence in fact shows, let us assume we find that the ratifiers intended to guarantee that blacks should be treated by law no worse than whites, but that it is unclear whether whites were intended to be protected from discrimination. On such evidence, the judge should protect only blacks from discrimination, and Allan Bakke would not have had a case. The reason is that the next higher level of generality above black equality, which is racial equality, is not shown to be a constitutional principle, and, therefore, there is nothing to be set against a current legislative majority's decision to favor blacks. Democratic choice must be accepted by the judge where the Constitution is silent. The test is the reasonableness of the distinction, and the level of generality chosen by the ratifiers determines that. If the evidence shows the ratifiers understood racial equality to have been the principle they were enacting, then Bakke *would* have a case.

To define a legal proposition or principle involves simultaneously stating its contents and its limits. When, for instance, you state what *is* contained within the clause of the First Amendment guarantee of the free exercise of religion, you necessarily state what is *not* contained within that clause. Because the First Amendment guarantees freedom of speech, judges are required reasonably to define what is speech and what is its freedom. Where the law stops, the legislator may move on to create more; but where the law stops, the judge must stop.

The neutral or nonpolitical application of principle has been discussed in connection with Wechsler's discussion of *Brown*. It is a requirement, like the others, addressed to the judge's integrity. Having derived and defined the principle to be applied, he must apply it consistently and without regard to his sympathy or lack of sympathy with the parties before him. This does not mean that the judge will never change the principle he has derived and defined. Anybody who has dealt extensively with law knows that a new case may seem to fall within a principle as stated and yet not fall within the rationale underlying it. As new cases present new patterns, the principle will often be restated and redefined. There is nothing wrong with that; it is, in fact, highly desirable. But the judge must be clarifying his own reasoning and verbal formulations and not trimming to arrive at results desired on grounds extraneous to the Constitution. This requires a fair degree of sophistication and self-consciousness on the part of the judge. The only external discipline to which the judge is subject is the scrutiny of professional observers who will be able to tell over a period of time whether or not he is displaying intellectual integrity.

* * *

The structure of government the Founders of this nation intended most certainly did not give courts a political role. The debates surrounding the Constitution focused much more upon theories of representation than upon the judiciary, which was thought to be a comparatively insignificant branch. There were, however, repeated attempts at the Constitutional Convention in Philadelphia to give judges a policy-making role. The plan of the Virginia delegation, which, amended and expanded, ultimately became the Constitution of the United States, included a proposal that the new national legislature be controlled by placing a veto power in a Council of Revision consisting of the executive and "a convenient number of the National Judiciary." That proposal was raised four times and defeated each time. Among the reasons, as reported in James Madison's notes, was the objection raised by Elbridge Gerry of Massachusetts that it "was quite foreign from the nature of ye office to make them judges of policy of public measures." Rufus King, also of Massachusetts, added that judges should "expound the law as it should come before them, free from the bias of having participated in its formation." Judges who create new constitutional rights are judges of the policy of public measures and are biased by having participated in the policy's formation.

The intention of the Convention was accurately described by Alexander Hamilton in *The Federalist* No. 78: "[T]he judiciary, from the nature of its functions, will always be the least dangerous to the political rights of the Constitution; because it will be least in a capacity to annoy or injure them." The political rights of the Constitution are, of course, the rights that make up democratic self-government. Hamilton obviously did not anticipate a judiciary that would injure those rights by adding to the list of subjects that were removed from democratic control. Thus, he could say that the courts were "beyond comparison the weakest of the three departments of power," and he appended a quotation from the "celebrated Montesquieu": "Of the three powers above mentioned [the others being the legislative and the executive], the JUDICIARY is next to nothing." This was true because judges were, as Rufus King said, merely to "expound" the law.

Even if evidence of what the Founders thought about the judicial role were unavailable, we would have to adopt the rule that judges must stick to the original meaning of the Constitution's words. If that method of interpretation were not common in the law, if James Madison and Justice Joseph Story had never endorsed it, if Chief Justice John Marshall had rejected it, we would have to invent the approach of original understanding in order to save the constitutional design. No other method of constitutional adjudication can confine courts to a defined sphere of authority and thus prevent them from assuming powers whose exercise alters, perhaps radically, the design of the American Republic. The philosophy of original understanding is thus a necessary inference from the structure of government apparent on the face of the U.S. Constitution.

* * *

We come now to the question of precedent. It is particularly important because, as Professor Henry Monaghan of Columbia University Law School notes, "much of the existing constitutional order is at variance with what we know of the original understanding." Some commentators have argued from this obvious truth that the approach of original understanding is impossible or fatally compromised, since they suppose it would require the Court to declare paper money unconstitutional and overturn the centralization accomplished by abandoning restrictions on congressional powers during the New Deal. But to say that prior courts have allowed, or initiated, deformations of the Constitution is not enough to create a warrant for present and future courts to do the same thing.

All serious constitutional theory centers upon the duties of judges, and that comes down to the question: What should the judge decide in the case now before him? Obviously, an originalist judge should not deform the Constitution further. Just as obviously, he should not attempt to undo all mistakes made in the past. At the center of the philosophy of original understanding, therefore, must stand some idea of when the judge is bound by prior decisions and when he is not.

Is judicial precedent an ironclad rule? It is not, and never has been. As Felix Frankfurter once explained, "*stare decisis* is a principle of policy and not a mechanical formula of adherence to the latest decision, however recent and questionable, when such adherence involves collision with a prior doctrine more embracing in its scope, intrinsically sounder, and verified by experience." Thus, in Justice Powell's words, "[i]t is... not only [the Court's] prerogative but also [its] duty to re-examine a precedent where its reasoning or understanding of the Constitution is fairly called into question." The Supreme Court frequently overrules its own precedents. *Plessy v. Ferguson*, and the rule of separate-but-equal in racial matters, lasted 58 years before it was dispatched in *Brown v. Board of Education*. In a period of 16 years the Court took three different positions with respect to the constitutionality of federal power to impose wage and price regulations on states and localities as employers. Indeed, Justice Blackmun explained in the last of these decisions that prior cases, even of fairly recent vintage, should be reconsidered if they "disserve principles of democratic self-governance." Every year the Court overrules a number of its own precedents.

The practice of overruling precedent is particularly common in constitutional law, the rationale being that it is extremely difficult for an incorrect constitutional ruling to be corrected through the amendment process. Almost all Justices have agreed with Felix Frankfurter's observation that "the ultimate touchstone of constitutionality is the Constitution itself and not what we have said about it." But that, of course, is only a partial truth. It is clear, first, that Frankfurter was talking about the Supreme Court's obligations with respect to its own prior decisions. Lower courts are not free to ignore what the Supreme Court has said about the Constitution, for that would introduce chaos into the legal system as courts of appeal refused to follow Supreme Court rulings and district courts disobeyed their appellate courts' orders. Second, what "the Constitution itself" says may, as in the case of paper money, be irretrievable, not simply because of "what [the Justices] have said about it," but because of what the nation has done or become on the strength of what the Court said.

To say that a decision is so thoroughly embedded in our national life that it should not be overruled, even though clearly wrong, is not necessarily to say that its principle should be followed in the future. Thus, the expansion of Congress's commerce, taxing, and spending powers has reached a point where it is not possible to state that, as a matter of articulated doctrine, there are any limits left. That does not mean, however, that the Court must necessarily repeat its mistake as congressional legislation attempts to reach new subject areas. Cases now on the books would seem to mean that Congress could, for example, displace state law on such subjects as marriage and divorce, thus ending such federalism as remains. But the Court could refuse to extend the commerce power so far, without overruling its prior decisions, thus leaving existing legislation in place but not giving generative power to the faulty principle by which that legislation was originally upheld. It will be said that this is a lawless approach, but that is not at all clear. The past decisions are beyond reach, but there remains a constitutional principle of federalism that should be regarded as law more profound than the implications of the past decisions. They cannot be overruled, but they can be confined to the subject areas they concern. When we cannot recover the transgressions of the past, then the best we can do is say to the Court, "Go and sin no more."

Finally, it should be said that those who adhere to a philosophy of original understanding are more likely to respect precedent than those who do not. As Justice Scalia has said, if revisionists can ignore "the most solemnly and democratically adopted text of the Constitution and its Amendments... on the basis of current values, what possible basis could there be for enforced adherence to a legal decision of the Supreme Court?" If you do not care about stability, if today's result is all-important, there is no occasion to respect either the constitutional text or the decisions of your predecessors.

NO

Leonard W. Levy

THE FRAMERS AND ORIGINAL INTENT

James Madison, Father of the Constitution and of the Bill of Rights, rejected the doctrine that the original intent of those who framed the Constitution should be accepted as an authoritative guide to its meaning. "As a guide in expounding and applying the provisions of the Constitution," he wrote in a well-considered and consistent judgment, "the debates and incidental decisions of the Convention can have no authoritative character." The fact that Madison, the quintessential Founder, discredited original intent is probably the main reason that he refused throughout his life to publish his "Notes of Debates in the Federal Convention," incomparably our foremost source for the secret discussions of that hot summer in Philadelphia in 1787.

We tend to forget the astounding fact that Madison's Notes were first published in 1840, fifty-three years after the Constitutional Convention had met. That period included the beginnings of the Supreme Court plus five years beyond the entire tenure of John Marshall as Chief Justice. Thus, throughout the formative period of our national history, the High Court, presidents, and Congress construed the Constitution without benefit of a record of the Convention's deliberations. Indeed, even the skeletal Journal of the Convention was not published until 1819. Congress could have authorized its publication anytime after President George Washington, who had presided at the 1787 Convention, deposited it at the State Department in 1796. Although the Journal merely revealed motions and votes, it would have assisted public understanding of the secret proceedings of the Convention, no records of which existed, other than the few spotty and jaundiced accounts by Convention members who opposed ratification. The Convention had, after all, been an assembly in which "America," as George Mason of Virginia said, had "drawn forth her first characters," and even Patrick Henry conceded that the Convention consisted of "the greatest, the best, and most enlightened of our citizens." Thomas Jefferson, in Paris, referred to the "assembly of demigods." The failure of the Framers to have officially preserved and published their proceedings seems inexplicable, especially in a nation that promptly turned matters of state into questions of constitutional law; but then, the Framers seem to have thought that "the original understanding at

Excerpted with permission of Macmillan Publishing Company, a division of Macmillan, Inc., from *Original Intent and the Framers' Constitution*, by Leonard W. Levy. Copyright © 1988 by Macmillan Publishing Company. Notes omitted.

Philadelphia," which Chief Justice William H. Rehnquist has alleged to be of prime importance, did not greatly matter. What mattered to them was the text of the Constitution, construed in light of conventional rules of interpretation, the ratification debates, and other contemporary expositions.

If the Framers, who met in executive sessions every day of their nearly four months of work, had wanted their country and posterity to construe the Constitution in the light of their deliberations, they would have had a stenographer present to keep an official record, and they would have published it. They would not have left the task of preserving their debates to the initiative of one of their members who retained control of his work and a proprietary interest in it. "Nearly a half century" after the convention, Madison wrote a preface to his Notes in which he explained why he had made the record. He had determined to preserve to the best of his ability "an exact account of what might pass in the Convention," because the record would be of value "for the History of a Constitution on which would be staked the happiness of a young people great even in its infancy, and possibly the cause of Liberty throughout the world." That seems to have been a compelling reason for publication as soon as possible, not posthumously—and Madison outlived all the members of the Convention. . . .

A constitutional jurisprudence of original intent is insupportable for reasons other than the fact that the records of the framing and ratification of both the Constitution and the Bill of Rights are inadequate because they are incomplete and inaccurate. Original intent also fails as a concept that can decide real cases. Original intent is an unreliable concept because it assumes the existence of one intent on a particular issue such as the meaning of executive powers or of the necessary and proper clause, the scope of the commerce clause, or the definition of the obligation of contracts. The entity we call "the Framers" did not have a collective mind, think in one groove, or possess the same convictions.

In fact, they disagreed on many crucial matters, such as the question whether they meant Congress to have the power to charter a bank. In 1789 Hamilton and Washington thought Congress had that power, but Madison and Randolph believed that it did not. Although the Journal of the Convention, except as read by Hamilton, supports Madison's view, all senators who had been at the Convention upheld the power, and Madison later changed his mind about the constitutionality of a bank. Clearly the Convention's "intent" on this matter lacks clarity; revelation is hard to come by when the Framers squabbled about what they meant. They often did, as political controversies during the first score of years under the Constitution revealed.

Sometimes Framers who voted the same way held contradictory opinions on the meaning of a particular clause. Each believed that his understanding constituted the truth of the matter. James Wilson, for example, believed that the ex post facto clause extended to civil matters, while John Dickinson held the view that it applied only to criminal cases, and both voted for the clause. George Mason opposed the same clause because he wanted the states to be free to enact ex post facto laws in civil cases, and he believed that the clause was not clearly confined to criminal cases; but Elbridge Gerry, who wanted to impose on the states a prohibition against retroactive civil legislation, opposed the clause because he thought it seemed limited to criminal cases. William Paterson changed his mind about the scope of the ex post facto clause. Seeking original intent in the opinions of the Framers is seeking a unanimity that did not exist on complex and divisive issues contested by strong-minded men. Madison was right when he spoke of the difficulty of verifying the intention of the Convention.

A serious problem even exists as to the identity of the Framers and as to the question whether the opinions of all are of equal importance in the determination of original intent. Who, indeed, were the Framers? Were they the fifty-five who were delegates at Philadelphia or only the thirty-nine who signed? If fathoming original intent is the objective, should we not also be concerned about the opinions of those who ratified the Constitution, giving it legitimacy? About 1,600 men attended the various state ratifying conventions, for which the surviving records are so inadequate. No way exists to determine their intent as a guide for judicial decisions; we surely cannot fathom the intent of the members of eight states for which no state convention records exist. The deficiencies of the records of the other five permit few confident conclusions and no basis for believing that a group mind can be located. Understanding ratifier intent is impossible except on the broadest kind of question: Did the people of the states favor scrapping the Articles of Confederation and favor, instead, the stronger Union proposed by the Constitution? Even as to that question, the evidence, which does not exist for a majority of the states, is unsatisfactorily incomplete, and it allows only rough estimates of the answers to questions concerning popular understanding of the meaning of specific clauses of the Constitution....

A CONSTITUTIONAL JURISPRUDENCE OF ORIGINAL INTENT?

A constitutional jurisprudence of original intent would be as viable and sound as Mr. Dooley's understanding of it. Mr. Dooley, Finley Peter Dunne's philosophical Irish bartender, believed that original intent was "what some dead Englishman thought Thomas Jefferson was goin' to mean whin he wrote th' Constitution." Acceptance of original intent as the foundation of constitutional interpretation is unrealistic beyond belief. It obligates us, even if we could grasp that intent, to interpret the Constitution in the way the Framers did in the context of conditions that existed in their time. Those conditions for the most part no longer exist and cannot be recalled with the historical arts and limited time available to the Supreme Court. Anyway, the Court resorts to history for a quick fix, a substantiation, a confirmation, an illustration, or a grace note; it does not really look for the historical conditions and meanings of a time long gone in order to determine the evidence that will persuade it to decide a case in one way rather than another. The Court, moreover, cannot engage in the sort of sustained historical analysis that takes professional historians some years to accomplish. In any case, for many reasons already described, concerning the inadequacies of the historical record and the fact that we cannot in most instances find a collective mind of the Framers, original intent analysis is not really possible, however desirable.

We must keep reminding ourselves that the most outspoken Framers disagreed with each other and did not necessarily reflect the opinions of the many who did not enter the debates. A point that Justice Rufus Peckham made for the Court in an 1897 case about legislative intent carries force with respect to the original intent of the Constitutional Convention. In reference to the difficulty of understanding an act by analyzing the speeches of the members of the body that passed it, Peckham remarked: "Those who did not speak may not have agreed with those who did; and those who spoke might differ from each other; the result being that the only proper way to construe a legislative act is from the language used in the act, and, upon occasion, by a resort to the history of the times when it was passed." We must keep reminding ourselves, too, that the country was deeply divided during the ratification controversy. And we must keep reminding ourselves that the Framers who remained active in national politics divided intensely on one constitutional issue after another—the removal power, the power to charter a corporation, the power to declare neutrality, the executive power, the power to enact excise and use taxes without apportioning them on population, the power of a treaty to obligate the House of Representatives, the power of judicial review, the power to deport aliens, the power to pass an act against seditious libel, the power of the federal courts to decide on federal common law grounds, the power to abolish judicial offices of life tenure, and the jurisdiction of the Supreme Court to decide suits against states without their consent or to issue writs of mandamus against executive officers. This list is not exhaustive; it is a point of departure. The Framers, who did not agree on their own constitutional issues, would not likely speak to us about ours with a single loud, clear voice....

CONCLUSIONS

Fifty years ago, in his fine study of how the Supreme Court used original intent (not what the Framers and ratifiers believed), Jacobus tenBroek asserted, rightly, that "the intent theory," as he called it, "inverts the judicial process." It described decisions of the Court as having been reached as a result of a judicial search for Framers' intent, "whereas, in fact, the intent discovered by the Court is most likely to be determined by the conclusion that the Court wishes to reach." Original intent analysis involves what tenBroek called "fundamental misconceptions of the nature of the judicial process." It makes the judge "a mindless robot whose task is the utterly mechanical function" of using original intent as a measure of constitutionality. In the entire history of the Supreme Court, as tenBroek should have added, no Justice employing the intent theory has ever written a convincing and reliable study. Lawyers making a historical point will cite a Court opinion as proof, but no competent historian would do that. He knows that judges cannot do their own research or do the right kind of research and that they turn to history to prove some point they have in mind. To paraphrase tenBroek, Justices mistakenly use original intent theory to depict a nearly fixed Constitution, to give the misleading impression that they have decided an issue of constitutionality by finding original intent, and to make a constitutional issue merely a historical question. The entire theory, tenBroek asserted, "falsely describes what the Court actually does," and it "hypothesizes a mathematically exact technique of discovery and a practically inescapable conclusion." That all added up, said tenBroek, to "judicial hokum."

If we could ascertain original intent, one may add, cases would not arise concerning that intent. They arise because the intent is and likely will remain uncertain; they arise because the Framers either had no discernible intent to govern the issue or their intent cannot control it because the problem before the Court would have been so alien to the Framers that only the spirit of some principle implied by them can be of assistance. The Framers were certainly vaguer on powers than on structure and vaguer still on rights.

If, as Robert H. Bork noticed, people rarely raise questions about original intent on issues involving powers or structure, the reason is likely that the Constitution provides the answer, or it has been settled conclusively by the Court, making inquiry futile or unnecessary. For example, the question of constitutional powers to regulate the economy has overwhelmingly been put beyond question by the 1937 "constitutional revolution, limited," in Edward S. Corwin's phrase. Not even the most conservative Justices on today's Court question the constitutionality of government controls. Congress has the constitutional authority under Court decisions to initiate a socialist economy; political restraints, not constitutional ones, prevent that. There are no longer any serious limits on the commerce powers of Congress. The government can take apart the greatest corporations, like Ma Bell; if it does not proceed against them, the reason is to be found in national defense needs and in politics, not in the Constitution.

The states are supplicants before the United States government, beneficiaries of its largesse like so many welfare recipients, unable to control their own policies, serving instead as administrative agencies of federal policies. Those federal policies extend to realms not remotely within the federal power to govern under the Constitution, except for the fact that the spending power, so called, the power to spend for national defense and general welfare can be exercised through programs of grants-in-aid to states and to over 75,000 substate governmental entities; they take federal tax money and obediently enforce the conditions laid down by Congress and by federal agencies for control of the expenditures. Federalism as we knew it has been replaced by a new federalism that even conservative Republican administrations enforce. The government today makes the New Deal look like a backer of Adam Smith's legendary free enterprise and a respecter of John C. Calhoun's state sovereignty.

Even conservative Justices on the Supreme Court accept the new order of things. William H. Rehnquist spoke for the Court in *PruneYard*, Sandra Day O'Connor in *Hawaii Housing Authority*, and the Court was unanimous in both. In the first of these cases, decided in 1980, the Court held that a state does not violate the property rights of a shopping center owner by authorizing the solicitation of petitions in places of business open to the public. Rehnquist, finding a reasonable police power regulation of private property, asserted that the public right to regulate the use of property is as fundamental as the right to property itself. One might have thought that as a matter of constitutional theory and of original intent, the property right was fundamental and the regulatory power was an exception to it that had to be justified. Rehnquist did not explain why the regulation was justifiable or

NO Leonard W. Levy / 143

reasonable; under its rational basis test the Court has no obligation to explain anything. It need merely believe that the legislature had some rational basis for its regulation....

The Constitution of the United States is our national covenant, and the Supreme Court is its special keeper. The Constitution's power of survival derives in part from the fact that it incorporates and symbolizes the political values of a free people. It creates a representative, responsible government empowered to serve the great objectives specified in the Preamble, while at the same time it keeps government bitted and bridled. Through the Bill of Rights and the great Reconstruction amendments, the Constitution requires that the government respect the freedom of its citizens, whom it must treat fairly. Courts supervise the process, and the Supreme Court is the final tribunal. "The great ideals of liberty and equality," wrote Justice Benjamin N. Cardozo, "are preserved against the assaults of opportunism, the expediency of the passing hour, the scorn and derision of those who have no patience with general principles, by enshrining them in constitutions, and consecrating to the task of their protection a body of defenders." Similarly, Justice Hugo L. Black once wrote for the Court, "Under our constitutional system, courts stand against any winds that blow, as havens of refuge for those who might otherwise suffer because they are helpless, weak, outnumbered, or because they are nonconforming victims of prejudice and public excitement."

The Court should have no choice but to err on the side of the constitutional liberty and equality of the individual, whenever doubt exists as to which side requires endorsement. Ours is so secure a system, precisely because it is free and dedicated to principles of justice, that it can afford to prefer the individual over the state. To interpose original intent against an individual's claim defeats the purpose of having systematic and regularized restraints on power; limitations exist for the minority against the majority, as Madison said. Original intent analysis becomes a treacherous pursuit when it turns the Constitution and the Court away from assisting the development of a still freer and more just society.

The history of Magna Carta throws dazzling light on a jurisprudence of original intent. Magna Carta approaches its 800th anniversary. It was originally "reactionary as hell," to quote the chief justice of West Virginia. But the feudal barons who framed it could not control its evolution. It eventually came to signify many things that are not in it and were not intended. Magna Carta is not remotely important for what it intended but for what it has become. It stands now for government by contract of the people, for fundamental law, for the rule of law, for no taxation without representation, for due process of law, for habeaus corpus, for equality before the law, for representative government, and for a cluster of the rights of the criminally accused. No one cares, or should, that the original document signifies none of this. The Constitution is comparably dynamic.

The Court has the responsibility of helping regenerate and fulfill the noblest aspirations for which this nation stands. It must keep constitutional law constantly rooted in the great ideals of the past yet in a state of evolution in order to realize them. Something should happen to a person who dons the black robe of a Justice of the Supreme Court of the United States. He or she comes under an obligation to strive for as much objectivity as is humanly attainable by putting aside personal opinions and preferences. Yet even the best and most impartial of Justices, those in whom the judicial temperament is most finely cultivated, cannot escape the influences that have tugged at them all their lives and inescapably color their judgment. Personality, the beliefs that make the person, has always made a difference in the Court's constitutional adjudication. There never has been a constitutional case before the Court in which there was no room for personal discretion to express itself.

We may not want judges who start with the answer rather than the problem, but so long as mere mortals sit on the Court and construe its majestic but murky words, we will not likely get any other kind. Not that the Justices knowingly or deliberately read their presuppositions into law. There probably has never been a member of the Court who consciously decided against the Constitution or was unable in his own mind to square his opinions with it. Most judges convince themselves that they respond to the words on parchment, illuminated, of course, by historical and social imperatives. The illusion may be good for their psyches or the public's need to know that the nine who sit on the nation's highest tribunal really become Olympians, untainted by considerations that move lesser beings into political office.

Even those Justices who start with the problem rather than the result cannot transcend themselves or transmogrify the obscure or inexact into impersonal truth. At bottom, constitutional law reflects great public policies enshrined in the form of supreme and fundamental commands. It is truer of constitutional law than of any other branch that "what the courts declare to have always been the law," as Holmes put it, "is in fact new. It is legislative in its grounds. The very considerations which judges most rarely mention, and always with an apology, are the secret root from which the law draws all the juices of life. I mean, of course, consideration of what is expedient for the community concerned." Result-oriented jurisprudence or, at the least, judicial activism is nearly inevitable —not praiseworthy, or desirable, but inescapable when the Constitution must be construed. Robert H. Bork correctly said that the best way to cope with the problem "is the selection of intellectually honest judges." One dimension of such honesty is capacity to recognize at the propitious moment a need for constitutional evolution, rather than keep the Constitution in a deepfreeze.

POSTSCRIPT

Should the Federal Courts Be Bound by the "Original Intent" of the Framers?

Bork's view of the limits of judicial power is often characterized as judicial self-restraint. It tends to be conservative and opposed to policies that alter the historical boundaries of the separation of powers, the federal division of power between the nation and the states, or long-observed standards regarding the extent of constitutional liberties and rights. A fuller statement of his position can be found in his book *The Tempting of America: The Political Seduction of the Law* (Free Press, 1990).

By contrast, Levy's position is usually defined as judicial activism because it permits elected officials to undertake, and judges to endorse, policies that extend the powers of government and the rights of persons beyond those contemplated by the authors of the Constitution and its amendments.

An interesting and intimate account of how the Supreme Court works can be found in William H. Rehnquist's book *The Supreme Court: How It Is* (William Morrow, 1987), the first interpretation of the highest court by a sitting chief justice. A short history and defense of judicial review, *The Court and the Constitution* (Houghton Mifflin, 1987), has been written by Alexander Cox, law professor, solicitor general, and original Watergate prosecutor. Cox is unsympathetic to the doctrine of original intent as embodying too narrow an interpretation of judicial power.

Several essays on opposing sides of the original intent debate can be found in Steven Anzovin and Janet Podell's book *The United States Constitution and the Supreme Court* (H. W. Wilson, 1988).

President Ronald Reagan's nomination of Judge Bork to the U.S. Supreme Court, and its rejection by the Senate, engendered a bitter controversy regarding who should sit on the Court and how the Constitution should be applied in cases before it. Opposing interpretations of this struggle can be found in Patrick B. McGuigan and Dawn M. Weyrich, *Ninth Justice: The Fight for Bork* (Free Congress Research and Educational Foundation, 1990), and Mark Gittenstein, *Matters of Principle: An Insider's Account of America's Rejection of Robert Bork's Nomination to the Supreme Court* (Simon & Schuster, 1992).

A more recent controversy centered on law professor Anita Hill's accusation of sexual harassment directed at Supreme Court nominee Clarence Thomas, who was ultimately confirmed. A variety of viewpoints from an African American perspective are collected in Robert Chrisman and Robert L. Allen, eds., *Court of Appeal: The Black Community Speaks Out on the Racial and Sexual Politics of Clarence Thomas vs. Anita Hill* (Ballantine Books, 1992).

PART 3

Social Change and Public Policy

Few topics are more emotional and divisive than those that involve social morality. Whatever consensus once existed on such issues as capital punishment, abortion, and equality of opportunity, that consensus has been shattered in recent years as Americans have lined up very clearly on opposing sides— and what is more important, they have taken those competing views into Congress, state legislatures, and the courts.

The issues in this section generate intense emotions because they ask us to clarify our values on a number of very personal concerns.

■ Will Mandatory Sentencing Reduce Crime?

■ Is Capital Punishment Justified?

■ Do We Need Tougher Gun Control Laws?

■ Is Affirmative Action Reverse Discrimination?

■ Should Hate Speech Be Punished?

■ Should Welfare Recipients Be Put to Work?

■ Do We Need National Health Care Insurance?

■ Should Women Have a Right to Abortion?

■ Does the Religious Right Threaten American Freedoms?

ISSUE 9

Will Mandatory Sentencing Reduce Crime?

YES: James Wootton, from "Truth in Sentencing: Why States Should Make Violent Criminals Do Their Time," *State Backgrounder* (December 30, 1993)

NO: Lois G. Forer, from *A Rage to Punish: The Unintended Consequences of Mandatory Sentencing* (W. W. Norton, 1994)

ISSUE SUMMARY

YES: James Wootton, the president of Safe Streets Alliance in Washington, D.C., argues that mandatory sentences effectively keep hardened criminals off the streets and sends a signal to would-be felons that they will pay heavily if they commit a crime.

NO: Judge Lois G. Forer contends that mandatory sentencing not only fails to deter crime, which is more a result of impulse than of calculation, but it disrupts families, increases welfare costs, and hurts the poor and minorities.

Few issues are of deeper concern to Americans than crime, and with good reason. Crimes of violence, such as homicide, rape, robbery, and assault, have nearly doubled since 1970, with no sign of letting up. Homicides by 18- to 24-year-olds have skyrocketed since the mid-1980s. Drugs, including dangerous, violence-inducing drugs like crack cocaine, are widespread. Particularly in the cities, many people now live behind triple-locked doors, afraid to walk the streets of their own neighborhoods, where drug wars and drive-by shootings are commonplace.

The perennial question is what to do about this plague of crime. A generation ago, the most popular view among social scientists was that crime was the result of poverty, ignorance, lack of opportunity, and racial discrimination. In a sense, criminals are themselves victims—victims of a pathological social environment. If that diseased environment can be properly treated through social programs, the experts believed, then we can eliminate the underlying causes of crime, and we no longer need to be obsessed with punishing it. More recently, however, some criminologists, along with the most of the public at large, have taken a more hard-nosed view of crime and criminals. As far back as 1975, political scientist James Q. Wilson concluded his book *Thinking About Crime* on this note:

> Wicked people exist. Nothing avails except to set them apart from innocent people. And many people, neither wicked nor innocent, but watchful, dissembling,

and calculating of their opportunities ponder our reaction to wickedness as a cue to what they might profitably do.

If criminals and would-be criminals are not so much victims as they are "calculating" individuals weighing costs against benefits, it follows that society ought to make the costs prohibitive and certain. A new era of "toughness" on crime thus began in the late 1970s. Several states enacted "determinate" sentencing laws, which limited the discretion of judges in handing down penalties. Touted as a kind of "truth in sentencing," the offender was now required to serve the entire sentence. This was followed by mandatory sentencing, the requirement of minimum prison terms for certain offenses that could not be reduced by parole or good behavior. Often this took the form of "sentencing guidelines." As set forth in Minnesota and some other states, a "grid" was developed specifying the length of prison stay for particular crimes committed under particular conditions. Many states also passed mandatory sentences for drug offenders.

In 1984 the federal government weighed in with its own versions of these laws. The Comprehensive Crime Control Act of 1984 prescribes stiff mandatory sentences for drug possession, and the Sentencing Reform Act, passed in the same year, took an approach similar to Minnesota's by drawing up detailed guidelines for sentencing. The federal Anti-Drug Abuse Acts of 1986 and 1988 and the 1990 federal crime bill added more layers of mandatory sentencing. Most recently, the much-debated crime bill passed by Congress in the summer of 1994 includes a "three strikes and you're out" provision requiring life imprisonment for those convicted of three violent crimes.

How well has all of this worked? It is hard to say. Crime rates continue to climb, though perhaps they might have climbed faster without mandatory sentencing. Critics charge that sentencing guidelines have altered American justice, replacing humane judicial discretion with a crabbed, soulless set of regulations resembling the income tax code. Defenders insist that these guidelines were necessary because the wide disparity of sentencing by judges made predictability—which is one element of justice—impossible. Whatever the merits of these arguments, one certain result of mandatory sentencing is the burgeoning prison population. Since 1970 the number of inmates in state and federal prisons has quintupled, and the number continues to grow at an annual rate of 12 percent. Prisons in the United States are so overcrowded that in some cases they have threatened the health and safety of inmates and have been a factor in setting off prison riots. The 1994 crime bill may provide some relief for these conditions. It authorizes almost $8 billion in state construction grants for prisons and boot camps.

In the following selections, James Wootton insists that mandatory sentencing not only keeps criminals off the streets but it also signals would-be criminals that the crime is not worth the price they will pay for it. Lois G. Forer argues that mandatory sentencing is neither just nor effective.

149

YES

James Wootton

TRUTH IN SENTENCING: WHY STATES SHOULD MAKE VIOLENT CRIMINALS DO THEIR TIME

Not surprisingly, Americans are increasingly alarmed at news stories of violent crimes committed by individuals who had received long sentences for other crimes and yet were released after serving only a small fraction of their time. This alarm is legitimate, because a high proportion of such early-release prisoners commit serious crimes after being released. If crime is to be reduced in America, this trend needs to be reversed. Experience shows clearly that the first step in fighting crime is to keep violent criminals off the street. Keeping violent criminals incarcerated for at least 85 percent of their sentences would be the quickest, surest route to safer streets, schools, and homes.[1]

Government statistics on release practices in 36 states and the District of Columbia in 1988 show that although violent offenders received an average sentence of seven years and eleven months imprisonment, they actually served an average of only two years and eleven months in prison—or only 37 percent of their imposed sentences.[2] The statistics also show that, typically, 51 percent of violent criminals were discharged from prison in two years or less, and 76 percent were back on the streets in four years or less.

Consider the median sentence and time served in prison for those released for the first time in 1988:[3]

Murder: Median sentence = 15 years/Median time served = 5.5 years
Rape: Median sentence = 8 years/Median time served = 3 years
Robbery: Median sentence = 6 years/Median time served = 2.25 years
Assault: Median sentence = 4 years/Median time served = 1.25 years

When these prisoners are released early, a high percentage commit more violent crimes. A three-year follow up of 108,850 state prisoners released in 1983 from institutions in eleven states found that within three years 60 percent of violent offenders were rearrested for a felony or serious misdemeanor, 42 percent were reconvicted, and 37 percent were reincarcerated. Of the violent offenders, 35 percent were rearrested for a new violent crime. Among nonviolent prisoners released, 19 percent were rearrested within three years for a new violent crime.

As a result of these lenient early-release practices and the high percentage of crimes committed by criminals released early, Americans are suffering a fearful epidemic of violent crime. Studies indicate that over 25 percent of all males admitted to prison were being reincarcerated after a new trial for a new offense before the prison term for the first offense had expired. Since 1960, the compounding effect of these crimes by prisoners or early-release prisoners has driven the violent crime rate up by over 500 percent. Now eight out of ten Americans are likely to be victims of violent crime at least once in their lives,[4] at a total cost of $140 billion.[5]

Not surprisingly, the fear of violent crime is intensifying. Polls indicate a growing loss of public confidence in their personal safety and the safety of their streets and neighborhoods. Some 90 percent of Americans think the crime problem is growing, and 43 percent say there is more crime in their neighborhood than there was a year ago.[6] The reason: despite rising arrest rates and prison overcrowding, 3.2 million convicted felons are out on parole or probation rather than in prison. Studies show that within three years, 62 percent of all prisoners released from prison are rearrested,[7] and 43 percent of felons on probation are rearrested for a felony.[8]

HIGH RECIDIVISM: THE FAILURE OF PAROLE

Releasing violent criminals from prison before they have completed their sentences is justified by proponents for one of three reasons: first, prisons are overcrowded and it is too costly to build more prisons; second, "good time" credits, which have the effect of reducing sentences, are and should be given to well-behaved prisoners; and third, prisoners sometimes can be rehabilitated, and so should be paroled.

The problem is that the evidence seriously questions the second and third rationales, and shows the first to be very short-sighted.

Recidivism among violent criminals is high. Consider a three-year follow-up of 108,850 state prisoners released in 1983 from institutions in eleven states, conducted by the Bureau of Justice Statistics.[9] The study, the conclusions of which are consistent with those of other such studies, found that within three years some 60 percent of violent offenders were rearrested for a felony or serious misdemeanor; 42 percent of all violent offenders released were reincarcerated. Of all the violent offenders released, 36 percent were rearrested for a violent crime. Among nonviolent prisoners released, 19 percent were rearrested within three years for a violent crime.

The prisoners in the study accounted for over 1.6 million arrest charges for the time before they had entered prison and for the three years afterwards. These included nearly 215,000 arrests for violent crimes before going to prison and 50,000 violent crimes within three years after release. Altogether they were arrested for:

- 14,467 homicides
- 7,073 kidnappings
- 23,174 rapes or sexual assaults
- 101,226 robberies
- 107,130 assaults

The U.S. Parole Board uses a sophisticated Salient Factor Score (SFS) to guide it in deciding who will be paroled. Unfortunately for law-abiding Americans, the Parole Board turns out to be over-optimistic. Of those classified by the Parole Board staff as "good risks" for parole, the Parole Board assumes that 18 percent will be rearrested and again sentenced to prison for over one year within five years of release. In addition, the Parole Board expects that 29 percent of "fair risks" who are paroled will be resentenced to over a year in prison within five years of release.[10]

Considering the government's—and the American people's—anxiety about risk, this parole policy is remarkable. Where else would such a high failure rate be tolerated, when it results in the death, rape, or injury of ordinary Americans? The Federal Aviation Administration certainly does not allow airplanes to fly with critical parts that fail 29 percent of the time. And the Food and Drug Administration does not allow drugs on the market that have dangerous side effects 18 percent of the time.

Twenty years ago, James Q. Wilson, then a professor of government at Harvard University, asked a basic question about rehabilitation:

If rehabilitation is the object, and if there is little or no evidence that available correctional systems will produce much rehabilitation, why should any offender be sent to any institution? But to turn them free on the grounds that society does not know how to make them better is to fail to protect society from those crimes they may commit again and to violate society's moral concern for criminality and thus to undermine society's conception of what constitutes proper conduct. [Because the correctional system had not re-

duced recidivism], we would view the correctional system as having a very different function—namely, to isolate and to punish. It is a measure of our confusion that such a statement will strike many enlightened readers today as cruel, even barbaric. It is not. It is merely a recognition that society at a minimum must be able to protect itself from dangerous offenders and to impose some costs (other than the stigma and inconvenience of an arrest and court appearance) on criminal acts; it is also frank admission that society really does not know how to do much else.[11]

Until there are dramatic improvements in the techniques of rehabilitation and identifying those who can safely be paroled, state legislators would be wise to follow Professor Wilson's admonition: society must protect itself from dangerous offenders and impose real costs on criminal acts. Or, as Douglas Jeffrey, executive vice president of the Claremont Institute says, "We need to put justice back into the criminal justice system by putting convicted criminals behind bars and keeping them there for appropriate periods of time."[12] If state legislators were to adopt that simple mission, today's unacceptable risks to law-abiding Americans would be reduced.

INCARCERATION SAVES MONEY

While full sentences may mean more spending on prison, lawmakers and tax-payers need to understand that early-release programs cost dollars rather than save them. A 1982 Rand Corporation study of prison inmates found that the average inmate had committed 187 crimes the year before being incarcerated.[13] When criminals are released early, many commit a similar volume of crimes when back on the streets.

The cost of crime committed by these early-release criminals is both direct and indirect. Taxpayers must finance the criminal justice system. Householders and businesses must buy private protection such as lighting, locks, dogs, fences, and alarm systems. They must buy insurance. The victims lose property and wages, and often incur heavy hospitalization costs.

In addition to the direct costs, there is the hidden cost of crime. Businesses, for instance, pass on to customers some of their costs for security and stolen merchandise. Households also must "pay" for crime by altering their behavior and life style.[14] It has been estimated that crime increases in the early 1980s caused "150,000 more New Yorkers to take taxis instead of public transportation; some 140,000 more New York City households sacrificed trips rather than leave their apartments unprotected. 50,000 put bars on their windows and 40,000 bought weapons. Even more difficult to assess are the costs of 'urban blight' such as abandoned buildings, unsafe schools, and inner city unemployment. Quite possibly the costs we can't count exceed the ones we can."[15] ...

INVESTING IN SAFETY

The imprisonment rate is higher in the United States than it is in other Western democracies mainly because Americans commit crime at a higher rate. The homicide rate in the United States is five times as high as in Europe; the rape rate is more than six times as high; and the robbery rate is four times as high.[16]

Given the higher crime rates in the United States, and the benefits to society

Table 1
Crimes Committed by Felons Not Incarcerated

One Criminal	Crimes Per Year
Burglar	76–118 burglaries
Robber	41–61 robberies
Thief	135–202 thefts
Auto Thief	76–100 auto thefts
Forger	62–98 frauds
Conman	127–283 frauds
Drug Dealer	880–1,299 drug deals

of incarcerating criminals, state and federal officials have underinvested in public safety. According to one estimate, more than 120,000 additional prison beds were needed across the nation at the close of 1990.[17] Some might argue that some inmates do not belong in prison, and should be replaced with hardened criminals. But 95 percent of Americans in prison are repeat or violent offenders.[18] Despite this enormous need for additional prison space, spending on corrections remains a very small percentage of state and local budgets. In fiscal year 1990, only 2.5 percent of the $975.9 billion in total expenditures by state and local governments went for corrections (about $24.7 billion). Investment in new prison construction is only a small fraction of that figure.[19] ...

WHY TRUTH IN SENTENCING HELPS

Truth in sentencing will increase the length of time convicted violent criminals are incarcerated. Currently violent criminals are serving 37 percent of the sentence that has been imposed. If required to serve at least 85 percent of their sentences, violent criminals would serve 2.3 times longer than they do now.

If the 55 percent of the estimated 800,000 current state and federal prisoners who are violent offenders were subject to serving 85 percent of their sentence, and assuming that those violent offenders would have committed ten violent crimes a year while on the street, then the number of crimes prevented each year by truth in sentencing would be 4,400,000.[20] That would be over two-thirds of the 6,000,000 violent crimes reported in the National Criminal Victims Survey for 1990.[21]

Targeting Hardened Criminals
Truth-in-sentencing laws would require state prison officials to retain more prisoners, at a higher cost to the state. But research shows that these prisoners are generally society's most dangerous predators.[22] In a landmark study, University of Pennsylvania criminologist Marvin Wolfgang compiled arrest records up to their 30th birthday for every male born and raised in Philadelphia in 1945 and 1958. He found that just 7 percent of each age group committed two-thirds of all violent crime, including three-fourths of the rapes and robberies and virtually all of the murders. Moreover, this 7 percent not only had five or more arrests by age 18 but went on committing felonies. Wolfgang and his colleagues estimate these criminals got away with about a dozen crimes.[23] Their studies suggest that about 75,000 new, young, persistent criminal predators are added to the population every year. They hit their peak rate of offenses at about age 16.[24]

In response to these findings, Alfred Regnery, who was Administrator of the Office of Juvenile Justice and Delinquency Prevention at the Justice Department from 1982 to 1986, funded projects in cities in which police, prosecutors, schools, and welfare and probation workers pooled information to focus on the "serious habitual offender." The program had a significant effect in many cities. Thanks to this Justice Department program, for example, Oxnard, California, was able to place the city's thirty most active serious habitual offenders behind bars, and violent crimes dropped 38 percent in 1987, more than double the drop in any other California city. By 1989, when all thirty of the active serious habitual offenders were behind bars, murders declined 60 percent compared with 1980, robberies 41 percent and burglaries 29 percent.[25]

Thus in conjunction with a criminal justice system that convicts and incarcerates the hardened criminals, a truth-in-sentencing policy will reduce crime by keeping these serious and habitual offenders in prison longer.

How Truth in Sentencing Deters Criminals
Incarceration incapacitates violent criminals, and directly benefits law-abiding Americans, by protecting families and also by yielding greater financial savings from reduced crime than the cost of incarceration itself. But stepped-up imprisonment also deters crime. Criminologist Isaac Ehrlich of the University of Chicago estimated that a one percent increase in arrest rates produces a one point decrease in crime rates, and a one percent increase in sentence length produces a one percent decrease in crime rates, for a combined deterrent and incapacitation effect of 1.1 percent.[26] Observed trends seem to support Ehrlich's broad conclusion and hence the claim of deterrence. When the rate of imprisonment per 100 crimes began dropping in the early 1960s, for in-

stance, the rate of crime per 100 population began to climb steeply.

A recent report by the Dallas-based National Center for Policy Analysis, written by Texas A&M economist Morgan Reynolds, makes a strong case for the deterrence value of longer sentences. According to Reynolds:

> Crime has increased as the expected costs of committing crimes has fallen. Today, for a burglary, for example, the chance of arrest is 7 percent. If you are unlucky enough to be one of the 7 percent arrested, relax; only 87 percent of arrestees are prosecuted. Of those, only 79 percent are convicted. Then only 25 percent of those convicted actually go to prison. Multiplying out all these probabilities gives your would-be burglar a 1.2 percent chance of going to jail.[27]

So, too many criminals do not go to jail for the crimes they commit. Reynolds points out that "once in prison, a burglar will stay there for about 13 months, but since more than 98 percent of burglaries never result in a prison sentence, the average expected sentence for each act of burglary is only 4.8 days. Similar calculations yield an expected punishment in 1990 of 1.8 years for murder, 60.5 days for rape, and 6.7 days for arson. Thus, for every crime, the expected punishment has declined over the decades. The decline continues between 1988 and 1990. When punishments rise, crime falls."[28] In short, Reynolds's argument is that raising expected punishment deters crime. Expected punishment is a function of the risk of being caught and convicted multiplied by the median time served. Therefore, everything being equal, increasing the length of sentence increases expected punishment, and hence a criminal is more likely to be deterred when the sentence is longer.

Reynolds also finds that since 1960, the expected punishment for committing a serious crime in Texas has dropped by more than two-thirds, while the number of serious crimes per 100,000 population in Texas has increased more than sixfold.[29]

While these data do not separate out the deterrent effect of longer sentences from the incapacitation effect, it is clear that longer sentences can generally be expected to reduce crime rates.

OBJECTIONS TO TRUTH-IN-SENTENCING LAWS

State truth-in-sentencing laws have great potential to combat violent crime. While academics and legislators in Washington and the states often focus on long-term solutions to the crime problem, such as social or economic conditions or the "root causes" of crime, the special merit of the truth-in-sentencing approach is simply that it keeps violent criminals off the streets while citizens, legislators, and professionals debate the merits of differing approaches in relative safety. In spite of its appeal to common sense, opponents of truth-in-sentencing legislation often make invalid objections. Some argue that truth in sentencing simply costs too much. But such an objection overlooks the opportunity cost of not keeping dangerous offenders in prison. For example, the cost of incarcerating a criminal is approximately $23,000 per year, but the cost of that criminal on the street is $452,000 per year. Some financial estimates are much higher. And, of course, for the families and victims of violent crime..., the human cost is beyond calculation. Others argue that the already large numbers of persons in American jails is an international scandal. While there are indeed are more criminals in America who serve more time than criminals in other countries, the fact remains that the violent crime rate in America is proportionately higher than in virtually all other countries. And if there is any scandal, it is the perpetuation of a failing criminal justice system that allows convicted rapists, kidnappers, and armed robbers back on the streets, ignoring the concerns of an American public that desperately needs security from predatory, violent criminals.

Beyond the questions of cost and the higher percentage of individuals being incarcerated, another objection to the enactment of truth-in-sentencing laws is that they ignore the "root causes" of crime. These root causes are often discussed in terms of persistent poverty, poor education, and deteriorating families. Liberal academics, of course, are not alone in addressing these maladies; and conservative social criticism, including recent analyses by scholars from The Heritage Foundation, have enriched the growing national debate on America's failing criminal justice system.[30] But an academic focus on "root causes," whatever its long-term impact on public policy, should not ignore the fact that violent crime itself immediately aggravates these social problems.

Beyond these general reservations, there are several other objections to truth in sentencing laws:

Objection #1: Truth in sentencing interferes with other policies.
Truth in-sentencing does not. For instance, it does not affect *habeas corpus*, mandatory minimum sentences, the

exclusionary rule, the death penalty, or gun control. Moreover, truth in sentencing is no threat to existing programs designed to divert criminals from jail or prison, such as community-based corrections, intensive probation, house arrest, restitution, or boot camps for first-time offenders. A judge or jury sentencing a convicted criminal to any of these alternatives would not be in conflict with truth in sentencing. But if a judge or jury imposes a prison sentence on a criminal with such a law on the books, another government official cannot later amend the sentence and send that person to an alternative program not involving incarceration. If a judge or jury feels comfortable permitting alternatives to prison for a criminal after listening to the evidence, learning the criminal's background, and hearing from the victim, then truth-in-sentencing requirements would be satisfied.

Objection #2: Truth in sentencing discriminates against minorities.
Some critics argue that the criminal justice system discriminates against black Americans, and so truth-in-sentencing rules will unfairly hit those inmates. On their face, the raw statistics are indeed disturbing. Blacks comprise only 12 percent of the population, but constitute 48.9 percent of state prisoners and 31.4 percent of federal prisoners. The impact of truth-in-sentencing law would depend on whether blacks or whites are disproportionately convicted of the crimes covered by the laws, and whether parole currently favors blacks or whites. However, these laws would be even-handed. All convicted offenders, regardless of race, would have to serve

85 percent of their sentences before being eligible for parole. A more significant question is whether the higher percentages of blacks in prison are the result of racial bias or of higher rates of crime. A number of studies have been conducted to answer that question and appear to demonstrate that it is higher rates of crime among blacks, and not bias, that accounts for their disproportionate representation in America's prisons.

CONCLUSION

The time has come for states to enact truth-in-sentencing laws. There are few viable alternatives that protect citizens from the immediate threat of violent crime. Parole, for example, is a failed experiment. The American people deserve better.

The task before America's state legislators and governors is to pass truth-in-sentencing legislation that would require violent criminals to serve the bulk of their sentences—85 percent is a good benchmark—and to provide the resources it will take to implement such laws. The federal government can encourage this commonsense approach. One such initiative is the Truth in Sentencing Act of 1993, H.R. 3584, introduced by Representatives Jim Chapman and Don Young. This bill would encourage each state to adopt truth-in-sentencing laws and would fund assistance to the states, amounting to $10.5 billion over five years, to help them implement such laws, including the building and operating of prisons. Trimming the federal bureaucracy, not tax increases, is the financing mechanism for these efforts.

The cost of doing nothing is unacceptably high. Crime is a leading concern for Americans. Political leaders and state legislators who can focus the public's attention on a common sense reform like truth in sentencing will be setting the terms of the national debate.

NOTES

1. See Bureau of Justice Statistics, U.S. Department of Justice, *National Corrections Reporting Program, 1988*, table 2–7 (1992).
2. See Bureau of Justice Statistics, *National Corrections Reporting Program, 1988*, table 2–4.
3. See Bureau of Justice Statistics, *National Corrections Reporting Program, 1988*, table 2–7.
4. See Bureau of Justice Statistics, U.S. Department of Justice, *Lifetime Likelihood of Victimization*, technical report, March 1987.
5. See U.S. Department of Justice, "The Case for More Incarceration," 1992, p. 16.
6. See CNN/Gallup Poll, cited in *USA Today*, October 28, 1993, p. 1A.
7. See Bureau of Justice Statistics, U.S. Department of Justice, Special Report, *Recidivism of Prisoners Released in 1983*, April 1989.
8. See Bureau of Justice Statistics, U.S. Department of Justice, Special Report, *Recidivism of Felons on Probation*, February 1992.
9. See Bureau of Justice Statistics, *Recidivism of Prisoners Released in 1983*. See also, Bureau of Justice Statistics, U.S. Department of Justice, Special Report, *Examining Recidivism*, February 1985.
10. See Peter B. Hoffman and James L. Beck, "Recidivism Among Released Federal Prisoners: Salient Factor Score and Five Year Follow-Up," *Criminal Justice and Behavior*, Vol. 12, No. 4 (December 1985), pp. 501–507.
11. See J. Q. Wilson, "If Every Criminal Knew He Would Be Punished If Caught," *The New York Times Magazine*, January 28, 1973, pp. 52–56.
12. Editor's note in Joseph M. and Anne Nutter Bissette, *Ten Myths About Crime and Justice* (Claremont, CA: The Claremont Institute, March 1992).
13. See generally Peter Greenwood et al., *Selective Incapacitation*, Report R-2815-NIJ, The Rand Corporation, Santa Monica, CA, 1982.
14. Edward Zedlewski, *Costs and Benefits of Sanction: A Synthesis of Recent Research*. Unpublished paper, National Institute of Justice, June 1992.
15. William W. Greer, "What Is The Cost of Rising Crime?" *New York Affairs*, January 1984, pp. 6–16.
16. "International Crime Rates," May 1988, NCJ-110776.
17. See Bureau of Justice Statistics, U.S. Department of Justice, *Prisoners in 1990*, table 9 (1991).

18. See Bureau of Justice Statistics, U.S. Department of Justice, *Prisons and Prisoners in the United States* (1992), p. 16.

19. See Bureau of the Census, U.S. Department of Commerce, *Government Finances: 1989–90* (1991), p. 2.

20. The median number of crimes reported in Rand Study was 15. See Greenwood et al., *op. cit.*

21. See U.S. Department of Justice, *Criminal Victimization in the United States, 1990*, p. 4.

22. Methvyn, *op. cit.*

23. See P. E. Tracy, M. E. Wolfgang, and R. M. Figlio, *Delinquency Careers in Two Birth Cohorts* (New York: Plenum Press, 1990), pp. 279–280.

24. *Ibid.*

25. Methvyn, *op. cit.*

26. See Isaac Ehrlich, "Participation in Illegitimate Activities: A Theoretical and Empirical Investigation," *Journal of Political Economy*, May/June 1973, pp. 521–564.

27. See Morgan O. Reynolds, "Why Does Crime Pay?" National Center for Policy Analysis *Backgrounder* No. 110 (1990), p.5.

28. *Ibid.*

29. See Morgan O. Reynolds, *Crime in Texas*, National Center for Policy Analysis Report No. 102 (1991), p. 4.

30. For an excellent summary of the relationship between crime and the deterioration of family life, particularly in urban areas, see Robert Rector, "A Comprehensive Urban Policy: How to Fix Welfare and Revitalize America's Inner Cities," Heritage Foundation *Memo to President-Elect Clinton* No. 12, January 18, 1993; see also Carl F. Horowitz, "An Empowerment Strategy For Eliminating Neighborhood Crime," Heritage Foundation *Backgrounder* No. 814, March 5, 1991.

NO

Lois G. Forer

THE COUNTER REFORMATION

The movement in American criminal law which is referred to here as the "counter reformation" was initiated to counteract the reforms of the criminal law begun in the 1950s. Its proponents sought to block and undo the decisions of the Warren Court, particularly those enforcing the constitutional rights of persons accused of crime.

The Counter-Reformation from which this term is derived was a movement within the Catholic Church to . . . reform the abuses of the Church, particularly corruption of the clergy, simony, and the selling of indulgences. Almost three centuries were required to achieve its goals.

The counter reform movement in American criminal law succeeded in barely four decades. Indeed, the death penalty which had been abolished in 1972 was restored four years later.

The dismantling of the reforms of the criminal law continues. The goal of the counter reformers is to transmogrify the criminal justice system of the United States to a system of crime control through the use of severe penalties: capital punishments and laws mandating long periods of incarceration. It has been accomplished in large part by decisions limiting the procedural rights of those accused of crime, and by the enactment of mandatory sentencing laws, sentencing guideline laws, and death penalty laws. The most striking and disruptive effects of these changes have been the massive overcrowding of jails and prisons at a cost of billions of dollars and loss of public confidence in the fairness of the law.

A comparable movement occurred simultaneously in the United Kingdom. In both nations prison populations rose alarmingly, commencing in the 1970s and 1980s. In England in 1986, the prison population was the highest of any of the member states of the Council of Europe: 95.3 per 100,000 of the population. Only Turkey's, with a rate of imprisonment of 102.3, was higher.

In the United States the rate of imprisonment . . . is even higher and increasing year by year, although the number of crimes has declined since 1991. . . .

* * *

A century and a half ago that perceptive observer of the American scene Alexis de Tocqueville noted, after visiting many prisons, "There are similar punishments and crimes called by the same name, but there are no two beings equal in regard to their morals." These obvious differences in morals and culpability have been deliberately eliminated from judicial consideration in sentencing.

Many lawyers, judges, and criminologists have ... taken issue with the choice of crimes covered under mandatory sentencing laws and the classifications of crimes under sentencing guidelines. One example is incest. In most guidelines, it is included in the category of child abuse and given a less severe rating than robbery. Robbery on public transportation is penalized more severely than robbery on a street or in a school room. The result is a greater disparity in sentences for similar crimes.

In a recent case in Minnesota, one of the first states to adopt guidelines, a judge departed from the guideline in sentencing an ex-priest convicted of sexual abuse of a child. This man was wanted for similar crimes in three states. The guideline sentence for this offense was two and a half years probation. The judge in imposing a prison sentence stated that he departed from the guidelines because the defendant showed no remorse, a permitted aggravating factor. The dangerous behavior of this man over a long period of time was not a factor that could be considered under the guidelines.

The classification of crimes under most mandatory laws and most guidelines is conceptual, based on the structure of crime codes that classify offenses as felonies of different grades and misdemeanors. Many of these codes were enacted decades ago and fail to take into account present conditions of life and new findings in the fields of psychology and psychiatry as to the nature of offenders and the lasting harm done to victims of sexual assault. Nor do they reflect the widespread harm done to individuals and communities from violations of environmental laws and pure food and drug laws. The commissions that created the guidelines pursuant to these laws did not consider dangerousness in establishing presumptive sentences. They were bemused by the theory of just deserts.

A more sensible method of calculating crime severity would be to structure the law to reflect public perceptions of harm and dangerousness in fixing penalties. Public opinion studies by criminologists of crime severity based not on the names of crimes but on factual situations describing the offender, the victim and the circumstances of the crime yield very different results.

Mandatory sentencing laws and guideline sentencing laws preclude judicial consideration of factors that most people consider highly relevant. The federal sentencing guidelines specifically exclude from consideration race, gender, age, education, vocational skills, and mental and emotional conditions, as well as physical conditions of the offender. Such a neutral sentencing scheme sounds fair. In operation it bears most heavily on women, minorities, the young, and the disadvantaged. Since blacks are disproportionately poorer and many have lower levels of education and job skills than most whites, the result has been to exacerbate the disproportionate racial composition of the prison population. Nonetheless, these statutes have been upheld by the United States Supreme Court.

During the Reagan-Bush years the composition of state legislatures and the Congress changed. The new legislators reflected the philosophy of the counter reformation and the theory of just deserts.

The membership of the United States Supreme Court also changed dramatically during this period. The minority views soon became the majority. Ignoring the doctrine of *stare decisis*, that prior decisions should be followed, and flouting their own much-professed strictures against "judicial activism," the majority of the Burger/Rehnquist Court promptly proceeded to erode, if not reverse, the decisions of the previous two decades. Rights of women, children, racial minorities, homosexuals, and those accused of crime were sharply curtailed. The rights of prisoners were also restricted. Despite vigorous challenges, guideline sentencing laws were upheld.

Whether these changes in pretrial and trial procedures and the limitations on appeals and habeas corpus brought about more convictions of those accused of crime probably cannot be accurately determined. There is no way of knowing whether these decisions contributed to prison overcrowding.

There can be no doubt, however, that legislation enacted embracing the theory of just deserts and fair and certain punishment is responsible in large part for the massive burgeoning of the prison population. Violent and property crime rates fell from 24 percent to 23 percent in 1992, down from 32 percent in 1975, while the prison population soared.

The United States Sentencing Commission in its Sentencing and Guidelines and Policy Statement, issued in April 1987, acknowledged not only that the prison population would increase as a result of the drug laws and the career offenders provision of the sentencing law but also that "The guidelines themselves, insofar as they reflect policy decisions made by the Commission... will lead to an increase in the prison population."

This was most probably not the intent of the legislators. Lawmakers in the states and in the Congress were frustrated by the rising incidence of street crime. Abetted by political rhetoric demanding stern punishment for criminals, they embraced the new penology to the plaudits of their constituents.

Lawmakers did not ask what the results of these laws would be. Indeed, vehement proponents of the new penology of just deserts and long prison sentences admitted they did not know what effect these changes in the law would bring about. Professor James Q. Wilson of Harvard, in proposing long prison sentences and severely limiting judicial discretion, wrote in 1977: "No one can know what effect any of these changes in sentencing policy will have on offenders or on society and its institutions."

Judges in criminal courts, probation officers, and prison officials were acutely aware that these laws would drastically increase the number of prisoners, that they would disrupt families, and place additional strains on the welfare system. But they were not consulted.

When judges in my court sought to discuss the practicalities of a proposed sentencing guideline law, they were told that if this law was not passed, a mandatory sentencing law would be enacted. So the judges remained silent. The legislature then enacted both a sentencing guideline statute and mandatory sentencing laws.

The theory behind these laws was that if potential felons knew in advance that the penalty for certain crimes was a long prison sentence or death, they would think carefully and refrain from violating the law. This was patently fallacious. Most street criminals act impulsively, without forethought. Even white-collar felons and professional criminals who carefully plot and plan their misdeeds are not deterred by knowledge of the severe penalties under the Racketeering Influence and Corrupt Organizations Act, popularly known as RICO. They think they can beat the law. Many do. Poor, ignorant offenders are far more likely to be caught and punished. Even when a long prison sentence is imposed on a white-collar offender "to send a message," it is usually revised and the offender is released after a relatively short time in prison. For example, Michael Milken served only twenty-two months of a ten-year sentence.

Proponents of just deserts also believed that if punishment was swift and certain, it would be an effective deterrent. Because American law requires that after a crime has been committed a suspect must be arrested, given a preliminary hearing, and a jury trial if he or she so desires, punishment cannot be swift. Because the law requires proof beyond a reasonable doubt, evidence must be presented, witnesses must testify; there is many a slip between arrest and conviction. Punishment cannot be certain. The Supreme Court has eroded the requirement of proof beyond a reasonable doubt with respect to the elements of a crime necessary for sentencing. But even this abandonment of constitutional rights does not ensure swift and certain punishment.

The United States Sentencing Commission explicitly adopted the new theory of just deserts rather than rehabilitation, stating: "Most observers of the criminal law agree that the ultimate aim of the law itself, and of punishment in particular, is the control of crime." This new policy has not succeeded. Crime has not been substantially reduced.

Even if the United States dispensed with constitutional requirements and adopted a penal system like that of Iran, where accusation is tantamount to conviction, and punishment—death or mutilation—follows inexorably without possibility of appeals or clemency, one must doubt whether impulsive street felons would stop to calculate the consequences....

These sentencing laws also wrought a drastic transformation in the practice of entering guilty pleas, often called plea bargaining. The United States Sentencing Commission has pointed out that 90 percent of all accused persons plead guilty. Since the adoption of guidelines and mandatory sentences, fewer defendants are willing to plead guilty knowing in advance the harsh sentences that will be imposed. Many prosecutors now oppose these laws because of the added burdens such trials impose.

Before the counter reformation, judges had the authority to fix sentences within the maximum limits set by statute, taking into account the circumstances of the crime and the characteristics of the offender. Guilty pleas were entered in open court. Judges imposed sentences on the basis of the facts placed on the record, presentence investigations, psychiatric evaluations if they were deemed appropriate, and any evidence defendants wished to offer. Guilty pleas are disparaged by many critics. I, however, believe that there is no reason to compel an accused who acknowledges guilt to plead not guilty and undergo a trial. When a guilty plea takes place in open court the defendant and the public are protected because an account of the facts is placed on the record, the judge explains the reason for the sentence, and the victims of the crime can be heard.

Under mandatory sentences and guidelines, plea bargaining takes place in secret, in the offices of the prosecutors. Because judges have no discretion in imposing sentence under mandatory laws and little discretion, if any, under guidelines, there is no incentive for an accused to plead guilty and hope for a lenient sentence based on extenuating circumstances or good character. The only official who has authority under these laws to decide what the penalty will be is the prosecutor, who can drop more serious charges and proceed on the less serious ones.

Sensible prosecutors charge all possible crimes for which there is reasonable evidence. Under prior practice at trial, the judge or jury would decide which charges had been proved. When a guilty plea was entered, the prosecutor was not under pressure to drop charges because the judge would impose the sentence. Now it is the prosecutor who, in effect, sets the sentence. Because the sentence for the crime is fixed by statute or guidelines, discretion has been transferred from the judge to the prosecutor. The public does not know what "deal" has been made or the basis for the decision. It is a secret process not unlike that of the hated Star Chamber* that was abolished in England in 1641.

The philosophy of just deserts gave new impetus and respectability to the rage to punish. Prior to the counter reformation, the emphasis was on rehabilitation, education, and crime prevention. Retribution or vengeance is now recognized as a legitimate motivation in sentencing. The criminal sanction and punishment are the preferred mode of dealing with difficult social, medical, and economic conditions.

Drug laws offer a telling example of the folly of relying on the criminal law to deal with what are essentially social and health problems. The government appears to have suffered a case of collective amnesia in forgetting the unsuccessful effort to deal with drinking through criminal laws.

More than three quarters of a century ago alcohol abuse was viewed as a moral issue to be controlled by the criminal law. Drinkers were treated as sinners who must be punished severely. In the grip of moral outrage the Congress passed the Volstead Act (1919) and the Eighteenth Amendment was adopted. The "demon rum" was pursued as a public menace, whether the beverage was wine or bathtub gin. These laws were expected to eliminate 75 percent of crime, poverty, and broken homes in the United States. When it became clear that these ends had not been fulfilled, barely a decade and a half later, common sense prevailed and the Twenty-First Amendment was enacted repealing the Eighteenth Amendment.

In New York, a similar fervor resulted in the Rockefeller laws, mandating prison sentences of from five to twenty years for possession of various quantities of drugs. These laws were not restricted to cocaine, heroin, and angel dust but also included marijuana. Alcohol and tobacco cause many more deaths than drugs. But punishment of sin, not public danger, was the motivation. The prison population of New York rose alarmingly.

The same moral fervor prevailed in the Reagan-Bush era. Drugs were considered the cause of violent crime and drug

*[The Star Chamber refers to a fifteenth-century court in England that was characterized by secrecy and often irresponsible arbitrariness and oppressiveness.—Eds.]

users, dealers, and producers in foreign countries were pursued with costly frenzy. Statistics reveal that 80 percent of drug offenders are non-violent.

Like the other laws of the counter reformation, drug laws have taken a heavy toll on poor black youth. The poor, ethnic minorities, and women are the three categories most seriously prejudiced by drug laws that prevent judges in sentencing from taking into account risk to the public and the social and medical problems of the offender. The result has been that one of every four black men is under some form of correctional control prison, probation, or parole. Women are prosecuted for using illegal drugs during pregnancy, imprisoned, and/or deprived of custody of their children.

A total of 220,000 persons were incarcerated for drug offenses in 1993. Seventy-five percent of new federal prisoners since 1987 are drug offenders; the length of their sentences has increased by 22 percent. The number of black inmates has increased by 55 percent, while white inmates increased by only 31 percent. The effect on the black communities in many cities has been devastating: 56 percent of all black males between the ages of eighteen and thirty-five in Baltimore and 40 percent of those in Washington, D.C., are either in prison or jail or on probation or parole or on arrest warrants, according to Jerome Miller, president of the National Center on Institutions and Alternatives. Only 26.4 percent of black drug offenders and 12.8 percent of white drug offenders had histories of violence. While the greatest burden of this misguided war on drugs has fallen on the black community, the burden on the taxpayers is very heavy.

As with alcohol laws, drug laws bear little relation to the nature of the substance or the danger to the public. Prohibited drugs include marijuana as well as crack cocaine and angel dust. All are punished harshly, even though by 1992 there were no reported cases of death from marijuana. All are considered illegal and all users are deemed sinners.

John Walters, former deputy director for supply reduction in the Office of National Drug Control Policy, maintained, "It's a moral question—the question of right and wrong." William P. Barr, former U.S. Attorney General, stated that building more prisons is "the morally right thing to do."

The cost to the taxpayers has been enormous. During the Bush administration, federal, state, and local governments spent $100 billion in the war on drugs. The federal drug budget was almost $1 billion, most of it spent on agents, prosecutors, and prisons. The courts are overwhelmed, attempting to process 1 million drug arrests a year; the incarceration of 75,000 drug offenders costs $3 billion a year. But cocaine use actually increased in 1991.

Belatedly, after the government has spent billions of dollars on drug enforcement with little appreciable success, knowledgeable persons are now recommending education rather than the heavy hand of the criminal law. But a similar understanding of other problems now confided solely to the criminal law is impeded by the conflation of crime and sin and the rage to punish.

The counter reformation, driven by the belief that punishment is the solution to all violations of law and all aberrant behavior, was remarkably effective in changing the criminal law during its short span of less than four decades. It succeeded in punishing with long terms of imprisonment more than 1.3

million persons at a cost of billions of dollars. More than 2,600 persons, some of whom are arguably innocent, have been condemned to death.

But the counter reformation did not reduce crime, eliminate unfairnesses in sentencing, or improve the quality of justice. Criminal law has a necessary but limited role in American life. It cannot solve all social and economic problems. Prison and the electric chair or lethal injection are not substitutes for families, homes, jobs, schools, health care, and other institutions and services. The theory of just deserts impedes a rational analysis of both offenses and offenders. It prevents judges from imposing appropriate penalties on offenders that treat them humanely, protect society, and are cost-effective.

The criminal justice system in the United States never achieved the goal of equal justice under law. It was always weighted heavily against the poor, the ignorant, and the disadvantaged. The reform movement that began in the 1950s mitigated many injustices. The counter reformation has exacerbated them. It has also filled the jails and prisons beyond capacity, placed hundreds on death row, and overwhelmed the courts with appeals from Draconian sentences.

POSTSCRIPT

Will Mandatory Sentencing Reduce Crime?

It may be said of crime—as Mark Twain said of the weather—that everyone talks about it but nobody does anything about it. Perhaps that is because the easy solutions only sound easy. If authorities are to "lock'em all up," where are they going to put them? The public applauds tough talk but seems unwilling to pay for new prison space. On the other hand, getting at the so-called root causes of crime—which supposedly include poverty and discrimination—is no easier. This approach assumes that these phenomena *are* the basic causes of crime. Yet the rate of violent crime was much lower during the poverty-ridden, racist decade of the 1930s than it was during the affluent and enlightened 1960s.

Dramatic increases in prison population and the rising cost of imprisonment have been accompanied by revelations of appalling conditions that cannot contribute to rehabilitation. Larry E. Sullivan, in *The Prison Reform Movement: Forlorn Hope* (Twayne, 1990), explores the possibilities of reforming prisons.

Much of the writings about crime and punishment in the last decade examines the possibility of alternatives to prison, particularly for people guilty of so-called victimless crimes, such as marijuana smoking, curfew violations, or public drunkenness. Restitution, community work service, monitored home confinement, and other sanctions are considered in Andrew R. Klein's *Alternative Sentencing: A Practitioner's Guide* (Anderson, 1988).

In addition to sentencing reform, Michael Tonry and Franklin E. Zimring, the editors of *Reform and Punishment: Essays on Criminal Sentencing* (University of Chicago Press, 1983), look at how the criminal justice system deals with the mentally ill, and they examine sentencing in European countries. Lawrence M. Friedman's *Crime and Punishment in American History* (Basic Books, 1993) is a popular history of the American justice system, although it concludes sadly that crime is "the price we pay" for living in a free society.

No matter what solutions to the crime problem are attempted, Forer and Wootton have helped set the terms of the debate. Wootton adopts the position set forth by criminologist James Q. Wilson 20 years ago with his famous observation that "wicked people exist." Forer, who characterizes this approach as "the counter-reformation," wants to recapture the spirit of the original reformation, which sought to combat crime by making American society more just and humane. The two goals, punishment and prevention, need not exclude each other, but today's limited resources may force us to decide where to place the emphasis.

ISSUE 10

Is Capital Punishment Justified?

YES: Robert W. Lee, from "Deserving to Die," *The New American* (August 13, 1990)

NO: Matthew L. Stephens, from "Instrument of Justice or Tool of Vengeance?" *Christian Social Action* (November 1990)

ISSUE SUMMARY

YES: Essayist Robert W. Lee argues that capital punishment is the only fair way for society to respond to certain heinous crimes.

NO: Matthew L. Stephens, a prison chaplain, contends that the death penalty is motivated by revenge, is arbitrary in its application, and is racist in its result.

Although capital punishment (the death penalty) is ancient, both the definition of a capital crime and the methods used to put convicted persons to death have changed dramatically. In eighteenth-century Massachusetts, for example, capital crimes included blasphemy and the worship of false gods. Slave states often imposed the death penalty upon blacks for crimes that were punished by only two or three years' imprisonment when committed by whites. It has been estimated that in this century approximately 10 percent of all legal executions have been for the crime of rape, 1 percent for all other crimes except murder (robbery, burglary, attempted murder, etc.), and nearly 90 percent for the commission of murder.

Long before the Supreme Court severely limited the use of the death penalty, executions in the United States were becoming increasingly rare. In the 1930s there were 1,667; the total for the 1950s was 717. In the 1960s the numbers fell even more dramatically. For example, seven persons were executed in 1965, one in 1966, and two in 1967. Put another way, in the 1930s and 1940s, there was 1 execution for every 60 or 70 homicides committed in states that had the death penalty; in the first half of the 1960s, there was 1 execution for every 200 homicides; and by 1966 and 1967, there were only 3 executions for approximately 20,000 homicides.

Then came the Supreme Court case of *Furman v. Georgia* (1972), which many thought—mistakenly—"abolished" capital punishment in America. Actually, only two members of the *Furman* majority thought that capital punishment *per se* violates the Eighth Amendment's injunction against "cruel and unusual punishment." The other three members of the majority took the view that capital punishment is unconstitutional only when applied in an arbitrary or a racially discriminatory manner, as they believed it was in this case. The four dissenters in the *Furman* case were prepared to uphold capital punishment both in general and in this particular instance. Not surprisingly, then, with a slight change of Court personnel—and with a different case before the Court —a few years later, the majority vote went the other way.

In the latter case, *Gregg v. Georgia* (1976), the majority upheld capital punishment under certain circumstances. In his majority opinion in the case, Justice Potter Stewart noted that the law in question (a new Georgia capital punishment statute) went to some lengths to avoid arbitrary procedures in capital cases. For example, Georgia courts were not given complete discretion in handing out death sentences to convicted murderers but had to consult a series of guidelines spelling out "aggravating circumstances," such as if the murder had been committed by someone already convicted of murder, if the murder endangered the lives of bystanders, and if the murder was committed in the course of a major felony. These guidelines, Stewart said, together with other safeguards against arbitrariness included in the new statute, preserved it against Eighth Amendment challenges.

Although the Court has upheld the constitutionality of the death penalty, it can always be abolished by state legislatures. However, that seems unlikely to happen in many states. If anything, the opposite is occurring. Almost immediately after the *Furman* decision of 1972, state legislatures began enacting new death penalty statutes designed to meet the objections raised in the case. By the time of the *Gregg* decision, 35 new death penalty statutes had been enacted.

In response to the public mood, Congress has put its own death penalty provisions into federal legislation. In 1988 Congress sanctioned the death penalty for drug kingpins convicted of intentionally killing or ordering anyone's death. More recently, in the 1994 crime bill, Congress authorized the death penalty for dozens of existing or new federal crimes, such as treason, kidnapping that results in death, or the murder of a federal law enforcement agent.

In the following selections, Robert W. Lee argues that capital punishment is an appropriate form of retribution for certain types of heinous offenses, while Matthew L. Stephens asserts that capital punishment is nothing but vengeance that falls disproportionately upon the poor and minorities.

YES
Robert W. Lee

DESERVING TO DIE

A key issue in the debate over capital punishment is whether or not it is an effective deterrent to violent crime. In at least one important respect, it unquestionably is: It simply cannot be contested that a killer, once executed, is forever deterred from killing again. The deterrent effect on others, however, depends largely on how swiftly and surely the penalty is applied. Since capital punishment has not been used with any consistency over the years, it is virtually impossible to evaluate its deterrent effect accurately. Abolitionists claim that a lack of significant difference between the murder rates for states with and without capital punishment proves that the death penalty does not deter. But the states with the death penalty on their books have used it so little over the years as to preclude any meaningful comparison between states. Through July 18, 1990 there had been 134 executions since 1976. Only 14 states (less than 40 percent of those that authorize the death penalty) were involved. Any punishment, including death, will cease to be an effective deterrent if it is recognized as mostly bluff. Due to costly delays and endless appeals, the death penalty has been largely turned into a paper tiger by the same crowd that calls for its abolition on the grounds that it is not an effective deterrent!

To allege that capital punishment, if imposed consistently and without undue delay, would not be a deterrent to crime is, in essence, to say that people are not afraid of dying. If so, as columnist Jenkin Lloyd Jones once observed, then warning signs reading "Slow Down," "Bridge Out," and "Danger— 40,000 Volts" are futile relics of an age gone by when men feared death. To be sure, the death penalty could never become a 100-percent deterrent to heinous crime, because the fear of death varies among individuals. Some race automobiles, climb mountains, parachute jump, walk circus high-wires, ride Brahma bulls in rodeos, and otherwise engage in endeavors that are more than normally hazardous. But, as author Bernard Cohen notes in his book *Law and Order,* "there are even more people who refrain from participating in these activities mainly because risking their lives is not to their taste."

MERIT SYSTEM

On occasion, circumstances *have* led to meaningful statistical evaluations of the death penalty's deterrent effect. In Utah, for instance, there have been three executions since the Supreme Court's 1976 ruling:

- Gary Gilmore faced a firing squad at the Utah State Prison on January 17, 1977. There had been 55 murders in the Beehive State during 1976 (4.5 per 100,000 population). During 1977, in the wake of the Gilmore execution, there were 44 murders (3.5 per 100,000), a 20 percent decrease.

- More than a decade later, on August 28, 1987, Pierre Dale Selby (one of the two infamous "hi-fi killers" who in 1974 forced five persons in an Ogden hi-fi shop to drink liquid drain cleaner, kicked a ballpoint pen into the ear of one, then killed three) was executed. During all of 1987, there were 54 murders (3.2 per 100,000). The count for January through August was 38 (a monthly average of 4.75). For September–December (in the aftermath of the Selby execution) there were 16 (4.0 per month, a nearly 16 percent decrease). For July and August there were six and seven murders, respectively. In September (the first month following Selby's demise) there were three.

- Arthur Gary Bishop, who sodomized and killed a number of young boys, was executed on June 10, 1988. For all of 1988 there were 47 murders (2.7 per 100,000, the fewest since 1977). During January–June, there were 26; for July–December (after the Bishop execution) the tally was 21 (a 19 percent difference).

In the wake of all three Utah executions, there have been notable decreases in both the number and the rate of murders within the state. To be sure, there are other variables that could have influenced the results, but the figures are there and abolitionists to date have tended simply to ignore them.

Deterrence should never be considered the *primary* reason for administering the death penalty. It would be both immoral and unjust to punish one man merely as an example to others. The basic consideration should be: Is the punishment deserved? If not, it should not be administered regardless of what its deterrent impact might be. After all, once deterrence supersedes justice as the basis for a criminal sanction, the guilt or innocence of the accused becomes largely irrelevant. Deterrence can be achieved as effectively by executing an innocent person as a guilty one (something that communists and other totalitarians discovered long ago). If a punishment administered to one person deters someone else from committing a crime, fine. But that result should be viewed as a bonus of justice properly applied, not as a reason for the punishment. The decisive consideration should be: Has the accused *earned* the penalty?

THE COST OF EXECUTION

The exorbitant financial expense of death penalty cases is regularly cited by abolitionists as a reason for abolishing capital punishment altogether. They prefer to ignore, however, the extent to which they themselves are responsible for the interminable legal maneuvers that run up the costs....

As presently pursued, death-penalty prosecutions *are* outrageously expensive. But, again, the cost is primarily due to redundant appeals, time-consuming delays, bizarre court rulings, and legal histrionics by defense attorneys:

Willie Darden, who had already survived three death warrants, was scheduled to die in Florida's electric chair on September 4, 1985 for a murder he had committed in 1973. Darden's lawyer made a last-minute emergency appeal to the Supreme Court, which voted against postponing the execution until a formal appeal could be filed. So the attorney (in what he later described as "last-minute ingenuity") then requested that the emergency appeal be technically transformed into a formal appeal. Four Justices agreed (enough to force the full court to review the appeal) and the execution was stayed. After additional years of delay and expense, Darden was eventually put out of our misery on March 15, 1988.

Ronald Gene Simmons killed 14 members of his family during Christmas week in 1987. He was sentenced to death, said he was willing to die, and refused to appeal. But his scheduled March 16, 1989 execution was delayed when a fellow inmate, also on death row, persuaded the Supreme Court to block it (while Simmons was having what he expected to be his last meal) on the grounds that the execution could have repercussions for other death-row inmates. It took the Court until April 24th of [1990] to reject that challenge. Simmons was executed on June 25th.

Robert Alton Harris was convicted in California of the 1978 murders of two San Diego teenagers whose car he wanted for a bank robbery. Following a seemingly interminable series of appeals, he was at last sentenced to die on April 3rd of [1990]. Four days earlier, a 9th U.S. Circuit Court of Appeals judge stayed the execution, largely on the claim that Harris was brain-damaged and therefore may possibly have been unable to "premeditate" the murders (as required under California law for the death penalty). On April 10th, the *Washington Times* reported that the series of tests used to evaluate Harris's condition had been described by some experts as inaccurate and "a hoax."

The psychiatric game is being played for all it is worth. On May 14th, Harris's attorneys argued before the 9th Circuit Court that he should be spared the death penalty because he received "inadequate" psychiatric advice during his original trial. In 1985, the Supreme Court had ruled that a defendant has a constitutional right to "a competent psychiatrist who will conduct an appropriate examination." Harris had access to a licensed psychiatrist, but now argues that—since the recent (highly questionable) evaluations indicated brain damage and other alleged disorders that the original psychiatrist failed to detect (and which may have influenced the jury not to impose the death sentence)—a new trial (or at least a re-sentencing) is in order. If the courts buy this argument, hundreds (perhaps thousands) of cases could be reopened for psychiatric challenge.

On April 2, 1974 William Neal Moore shot and killed a man in Georgia. Following his arrest, he pleaded guilty to armed robbery and murder and was convicted and sentenced to death. On July 20, 1975 the Georgia Supreme Court denied his petition for review. On July 16, 1976 the U.S. Supreme

Court denied his petition for review. On May 13, 1977 the Jefferson County Superior Court turned down a petition for a new sentencing hearing (the state Supreme Court affirmed the denial, and the U.S. Supreme Court again denied a review). On March 30, 1978 a Tattnall County Superior Court judge held a hearing on a petition alleging sundry grounds for a writ of *habeas corpus*, but declined on July 13, 1978 to issue a writ. On October 17, 1978 the state Supreme Court declined to review that ruling. Moore petitioned the U.S. District Court for Southern Georgia. After a delay of more than two years, a U.S. District Court judge granted the writ on April 29, 1981. After another two-year delay, the 11th U.S. Circuit Court of Appeals upheld the writ on June 23, 1983. On September 30, 1983 the Circuit Court reversed itself and ruled that the writ should be denied. On March 5, 1984 the Supreme Court rejected the case for the third time.

Moore's execution was set for May 24, 1984. On May 11, 1984 his attorneys filed a petition in Butts County Superior Court, but a writ was denied. The same petition was filed in the U.S. District Court for Georgia's Southern District on May 18th, but both a writ and a stay of execution were denied. Then, on May 23rd (the day before the scheduled execution) the 11th Circuit Court of Appeals granted a stay. On June 4, 1984 a three-judge panel of the Circuit Court voted to deny a writ. After another delay of more than three years, the Circuit Court voted 7 to 4 to override its three-judge panel and rule in Moore's favor. On April 18, 1988, the Supreme Court accepted the case. On April 17, 1989 it sent the case back to the 11th Circuit Court for review in light of new restrictions that the High Court had placed on *habeas corpus*. On September 28, 1989 the Circuit Court ruled 6 to 5 that Moore had abused the writ process. On December 18, 1989 Moore's attorneys again appealed to the Supreme Court.

Moore's case was described in detail in *Insight* magazine for February 12, 1990. By the end of [1989] his case had gone through 20 separate court reviews, involving some 118 state and federal judges. It had been to the Supreme Court and back four times. There had been a substantial turnover of his attorneys, creating an excuse for one team of lawyers to file a petition claiming that all of the prior attorneys had given ineffective representation. No wonder capital cases cost so much!

Meanwhile, the American Bar Association proposes to make matters even worse by requiring states (as summarized by *Insight*) "to appoint two lawyers for every stage of the proceeding, require them to have past death penalty experience and pay them at 'reasonable' rates to be set by the court."

During an address to the American Law Institute on May 16, 1990, Chief Justice Rehnquist asserted that the "system at present verges on the chaotic" and "cries out for reform." The time expended between sentencing and execution, he declared, "is consumed not by structured review ... but in fits of frantic action followed by periods of inaction." He urged that death row inmates be given one chance to challenge their sentences in state courts, and one challenge in federal courts, period.

LIFETIME TO ESCAPE

Is life imprisonment an adequate substitute for the death penalty? Presently, according to the polls, approximately three-fourths of the American people favor capital punishment. But abolitionists try to discount that figure by claiming that support for the death penalty weakens when life imprisonment without the possibility of parole is offered as an alternative. (At other times, abolitionists argue that parole is imperative to give "lifers" some hope for the future and deter their violent acts in prison.)

Life imprisonment is a flawed alternative to the death penalty, if for no other reason than that so many "lifers" escape. Many innocent persons have died at the hands of men previously convicted and imprisoned for murder, supposedly for "life." The ways in which flaws in our justice system, combined with criminal ingenuity, have worked to allow "lifers" to escape include these recent examples:

- On June 10, 1977, James Earl Ray, who was serving a 99-year term for killing Dr. Martin Luther King Jr., escaped with six other inmates from the Brushy Mountain State Prison in Tennessee (he was captured three days later).
- Brothers Linwood and James Briley were executed in Virginia on October 12, 1984 and April 18, 1985, respectively. Linwood had murdered a disc jockey in 1979 during a crime spree. During the same spree, James raped and killed a woman (who was eight months pregnant) and killed her five-year-old son. On May 31, 1984, the Briley brothers organized and led an escape of five death-row inmates (the largest death-row breakout in U.S. history). They were at large for 19 days.

- On August 1, 1984 convicted murderers Wesley Allen Tuttle and Walter Wood, along with another inmate, escaped from the Utah State Prison. All were eventually apprehended. Wood subsequently sued the state for $2 million for violating his rights by allowing him to escape. In his complaint, he charged that, by allowing him to escape, prison officials had subjected him to several life-threatening situations: "Because of extreme fear of being shot to death, I was forced to swim several irrigation canals, attempt to swim a 'raging' Jordan River and expose myself to innumerable bites by many insects. At one point I heard a volley of shotgun blasts and this completed my anxiety."
- On April 3, 1988 three murderers serving life sentences without the chance of parole escaped from the maximum-security West Virginia Penitentiary. One, Bobby Stacy, had killed a Huntington police officer in 1981. At the time, he had been free on bail after having been arrested for shooting an Ohio patrolman.
- On November 21, 1988 Gonzalo Marrero, who had been convicted of two murders and sentenced to two life terms, escaped from New Jersey's Trenton state prison by burrowing through a three-foot-thick cell wall, then scaling a 20-foot outer wall with a makeshift ladder.
- In August 1989 Arthur Carroll, a self-proclaimed enforcer for an East Oakland street gang, was convicted of murdering a man. On September 28th, he was sentenced to serve 27-years-to-life in prison. On October 10th he was transferred to San Quentin prison. On October 25th he was set free after a paperwork snafu led officials to believe

that he had served enough time. An all-points bulletin was promptly issued.

- On February 11, 1990 six convicts, including three murderers, escaped from their segregation cells in the maximum security Joliet Correctional Center in Illinois by cutting through bars on their cells, breaking a window, and crossing a fence. In what may be the understatement of the year, a prison spokesman told reporters: "Obviously, this is a breach of security."

Clearly, life sentences do not adequately protect society, whereas the death penalty properly applied does so with certainty.

EQUAL OPPORTUNITY EXECUTION

Abolitionists often cite statistics indicating that capital punishment has been administered in a discriminatory manner, so that the poor, the black, the friendless, etc., have suffered a disproportionate share of executions. Even if true, such discrimination would not be a valid reason for abandoning the death penalty unless it could be shown that it was responsible for the execution of *innocent* persons (which it has not been, to date). Most attempts to pin the "discrimination" label on capital convictions are similar to one conducted at Stanford University a few years ago, which found that murderers of white people (whether white or black) are more likely to be punished with death than are killers of black people (whether white or black). But the study also concluded that blacks who murdered whites were somewhat *less* likely to receive death sentences than were whites who killed whites.

Using such data, the ACLU attempted to halt the execution of Chester Lee Wicker in Texas on August 26, 1986. Wicker, who was white, had killed a white person. The ACLU contended that Texas unfairly imposes the death penalty because a white is more likely than a black to be sentenced to death for killing a white. The Supreme Court rejected the argument. On the other hand, the execution of Willie Darden in Florida attracted worldwide pleas for amnesty from sundry abolitionists who, ignoring the Stanford study, claimed that Darden had been "railroaded" because he was black and his victim was white.

All criminal laws—in all countries, throughout all human history—have tended to be administered in an imperfect and uneven manner. As a result, some elements in society have been able to evade justice more consistently than others. But why should the imperfect administration of justice persuade us to abandon any attempt to attain it?

The most flagrant example if discrimination in the administration of the death penalty does not involve race, income, or social status, but gender. Women commit around 13 percent of the murders in America, yet, from 1930 to June 30, 1990, only 33 of the 3991 executions (less than 1 percent) involved women. Only one of the 134 persons executed since 1976 (through July 18th [1990]) has been a woman (Velma Barfield in North Carolina on November 2, 1984). One state governor commuted the death sentence of a woman because "humanity does not apply to women the inexorable law that it does to men."

According to L. Kay Gillespie, professor of sociology at Weber State College in Utah, evidence indicates that women who cried during their trials had a better chance of getting away with murder and avoiding the death penalty. Perhaps the

National Organization for Women can do something about this glaring example of sexist "inequality" and "injustice." In the meantime, we shall continue to support the death penalty despite the disproportionate number of men who have been required to pay a just penalty for their heinous crimes.

FORGIVE AND FORGET?

Another aspect of the death penalty debate is the extent to which justice should be tempered by mercy in the case of killers. After all, abolitionists argue, is it not the duty of Christians to forgive those who trespass against them? In Biblical terms, the most responsible sources to extend mercy and forgiveness are (1) God and (2) the victim of the injustice. In the case of murder, so far as *this* world is concerned, the victim is no longer here to extend mercy and forgiveness. Does the state or any other earthly party have the right or authority to intervene and tender mercy on behalf of a murder victim? In the anthology *Essays on the Death Penalty*, the Reverend E. L. H. Taylor clarifies the answer this way: "Now it is quite natural and proper for a man to forgive something you do to *him*. Thus if somebody cheats me out of $20.00 it is quite possible and reasonable for me to say, 'Well, I forgive him, we will say no more about it.' But what would you say if somebody had done you out of $20.00 and I said, 'That's all right. I forgive him on your behalf'?"

The point is simply that there is no way, in *this* life, for a murderer to be reconciled to his victim, and secure the victim's forgiveness. This leaves the civil authority with no other responsible alternative but to adopt *justice* as the standard for assigning punishment in such cases.

Author Bernard Cohen raises an interesting point: " ... if it is allowable to deprive a would-be murderer of his life, in order to forestall his attack, why is it wrong to take away his life after he has successfully carried out his dastardly business?" Does anyone question the right of an individual to kill an assailant should it be necessary to preserve his or her life or that of a loved one?

Happily, however, both scripture and our legal system uphold the morality and legality of taking the life of an assailant, if necessary, *before* he kills us. How, then, can it be deemed immoral for civil authority to take his life *after* he kills us?

INTOLERANT VICTIMS?

Sometimes those who defend the death penalty are portrayed as being "intolerant." But isn't one of our real problems today that Americans are *too tolerant* of evil? Are we not accepting acts of violence, cruelty, lying, and immorality with all too little righteous indignation? Such indignation is not, as some would have us believe, a form of "hatred." In *Reflections on the Psalms*, C. S. Lewis discussed the supposed spirit of "hatred" that some critics claimed to see in parts of the Psalms: "Such hatreds are the kind of thing that cruelty and injustice, by a sort of natural law, produce. ... Not to perceive it at all— not even to be tempted to resentment—to accept it as the most ordinary thing in the world—argues a terrifying insensibility. Thus the absence of anger, especially that sort of anger which we call indignation, can, in my opinion, be a most alarming symptom."

When mass murderer Ted Bundy was executed in Florida on January 24, 1989, a crowd of some 2000 spectators gathered across from the prison to cheer and celebrate. Many liberal commentators were appalled. Some contended that it was a spectacle on a par with Bundy's own callous disrespect for human life. One headline read: "Exhibition witnessed outside prison was more revolting than execution." What nonsense! As C. S. Lewis observed in his commentary on the Psalms: "If the Jews cursed more bitterly than the Pagans this was, I think, at least in part because they took right and wrong more seriously." It is long past time for us all to being taking right and wrong more seriously....

SEEDS OF ANARCHY

As we have seen, most discussions of the death penalty tend to focus on whether it should exist for murder or be abolished altogether. The issue should be reframed so that the question instead becomes whether or not it should be imposed for certain terrible crimes in addition to murder (such as habitual lawbreaking, clearly proven cases of rape, and monstrous child abuse).

In 1953 the renowned British jurist Lord Denning asserted: "Punishment is the way in which society expresses its denunciation of wrongdoing; and in order to maintain respect for law, it is essential that the punishment for grave crimes shall adequately reflect the revulsion felt by a great majority of citizens for them." Nineteen years later, U.S. Supreme Court Justice Potter Stewart noted (while nevertheless concurring in the Court's 1972 opinion that temporarily banned capital punishment) that the "instinct for retribution is part of the nature of man and channeling that instinct in the administration of criminal justice serves an important purpose in promoting the stability of a society governed by law. When people begin to believe that organized society is unwilling or unable to impose upon criminal offenders the punishment they 'deserve,' then there are sown the seeds of anarchy—of self-help, vigilante justice, and lynch law."

To protect the innocent and transfer the fear and burden of crime to the criminal element where it belongs, we must demand that capital punishment be imposed when justified and expanded to cover terrible crimes in addition to murder.

NO   Matthew L. Stephens

INSTRUMENT OF JUSTICE OR
TOOL OF VENGEANCE?

When we look at capital punishment as an instrument of the administration of justice, we must ask: 1) Is capital punishment evenly applied to all cases of murder? 2) Will those charged in a capital punishment case have both the best lawyers and defense available to them? 3) Is the cost of carrying out the death penalty worth the money spent to execute one person? and, 4) Is capital punishment a deterrent to murder? After all, the latter is ultimately the question our society must answer. If it works, we must carry it out: if it doesn't, it is a ghastly and irrevocable error.

APPLYING THE DEATH PENALTY

In the United States, we experience the tragedy of over 20,000 homicides each year. These statistics are constantly increasing due to the devastating effects of drugs, racism and poverty. Yet, we choose, as a society, only 200, (or 1 percent of all murderers) to receive the ultimate punishment of death. When one looks at the criteria for selecting this nominal fraction of all murderers, the real issues come to light. Who are these people? What is their economic and racial background? What are their legal resources and representation? What is their intellectual capacity?

The facts are clear. Those on death row are the poorest of the poor. They are disproportionately "people of color": African American (40.7 percent), Hispanic (5.72 percent), Native American (1.49 percent) and Asian (0.61 percent), as compared to European/Caucasian. This means approximately 50 percent of all death row inmates are people of color in a society in which all of these populations constitute significant minorities.

Additionally, it is estimated that over one-third of all death row inmates are mentally retarded (with IQ's of less than 70), and that nearly half are functionally illiterate.

It is these poor and oppressed children of God who become the victims of our society's anger and need for revenge. The death penalty is clearly *not* equally applied under the law, or under the more significant mandate of moral, ethical and spiritual values of a nation founded on these principles.

In a society that champions human rights and individual dignity in all of our creeds, we are far behind the rest of the so-called "civilized" western world in showing compassion to the poor and oppressed of our country. There are only two countries that still engage the death penalty as justice: South Africa and the United States. Recently, the South African government officially put a "hold" on death sentences and executions.

There is overwhelming evidence that race is the single most important factor in choosing those who will be sentenced to death. Of the more than 3,000 people executed since 1930, nearly half were people of color. Eighty-five percent of those executed since 1977, when new death penalty statutes were passed, were punished for crimes against white victims. This is true despite the fact that the homicide rate for people of color is roughly 50 percent higher than that of the majority community.

Take, for example, the state of Ohio where 842 people have been executed since 1884. Of this number, only one white man was executed for killing a black person. In 1989, there were 100 people on death row in Ohio: 51 black men, 45 white men and 4 black women. Ohio has not executed anyone since the state reinstituted the death penalty, but the first execution will probably take place soon. Keep in mind that the minimum age for death sentencing in Ohio is 18.

Consider the historic case of Willie Jasper Darden, executed March 15, 1988 in Florida's electric chair. He was 54 years old. Willie Darden was sentenced to death for the murder of a furniture store owner in Lakeland, Florida. Darden proclaimed his innocence from the moment of his arrest until the moment of his execution, over 14 years later. Significant doubt of Darden's guilt remains.

Willie Darden was tried by an all-white jury in Inverness, Florida, a county with a history of racial segregation and oppression. The prosecutor's opening remarks in the trial demonstrate the racial implications of this case:

> "... The testimony is going to show, I think very shortly, when the trial starts, that the victims in this case were white. And of course, Mr. Darden, the defendant, is black. Can each of you tell me you can try Mr. Darden as if he was white?"

Throughout the trial, the prosecutor characterized Darden as subhuman, saying such things as, "Willie Darden is an animal who should be placed on a leash." The US Supreme Court sharply criticized this misconduct, but refused to find that it unfairly influenced the trial.

In the face of evidence that those who kill whites in Florida are nearly five times more likely to be sentenced to death than those who kill blacks, the prosecution of Willie Darden becomes the story of a man who may well have been innocent, but whose protestations were overshadowed by the color of his victim and himself.

Finally, consider the case of Delbert Tibbs who went from Chicago Theological Seminary to Florida's death row. Luckily, he did not "graduate" from either. Deciding to take some time off from his studies, he hitchhiked across country. "White boys could drop out to 'find themselves,'" says Tibbs, "but nobody ever heard of a black man needing to do the same thing." His journey ended abruptly when, being in the wrong place at the wrong time, he was arrested and later convicted for the rape of a 16-year-old girl and the murder of her boyfriend in 1974. He was sentenced to death.

It was only with the assistance of the National Council of Churches Defense Fund attorneys that on appeal, his conviction was overturned on the grounds that it was not supported by the weight of the evidence. However, he was never said to be innocent of the crime. In spite of a US Supreme Court decision that he could be retried, the state decided not to reopen the case on the grounds that the police investigation of the crime was tainted from the start. The original prosecutor said, "If there is a retrial, I will appear as a witness for Mr. Tibbs." Today, Delbert Tibbs devotes his life to his family and to anti-death penalty work across the nation and around the world.

It is more than clear that race is the single-most contributing factor to one being dealt the death penalty. In combination with poverty, lack of adequate legal representation and the drive of society for vengeance, people of color are the common victims of this catharsis of hate and cycle of violence.

QUALITY OF LEGAL REPRESENTATION

The quality of legal representation of indigent defendants in capital cases is of widespread concern. Most capital defendants cannot afford to pay for their own counsel and are represented by court-appointed lawyers in private practice, or by public defenders. Many times they are given inexperienced counsel, ill-equipped to handle such cases and working with severely limited resources. Many public defenders' offices are overextended with caseloads and cannot devote the time necessary to defend a capital case.

In rural areas, lawyers handling capital cases have little or no experience in criminal law; many are ignorant of the special issues relating to capital punishment. A recent study found that capital defendants in Texas with court-appointed lawyers were more than twice as likely to receive death sentences than those who retained counsel. The trial lawyers of a number of executed prisoners were found to have spent very little time preparing the case for trial. Often, they failed to interview potentially important witnesses or to raise mitigating factors at the proper times.

A good example of this problem is the case of John Young, a black man executed in Georgia. He was convicted in 1976 of murdering three elderly people while under the influence of drugs. He was 18-years-old. His trial lawyer was disbarred from legal practice within days after the trial and left the state of Georgia.

When the lawyer learned of the execution, he came forward and submitted an affidavit to the court in which he admitted spending hardly any time preparing for the case, due to personal problems. He admitted he did not investigate his client's background or raise any mitigating circumstances at the sentencing stage of the trial that might have influenced the jury's decision. These circumstances included the fact that at the age of three, John Young had seen his mother murdered while he was lying in bed with her. He later was placed with an alcoholic relative who turned him out on the street to survive at an early age.

The US District Court and the Court of Appeals ruled that they could not consider the lawyer's affidavit as new evidence because it should have been presented earlier. John Young died because of inadequate defense counsel. (Reference: Amnesty International "USA: The Death Penalty Briefing.")

THE COST OF CAPITAL PUNISHMENT

Certainly there is the moral cost of taking a life, to make up for the taking of another life. There is no real way to replace one life with the death of another. Yet when capital punishment is the choice of the courts, this is exactly what has been decided.

The moral issue here is: Do we have the right to kill, or is that the right of God only? This does not excuse one who takes the life of another. That is clearly wrong. They will have to answer to the vengeance of their God. We do have the right to demand restitution and protection in the form of taking away the freedom of that individual found guilty of taking a life.

Taking freedom from individuals who kill others has also been shown to be less costly than executing them through our court system. The current debate on side-stepping a lengthy appeal process is nothing more than a rationale to expedite the death sentence while saving money.

In 1972, the Supreme Court of the United States, in *Furmon vs. Georgia* held that "arbitrary and capricious" application of capital punishment violated the Eighth Amendment prohibition against cruel and unusual punishment. This means that a defendant has to be prosecuted and convicted in a way that is extraordinarily righteous and free of any kind of prejudice.

This "super" due process requirement has made the prosecutions of capital cases enormously expensive. In a recent University of California at Davis Law Review article, Margaret Garey calculated that it costs a minimum of $500,000 to complete a capital case in California. It costs approximately $30,000 per year to house an inmate in the California system.

Between August of 1977 and December of 1985, only 10 percent (190 of 1,847 cases) resulted in the death sentence. Data from New York State suggests that if it adapted capital punishment, the cost would be $1,828,000 per capital trial. Assuming even a 0.75 percent failure rate, it would cost about $7.3 million to sentence one person to death in New York, compared with $4.5 million ($500,000 × 0.90 percent failure rate) to sentence one person to death in California. (Reference: "Price of Executions Is Just Too High," Richard Moran and Joseph Ellis, *Wall Street Journal*, 1986.)

Cost effectiveness is a weak argument when talking about the value of human life. However, even when put on such a shallow rationale as cost-analysis, the death penalty does not hold up.

It has cost the state of Florida $57 million to execute 18 men. It is estimated that this is six times the cost of life imprisonment. A report from the *Miami Herald* said that keeping a prisoner in jail for life would cost the state $515,964 based on a 40-year life span in prison. It would cost $3.17 million for each execution. The newspaper broke the cost of execution down to show $36,000 to $116,700 for trial and sentencing; $69,480 to $160,000 for mandatory state review, which is not required in non-capital trials; $274,820 to $1 million for additional appeals; $37,600 to $312,000 for jail costs, and $845,000 for the actual execution.

These figures should make us ask ourselves: Is the need for our vengeance worth all this money when the possibility that we still convict and execute the wrong person exists? What really guides our conscience—the money or the moral issue of state murder and street murder? Whatever side moves us, we must see that the cost of capital punishment is too high. (Reference: "The Cost of the Death Penalty," Illinois Coalition Against the Death Penalty.)

A DETERRENT TO MURDER?

Since capital punishment has been reinstated as a legal sentence of the law, there is no proof that shows murder has declined in any of the states in which it is being used. In fact, some states show an increase in violent crimes.

People who favor the death penalty often believe it helps reduce the number of violent crimes. This may be true if the person who considers homicide would make a rational decision in anticipation of the consequences. This rarely happens because most homicides happen in the "heat of passion," anger, and under the influence of drugs or alcohol.

Studies show that murder rates in states with capital punishment, such as Illinois, differ little from the states that do not have capital punishment, such as Michigan. In 1975, the year before Canada abolished the death penalty, the homicide rate was 3.09 per 100,000 persons. In 1986, that rate was down to 2.19 per 100,000 persons, the lowest in 15 years. In some states, the use of capital punishment increased the crime rate. In New York, between 1903 and 1963, executions were followed by a slight rise in the state's homicide rate.

The recent cry for the death penalty in our country comes more from the need for revenge than for justice.... Could it be that violence begets violence? Could it be that as long as the state is killing, we are sending a message that killing is the way to solve problems?

With all of the various factors we have considered, it is clear, even to the casual observer, that the death penalty does not work. It cannot be taken back, and it is arbitrary in its application and racist in its result. People of faith must take a stand. We must choose the day when we will transform instead of kill, when we will "do justice and love mercy and walk humbly with our God" instead of perpetuating a system that is evil, barbaric, costly and ineffective.

POSTSCRIPT

Is Capital Punishment Justified?

In their arguments, Lee and Stephens cite some of the same facts and figures but draw opposite conclusions. Both, for example, note how expensive it is to keep prisoners on death row for so many years while appeals continue. Lee, however, draws from this the conclusion that appeals should be limited, while Stephens uses it to show that it costs taxpayers less to keep a felon in prison for life than to try to kill him.

Note that Lee does not rest his case for capital punishment on deterrence. He calls deterrence a "bonus" but not a primary justification. What really counts, he says, is whether or not the accused has "earned" the death penalty. For a similar argument developed at greater length, see Walter Berns, *For Capital Punishment: Crime and the Morality of the Death Penalty* (Basic Books, 1979). Directly opposed to the contention that capital punishment is moral is the view of the late judge Lois G. Forer: "Killing human beings when carried out by government as a matter of policy is, I believe, no less abhorrent than any other homicide." Forer's case against capital punishment is presented in her book *A Rage to Punish: The Unintended Consequences of Mandatory Sentencing* (W. W. Norton, 1994). For a moving account of how one condemned man was put into the electric chair *twice* (the first time the jolt was not enough to kill him) after losing a Supreme Court appeal based on "double jeopardy" and "cruel and unusual punishment," see chapter 10 of Fred W. Friendly and Martha Elliott, *The Constitution: That Delicate Balance* (Random House, 1984).

There is little dispute over the proposition that the manner of execution should be as painless as possible (no one is drawn and quartered in civilized society), although there is no unanimity of opinion about whether death by electrocution, gas, or hanging best meets that test. Some states, such as Texas and New Jersey, have adopted the method of fatal injections, though the experience with its use in Texas has raised doubts about its painlessness. It may well be that the firing squad, perhaps the most violent means of execution permitted in the United States, could also be the quickest and most painless.

ISSUE 11

Do We Need Tougher Gun Control Laws?

YES: Carl T. Bogus, from "The Strong Case for Gun Control," *The American Prospect* (Summer 1992)

NO: Daniel D. Polsby, from "The False Promise of Gun Control," *The Atlantic Monthly* (March 1994)

ISSUE SUMMARY

YES: Writer Carl Bogus argues that even local gun control laws will reduce the number of gun-related crimes.

NO: Professor of law Daniel D. Polsby contends that not only does gun control not work, it may actually increase the incidence of robbery and other gun-related crimes.

During evening rush hour one day in December 1993, a man named Colin Ferguson boarded a Long Island Railroad train in New York City. When the train reached Long Island, Ferguson pulled out a 9-millimeter pistol and walked down the aisle methodically shooting people in the head. Six people died and 19 others were seriously wounded.

Ferguson's pistol had a 15-round magazine, meaning that he could fire 15 shots before he had to reload his gun. After finishing one magazine, he punched in a new clip and began firing again. (He was finally tackled and subdued by passengers.) He had purchased the pistol, a Ruger P-89, nine months earlier in a hunting-and-fishing store in California. California has a 15-day waiting period before anyone can buy a gun, during which time a background check is run on the purchaser; in Ferguson's case, the gun store added an extra day for good measure. Ferguson supplied all the information requested, then waited. Nothing suspicious showed up during the check, so he walked away with his Ruger after 16 days.

California's gun control law is one of the toughest state laws in America, much tougher than the federal law passed just one month before Ferguson's shooting spree. In November 1993, after seven years of wrangling, Congress finally passed the Brady Bill. For several years, James Brady, a press secretary to President Ronald Reagan who was partially paralyzed by a bullet intended for Reagan in 1981, had been heading a campaign to regulate handguns. The National Rifle Association (NRA) and other opponents of gun control had fought hard against any such legislation, and Republican presidents had largely agreed with the NRA position that the best way to curb gun violence is not to ban guns but to stiffen penalties against those who use them illegally. But President Bill Clinton threw his support behind the Brady Bill, and during a signing ceremony he and Brady congratulated each other on finally making a breakthrough into meaningful federal gun control.

But was it meaningful—or largely symbolic? The Brady Law requires a *five*-day waiting period on handgun purchase, 11 days fewer than Ferguson had to wait in California. One month after the signing ceremony, there was already talk in Congress about the need for "Brady 2," a more sweeping control on handguns. As sponsored by Ohio senator Howard Metzenbaum (D), this bill would require a person to obtain a license, similar to a driver's license, before he or she could own a handgun. Among its other provisions, the bill would require people to show that they had passed courses in firearms safety before they could obtain a license to purchase a handgun.

"Brady 2" was given little chance of passage—if anything, it lent credibility to the gun lobby's charge of "give them this and they'll just want more"— but the bill also contained a ban on assault weapons that eventually worked its way into the crime bill passed by Congress in 1994. An assault weapon is one with a magazine capable of holding many rounds that can be fired off each time the trigger is pulled. The 1994 crime law puts a 10-year ban on the manufacture and sale of 19 types of assault weapons as well as copycat models and certain other guns with features similar to assault weapons. This moves federal gun control much further than it has ever gone. But again, the question remains: Is this regulation simply symbolic, or will it have any meaningful effect on the level of gun violence in America?

Advocates of gun control regard the latest crime bills as at least a step in the right direction. They often call attention to countries like the United Kingdom and Japan, which have very tough firearm laws and very low murder rates. Opponents of gun control reply that the low murder rates in those countries are actually the result of their cultures and criminal justice systems. They point to countries like Switzerland, New Zealand, and Israel, where firearms are practically unrestricted yet murder rates are also very low. There are, indeed, a mass of variables to consider when trying to correlate firearm possession with the risk of death by firearms. Do the firearms cause the risk, or does the risk cause the firearms? Perhaps in some way the two feed into each other. People may arm themselves partly because they fear crime, yet a proliferation of arms in society may help to cause crime.

In the following selections, law professor Daniel Polsby and essayist Carl Bogus wrestle with these problems of causality and reach very different conclusions. Bogus presents evidence suggesting that, even with other demographic factors held nearly constant, there is less gun-related crime in areas that have gun control. Polsby, however, argues that gun control, by keeping guns out of the hands of law-abiding citizens, may tempt criminals to a more indiscriminate use of firearms.

YES

Carl T. Bogus

THE STRONG CASE FOR GUN CONTROL

While abhorring violence, Americans generally believe that gun control cannot do much to reduce it. A majority of Americans questioned in a 1992 CBS–*New York Times* poll responded that banning handguns would only keep them away from law-abiding citizens rather than reduce the amount of violent crime. Many serious scholars have accepted the argument that the huge number of guns already in circulation would make any gun control laws ineffective. Until recently, it has been difficult to answer these objections. But in the past few years, new research has demonstrated that some gun control laws do work, dramatically reducing murder rates.

Gun violence is a plague of such major proportions that its destructive power is rivaled only by wars and epidemics. During the Vietnam War, more than twice as many Americans were shot to death in the United States as died in combat in Vietnam. Besides the 34,000 Americans killed by guns each year, more than 60,000 are injured—many seriously—and about a quarter of a million Americans are held up at gunpoint.

Measures that demonstrably reduce gun violence would gain wide public support. But that has been exactly the problem: A public that approves of gun control by wide margins also is skeptical about its effectiveness and even its constitutionality. Both of these sources of doubt can now be put to rest.

A TALE OF TWO CITIES

Perhaps the most dramatic findings about the efficacy of gun control laws come from a study comparing two cities that have followed different policies for regulating handguns: Seattle, Washington and Vancouver, British Columbia.[1] Only 140 miles apart, the two cities are remarkably alike despite being located on opposite sides of an international border. They have populations nearly identical in size and, during the study period (1980–86), had similar socioeconomic profiles. Seattle, for example, had a 5.8 percent unemployment rate while Vancouver's was 6.0 percent. The median household income in Seattle was $16,254; in Vancouver, adjusted in U.S. dollars, it was $16,681. In racial and ethnic makeup, the two cities are also similar. Whites represent 79 percent of Seattle's inhabitants and 76 percent of Vancouver's. The principal racial difference is that Asians make up a larger share of Vancouver's population (22 percent versus 7 percent). The two cities share not only a common frontier history but a current culture as well. Most of the top ten television shows in one city, for example, also rank among the top ten in the other.

As one might expect from twin cities, burglary rates in Seattle and Vancouver were nearly identical. The aggravated assault rate was, however, slightly higher in Seattle. On examining the data more closely, the Sloan study found "a striking pattern." There were almost identical rates of assaults with knives, clubs and fists, but there was a far greater rate of assault with firearms in Seattle. Indeed, the firearm assault rate in Seattle was nearly eight times higher than in Vancouver [see Figure 1].

The homicide rate was also markedly different in the two cities. During the seven years of the study, there were 204 homicides in Vancouver and 388 in Seattle—an enormous difference for two cities with comparable populations. Further analysis led to a startling finding: the entire difference was due to gun-related homicides. The murder rates with knives—and all other weapons excluding firearms—were virtually identical, but the rate of murders involving guns was five times greater in Seattle [see Figure 2]. That alone accounted for Seattle having nearly twice as many homicides as Vancouver.

People in Seattle may purchase a handgun for any reason after a five-day waiting period; 41 percent of all households have handguns. Vancouver on the other hand, requires a permit for handgun purchases and issues them

Figure 1

Aggravated Assaults per 100,000 People, 1980–1983, by Weapon

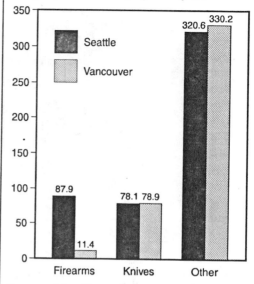

Source: John Henry Sloan, et al., "Handgun Regulations, Crime, Assaults, and Homicide," *The New England Journal of Medicine*, Nov. 10, 1988, pp. 1256–62. Reprinted by permission.

only to applicants who have a lawful reason to own a handgun and who, after a careful investigation, are found to have no criminal record and to be sane. Self-defense is not a valid reason to own a handgun, and recreational uses of handguns are strictly regulated. The penalty for illegal possession is severe— two years' imprisonment. Handguns are present in only 12 percent of Vancouver's homes.

The Seattle-Vancouver study provides strong evidence for the efficacy of gun control. Sloan and his colleagues concluded that the wider proliferation of handguns in Seattle was the sole cause of the higher rate of murders and assaults. The study answered other important questions as well.

Figure 2

Murders per 100,000 People, 1980–1986, by Weapon

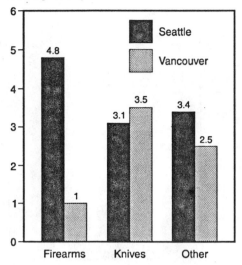

Source: John Henry Sloan, et al., "Handgun Regulations, Crime, Assaults, and Homicide," *The New England Journal of Medicine*, Nov. 10, 1988, pp. 1256–62. Reprinted by permission.

- *Do handguns deter crime?* If handguns deter burglary, the burglary rate in Seattle—where so many more homes have handguns—should have been lower than the burglary rate in Vancouver. But it was not.
- *How often are handguns used for self-defense?* Less than 4 percent of the homicides in both cities resulted from acts of self-defense.
- Perhaps most important: *If handguns are unavailable, will people merely use other weapons instead?* The answer must be "no." Otherwise, the cities would have had similar total murder rates and Vancouver would have had higher rates of homicide with other weapons.

* * *

A more recent study measured gun control legislation more directly.[2] In 1976 the District of Columbia enacted a new gun control law. Residents who lawfully owned firearms had sixty days to reregister them. After the sixty-day period, newly acquired handguns became illegal. Residents could continue to register rifles and shotguns, provided they purchased them from licensed dealers and complied with other regulations.

The researchers compared gun-related violence in the nine years prior to the law's enactment with the following nine years. They also compared the experience within the District with that of the immediately surrounding metropolitan area. The law was, of course, only in force within the boundaries of the District itself and not in contiguous areas of Maryland and Virginia that belong to the same metropolitan area, as the Census Bureau defines it.

The results of the study were surprising even to the most ardent gun control advocates. Within the District, gun-related homicides fell by more than 25 percent and gun-related suicides declined by 23 percent. Meanwhile, there was no statistically significant change in either gun-related homicides or suicides in the adjacent areas. Here again the data demonstrated that people did not switch to other weapons: within the District there was no statistically significant change in either homicides or suicides with other weapons.

Perhaps most surprising of all was the suddenness of the change. Any decline in murders and suicides was expected to be gradual, as the number of weapons in the district slowly shrank. Yet homicides and suicides abruptly declined when the law went into effect. The D.C. law, therefore, had a significant and virtually immediate benefit.

The D.C. study demonstrates that gun control can work in the United States. Despite the similarities between Seattle and Vancouver, some critics of the Sloan study have suggested that Canada and the United States are sufficiently different to make extrapolations questionable. The D.C. study shows that even local gun control laws can be effective in the U.S. Previously, the prevailing opinion was that only national legislation could be effective. Critics said that if local laws blocked handgun purchases, buyers would simply import one from a nearby area. Many people probably do just that, and there is little doubt that national legislation would be far more effective.

Washington D.C.'s gun control law has not transformed the city into a utopia. It has remained a violent city and—along with many other large cities—its murder rate rose sharply in the last few years of the study (1986–88), when the use of "crack" cocaine was increasing. Yet the fact remains that for the full nine-year period after the gun control law was enacted, the mean D.C. murder rate was more than 25 percent lower and its mean suicide rate was 23 percent lower than in the preceding nine years. The effect of the law was not only immediate but sustained as well.

WHY GUN CONTROL WORKS

The gun lobby is fond of saying, "If guns are outlawed, only outlaws will have guns." What's wrong with this picture?

The National Rifle Association (NRA) slogan leads us to envision two groups —solid citizens and hardened criminals —but the real world cannot be neatly divided into good guys and bad guys. Many people are law-abiding citizens until they become inflamed in a domestic dispute, a drunken argument in a bar, even a fender-bender on the highway. Murder is usually an act of rage; it is more often impulsive than premeditated. In fact, 80 percent of all murders occur during altercations and 71 percent involve acquaintances, including lovers, family members, and neighbors. Only 29 percent of those arrested for murder are previously convicted felons.

Rage can pass quickly, but if there is a gun available, even a few seconds may not be soon enough. Of course, enraged lovers and brawlers use other weapons, but it is better to be attacked with anything other than a gun. Guns are, by far, the most lethal weapons. The second deadliest is the knife, but knife attacks result in death only one-fifth as often as those with guns.

For the same reason that it is better to face a knife than a gun in a lover's quarrel, it is better to be robbed at knife point rather than gunpoint. There are good reasons to believe that reducing the number of guns in the general population will reduce them in the hands of muggers and robbers. Prison inmates report that they acquired one-third of their guns by stealing them, typically in home burglaries. There are also people at the margin—not yet career criminals but drifting in that direction—who are more inclined to have guns if they are cheap and readily available. And since handguns are lawful almost everywhere, these people do not even have to cross a psychological Rubicon to get a gun.

* * *

Many of the people at the margin are youngsters. Nearly 70 percent of all serious crimes are committed by boys and young men, ages fourteen to twenty-four. Many of them are not yet career criminals. They are the children of despair, kids from dysfunctional families and impoverished communities who thirst for a feeling of importance. They are angry, immature, and unstable. In the 1950s, they carried switchblades, but since the early 1960s they have increasingly been carrying handguns. Packing a gun makes them feel like men, and it just takes a little alcohol or drugs, a buddy's dare, or a moment of bravado to propel them into their first mugging or holdup of a convenience store. Many juvenile robbers say that they did not intend to commit a robbery when they went out. The nation will be a less dangerous place if these kids go out without guns.

There is a frightening increase in the number of youngsters carrying guns. The National Adolescent Student Health Survey discovered that by 1987, nearly 2 percent of all eighth and tenth graders across the nation said that they carried a gun to school within the past year. A third of those said they took a gun to school with them every day, which translates into more than 100,000 students packing a pistol all the time. In just the first two months of 1992, more than a hundred firearms were confiscated in New York City schools.

And kids are not just carrying guns, they are using them. New York City was shaken earlier this year when, moments before Mayor David Dinkins was to give a speech to the students at Brooklyn's Thomas Jefferson High School, a fifteen-year-old pulled out a Smith & Wesson .38 and killed two other students. Had it not been for the mayor's presence at the school, the shootings might not have been front-page news.

It is somewhat disingenuous to be shocked about youths with handguns.

Kids emulate adults. They live in a society that has not attached a sense of gravity to owning handguns. In half of the fifty states, handguns are completely unregulated; anyone may walk into a gun shop and buy a handgun just as easily as a quart of milk at a grocery. Most of the other states have only modest handgun regulations; four states, for example, have forty-eight hour waiting periods. Except in a very few locales, automobiles are regulated far more rigorously than handguns.

There are 35 million handguns in the United States; a quarter of all homes have at least one handgun in them. We can tell a teenage boy that he is really safer if he does not pack a gun. But why should he believe adults who keep handguns in their nightstand drawers, even though they have been told that a gun in the home is six times more likely to be used to shoot a family member than an intruder?

For more than a decade some observers, such as Charles Silberman, have noted a rising tide of savagery. Today, for example, my morning newspaper carries a report about a robbery at a local McDonald's restaurant. A man with a pistol demanded the restaurant's cash, which the manager immediately gave him. The robber then told the manager and two other employees to lie down, and proceeded to shoot two to death while one of the three ran away. Not long ago it would have been extraordinarily rare for a robber—with the money in his hand—to kill his victims gratuitously; now it seems commonplace. We may wonder what impels someone to top off a robbery with a double murder, but whatever the motive, the handgun makes that act possible.

* * *

We are also witnessing a bewildering escalation in suicides. In 1960 there were about 19,000 suicides in the United States; now there are more than 30,000 each year. (This represents a rise in the suicide rate from 10.6 per 100,000 in 1960 to 12.4 per 100,000 in 1988.) Nearly two-thirds of all suicides in the United States are committed with firearms, more than 80 percent of those with handguns. The rising number of suicides is due almost completely to firearm suicides. While the number of suicides with other weapons has remained relatively stable (even slightly declining over the past two decades), the number of firearm suicides has more than doubled since 1960.

Why should that be so? If someone really wants to kill himself, is he not going to find a way to do so regardless of whether a handgun is available? This is something of a trick question. The rabbit in the hat is the phrase "really wants to kill himself" because suicide, like murder, is often an impulsive act, particularly among the 2,000 to 3,000 American teenagers who commit suicide each year. If an individual contemplating suicide can get through the moment of dark despair, he may reconsider. And if a gun is not available, many potential suicides will resort to a less lethal method, survive, and never attempt suicide again. Nothing is as quick and certain as a gun. The desire to die need only last as long as it takes to pull a trigger, and the decision is irrevocable.

In the Seattle-Vancouver study' the researchers found a 40-percent higher suicide rate among the fifteen- to twenty-five-olds in Seattle, a difference they discovered was due to a firearm suicide rate that is ten times higher among Seattle

adolescents. Other research reveals that a potentially suicidal adolescent is *seventy-five times* as likely to kill himself when there is a gun in the house.[3]

This is the one area, however where the type of gun may not matter. While more than 80 percent of all gun-related suicides are with handguns, research suggests that when handguns are not available, people attempting suicide may just as readily use long guns. But many homes only have a handgun, and reducing the number of homes with handguns will therefore reduce the number of suicides.

WHAT KIND OF GUN CONTROL WORKS?

No one suggests that gun control legislation will be a panacea. Nevertheless, the strong evidence is that the right kind of gun control legislation can reduce murders, suicides, and accidents substantially in the United States.

First and foremost, gun control means controlling handguns. Handguns account for only about one-third of all firearms in general circulation, but they are used in more than 75 percent of all gun-related homicides and more than 80 percent of all gun-related robberies. No other weapon is used nearly so often to murder: While handguns are used in half of all murders in America, knives are used in 18 percent, shotguns in 6 percent, rifles in 4 percent.

Two basic approaches are available to regulate handguns. One is to allow anyone to have a handgun, except for individuals in certain prohibited categories such as convicted felons, the mentally ill, drunkards, and the like. This approach is fatally flawed. The vast majority of people who end up abusing handguns do not have records that place them in a high-risk category. Whenever someone commits a murder, we can in retrospect always say that the murderer was mentally unstable, but it is not easy to check potential handgun purchasers for signs of instability or smoldering rage. There is no test to give. Many mentally unstable individuals have no record of psychiatric treatment and, even if they do, their records are confidential. Because we want to encourage people who need psychological help to seek treatment, legislation that would open psychiatric records to the government or place them in some national data bank would be counterproductive. Moreover, even someone who clearly falls into a prohibited category, such as a convicted felon, can easily circumvent this system by sending a surrogate to purchase a handgun for him.

* * *

The second approach, known as a need-based or a restrictive permitting system, allows only people who fall within certain categories to own handguns. Handgun permits are, of course, issued to law enforcement personnel, but among the general population someone who wants a handgun permit must demonstrate a special need. Simply wanting a handgun for self-defense is not enough, but someone who can provide a sufficiently concrete reason to fear attack would be granted a handgun permit. Sportsmen can obtain special permits, but their handguns must be kept under lock and key at a gun club. It may inconvenience them, but when public safety is balanced against recreation, public safety must win out.

Many states have similar systems for permits to carry a concealed weapon in public, but in the United States only New Jersey and a few cities have true need-based permitting systems for handgun possession. Canada adopted this system nationally in 1978....

Handgun registration should be part of a restrictive permitting system. Owners should be required to register their handguns, and a permanent identification number should be engraved on every handgun. All transfers should be recorded. Everyone who has a driver's license or owns a car understands such a system, and even 78 percent of gun owners in America favor the registration of handguns, according to a 1991 Gallup poll.

* * *

With one exception, long guns do not present the same kind of threat to public safety as handguns. The exception, of course, is assault weapons. We remember how Patrick Purdy fired his AK-47 into a schoolyard in Stockton, California. In less than two minutes, he fired 106 rounds at children and teachers, killing five and wounding twenty-nine.

The NRA argues that it is impossible to differentiate an assault weapon from a standard hunting rifle—and to some extent it is right. Both hunting rifles and the assault weapons that are sold to the general public are semi-automatic. With a semi-automatic, firing repeat rounds requires pulling the trigger back for each one; with an automatic weapon, one must only pull the trigger back once and keep it depressed. This, however, is an inconsequential difference. A thirty-round magazine can be emptied in two seconds with a fully automatic weapon and in five seconds with a semi-automatic.

The way to regulate long guns, therefore, is to limit the size of magazines. Civilians should not be permitted to have magazines that hold more than five rounds. This simply means that after firing five rounds one must stop, remove the empty magazine and either reload it or insert another full magazine. No hunter worth his salt blasts away at a deer as if he were storming the beach at Guadalcanal, and therefore this is no real inconvenience for hunters. But as Patrick Purdy demonstrated with his seventy-five-round magazine in Stockton, large-capacity magazines pose an unreasonable danger to public safety and should not be available to civilians.

The gun lobby urges that instead of regulating handguns (or assault weapons), severe and mandatory penalties should be imposed on persons who violate firearm laws. The weight of the evidence, however, suggests that these laws are not as effective. In 1987, for example, Detroit enacted an ordinance that imposed mandatory jail sentences on persons convicted of unlawfully concealing a handgun or carrying a firearm within the city. The strategy was to allow the general population to keep guns in their homes and offices but to reduce the number of people carrying guns on the streets. After evaluating the law, researchers concluded that, at best, "the ordinance had a relatively small preventive effect on the incidence of homicides in Detroit."[4] The researchers were, in fact, dubious that there was any effect. An analysis of the case histories of more than a thousand persons charged under the ordinance revealed that only 3 percent spent time in prison. With overcrowded jails, judges choose instead to incarcerate people convicted of more serious crimes. This is consistent with other studies of mandatory sentencing laws.[5] ...

* * *

Blame for the failure of gun control is generally laid at the feet of the NRA, but the problem is not so much a zealous minority as it is a quiescent majority. There has not been a sufficiently clear understanding of why the majority of Americans want gun control but do not want it enough to make it a priority in the voting booth. Much effort has been wasted describing the magnitude and horror of gun violence in America. The gun lobby has taken one broadside after another—from television network specials and newsweekly cover stories— all to no avail.

In talking about the horror of gun violence however, the news media are preaching to the converted. Americans are aware of the level of gun violence, and they detest it. But news specials decrying gun violence may unwittingly have the same effect as the entertainment media's glorification of gun violence. They only reinforce a sense of hopelessness. If things could be different, Americans think, they would be. Otherwise, the carnage would not be tolerated. The media portrayals may also have a numbing effect. Research shows that if people are frightened but believe there is no way to escape or to improve conditions, the fear becomes debilitating.

Majority passivity is rooted in the belief that the status quo is immutable. It is this attitude that gun control advocates must try to change, by communicating the evidence that gun control laws do work. Americans know how bad gun violence is; they must now hear the evidence that reducing the violence is possible.

NOTES

1. John Henry Sloan, et al., "Handgun Regulations, Crime, Assaults, and Homicide," *The New England Journal of Medicine*, Nov. 10, 1988, pp. 1256–62.

2. Colin Liftin, et al., "Effects of Restrictive Licensing of Handguns on Homicide and Suicide in the District of Columbia," *The New England Journal of Medicine*, Dec. 5, 1991, pp. 1615–1649.

3. David A. Brent, et al., "The Presence and Accessibility of Firearms in the Homes of Adolescent Suicides," *Journal of the American Medical Association*, Dec. 4, 1991, pp. 2989–93.

4. Patrick W. O'Carroll, "Preventing Homicide: An Evaluation of the Efficacy of a Detroit Gun Ordinance," *American Journal of Public Health*, May 1991, pp. 576–81.

5. Alan Lizotte and Marjorie A. Zatz, "The Use and Abuse of Sentence Enhancement for Firearms Offenses in California," *Law and Contemporary Problems* (1986), pp. 199–221.

NO
Daniel D. Polsby

THE FALSE PROMISE OF GUN CONTROL

During the 1960s and 1970s the robbery rate in the United States increased sixfold, and the murder rate doubled; the rate of handgun ownership nearly doubled in that period as well. Handguns and criminal violence grew together apace, and national opinion leaders did not fall to remark on the coincidence.

It has become a bipartisan article of faith that more handguns cause more violence. Such was the unequivocal conclusion of the National Commission on the Causes and Prevention of Violence in 1969, and such is now the editorial opinion of virtually every influential newspaper and magazine, from *The Washington Post* to *The Economist* to the *Chicago Tribune.* Members of the House and Senate who have not dared to confront the gun lobby concede the connection privately. Even if the National Rifle Association [NRA] can produce blizzards of angry calls and letters to the Capitol virtually overnight, House members one by one have been going public, often after some new firearms atrocity at a fast-food restaurant or the like. And last November they passed the Brady bill.

Alas, however well accepted, the conventional wisdom about guns and violence is mistaken. Guns don't increase national rates of crime and violence —but the continued proliferation of gun-control laws almost certainly does. Current rates of crime and violence are a bit below the peaks of the late 1970s, but because of a slight oncoming bulge in the at-risk population of males aged fifteen to thirty-four, the crime rate will soon worsen. The rising generation of criminals will have no more difficulty than their elders did in obtaining the tools of their trade. Growing violence will lead to calls for laws still more severe. Each fresh round of legislation will be followed by renewed frustration.

Gun-control laws don't work. What is worse, they act perversely. While legitimate users of firearms encounter intense regulation, scrutiny, and bureaucratic control, illicit markets easily adapt to whatever difficulties a free society throws in their way. Also, efforts to curtail the supply of firearms inflict collateral damage on freedom and privacy interests that have long been considered central to American public life. Thanks to the seemingly never-ending war on drugs and long experience attempting to suppress prostitution and pornography, we know a great deal about how illicit markets function and how costly to the public attempts to control them can be. It is essential that we make use of this experience in coming to grips with gun control.

The thousands of gun-control laws in the United States are of two general types. The older kind sought to regulate how, where, and by whom firearms could be carried. More recent laws have sought to make it more costly to buy, sell, or use firearms (or certain classes of firearms, such as assault rifles, Saturday-night specials, and so on) by imposing fees, special taxes, or surtaxes on them. The Brady bill is of both types: it has a background-check provision, and its five-day waiting period amounts to a "time tax" on acquiring handguns. All such laws can be called scarcity-inducing, because they seek to raise the cost of buying firearms, as figured in terms of money, time, nuisance, or stigmatization.

Despite the mounting number of scarcity-inducing laws, no one is very satisfied with them. Hobbyists want to get rid of them, and gun-control proponents don't think they go nearly far enough. Everyone seems to agree that gun-control laws have some effect on the distribution of firearms. But it has not been the dramatic and measurable effect their proponents desired.

Opponents of gun control have traditionally wrapped their arguments in the Second Amendment to the Constitution. Indeed, most modern scholarship affirms that so far as the drafters of the Bill of Rights were concerned the right to bear arms was to be enjoyed by everyone, not just a militia, and that one of the principal justifications for an armed populace was to secure the tranquillity and good order of the community. But most people are not dedicated antiquitarians, and would not be impressed by the argument "I admit that my behavior is very dangerous to public safety, but the Second Amendment says I have a right to do it anyway." That would be a case for repealing the Second Amendment, not respecting it.

FIGHTING THE DEMAND CURVE

Everyone knows that possessing a handgun makes it easier to intimidate, wound, or kill someone. But the implication of this point for social policy has not been so well understood. It is easy to count the bodies of those who have been killed or wounded with guns, but not easy to count the people who have avoided harm because they had access to weapons. Think about uniformed police officers, who carry handguns in plain view not in order to kill people but simply to daunt potential attackers. And it works. Criminals generally do not single out police officers for opportunistic attack. Though officers can expect to draw their guns from time to time, few even in big-city departments will actually fire a shot (except in target practice) in the course of a year. This observation points to an important truth: people who are armed make comparatively unattractive victims. A criminal might not know if any one civilian is armed, but if it becomes known that a large number of civilians do carry weapons, criminals will become warier.

Which weapons laws are the right kinds can be decided only after considering two related questions. First, what is the connection between civilian possession of firearms and social violence? Second, how can we expect gun-control laws to alter people's behavior? Most recent scholarship raises serious questions about the "weapons increase violence" hypothesis. The second question is emphasized here, because it is routinely overlooked and often mocked when noticed; yet it is crucial. Rational gun control requires understanding not only the relationship between weapons and violence but also the relationship between laws and people's behavior. Some things are very hard to accomplish with laws. The purpose of a law and its likely effects are not always the same thing. Many statutes are notorious for the way in which their unintended effects have swamped their intended ones.

In order to predict who will comply with gun-control laws, we should remember that guns are economic goods that are traded in markets. Consumers' interest in them varies. For religious, moral, aesthetic, or practical reasons, some people would refuse to buy firearms at any price. Other people willingly pay very high prices for them.

Handguns, so often the subject of gun-control laws, are desirable for one purpose—to allow a person tactically to dominate a hostile transaction with another person. The value of a weapon to a given person is a function of two factors: how much he or she wants to dominate a confrontation if one occurs, and how likely it is that he or she will actually be in a situation calling for a gun.

Dominating a transaction simply means getting what one wants without being hurt. Where people differ is in how likely it is that they will be involved in a situation in which a gun will be valuable. Someone who *intends* to engage in a transaction involving a gun—a criminal, for example—is obviously in the best possible position to predict that likelihood. Criminals should therefore be will-

ing to pay more for a weapon than most other people would. Professors, politicians, and newspaper editors are, as a group, at very low risk of being involved in such transactions, and they thus systematically underrate the value of defensive handguns. (Correlative, perhaps, is their uncritical readiness to accept studies that debunk the utility of firearms for self-defense.) The class of people we wish to deprive of guns, then, is the very class with the most inelastic demand for them —criminals—whereas the people most likely to comply with gun-control laws don't value guns in the first place.

DO GUNS DRIVE UP CRIME RATES?

Which premise is true—that guns increase crime or that the fear of crime causes people to obtain guns? Most of the country's major newspapers apparently take this problem to have been solved by an article published by Arthur Kellermann and several associates in the October 7, 1993, *New England Journal of Medicine*. Kellermann is an emergency-room physician who has published a number of influential papers that he believes discredit the thesis that private ownership of firearms is a useful means of self-protection. (An indication of his wide influence is that within two months the study received almost 100 mentions in publications and broadcast transcripts indexed in the Nexis data base.) For this study Kellermann and his associates identified fifteen behavioral and fifteen environmental variables that applied to a 388-member set of homicide victims, found a "matching" control group of 388 nonhomicide victims, and then ascertained how the two groups differed in gun ownership. In interviews Kellermann made clear his belief that owning a handgun markedly increases a person's risk of being murdered.

But the study does not prove that point at all. Indeed, as Kellermann explicitly conceded in the text of the article, the causal arrow may very well point in the other direction: the threat of being killed may make people more likely to arm themselves. Many people at risk of being killed, especially people involved in the drug trade or other illegal ventures, might well rationally buy a gun as a precaution, and be willing to pay a price driven up by gun-control laws. Crime, after all, is a dangerous business. Peter Reuter and Mark Kleiman, drug-policy researchers, calculated in 1987 that the average crack dealer's risk of being killed was far greater than his risk of being sent to prison. (Their data cannot, however, support the implication that ownership of a firearm causes or exacerbates the risk of being killed.)

Defending the validity of his work, Kellermann has emphasized that the link between lung cancer and smoking was initially established by studies method- ologically no different from his. Gary Kleck, a criminology professor at Florida State University, has pointed out the flaw in this comparison. No one ever thought that lung cancer causes smoking, so when the association between the two was es- tablished the direction of the causal arrow was not in doubt. Kleck wrote that it is as though Kellermann, trying to discover how diabetics differ from other people, found that they are much more likely to possess insulin than nondiabetics, and concluded that insulin is a risk factor for diabetes.

The New York Times, the *Los Angeles Times*, *The Washington Post*, *The Boston Globe*, and the *Chicago Tribune* all gave prominent coverage to Kellermann's study as soon as it appeared, but none saw fit to discuss the study's limitations. A few, in order to introduce a hint of balance, mentioned that the NRA, or some member of its staff, disagreed with the study. But readers had no way of knowing that Kellermann himself had registered a disclaimer in his text. "It is possible," he conceded. "that reverse causation accounted for some of the association we observed between gun ownership and homicide." Indeed, the point is stronger than that: "reverse causation" may account for *most* of the association between gun ownership and homicide. Kellermann's data simply do not allow one to draw any conclusion.

If firearms increased violence and crime, then rates of spousal homicide would have skyrocketed, because the stock of privately owned handguns has increased rapidly since the mid-1960s. But according to an authoritative study of spousal homicide in the *American Journal of Public Health,* by James Mercy and Linda Saltzman, rates of spousal homicide in the years 1976 to 1985 fell. If firearms increased violence and crime, the crime rate should have increased throughout the 1980s, while the national stock of privately owned handguns increased by more than a million units in every year of the decade. It did not. Nor should the rates of violence and crime in Switzerland, New Zealand, and Israel be as low as they are, since the number of firearms per civilian household is comparable to that in the United States. Conversely, gun-controlled Mexico and South Africa should be islands of peace instead of having murder rates more than twice as high as those [in the United States]. The determinants of crime and law-abidingness are, of course, complex matters, which are not fully understood and certainly not explicable in terms of a country's laws. But gun-control enthusiasts, who have made capital out of the low murder rate in England, which is largely disarmed, simply ignore the counterexamples that don't fit their theory.

If firearms increased violence and crime, Florida's murder rate should not have been falling since the introduction, seven years ago, of a law that makes it easier for ordinary citizens to get permits to carry concealed handguns. Yet the murder rate has remained the same or fallen every year since the law was enacted, and it is now lower than the national murder rate (which has been rising). As of last November 183,561 permits had been issued, and only seventeen of the permits had been revoked because the holder was involved in a firearms offense. It would be precipitate to claim that the new law has "caused" the murder rate to subside. Yet here is a situation that doesn't fit the hypothesis that weapons increase violence.

If firearms increased violence and crime, programs of induced scarcity would suppress violence and crime. But —another anomaly—they don't. Why not? A theorem, which we could call the futility theorem, explains why gun-control laws must either be ineffectual or in the long term actually provoke more violence and crime. Any theorem depends on both observable fact and assumption. An assumption that can be made with confidence is that the higher the number of victims a criminal assumes to be armed, the higher will be the risk—the price—of assaulting them. By definition, gun-control laws should make weapons scarcer and thus more expensive. By our prior reasoning about

demand among various types of consumers, after the laws are enacted criminals should be better armed, compared with noncriminals, than they were before. Of course, plenty of noncriminals will remain armed. But even if many noncriminals will pay as high a price as criminals will to obtain firearms, a larger number will not.

Criminals will thus still take the same gamble they already take in assaulting a victim who might or might not be armed. But they may appreciate that the laws have given them a freer field, and that crime still pays—pays even better, in fact, than before. What will happen to the rate of violence? Only a relatively few gun-mediated transactions —currently, five percent of armed robberies committed with firearms—result in someone's actually being shot (the statistics are not broken down into encounters between armed assailants and unarmed victims, and encounters in which both parties are armed). It seems reasonable to fear that if the number of such transactions were to increase because criminals thought they faced fewer deterrents, there would be a corresponding increase in shootings. Conversely, if gun-mediated transactions declined—if criminals initiated fewer of them because they feared encountering an armed victim or an armed good Samaritan—the number of shootings would go down. The magnitude of these effects is, admittedly, uncertain. Yet it is hard to doubt the general tendency of a change in the law that imposes legal burdens on buying guns. The futility theorem suggests that gun-control laws, if effective at all, would unfavorably affect the rate of violent crime.

The futility theorem provides a lens through which to see much of the debate. It is undeniable that gun-control laws work—to an extent. Consider, for example, California's background-check law, which in the past two years has prevented about 12,000 people with a criminal record or a history of mental illness or drug abuse from buying handguns. In the same period Illinois's background-check law prevented the delivery of firearms to more than 2,000 people. Surely some of these people simply turned to an illegal market, but just as surely not all of them did. The laws of large numbers allow us to say that among the foiled thousands, some potential killers were prevented from getting a gun. We do not know whether the number is large or small, but it is implausible to think it is zero. And, as gun-control proponents are inclined to say, "If only one life is saved..."

The hypothesis that firearms increase violence does predict that if we can slow down the diffusion of guns, there will be less violence; one life, or more, *will* be saved. But the futility theorem asks that we look not simply at the gross number of bad actors prevented from getting guns but at the effect the law has on *all* the people who want to buy a gun. Suppose we succeed in piling tax burdens on the acquisition of firearms. We can safely assume that a number of people who might use guns to kill will be sufficiently discouraged not to buy them. But we cannot assume this about people who feel that they must have guns in order to survive financially and physically. A few lives might indeed be saved. But the overall rate of violent crime might not go down at all. And if guns are owned predominantly by people who have good reason to think they will use them, the rate might even go up.

Are there empirical studies that can serve to help us choose between the futility theorem and the hypothesis that guns increase violence? Unfortunately, no: the best studies of the effects of gun-control laws are quite inconclusive. Our statistical tools are too weak to allow us to identify an effect clearly enough to persuade an open-minded skeptic. But it is precisely when we are dealing with undetectable statistical effects that we have to be certain we are using the best models available of human behavior....

ADMINISTERING PROHIBITION

Assume for the sake of argument that to a reasonable degree of criminological certainty, guns are every bit the public-health hazard they are said to be. It follows, and many journalists and a few public officials have already said, that we ought to treat guns the same way we do smallpox viruses or other critical vectors of morbidity and mortality—namely, isolate them from potential hosts and destroy them as speedily as possible. Clearly, firearms have at least one characteristic that distinguishes them from smallpox viruses: nobody wants to keep smallpox viruses in the nightstand drawer. Amazingly enough, gun-control literature seems never to have explored the problem of getting weapons away from people who very much want to keep them in the nightstand drawer.

Our existing gun-control laws are not uniformly permissive, and, indeed, in certain places are tough even by international standards. Advocacy groups seldom stress the considerable differences among American jurisdictions, and media reports regularly assert that firearms are readily available to anybody anywhere in the country. This is not the case. For example, handgun restrictions in Chicago and the District of Columbia are much less flexible than the ones in the United Kingdom. Several hundred thousand British subjects may legally buy and possess sidearms, and anyone who joins a target-shooting club is eligible to do so. But in Chicago and the District of Columbia, excepting peace officers and the like, only grandfathered registrants may legally possess handguns. Of course, tens or hundreds of thousands of people in both those cities—nobody can be sure how many—do in fact possess them illegally.

Although there is, undoubtedly, illegal handgun ownership in the United Kingdom, especially in Northern Ireland (where considerations of personal security and public safety are decidedly unlike those elsewhere in the British Isles), it is probable that Americans and Britons differ in their disposition to obey gun-control laws: there is reputed to be a marked national disparity in compliance behavior. This difference, if it exists, may have something to do with the comparatively marginal value of firearms to British consumers. Even before it had strict firearms regulation, Britain had very low rates of crimes involving guns; British criminals, unlike their American counterparts, prefer burglary (a crime of stealth) to robbery (a crime of intimidation).

Unless people are prepared to surrender their guns voluntarily, how can the U.S. government confiscate an appreciable fraction of our country's nearly 200 million privately owned firearms? We know that it is possible to set up weapons-free zones in certain locations —commercial airports and many courthouses and, lately, some troubled big-city high schools and housing projects. The sacrifices of privacy and convenience, and the costs of paying guards, have been thought worth the (perceived) gain in security. No doubt it would be possible, though it would probably not be easy, to make weapons-free zones of shopping centers, department stores, movie theaters, ball parks. But it is not obvious how one would cordon off the whole of an open society.

Voluntary programs have been ineffectual. From time to time community-action groups or police departments have sponsored "turn in your gun" days, which are nearly always disappointing. Sometimes the government offers to buy guns at some price. This approach has been endorsed by Senator Chafee and the *Los Angeles Times*. Jonathan Alter, of *Newsweek*, has suggested a variation on this theme: youngsters could exchange their guns for a handshake with Michael Jordan or some other sports hero. If the price offered exceeds that at which a gun can be bought on the street, one can expect to see plans of this kind yield some sort of harvest—as indeed they have. But it is implausible that these schemes will actually result in a less-dangerous population. Government programs to buy up surplus cheese cause more cheese to be produced without affecting the availability of cheese to people who want to buy it. So it is with guns....

The solution to the problem of crime lies in improving the chances of young men. Easier said than done, to be sure. No one has yet proposed a convincing program for checking all the dislocating forces that government assistance can set in motion. One relatively straightforward change would be reform of the educational system. Nothing guarantees prudent behavior like a sense of the future, and with average skills in reading, writing, and math, young people can realistically look forward to constructive employment and the straight life that steady work makes possible.

But firearms are nowhere near the root of the problem of violence. As long as people come in unlike sizes, shapes, ages, and temperaments, as long as they diverge in their taste for risk and their willingness and capacity to prey on other people or to defend themselves from predation, and above all as long as some people have little or nothing to lose by spending their lives in crime, dispositions to violence will persist.

This is what makes the case for the right to bear arms, not the Second Amendment. It is foolish to let anything ride on hopes for effective gun control. As long as crime pays as well as it does, we will have plenty of it, and honest folk must choose between being victims and defending themselves.

POSTSCRIPT

Do We Need Tougher Gun Control Laws?

The Constitution's Second Amendment reads: "A well regulated Militia, being necessary to the security of a free State, the right of the people to keep and bear Arms, shall not be infringed." At the time this was written, a clear right to bear arms existed in England. Alexander Hamilton referred to the people as the "unorganized militia," and even some scholars today who favor gun control think that it violates the Second Amendment. Nevertheless, the Supreme Court has stated and reaffirmed that the amendment "guarantees no right to keep and bear a firearm that does not have some reasonable relationship to the preservation or efficiency of a well-regulated militia."

As far back as 1976, Barry Bruce-Briggs anticipated some of the arguments made by Polsby. See "The Great American Gun War," *The Public Interest* (Fall 1976). For a similar view, see Don B. Kates, Jr., *Restricting Handguns: The Liberal Skeptics Speak Out* (North River Press, 1979). Neal Bernards, *Gun Control* (Lucent Books, 1991) and David E. Newton, *Gun Control: An Issue for the Nineties* (Enslow Publications, 1992) are both attempts to summarize fairly the chief arguments for and against gun control. To put the issue of guns in a larger historical perspective, readers may wish to examine the impact of the American frontier, with its gun-slinging heroes and villains, on modern American culture. Richard Slotkin's *Gunfighter Nation* (Atheneum, 1992) is an illuminating study of this enduring American myth.

It is difficult to predict the future of gun control in the United States. Advocates have been much encouraged by their victories in 1993 and 1994, but the gun lobby is now in a position to say that enough is enough. As it is, these victories were hard won. The opposition of southern and western Democrats to the assault weapons ban in the crime bill was so adamant that Democratic president Bill Clinton was forced to appeal to Republicans for support. It was a handful of Republican moderates who provided the remaining votes to get the crime bill passed. And they may yet suffer for it. The gun lobby, which can flood congressional offices with mail, faxes, and phone calls, remains a force to be reckoned with.

ISSUE 12

Is Affirmative Action Reverse Discrimination?

YES: Shelby Steele, from *The Content of Our Character* (St. Martin's Press, 1990)

NO: Stanley Fish, from "Reverse Racism, or How the Pot Got to Call the Kettle Black," *The Atlantic Monthly* (November 1993)

ISSUE SUMMARY

YES: Associate professor of English Shelby Steele argues that affirmative action demoralizes both blacks and whites and that racial preferences do not empower blacks.

NO: Professor of law Stanley Fish asserts that affirmative action is justified as a remedy for the effects of past discrimination because it ultimately eliminates the advantages that whites have historically held over blacks.

"We didn't land on Plymouth Rock, my brothers and sisters—Plymouth Rock landed on *us!*" Malcolm X's observation is borne out by the facts of American history. Snatched from their native land, transported thousands of miles—in a nightmare of disease and death—and sold into slavery, blacks were reduced to the legal status of farm animals. Even after emancipation, blacks were segregated from whites—in some states by law, and by social practice almost everywhere. American apartheid continued for another century.

In 1954 the Supreme Court declared state-compelled segregation in schools unconstitutional, and it followed up that decision with others that struck down many forms of official segregation. Still, discrimination survived, and in most southern states blacks were either discouraged or prohibited from exercising their right to vote. Not until the 1960s was compulsory segregation finally and effectively challenged. Between 1964 and 1968 Congress passed the most sweeping civil rights legislation since the end of the Civil War. It banned discrimination in employment, public accommodations (hotels, motels, restaurants, etc.), and housing; it also guaranteed voting rights for blacks and even authorized federal officials to take over the job of voter registration in areas suspected of disenfranchising blacks. Today, several agencies in the federal government exercise sweeping powers to enforce these civil rights measures.

But is that enough? Equality of condition between blacks and whites seems as elusive as ever. The black unemployment rate is double that of whites, and the percentage of black families living in poverty is nearly four times that of whites. Only a small percentage of blacks ever make it into medical school or law school.

Advocates of affirmative action have focused upon these *de facto* differences to bolster their argument that it is no longer enough just to stop discrimination. The damage done by three centuries of racism now has to be remedied, they argue, and effective remediation requires a policy of "affirmative action." At the heart of affirmative action is the use of "numerical goals." Opponents call them "racial quotas." Whatever the name, what they imply is the setting aside of a certain number of jobs or positions for blacks or other historically oppressed groups. Opponents charge that affirmative action really amounts to reverse discrimination, that it penalizes innocent people simply because they are white, that it often results in unqualified appointments, and that it ends up harming instead of helping blacks.

Affirmative action has had an uneven history in U.S. federal courts. In *Regents of the University of California v. Allan Bakke* (1978), which marked the first time the Supreme Court directly dealt with the merits of affirmative action, a 5–4 majority ruled that a white applicant to a medical school had been wrongly excluded due to the school's affirmative action policy; yet the majority also agreed that "race-conscious" policies may be used in admitting candidates—as long as they do not amount to fixed quotas. The ambivalence of *Bakke* has run through the Court's treatment of the issue since 1978. Decisions have gone one way or the other depending on the precise circumstances of the case (such as whether it was a federal or state policy, whether or not it was mandated by a congressional statute, and whether quotas were required or simply permitted). In recent years, however, most of the Court's decisions seem to have run against affirmative action programs.

In the following selections, Shelby Steele contends that affirmative action has not solved the problem of inequality but has simply resulted in a kind of reverse racism, while Stanley Fish contends that such programs are necessary to undo the damage caused by centuries of slavery and segregation.

YES
Shelby Steele

AFFIRMATIVE ACTION: THE PRICE OF PREFERENCE

[I]n theory, affirmative action certainly has all the moral symmetry that fairness requires—the injustice of historical and even contemporary white advantage is offset with black advantage; preference replaces prejudice, inclusion answers exclusion. It is reformist and corrective, even repentant and redemptive. And I would never sneer at these good intentions. Born in the late forties in Chicago, I started my education (a charitable term in this case) in a segregated school and suffered all the indignities that come to blacks in a segregated society. My father, born in the South, only made it to the third grade before the white man's fields took permanent priority over his formal education. And though he educated himself into an advanced reader with an almost professorial authority, he could only drive a truck for a living and never earned more than ninety dollars a week in his entire life. So yes, it is crucial to my sense of citizenship, to my ability to identify with the spirit and the interests of America, to know that this country, however imperfectly, recognizes its past sins and wishes to correct them.

Yet good intentions, because of the opportunity for innocence they offer us, are very seductive and can blind us to the effects they generate when implemented. In our society, affirmative action is, among other things, a testament to white goodwill and to black power, and in the midst of these heavy investments, its effects can be hard to see. But after twenty years of implementation, I think affirmative action has shown itself to be more bad than good and that blacks—whom I will focus on in this essay—now stand to lose more from it than they gain.

In talking with affirmative action administrators and with blacks and whites in general, it is clear that supporters of affirmative action focus on its good intentions while detractors emphasize its negative effects. Proponents talk about "diversity" and "pluralism"; opponents speak of "reverse discrimination," the unfairness of quotas and set-asides. It was virtually impossible to find people outside either camp. The closest I came was a white male manager at a large computer company who said, "I think it amounts to reverse discrimination, but I'll put up with a little of that for a little more diversity." I'll live with a little of the effect to gain a little of the intention, he seemed to be saying. But this only makes him a halfhearted supporter of affirmative action. I think many people who don't really like affirmative action support it to one degree or another anyway.

I believe they do this because of what happened to white and black Americans in the crucible of the sixties when whites were confronted with their racial guilt and blacks tasted their first real power. In this stormy time white absolution and black power coalesced into virtual mandates for society. Affirmative action became a meeting ground for these mandates in the law, and in the late sixties and early seventies it underwent a remarkable escalation of its mission from simple anti-discrimination enforcement to social engineering by means of quotas, goals, timetables, set-asides and other forms of preferential treatment.

Legally, this was achieved through a series of executive orders and EEOC [Equal Employment Opportunity Commission] guidelines that allowed racial imbalances in the workplace to stand as proof of racial discrimination. Once it could be assumed that discrimination explained racial imbalances, it became easy to justify group remedies to presumed discrimination, rather than the normal case-by-case redress for proven discrimination. Preferential treatment through quotas, goals, and so on is designed to correct imbalances based on the assumption that they always indicate discrimination. This expansion of what constitutes discrimination allowed affirmative action to escalate into the business of social engineering in the name of anti-discrimination, to push society toward statistically proportionate racial representation, without any obligation of proving actual discrimination.

What accounted for this shift, I believe, was the white mandate to achieve a new racial innocence and the black mandate to gain power. Even though blacks had made great advances during the sixties without quotas, these mandates, which came to a head in the very late sixties, could no longer be satisfied by anything less than racial preferences. I don't think these mandates in themselves were wrong, since whites clearly needed to do better by blacks and blacks needed more real power in society. But, as they came together in affirmative action, their effect was to distort our understanding of racial discrimination in a way that allowed us to offer the remediation of preference on the basis of mere color rather than actual injury. By making black the color of preference, these mandates have reburdened society with the very marriage of color and preference (in reverse) that we set out to eradicate. The old sin is reaffirmed in a new guise.

But the essential problem with this form of affirmative action is the way it leaps over the hard business of developing a formerly oppressed people to the point where they can achieve proportionate representation on their own (given equal opportunity) and goes straight for the proportionate representation. This may satisfy some whites of their innocence and some blacks of their power, but it does very little to truly uplift blacks.

A white female affirmative action officer at an Ivy League university told me what many supporters of affirmative action now say: "We're after diversity. We ideally want a student body where racial and ethnic groups are represented according to their proportion in society." When affirmative action escalated into social engineering, diversity became a golden word. It grants whites an egalitarian fairness (innocence) and blacks an entitlement to proportionate representation (power). *Diversity* is a term that applies democratic principles to races and cultures rather than to citizens, despite the fact that there is nothing to indicate that real diversity is the same thing as proportionate representation. Too often the result of this on campuses (for example) has been a democracy of colors rather than of people, an artificial diversity that gives the appearance of an educational parity between black and white students that has not yet been achieved in reality. Here again, racial preferences allow society to leapfrog over the difficult problem of developing blacks to parity with whites and into a cosmetic diversity that covers the blemish of disparity—a full six years after admission, only about 26 percent of black students graduate from college.

Racial representation is not the same thing as racial development, yet affirmative action fosters a confusion of these very different needs. Representation can be manufactured; development is always hard-earned. However, it is the music of innocence and power that we hear in affirmative action that causes us to cling to it and to its distracting emphasis on representation. The fact is that after twenty years of racial preferences, the gap between white and black median income is greater than it was in the seventies. None of this is to say that blacks don't need policies that ensure our right to equal opportunity, but what we need more is the development that will let us take advantage of society's efforts to include us.

I think that one of the most troubling effects of racial preferences for blacks is a kind of demoralization, or put another way, an enlargement of self-doubt. Under affirmative action the quality that earns us preferential treatment is an implied inferiority. However this inferiority is explained—and it is easily enough explained by the myriad deprivations that grew out of our oppression—it is still inferiority. There are explanations, and then there is the fact. And the fact must be borne by the individual as a condition apart from the explanation, apart even from the fact that others like himself also bear this condition. In integrated situations where blacks must compete with whites who may be better prepared, these explanations may quickly wear thin and expose the individual to racial as well as personal self-doubt.

All of this is compounded by the cultural myth of black inferiority that blacks have always lived with. What this means in practical terms is that when blacks deliver themselves into integrated situations, they encounter a nasty little reflex in whites, a mindless, atavistic reflex that responds to the color black with alarm. Attributions may follow this alarm if the white cares to indulge them, and if they do, they will most likely be negative—one such attribution is intellectual ineptness. I think this reflex and the attributions that may follow it embarrass most whites today, therefore, it is usually quickly repressed. Nevertheless, on an equally atavistic level, the black will be aware of the reflex his color triggers and will feel a stab of horror at seeing himself reflected in this way. He, too, will do a quick repression, but a lifetime of such stabbings is what constitutes his inner realm of racial doubt.

The effects of this may be a subject for another essay. The point here is that the implication of inferiority that racial preferences engender in both the white and black mind expands rather than contracts this doubt. Even when the black sees no implication of inferiority in racial preferences, he knows that whites do, so that—consciously or unconsciously—the result is virtually the same. The effect of preferential treatment —the lowering of normal standards to increase black representation—puts blacks at war with an expanded realm of debilitating doubt, so that the doubt itself becomes an unrecognized preoccupation that undermines their ability to perform, especially in integrated situations. On largely white campuses, blacks are five times more likely to drop out than whites. Preferential treatment, no matter how it is justified in the light of day, subjects blacks to a midnight of self-doubt, and so often transforms their advantage into a revolving door.

Another liability of affirmative action comes from the fact that it indirectly encourages blacks to exploit their own past victimization as a source of power and privilege. Victimization, like implied inferiority, is what justifies preference, so that to receive the benefits of preferential treatment one must, to some extent, become invested in the view of one's self as a victim. In this way, affirmative action nurtures a victim-focused identity in blacks. The obvious irony here is that we become inadvertently invested in the very condition we are trying to overcome. Racial preferences send us the message that there is more power in our past suffering than our present achievements —none of which could bring us a *preference* over others.

When power itself grows out of suffering, then blacks are encouraged to expand the boundaries of what qualifies as racial oppression, a situation that can lead us to paint our victimization in vivid colors, even as we receive the benefits of preference. The same corporations and institutions that give us preference are also seen as our oppressors. At Stanford University minority students— some of whom enjoy as much as $15,000 a year in financial aid—recently took over the president's office demanding, among other things, more financial aid. The power to be found in victimization, like any power, is intoxicating and can lend itself to the creation of a new class of super-victims who can feel the pea of victimization under twenty mattresses. Preferential treatment rewards us for being underdogs rather than for moving beyond that status—a misplacement of incentives that, along with its deepening of our doubt, is more a yoke than a spur.

But, I think, one of the worst prices that blacks pay for preference has to do with an illusion. I saw this illusion at work recently in the mother of a middle-class black student who was going off to his first semester of college. "They owe us this, so don't think for a minute that you don't belong there." This is the logic by which many blacks, and some whites, justify affirmative action —it is something "owed," a form of reparation. But this logic overlooks a much harder and less digestible reality, that it is impossible to repay blacks living today for the historic suffering of the race. If all blacks were given a million dollars tomorrow morning it would not amount to a dime on the dollar of three centuries of oppression, nor would it obviate the residues of that oppression that we still carry today. The concept of historic reparation grows out of man's need to impose a degree of justice on the world that simply does not exist. Suffering can be endured and overcome, it cannot be repaid. Blacks cannot be repaid for the injustice done to the race, but we can be corrupted by society's guilty gestures of repayment.

Affirmative action is such a gesture. It tells us that racial preferences can do for us what we cannot do for ourselves. The corruption here is in the hidden incentive *not* to do what we believe preferences will do. This is an incentive to be reliant on others just as we are struggling for self-reliance. And it keeps alive the illusion that we can find some deliverance in repayment. The hardest thing for any sufferer to accept is that his suffering excuses him from very little and never has enough currency to restore him. To think otherwise is to prolong the suffering.

Several blacks I spoke with said they were still in favor of affirmative action because of the "subtle" discrimination blacks were subject to once on the job. One photojournalist said, "They have ways of ignoring you." A black female television producer said, "You can't file a lawsuit when your boss doesn't invite you to the insider meetings without ruining your career. So we still need affirmative action." Others mentioned the infamous "glass ceiling" through which blacks can see the top positions of authority but never reach them. But I don't think racial preferences are a protection against this subtle discrimination; I think they contribute to it.

In any workplace, racial preferences will always create two-tiered populations composed of preferreds and unpreferreds. This division makes automatic a perception of enhanced competence for the unpreferreds and of questionable competence for the preferreds—the former earned his way, even though others were given preference, while the latter made it by color as much as by competence. Racial preferences implicitly mark whites with an exaggerated superiority just as they mark blacks with an exaggerated inferiority. They not only reinforce America's oldest racial myth but, for blacks, they have the effect of stigmatizing the already stigmatized.

I think that much of the "subtle" discrimination that blacks talk about is often (not always) discrimination against the stigma of questionable competence that affirmative action delivers to blacks. In this sense, preferences scapegoat the very people they seek to help. And it may be that at a certain level employers impose a glass ceiling, but this may not be against the race so much as against the race's reputation for having advanced by color as much as by competence. Affirmative action makes a glass ceiling virtually necessary as a protection against the corruptions of preferential treatment. This ceiling is the point at which corporations shift the emphasis from color to competency and stop playing the affirmative action game. Here preference backfires for blacks and becomes a taint that holds them back. Of course, one could argue that this taint, which is, after all, in the minds of whites, becomes nothing more than an excuse to discriminate against blacks. And certainly the result is the same in either case—blacks don't get past the glass ceiling. But this argument does not get around the fact that racial preferences now taint this color with a new theme of suspicion that makes it even more vulnerable to the impulse in others to discriminate. In this crucial yet gray area of perceived competence, preferences make whites look better than they are and blacks worse, while doing nothing whatever to stop the very real discrimination that blacks may encounter. I don't wish to justify the glass ceiling here, but only to suggest the very subtle ways that affirmative action revives rather than extinguishes the old rationalizations for racial discrimination.

In education, a revolving door; in employment, a glass ceiling.

I believe affirmative action is problematic in our society because it tries to function like a social program. Rather than ask it to ensure equal opportunity we have demanded that it create parity between the races. But preferential treatment does not teach skills, or educate, or instill motivation. It only passes out entitlement by color, a situation that in my profession has created an unrealistically high demand for black professors. The social engineer's assumption is that this high demand will inspire more blacks to earn Ph.D.'s and join the profession. In fact, the number of blacks earning Ph.D.'s has declined in recent years. A Ph.D. must be developed from preschool on. He requires family and community support. He must acquire an entire system of values that enables him to work hard while delaying gratification. There are social programs, I believe, that can (and should) help blacks *develop* in all these areas, but entitlement by color is not a social program; it is a dubious reward for being black. . . .

Preferences are inexpensive and carry the glamour of good intentions—change the numbers and the good deed is done. To be against them is to be unkind. But I think the unkindest cut is to bestow on children like my own an undeserved advantage while neglecting the development of those disadvantaged children on the East Side of my city who will likely never be in a position to benefit from a preference. Give my children fairness; give disadvantaged children a better shot at development—better elementary and secondary schools, job training, safer neighborhoods, better financial assistance for college, and so on. Fewer blacks go to college today than ten years ago; more black males of college age are in prison or under the control of the criminal justice system than in college. This despite racial preferences.

The mandates of black power and white absolution out of which preferences emerged were not wrong in themselves. What was wrong was that both races focused more on the goals of these mandates than on the means of the goals. Blacks can have no real power without taking responsibility for their own educational and economic development. Whites can have no racial innocence without earning it by eradicating discrimination and helping the disadvantaged to develop. Because we ignored the means, the goals have not been reached, and the real work remains to be done.

NO

Stanley Fish

REVERSE RACISM, OR HOW THE POT GOT TO CALL THE KETTLE BLACK

I take my text from George Bush, who, in an address to the United Nations on September 23, 1991, said this of the UN resolution equating Zionism with racism: "Zionism... is the idea that led to the creation of a home for the Jewish people.... And to equate Zionism with the intolerable sin of racism is to twist history and forget the terrible plight of Jews in World War II and indeed throughout history." What happened in the Second World War was that six million Jews were exterminated by people who regarded them as racially inferior and a danger to Aryan purity. What happened after the Second World War was that the survivors of that Holocaust established a Jewish state—that is, a state centered on Jewish history, Jewish values, and Jewish traditions: in short, a Jewocentric state. What President Bush objected to was the logical sleight of hand by which these two actions were declared equivalent because they were both expressions of racial exclusiveness. Ignored, as Bush said, was the *historical* difference between them—the difference between a program of genocide and the determination of those who escaped it to establish a community in which they would be the makers, not the victims, of the laws.

Only if racism is thought of as something that occurs principally in the mind, a falling-away from proper notions of universal equality, can the desire of a victimized and terrorized people to band together be declared morally identical to the actions of their would-be executioners. Only when the actions of the two groups are detached from the historical conditions of their emergence and given a purely abstract description can they be made interchangeable. Bush was saying to the United Nations, "Look, the Nazis' conviction of racial superiority generated a policy of systematic genocide; the Jews' experience of centuries of persecution in almost every country on earth generated a desire for a homeland of their own. If you manage somehow to convince yourself that these are the same, it is you, not the Zionists, who are morally confused, and the reason you are morally

From Stanley Fish, "Reverse Racism, or How the Pot Got to Call the Kettle Black," *The Atlantic Monthly* (November 1993). Adapted from Stanley Fish, *There Is No Such Thing as Free Speech and It's a Good Thing, Too* (Oxford University Press, 1994). Copyright © 1994 by Stanley Fish. Reprinted by permission of Oxford University Press.

confused is that you have forgotten history."

A KEY DISTINCTION

What I want to say, following Bush's reasoning, is that a similar forgetting of history has in recent years allowed some people to argue, and argue persuasively, that affirmative action is reverse racism. The very phrase "reverse racism" contains the argument in exactly the form to which Bush objected: In this country whites once set themselves apart from blacks and claimed privileges for themselves while denying them to others. Now, on the basis of race, blacks are claiming special status and reserving for themselves privileges they deny to others. Isn't one as bad as the other? The answer is no. One can see why by imagining that it is not 1993 but 1955, and that we are in a town in the South with two more or less distinct communities, one white and one black. No doubt each community would have a ready store of dismissive epithets, ridiculing stories, self-serving folk myths, and expressions of plain hatred, all directed at the other community, and all based in racial hostility. Yet to regard their respective racisms— if that is the word—as equivalent would be bizarre, for the hostility of one group stems not from any wrong done to it but from its wish to protect its ability to deprive citizens of their voting rights, to limit access to educational institutions, to prevent entry into the economy except at the lowest and most menial levels, and to force members of the stigmatized group to ride in the back of the bus. The hostility of the other group is the result of these actions, and whereas hostility and racial anger are unhappy facts wherever they are found, a distinction must surely be made between the ideological hostility of the oppressors and the experience-based hostility of those who have been oppressed.

Not to make that distinction is, adapting George Bush's words, to twist history and forget the terrible plight of African-Americans in the more than 200 years of this country's existence. Moreover, to equate the efforts to remedy that plight with the actions that produced it is to twist history even further. Those efforts, designed to redress the imbalances caused by long-standing discrimination, are called affirmative action; to argue that affirmative action, which gives preferential treatment to disadvantaged minorities as part of a plan to achieve social equality, is no different from the policies that created the disadvantages in the first place is a travesty of reasoning. "Reverse racism" is a cogent description of affirmative action only if one considers the cancer of racism to be morally and medically indistinguishable from the therapy we apply to it. A cancer is an invasion of the body's equilibrium, and so is chemotherapy; but we do not decline to fight the disease because the medicine we employ is also disruptive of normal functioning. Strong illness, strong remedy: the formula is as appropriate to the health of the body politic as it is to that of the body proper....

A TILTED FIELD

... [I]nsincerity and hollowness of promise infect another formula that is popular with the anti-affirmative-action crowd: the formula of the level playing field. Here the argument usually takes the form of saying "It is undemocratic to give one class of citizens advantages at the expense of other citizens; the truly democratic way is to have a level playing field to which everyone has access and where everyone has a fair and equal chance to succeed on the basis of his or her merit." Fine words—but they conceal the facts of the situation as it has been given to us by history: the playing field is already tilted in favor of those by whom and for whom it was constructed in the first place. If mastery of the requirements for entry depends upon immersion in the cultural experiences of the mainstream majority, if the skills that make for success are nurtured by institutions and cultural practices from which the disadvantaged minority has been systematically excluded, if the language and ways of comporting oneself that identify a player as "one of us" are alien to the lives minorities are forced to live, then words like "fair" and "equal" are cruel jokes, for what they promote and celebrate is an institutionalized unfairness and a perpetuated inequality. The playing field is already tilted, and the resistance to altering it by the mechanisms of affirmative action is in fact a determination to make sure that the present imbalances persist as long as possible.

One way of tilting the field is the Scholastic Aptitude Test [SAT]. This test figures prominently in Dinesh D'Souza's book *Illiberal Education* (1991), in which one finds many examples of white or Asian students denied admission to colleges and universities even though their SAT scores were higher than the scores of some others—often African-Americans—who were admitted to the same institution. This, D'Souza says, is evidence that as a result of affirmative-action policies colleges and universities tend "to depreciate the importance of merit criteria in admissions." D'Souza's assumption—and it is one that many would share—is that the test does in fact

measure *merit*, with merit understood as a quality objectively determined in the same way that body temperature can be objectively determined.

In fact, however, the test is nothing of the kind. Statistical studies have suggested that test scores reflect income and socioeconomic status. It has been demonstrated again and again that scores vary in relation to cultural background; the test's questions assume a certain uniformity in educational experience and lifestyle and penalize those who, for whatever reason, have had a different experience and lived different kinds of lives. In short, what is being measured by the SAT is not absolutes like native ability and merit but accidents like birth, social position, access to libraries, and the opportunity to take vacations or take SAT prep courses.

Furthermore, as David Owen notes in *None of the Above: Behind the Myth of Scholastic Aptitude* (1985), the "correlation between SAT scores and college grades . . . is lower than the correlation between weight and height; in other words you would have a better chance of predicting a person's height by looking at his weight than you would of predicting his freshman grades by looking only at his SAT scores." Everywhere you look in the SAT story, the claims of fairness, objectivity, and neutrality fall away, to be replaced by suspicions of specialized measures and unfair advantages.

Against this background a point that in isolation might have a questionable force takes on a special and even explanatory resonance: the principal deviser of the test was an out-and-out racist. In 1923 Carl Campbell Brigham published a book called *A Study of American Intelligence*, in which, as Owen notes, he declared, among other things, that we faced in America "a possibility of racial admixture... infinitely worse than that faced by any European country today, for we are incorporating the Negro into our racial stock, while all of Europe is comparatively free of this taint." Brigham had earlier analyzed the Army Mental Tests using classifications drawn from another racist text, Madison Grant's *The Passing of the Great Race*, which divided American society into four distinct racial strains, with Nordic, blue-eyed, blond people at the pinnacle and the American Negro at the bottom. Nevertheless, in 1925 Brigham became a director of testing for the College Board, and developed the SAT. So here is the great SAT test, devised by a racist in order to confirm racist assumptions, measuring not native ability but cultural advantage, an uncertain indicator of performance, an indicator of very little except what money and social privilege can buy. And it is in the name of this mechanism that we are asked to reject affirmative action and reaffirm "the importance of merit criteria in admissions."

THE REALITY OF DISCRIMINATION

Nevertheless, there is at least one more card to play against affirmative action, and it is a strong one. Granted that the playing field is not level and that access to it is reserved for an already advantaged elite, the disadvantages suffered by others are less racial—at least in 1993—than socioeconomic. Therefore shouldn't, as D'Souza urges, "universities... retain their policies of preferential treatment, but alter their criteria of application from race to socioeconomic disadvantage," and thus avoid the unfairness of current policies that reward middle-class or affluent blacks at the expense of poor whites? One answer to

this question is given by D'Souza himself when he acknowledges that the overlap between minority groups and the poor is very large—a point underscored by the former Secretary of Education Lamar Alexander, who said, in response to a question about funds targeted for black students, "Ninety-eight percent of race-specific scholarships do not involve constitutional problems." He meant, I take it, that 98 percent of race-specific scholarships were also scholarships to the economically disadvantaged.

Still, the other two percent—non-poor, middle-class, economically favored blacks—are receiving special attention on the basis of disadvantages they do not experience. What about them? The force of the question depends on the assumption that in this day and age race could not possibly be a serious disadvantage to those who are otherwise well positioned in the society. But the lie was given dramatically to this assumption in a 1991 broadcast of the ABC program *PrimeTime Live*. In a stunning fifteen-minute segment reporters and a camera crew followed two young men of equal education, cultural sophistication, level of apparent affluence, and so forth around St. Louis, a city where neither was known. The two differed in only a single respect: one was white, the other black. But that small difference turned out to mean everything. In a series of encounters with shoe salesmen, record-store employees, rental agents, landlords, employment agencies, taxicab drivers, and ordinary citizens, the black member of the pair was either ignored or given a special and suspicious attention. He was asked to pay more for the same goods or come up with a larger down payment for the same car, was turned away as a prospective tenant, was rejected as a prospective taxicab fare, was treated with contempt and irritation by clerks and bureaucrats, and in every way possible was made to feel inferior and unwanted.

The inescapable conclusion was that alike though they may have been in almost all respects, one of these young men, because he was black, would lead a significantly lesser life than his white counterpart: he would be housed less well and at greater expense; he would pay more for services and products when and if he was given the opportunity to buy them; he would have difficulty establishing credit; the first emotions he would inspire on the part of many people he met would be distrust and fear; his abilities would be discounted even before he had a chance to display them; and, above all, the treatment he received from minute to minute would chip away at his self-esteem and self-confidence with consequences that most of us could not even imagine. As the young man in question said at the conclusion of the broadcast, "You walk down the street with a suit and tie and it doesn't matter. Someone will make determinations about you, determinations that affect the quality of your life." ...

WHY ME?

When all is said and done, however, one objection to affirmative action is unanswerable on its own terms, and that is the objection of the individual who says, "Why me? Sure, discrimination has persisted for many years, and I acknowledge that the damage done has not been removed by changes in the law. But why me? I didn't own slaves; I didn't vote to keep people on the back of the bus; I didn't turn water hoses on civil-rights marchers. Why, then, should I be the one who doesn't get the job or who doesn't get the scholarship or who gets bumped back to the waiting list?"

I sympathize with this feeling, if only because in a small way I have had the experience that produces it. I was recently nominated for an administrative post at a large university. Early signs were encouraging, but after an interval I received official notice that I would not be included at the next level of consideration, and subsequently I was told unofficially that at some point a decision had been made to look only in the direction of women and minorities. Although I was disappointed, I did not conclude that the situation was "unfair," because the policy was obviously not directed at me—at no point in the proceedings did someone say, "Let's find a way to rule out Stanley Fish." Nor was it directed even at persons of my race and sex—the policy was not intended to disenfranchise white males. Rather, the policy was driven by other considerations, and it was only as a by-product of those considerations—not as the main goal—that white males like me were rejected. Given that the institution in question has a high percentage of minority students, a very low percentage of minority faculty, and an even lower percentage of minority administrators, it made perfect sense to focus on women and minority candidates, and within that sense, not as the result of prejudice, my whiteness and maleness became disqualifications. ...

TIIE NEW BIGOTRY

... The sleight-of-hand logic that first abstracts events from history and then assesses them from behind a veil of willed ignorance gains some of its plausibility from another key word in the anti-affirmative-action lexicon. That word is "individual," as in "The American way is to focus on the rights of individuals rather than groups." Now, "individual" and "individualism" have been honorable words in the American political vocabulary, and they have often been well employed in the fight against various tyrannies. But like any other word or concept, individualism can be perverted to serve ends the opposite of those it originally served, and this is what has happened when in the name of individual rights, millions of individuals are enjoined from redressing historically documented wrongs. How is this managed? Largely in the same way that the invocation of fairness is used to legitimize an institutionalized inequality. First one says, in the most solemn of tones, that the protection of individual rights is the chief obligation of society. Then one defines individuals as souls sent into the world with equal entitlements as guaranteed either by their Creator or by the Constitution. Then one pretends that nothing has happened to them since they stepped onto the world's stage. And then one says of these carefully denatured souls that they will all be treated in the same way, irrespective of any of the differences that history has produced. Bizarre as it may seem, individualism in this argument turns out to mean that everyone is or should be the *same*. This dismissal of individual difference in the name of the individual would be funny were its consequences not so serious: it is the mechanism by which imbalances and inequities suffered by millions of people through no fault of their own can be sanitized and even celebrated as the natural workings of unfettered democracy.

"Individualism," "fairness," "merit" —these three words are continually misappropriated by bigots who have learned that they need not put on a white hood or bar access to the ballot box in order to secure their ends. Rather, they need only clothe themselves in a vocabulary plucked from its historical context and made into the justification for attitudes and policies they would not acknowledge if frankly named.

POSTSCRIPT

Is Affirmative Action Reverse Discrimination?

Much of the argument between Steele and Fish turns on the question of "color blindness." To what extent should our laws be color-blind? During the 1950s and early 1960s, civil rights leaders were virtually unanimous on this point. Martin Luther King, Jr., in a speech given at a civil rights march on Washington, said, "I have a dream that my four little children will one day live in a nation where they will not be judged by the color of their skin but by the content of their character." This was the consensus view in 1963, but today, as Fish seems to be suggesting, does that statement need to be qualified? In order to *bring about* color blindness, it may be necessary to become temporarily color-conscious. But for how long? And is there a danger that this temporary color consciousness may become a permanent policy?

Robert M. O'Neil, in *Discriminating Against Discrimination* (Indiana University Press, 1975), discusses his studies of preferential admissions to universities and voices support for preferential treatment without racial quotas. Law professor Stephen Carter recounts his own experience as an African American dealing with affirmative action—an intended benefit that he rejected —and expresses his concerns about it in *Reflections of An Affirmative Action Baby* (Basic Books, 1991). The focus of Allan P. Sindler's *Bakke, DeFunis, and Minority Admissions* (Longman, 1978) is on affirmative action in higher education, as is Nicholas Capaldi's *Out of Order: Affirmative Action and the Crisis of Doctrinaire Liberalism* (Prometheus Books, 1985). A more general discussion is found in Thomas Sowell's *Civil Rights: Rhetoric or Reality?* (William Morrow, 1984). Chapter 13 of *The Constitution: That Delicate Balance* (Random House, 1984) by Fred W. Friendly and Martha J. H. Elliott provides an account of the events leading up to the landmark *Bakke* case on affirmative action.

Affirmative action is one of those issues, like abortion, in which the opposing sides seem utterly intransigent. It is hard to imagine any compromise acceptable to both sides of the controversy. But there may be a large middle sector of opinion that is simply weary of the whole controversy and may be willing to support any expedient solution worked out by pragmatists in the executive and legislative branches of the government.

ISSUE 13

Should Hate Speech Be Punished?

YES: Charles R. Lawrence III, from "If He Hollers Let Him Go: Regulating Racist Speech on Campus," *Duke Law Journal* (June 1990)

NO: Nadine Strossen, from "Regulating Racist Speech on Campus: A Modest Proposal?" *Duke Law Journal* (June 1990)

ISSUE SUMMARY

YES: Charles Lawrence III, a professor of law, believes that speech should be impermissible when, going beyond insult, it inflicts injury on its victims.

NO: Nadine Strossen, executive director of the American Civil Liberties Union, concludes that any limits on free speech threatens the expression of all unpopular ideas.

In 1942, on a busy public street in Rochester, New Hampshire, a man named Walter Chaplinsky was passing out literature promoting the Jehovah's Witnesses, which would have been all right except that the literature denounced all other religions as "rackets." As might be expected, Chaplinsky's activities caused a stir. The city marshall warned Chaplinsky that he was on the verge of creating a riot and told him that he ought to leave, whereupon Chaplinsky answered him in these words: "You are a Goddamned racketeer . . . a damned Fascist, and the whole government of Rochester are Fascists or agents of Fascists." Chaplinsky was arrested for disturbing the peace and he appealed on the grounds that his First Amendment right to free speech had been violated. The Supreme Court of the United States ruled unanimously against him. In *Chaplinsky v. New Hampshire* (1942) the Court said that his words were "fighting words," not deserving of First Amendment protection because they were "likely to provoke the average person to retaliation."

In 1984 a Texan named Gregory Lee Johnson stood in front of Dallas City Hall, doused an American flag in kerosene, and set it on fire while chanting, "Red, white, and blue, we spit on you." When he was arrested for flag desecration, he appealed to the Supreme Court on grounds of free speech—and won. In *Texas v. Johnson* (1989) the Court ruled that flag-burning was a form of "symbolic speech" protected by the First Amendment.

So Chaplinsky used his mouth and was punished for it, and Johnson burned a flag and was not. How do we square these decisions, or should we? What about cases today? If flag-burning is symbolic speech, what about cross-burning? If a state can punish a person for calling someone a "Goddamned racketeer," can it also punish someone for shouting racial epithets?

Some municipalities have enacted laws that punish "hate speech" directed at women and minorities. The intention of these codes and laws is to ensure at least a minimum of civility in places where people of very diverse backgrounds must live and work together. But do they infringe upon essential freedoms?

In 1992 the Supreme Court confronted this issue in a case testing the constitutionality of a St. Paul, Minnesota, statute punishing anyone who displays symbols attacking people because of their "race, color, creed, religion, or gender." A group of St. Paul teenagers had burned a cross in the yard of a black family. Prosecutors used this newly enacted law, which raised the essential issues in the case: Did the statute violate freedoms guaranteed by the First Amendment? If so, why? In its decision of *R. A. V. v. St. Paul* (1992), the Court gave a unanimous answer to the first question. All nine justices agreed that the statute was indeed a violation of the First Amendment. But on the second question—*why* was it a violation?—the Court was deeply divided. Four members thought that it was unconstitutional because it was "overbroad," that is, worded in such general language that it would reach beyond the narrow bounds of speech activities that the Court has deemed punishable. But the majority, in an opinion by Justice Antonin Scalia, struck down the statute for a very different reason: because it contained "content discrimination." By punishing speech that attacks people because of their "race, color, creed, religion, or gender," it was prohibiting speech "solely on the basis of the subjects the speech addresses." A statute punishing speech may not single out specific categories like race or creed for protection, for to do so is to involve the state in deciding which sorts of people deserve protection against "hate speech."

A related controversy that has inflamed American college campuses in recent years also involves questions of "content discrimination." The term *politically correct* (p.c.) is a sarcastic term used by opponents of the new campus speech codes and other efforts to punish verbal attacks on minorities. It implies that the codes discriminate according to speech content because they punish mainly the kinds of speech whose contents offend some liberals, but seldom punish speech that particularly offends conservatives. Critics charge that the net effect is to inhibit dissent from liberal views.

In the following selections, Charles Lawrence III argues that speech can inflict injury and curtail the freedom of the victims of hate. Nadine Strossen believes that such restrictions on expression endanger the freedom of all. Although their debate focuses on campus speech, it is applicable to every area in which controversial and hurtful ideas may be expressed.

YES

Charles R. Lawrence III

REGULATING RACIST SPEECH
ON CAMPUS

RACIST SPEECH AS THE FUNCTIONAL EQUIVALENT
OF FIGHTING WORDS

Much recent debate over the efficacy of regulating racist speech has focused on the efforts by colleges and universities to respond to the burgeoning incidents of racial harassment on their campuses. At Stanford, where I teach, there has been considerable controversy over the questions whether racist and other discriminatory verbal harassment should be regulated and what form that regulation should take. Proponents of regulation have been sensitive to the danger of inhibiting expression, and the current regulation (which was drafted by my colleague Tom Grey) manifests that sensitivity. It is drafted somewhat more narrowly than I would have preferred, leaving unregulated hate speech that occurs in settings where there is a captive audience, speech that I would regulate. But I largely agree with this regulation's substance and approach. I include it here as one example of a regulation of racist speech that I would argue violates neither first amendment precedent nor principle. The regulation reads as follows:

Fundamental Standard Interpretation: Free Expression and Discriminatory Harassment

1. Stanford is committed to the principles of free inquiry and free expression. Students have the right to hold and vigorously defend and promote their opinions, thus entering them into the life of the University, there to flourish or wither according to their merits. Respect for this right requires that students tolerate even expression of opinions which they find abhorrent. Intimidation of students by other students in their exercise of this right, by violence or threat of violence, is therefore considered to be a violation of the Fundamental Standard.

2. Stanford is also committed to principles of equal opportunity and non-discrimination. Each student has the right to equal access to a Stanford education, without discrimination on the basis of sex, race, color, handicap, religion, sexual orientation, or national and ethnic origin. Harassment

of students on the basis of any of these characteristics contributes to a hostile environment that makes access to education for those subjected to it less than equal. Such discriminatory harassment is therefore considered to be a violation of the Fundamental Standard.

3. This interpretation of the Fundamental Standard is intended to clarify the point at which protected free expression ends and prohibited discriminatory harassment begins. Prohibited harassment includes discriminatory intimidation by threats of violence, and also includes personal vilification of students on the basis of their sex, race, color, handicap, religion, sexual orientation, or national and ethnic origin.

4. Speech or other expression constitutes harassment by personal vilification if it:

   a. is intended to insult or stigmatize an individual or a small number of individuals on the basis of their sex, race, color, handicap, religion, sexual orientation, or national and ethnic origin; and

   b. is addressed directly to the individual or individuals whom it insults or stigmatizes; and

   c. makes use of insulting or "fighting" words or non-verbal symbols.

In the context of discriminatory harassment by personal vilification, insulting or "fighting" words or non-verbal symbols are those "which by their very utterance inflict injury or tend to incite to an immediate breach of the peace," and which are commonly understood to convey direct and visceral hatred or contempt for human beings on the basis of their sex, race, color, handicap, religion, sexual orientation, or national and ethnic origin.

This regulation and others like it have been characterized in the press as the work of "thought police," but it does nothing more than prohibit intentional face-to-face insults, a form of speech that is unprotected by the first amendment. When racist speech takes the form of face-to-face insults, catcalls, or other assaultive speech aimed at an individual or small group of persons, then it falls within the "fighting words" exception to first amendment protection. The Supreme Court has held that words that "by their very utterance inflict injury or tend to incite an immediate breach of the peace" are not constitutionally protected.

Face-to-face racial insults, like fighting words, are undeserving of first amendment protection for two reasons. The first reason is the immediacy of the injurious impact of racial insults. The experience of being called "nigger, "spic," "Jap," or "kike" is like receiving a slap in the face. The injury is instantaneous. There is neither an opportunity for intermediary reflection on the idea conveyed nor an opportunity for responsive speech. The harm to be avoided is both clear and present. The second reason that racial insults should not fall under protected speech relates to the purpose underlying the first amendment. If the purpose of the first amendment is to foster the greatest amount of speech, then racial insults disserve that purpose. Assaultive racist speech functions as a preemptive strike. The racial invective is experienced as a blow, not a proffered idea, and once the blow is struck, it is unlikely that dialogue will follow. Racial insults are undeserving of first amendment protection because the perpetrator's intention is not to discover truth or initiate dialogue but to injure the victim.

The fighting words doctrine anticipates that the verbal "slap in the face" of insulting words will provoke a violent response with a resulting breach of the peace. When racial insults are hurled at minorities, the response may be silence or flight rather than a fight, but the preemptive effect on further speech is just as complete as with fighting words. Women and minorities often report that they find themselves speechless in the face of discriminatory verbal attacks. This inability to respond is not the result of oversensitivity among these groups, as some individuals who oppose protective regulation have argued. Rather, it is the product of several factors, all of which reveal the non-speech character of the initial preemptive verbal assault. The first factor is that the visceral emotional response to personal attack precludes speech. Attack produces an instinctive, defensive psychological reaction. Fear, rage, shock, and flight all interfere with any reasoned response. Words like "nigger," "kike," and "faggot" produce physical symptoms that temporarily disable the victim, and the perpetrators often use these words with the intention of producing this effect. Many victims do not find words of response until well after the assault when the cowardly assaulter has departed.

A second factor that distinguishes racial insults from protected speech is the preemptive nature of such insults—the words by which to respond to such verbal attacks may never be forthcoming because speech is usually an inadequate response. When one is personally attacked with words that denote one's subhuman status and untouchability, there is little

(if anything) that can be said to redress either the emotional or reputational injury. This is particularly true when the message and meaning of the epithet resonates with beliefs widely held in society. This preservation of widespread beliefs is what makes the face-to-face racial attack more likely to preempt speech than are other fighting words. The racist name-caller is accompanied by a cultural chorus of equally demeaning speech and symbols.

The subordinated victim of fighting words also is silenced by her relatively powerless position in society. Because of the significance of power and position, the categorization of racial epithets as "fighting words" provides an inadequate paradigm; instead one must speak of their "functional equivalent." The fighting words doctrine presupposes an encounter between two persons of relatively equal power who have been acculturated to respond to face-to-face insults with violence. The fighting words doctrine is a paradigm based on a white male point of view. In most situations, minorities correctly perceive that a violent response to fighting words will result in a risk to their own life and limb. Since minorities are likely to lose the fight, they are forced to remain silent and submissive. This response is most obvious when women submit to sexually assaultive speech or when the racist name-caller is in a more powerful position—the boss on the job or the mob. Certainly, we do not expect the black women crossing the Wisconsin campus to turn on their tormentors and pummel them. Less obvious, but just as significant, is the effect of pervasive racial and sexual violence and coercion on individual members of subordinated groups who must learn the survival techniques of suppressing and disguising rage and anger at an early age.

One of my students, a white, gay male, related an experience that is quite instructive in understanding the inadequacy and potential of the "fighting words" doctrine. In response to my request that students describe how they experienced the injury of racist speech, Michael told a story of being called "faggot" by a man on a subway. His description included all of the speech inhibiting elements I have noted previously. He found himself in a state of semi-shock, nauseous, dizzy, unable to muster the witty, sarcastic, articulate rejoinder he was accustomed to making. He suddenly was aware of the recent spate of gay-bashing in San Francisco, and how many of these had escalated from verbal encounters. Even hours later when the shock resided and his facility with words returned, he realized that any response was inadequate to counter the hundreds of years of societal defamation that one word—"faggot"—carried with it. Like the word "nigger" and unlike the word "liar," it is not sufficient to deny the truth of the word's application, to say, "I am not a faggot." One must deny the truth of the word's meaning, a meaning shouted from the rooftops by the rest of the world a million times a day. Although there are many of us who constantly and in myriad ways seek to counter the lie spoken in the meaning of hateful words like "nigger" and "faggot," it is a nearly impossible burden to bear when one encounters hateful speech face-to-face....

Understanding the Injury Inflicted by Racist Speech

There can be no meaningful discussion about how to reconcile our commitment to equality and our commitment to free speech until we acknowledge that racist speech inflicts real harm and that this harm is far from trivial. I should state that more strongly: To engage in a debate about the first amendment and racist speech without a full understanding of the nature and extent of the harm of racist speech risks making the first amendment an instrument of domination rather than a vehicle of liberation. Not everyone has known the experience of being victimized by racist, misogynist, and homophobic speech, and we do not share equally the burden of the societal harm it inflicts. Often we are too quick to say we have heard the victims' cries when we have not; we are too eager to assure ourselves we have experienced the same injury, and therefore we can make the constitutional balance without danger of mismeasurement. For many of us who have fought for the rights of oppressed minorities, it is difficult to accept that— by underestimating the injury from racist speech—we too might be implicated in the vicious words we would never utter. Until we have eradicated racism and sexism and no longer share in the fruits of those forms of domination, we cannot justly strike the balance over the protest of those who are dominated. My plea is simply that we listen to the victims.

Members of my own family were involved in a recent incident at a private school in Wilmington, Delaware that taught me much about both the nature of the injury racist speech inflicts and the lack of understanding many whites have of that injury....

[In the next section, not reprinted here, Lawrence recounts an incident involving racist cartoons, threats, and epithets scrawled on the wall of a soccer field at a private school where his sister taught. The perpetrators were discovered and expelled.—Eds.]

When I visited my sister's family a few days after this incident, the injury they had suffered was evident. The wounds were fresh. My sister, a care-giver by nature and vocation, was clearly in need of care. My nephews were quiet. Their faces betrayed the aftershock of a recently inflicted blow and a newly discovered vulnerability. I knew the pain and scars were no less enduring because the injury had not been physical. And when I talked to my sister, I realized the greatest part of her pain came not from the incident itself but rather from the reaction of white parents who had come to the school in unprecedented numbers to protest the offending students' expulsion. "It was only a prank." "No one was physically attacked." "How can you punish these kids for mere words, mere drawings." Paula's pain was compounded by the failure of these people, with whom she had lived and worked, to recognize that she had been hurt, to understand in even the most limited way the reality of her pain and that of her family.

Many people called the incident "isolated." But black folks know that no racial incident is "isolated" in America. That is what makes the incidents so horrible, so scary. It is the knowledge that they are not the isolated unpopular speech of a dissident few that makes them so fright-ening. These incidents are manifestations of an ubiquitous and deeply ingrained cultural belief system, an American way of life. Too often in recent months, as I have debated this issue with friends and colleagues, I have heard people speak of the need to protect "offensive" speech. The word offensive is used as if we were speaking of a difference in taste, as if I should learn to be less sensitive to words that "offend" me. I cannot help but believe that those people who speak of offense—those who argue that this speech must go unchecked—do not understand the great difference between offense and injury.... There is a great difference between the offensiveness of words that you would rather not hear—because they are labeled dirty, impolite, or personally demeaning—and the *injury* inflicted by words that remind the world that you are fair game for physical attack, evoke in you all of the millions of cultural lessons regarding your inferiority that you have so painstakingly repressed, and imprint upon you a badge of servitude and subservience for all the world to see. It is instructive that the chief proponents for sanctioning people who inflict these injuries are women and people of color, and there are few among these groups who take the absolutist position that any regulation of this speech is too much.

NO

Nadine Strossen

REGULATING RACIST SPEECH ON CAMPUS: A MODEST PROPOSAL?

What is disquieting about Professor [Charles] Lawrence's article [in the *Duke Law Journal* (June 1990)] is not the relatively limited Stanford code [prohibiting certain kinds of speech] he defends, but rather his simultaneous defense of additional, substantially more sweeping, speech prohibitions.

The rationales that Professor Lawrence advances for the regulations he endorses are so open-ended that, if accepted, they would appear to warrant the prohibition of *all* racist speech, and thereby would cut to the core of our system of free expression.

Although Professor Lawrence's specific proposed code appears relatively modest, his supporting rationales depend on nothing less immodest than the abrogation of the traditional distinctions between speech and conduct and between state action and private action. He equates private racist speech with governmental racist conduct. This approach offers no principled way to confine racist speech regulations to the particular contours of the Stanford code, or indeed to any particular contours at all. Professor Lawrence apparently acknowledges that, if accepted, his theories could warrant the prohibition of *all* private racist speech. Moreover, although he stresses the particular evils of racism, he also says that "much of my analysis applies to violent pornography and homophobic hate speech." Thus, Professor Lawrence himself demonstrates that traditional civil libertarians are hardly paranoiac when we fear that any specific, seemingly modest proposal to regulate speech may in fact represent the proverbial "thin edge of the wedge" for initiating broader regulations.

As just explained, the relatively narrow Stanford code that Professor Lawrence endorses is incongruous with his broad theoretical rationale. The Stanford code also is at odds with Professor Lawrence's pragmatic rationale. The harms of racist speech that he seeks to redress largely remain untouched by the rule. For example, Professor Lawrence movingly recounts the pain suffered by his sister's family as a result of racist expression, as well as the anxiety he endured as a boy even from the *possibility* of racist expression. Yet the Stanford code clearly would not apply to any of the unspoken racist expressions that may lurk beneath the surface of much parlance in American life. Moreover, the regulation also would not apply unless the speech was directly targeted at a specific victim. Therefore, it would not have relieved Professor Lawrence or his family of the traumas they experienced. Furthermore, the Stanford code would not address the racist incident at Stanford that led to its adoption. Likewise, many additional campus racist incidents catalogued by Professor Lawrence and others would be beyond the scope of the Stanford code....

Fighting Words.
The fighting words doctrine is the principal model for the Stanford code, which Professor Lawrence supports. However, this doctrine provides a constitutionally shaky foundation for several reasons: it has been substantially limited in scope and may no longer be good law; even if the Supreme Court were to apply a narrowed version of the doctrine, such an application would threaten free speech principles; and, as actually implemented, the fighting words doctrine suppresses protectible speech and entails the inherent danger of discriminatory application to speech by members of minority groups and dissidents.

Although the Court originally defined constitutionally regulable fighting words in fairly broad terms in *Chaplinsky v. New Hampshire,* subsequent decisions have narrowed the definition to such a point that the doctrine probably would not apply to any of the instances of campus racist speech that Professor Lawrence and others seek to regulate. As originally formulated in *Chaplinsky,* the fighting words doctrine excluded from first amendment protection "insulting or 'fighting' words, those which by their very utterance inflict injury *or* tend to incite an immediate breach of the peace."

In light of subsequent developments, it is significant to note that the first prong of *Chaplinsky's* fighting words definition, words "which by their very utterance inflict injury," was dictum. The Court's actual holding was that the state statute at issue was justified by the state's interest in preserving the public peace by prohibiting "words likely to cause an average addressee to fight." The Court stressed that "no words were forbidden except such as have a direct tendency to cause acts of violence by the person to whom, individually, [they are] addressed." The Court also held that the statute had been applied appropriately to Mr. Chaplinsky, who had called a city marshal "a God damned racketeer" and "a damned Fascist." It explained that these "epithets [are] likely to provoke the average person to retaliation, and thereby cause a breach of the peace."

In *Gooding v. Wilson,* the Court substantially narrowed *Chaplinsky's* definition of fighting words by bringing that definition into line with *Chaplinsky's* actual holding. In *Gooding,* as well as in every subsequent fighting words case, the Court disregarded the dictum in which the first prong of *Chaplinsky's* definition was set forth and treated only those words that "tend to incite an immediate breach of the peace" as fighting words. Consistent with this narrowed definition, the Court has invalidated regulations that hold certain words to be per se proscribable and insisted that each challenged utterance be evaluated contextually. Thus, under the Court's current view, even facially valid laws that restrict fighting words may be applied constitutionally only in circumstances where their utterance almost certainly will lead to immediate violence. . . .

The Proposed Regulations Would Endanger Fundamental Free Speech Principles

The various proposed campus hate speech regulations, including the Stanford code that Professor Lawrence endorses, are inconsistent with current Supreme Court doctrine prescribing permissible limits on speech. More importantly, they jeopardize basic free speech principles. Whereas certain conduct may be regulable, speech that advocates such conduct is not, and speech may not be regulated on the basis of its content, even if many of us strongly disagree with—or are repelled by—that content.

Protection of Speech Advocating Regulable Conduct.

Civil libertarians, scholars, and judges consistently have distinguished between speech advocating unlawful conduct and the unlawful conduct itself. Although this distinction has been drawn in numerous different factual settings, the fundamental underlying issues always are the same. For example, within recent years, some pro-choice activists have urged civil libertarians and courts to make an exception to free speech principles in order to restrain the expressive conduct of anti-abortion activists. Instead, civil libertarians have persuaded courts to prohibit assaults, blockages of clinic entrances, trespasses, and other illegal conduct by anti-choice activists. Similarly, civil libertarians and courts have rejected pleas by some feminists to censor pornography that reflects sexist attitudes. Instead, civil libertarians have renewed their efforts to persuade courts and legislatures to invalidate sexist actions. A

decade ago, civil libertarians and several courts—including the Supreme Court—rejected the plea of Holocaust survivors in Skokie, Illinois to prohibit neo-Nazis from demonstrating. Instead, civil libertarians successfully have lobbied for the enactment and enforcement of laws against anti-Semitic vandalism and other hate-inspired conduct.

A pervasive weakness in Professor Lawrence's analysis is his elision of the distinction between racist speech, on the one hand, and racist conduct, on the other. It is certainly true that racist speech, like other speech, may have some causal connection to conduct. As Justice [Oliver W.] Holmes observed [in *Gitlow v. New York*], "[e]very idea is an incitement" to action. However, as Justice Holmes also noted, to protect speech that advocates conduct you oppose does not "indicate that you think the speech impotent, . . . or that you do not care wholeheartedly for the result." Rather, this protection is based on the critical distinction between speech that has a direct and immediate link to unlawful conduct and all other speech, which has less direct and immediate links. . . .

Proscription on Content-Based Speech Regulations.

The indivisibility of free speech. It is important to place the current debate about campus racist speech in the context of earlier efforts to censor other forms of hate speech, including sexist and anti-Semitic speech. Such a broadened perspective suggests that consistent principles should be applied each time the issue resurfaces in any guise. Every person may find one particular type of speech especially odious and one message that most sorely tests his or her dedication to free speech values. But for each person who would exclude racist speech from the general proscription against content-based speech regulations, recent experience shows that there is another who would make such an exception only for anti-choice speech, another who would make it only for sexist speech, another who would make it only for anti-Semitic speech, another who would make it only for flag desecration, and so on. . . .

In light of the universal condemnation of racial discrimination and the world-wide regulation of racist speech, it certainly is tempting to consider excepting racist speech from first amendment protection. Episodes of racist speech . . . make a full commitment to free speech at times seem painful and difficult. Civil libertarians find such speech abhorrent, given our dedication to eradicating racial discrimination and other forms of bigotry. But experience has confirmed the truth of the indivisibility principle articulated above: History demonstrates that if the freedom of speech is weakened for one person, group, or message, then it is no longer there for others. . . .

The slippery slope dangers of banning racist speech. To attempt to craft free speech exceptions only for racist speech would create a significant risk of a slide down the proverbial "slippery slope." To be sure, lawyers and judges are capable of—indeed, especially trained in—drawing distinctions between similar situations. Therefore, I agree with Professor Lawrence and other critics of the absolutist position that slippery slope dangers should not be exaggerated. It is probably hyperbole to contend that if we ever stepped off the mountaintop where all speech is protected regardless of its content, then inevitably we would end up in the abyss where the government controls all our words. On the other hand, critics of absolutism should not minimize the real danger: We would have a difficult time limiting our descent to a single downward step by attempting to prohibit only racist expression on campus. Applicable rules and supporting rationales would need to be crafted carefully to distinguish this type of speech from others.

First, we must think hard about the groups that should be protected. Should we regulate speech aimed only at racial and ethnic groups? . . . Or should we also bar insults of religious groups, women, gays and lesbians, individuals with disabilities, Vietnam War veterans, and so on, as do the rules adopted by Stanford? . . .

Second, we must carefully define proscribable harassing speech to avoid encompassing the important expression that inevitably is endangered by any hate speech restriction. Censorial consequences could result from many proposed or adopted university policies, including the Stanford code, which sanctions speech intended to "insult or stigmatize" on the basis of race or other prohibited grounds. . . .

An exaggerated concern with racist speech creates a risk of elevating symbols over substance in two problematic respects. First, it may divert our attention from the causes of racism to its symptoms. Second, a focus on the hateful message conveyed by particular speech may distort our view of fundamental neutral principles applicable to our system of free expression generally. We should not let the racist veneer in which expression is cloaked obscure our recognition of how important free expression is and of how effectively it has advanced racial equality.

POSTSCRIPT

Should Hate Speech Be Punished?

Many forms of hate speech are punished in other countries, but other democracies do not have the American tradition of freedom of opinion and expression. At the same time, the United States has more races, religions and nationalities than other countries, giving rise to suspicion, prejudice, and hostility.

One the one hand, this diversity has given rise to sharp political disagreement on issues relating to race, religion, women, homosexuals, and others. On the other hand, this diversity has stimulated greater sensitivity to the claims of these groups for equal treatment and social justice. Free speech on controversial issues risks giving offense. At what point, if any, does giving offense curtail the liberty of the offended group? Should such speech be punished?

Nowhere have these questions provoked greater controversy than on college campuses. Do college codes inhibiting or punishing racist, sexist, or other biased speech protect the liberty of the victims of these insults or injuries? Or do they prevent the examination of disapproved beliefs and threaten the suppression of other unpopular ideas?

In 1993, the Supreme Court unanimously upheld a Wisconsin law that increased the punishment for crimes motivated by hate based on race, sex, and other categories enumerated in the law. Does this Supreme Court ruling on the Wisconsin law restrict or inhibit free expression? The American Civil Liberties Union said it did not; the Wisconsin Supreme Court and some civil libertarians said it did.

One of those civil libertarians was Nat Hentoff; see *Free Speech for Me— But Not for Thee: How the American Left and Right Relentlessly Censor Each Other* (HarperCollins, 1992). Less absolutist in defending all speech is Cass R. Sunstein, *Democracy and the Problem of Free Speech* (The Free Press, 1993), who attempts to define a distinction between protected and unprotected speech.

The defense of limits on what the authors call "assaultive speech" can be found in the essays in Mari J. Matsuda et al., *Words That Wound: Critical Race Theory, Assaultive Speech, and the First Amendment* (Westview Press, 1993).

"Are longer sentences for hate crimes constitutional?" is the question probed in the title of the January 8, 1993, issue of *Researcher*, which provides an impartial examination of hate crimes laws and the constitutional and moral questions that they raise.

ISSUE 14

Should Welfare Recipients Be Put to Work?

YES: Mickey Kaus, from *The End of Equality* (Basic Books, 1992)

NO: Richard A. Cloward and Frances Fox Piven, from "Punishing the Poor, Again: The Fraud of Workfare," *The Nation* (May 24, 1993)

ISSUE SUMMARY

YES: Magazine editor Mickey Kaus believes that replacing welfare payments with jobs will benefit poor people by creating self-respect, restoring family and community cohesion, and reducing crime and poverty.

NO: Social scientists Richard A. Cloward and Francis Fox Piven maintain that workfare will greatly increase welfare costs without providing adequate employment or raising the living standards of the poor.

The Great Depression that began with the stock market crash of 1929 and continued through the 1930s led to the adoption of far-reaching government policies designed to put people to work. These in turn led to the Social Security Act in 1935, to provide some measure of economic protection for retired workers and their survivors, disabled workers, and the unemployed.

Social Security insured only working people, and neither it nor Aid to Families with Dependent Children nor public housing programs met the needs of the poorest people. President Franklin D. Roosevelt called attention in 1937 to the plight of "one-third of a nation, ill-housed, ill-clad, ill-nourished," and, a generation later, President Lyndon B. Johnson proposed a War on Poverty "to lift this forgotten fifth of our nation above the poverty line." Almost surely the proportion was less than it had been, but it was clear that poverty remained widespread and deeply rooted in American society.

It was during Johnson's presidency that the federal government initiated food stamps, Medicaid for the poor, Medicare for the elderly, Head Start educational programs for underprivileged children, and the Job Corps. Still later came Supplemental Security Income for the blind, disabled, and low-income aged.

During the Reagan and Bush presidencies, federal welfare programs were cut back to some extent. But most survived and continue to provide benefits for millions of poor people. There are now at least 75 different welfare programs for the needy. In 1993 Aid to Families with Dependent Children (AFDC) cost $22 billion, food stamps $24 billion, and Medicaid $120 billion.

In four-and-a-half years (from July 1989 to December 1993), the number of people receiving AFDC assistance increased by more than one-third. In 1994 one out of every ten Americans received food stamps.

Women and children are the most likely recipients of all types of welfare payments. One of every seven children in the United States receives AFDC support. Millions of women who are single, divorced, separated, or widowed receive welfare benefits. Because they are unemployed or working at unskilled, part-time jobs, they fall below the poverty level.

Both conservatives and liberals seek to break the cycle of poverty. The harshest critics of welfare believe that welfare perpetuates poverty and that ending welfare is a necessary first step to reducing poverty. Others maintain that the problem is better dealt with by the states. Senator Nancy Kassebaum (R-Kansas) proposes that the federal government should assume the total cost of Medicaid, leaving the states to reform and fund AFDC and other programs for women, infants, and children.

Some states have begun changing the rules. Colorado, Florida, Iowa, Vermont, and Wisconsin have adopted time limits for welfare assistance, and similar proposals have received national attention. President Bill Clinton, while campaigning for president and in his 1994 State of the Union message, urged a two-year limit for welfare recipients, with public and private efforts to find employment for all able-bodied adults.

Such programs, called workfare, are looked upon as a practical alternative to welfare. Because welfare payments may equal or exceed unskilled job pay, many do not now seek work. If workfare is implemented, advocates claim, unemployed adults will find jobs before their welfare payments are stopped. Critics of workfare feel that these programs are unrealistic. They point out that many year-round, full-time workers receive wages that are below the poverty level. AFDC mothers will be fortunate to get any employment, and it is likely to be part-time, pay poorly, and lack health and pension benefits.

There is widespread agreement among Americans that welfare should not be a way of life and that neither the nation nor the states can afford the escalating costs. Is replacing welfare with workfare the solution? *New Republic* magazine editor Mickey Kaus believes that welfare time limits and putting poor people to work will restore family and community cohesion and reduce crime and poverty. Social scientists Richard Cloward and Francis Fox Piven characterize workfare as a symbolic charade that will be costlier than welfare and that will not end poverty.

YES   Mickey Kaus

THE CURE FOR THE
CULTURE OF POVERTY

Welfare may not have been a sufficient condition for the growth of the underclass, but it's hard to see how contemporary liberals can deny that it was a necessary condition.... Which raises the obvious question: could altering this necessary ingredient somehow "de-enable" the underclass?

Certainly, if we're looking for a political handle on underclass culture, there is none bigger than the benefit programs that constitute the economic basis—the "mode of production," a Marxist might say—of the ghetto. In the average "extreme social problem" neighborhood, 34 percent of the households are on welfare. According to the Congressional Budget Office, cash welfare (mainly AFDC [Aid to Families with Dependent Children]) is some 65 percent of the above-ground income of single mothers in the bottom fifth of the income distribution—up from 45 percent in 1970. A second, hidden chunk of ghetto GNP is illegal income, including income from the sale of drugs. But after interviewing urban welfare mothers in confidence about where they really get their money, Christopher Jencks and Kathryn Edin report that AFDC and food stamps account for 57 percent of their incomes. Work accounts for 12 percent, crime only 9 percent. Even assuming crime is a bigger factor than that (especially for young ghetto men), it's not a factor the larger society has been able to control. Welfare is something society *can* control....

* * *

Changing welfare... offers a chance to transform the economic role of the ghetto poor without tying them to their dying neighborhoods. Instead of attempting to somehow teach mainstream culture to people who spend most of their day immersed in ghetto culture, we could make ghetto culture economically unsustainable.

In this respect, the implications of the "enabling" theory of welfare are far more radical, and perhaps nastier, than those of the "bribe" version. For decades, Money Liberal reformers have assumed that if you extended welfare to two-parent families, then AFDC's "bribes" (or "incentives") would no longer pull families apart. The poor would never willingly have illegitimate babies and go on welfare if they could get married and go on welfare.

But if the "enabling" theory is correct, the culture of poverty is now so entrenched that young girls will keep on having illegitimate babies and going on welfare even if they could form two-parent families and still get their checks. If that's true, it isn't enough to extend benefits to intact families (which indeed has had little effect on the underclass in the states where it's been tried). You have to somehow *deny* benefits to one-parent families, unplug the underclass culture's life support system. In short, you have to re-make FDR's [President Franklin D. Roosevelt's] 1935 choice—this time applying it to able-bodied single parents along with everyone else.

That means something like this: replacing AFDC and all other cash-like welfare programs that assist the able-bodied poor (including "general relief" and food stamps) with a single, simple offer from the government—an offer of employment for every American citizen over eighteen who wants it, in a useful public job at a wage slightly below the minimum wage for private sector work. The government would supplement the wages of all low-wage jobs, both public and private, to ensure that every American who works full-time has enough money to raise a normal-sized family with dignity, out of poverty.

In this system, if you could work and needed money, the government would not give you a check (welfare). It wouldn't give you a check and then try to cajole, instruct, and threaten you into working it off ("workfare") or "training it off." It would give you the location of several government job sites. If you showed up and worked, you would be paid for your work. If you don't show up, you don't get paid. Simple.

Unlike welfare, these public, WPA*-style jobs would be available to everybody, men as well as women, single or married, mothers and fathers alike. No perverse "anti-family" incentives. It wouldn't even be necessary to limit the public jobs to the poor. If Donald Trump showed up, he could work too. But he wouldn't. Most Americans wouldn't. There'd be no need to "target" the program to the needy. The low wage itself would guarantee that those who took the jobs would be those who needed them, while preserving the incentive to look for better work in the private sector.

Perhaps most important for Civic Liberals (as for FDR), such work-relief wouldn't carry the stigma of a cash dole. Those who worked in the neo-WPA jobs would be earning their money. They could hold their heads up. They would also have something most unemployed underclass members desperately need: a supervisor they could give as a job reference to other employers. Although some WPA workers could be promoted to higher-paying public service positions, for most of them movement into the private sector would take care of itself. If you have to work anyway, why do it for $4 an hour? The whole problem of "work incentives" that obsesses current welfare policy dwindles into insignificance when what you're offering is work itself, rather than a dole that people have to then be "incentivized" (that is, bribed) into leaving.

*[Works Progress Administration, a public jobs program created during the Roosevelt administration. —Eds.]

Those who didn't take advantage of the neo-WPA jobs, however, would be on their own as far as income assistance went. No cash doles. Mothers included. The key welfare question left unresolved by the New Deal—do we expect single mothers with children to work?—would be resolved cleanly and clearly in favor of work. The government would announce that after a certain date able-bodied single women who bear children would no longer qualify for cash payments. Young women contemplating single motherhood couldn't count on AFDC to sustain them. As mothers, they would have to work like everyone else. The prospect of juggling motherhood and a not-very-lucrative public job would make them think twice. . . . But the public jobs would . . . also offer both mothers and non-mothers a way out of poverty.

Most American mothers, 67 percent, now work. Most single mothers work. Today's liberals are eager to acknowledge these facts of modern life when it suits their purposes—when arguing for parental leave, or deriding Phyllis Schlafly's "Ozzie and Harriet" vision of the ideal family. But they can't have it both ways. If mothers are expected to work, they're expected to work.

If poor mothers are to work, of course, day care must be provided for their children whenever it's needed, funded by the government if necessary. To avoid creating a day-care ghetto for low-income kids, this service will have to be integrated into the larger system of child care for other American families. That will be expensive. But it won't necessarily be as expensive as you might think. When free day care has been offered to welfare mothers who work, demand has fallen below predictions. "It is never utilized to the extent people thought it would be," says Barbara Goldman of the Manpower Demonstration Research Corporation (MDRC). Most welfare mothers, it seems, prefer to make their own arrangements. (Whether those arrangements are any good is another question. The government might want to take steps to actually encourage day care, as part of an "acculturation" campaign to get underclass kids out of the home and into classrooms at an early age.)

What happens if a poor single mother is offered decent day care, and a WPA-style job, and she refuses them? The short answer is that nothing happens. There's no penalty. Also no check. Perhaps she will discover some other, better way of feeding herself and her family. If, on the other hand, her children are subsequently discovered living in squalor and filth, then she has neglected a basic task of parenthood. She is subject to the laws that already provide for removal of a child from an unfit home. The long answer, then, is that society will also have to construct new institutions, such as orphanages, to care for the children whose parents so fail them.

Will people be allowed to starve? The state's basic obligation, in this scheme, is to provide decent work for all who are able and a decent income for the disabled. There will be able-bodied people—not only mothers—who need money but who don't take advantage of the WPA jobs. Many ghetto men, at least initially, may prefer the world of crime, hustle, and odd jobs to working for "chump change." (One advantage of the Work Ethic State would be that criminals could be treated as criminals, without residual guilt about the availability of employment.) Others —the addled and addicted—will simply fail at working, or not even try.

The first underclass generation *off* welfare will be the roughest. Those people who fail at work will be thrown into the world of austere public in-kind guarantees—homeless shelters, soup kitchens—and of charitable organizations. This aid will be stigmatizing (as it must be if work is to be honored). It will be frankly paternalistic. But it could also be compassionate. Nobody would starve. The government could (and should) offer to subsidize all the counseling, therapy, and job training it could afford, in order to help people back on their feet. The one thing it would not offer them is cash.

What if women take the jobs but still don't form two-parent families? Suppose the work-for-welfare swap goes well. A life on welfare becomes impossible. Young women who would previously have had children and gone on welfare now go to work, have children, and put them in day care. But has the underclass culture really been transformed if these women don't form stable two-parent families? After all, as [Nicholas] Lemann reminds us, many of the black family patterns we lament today were in evidence before AFDC, when black women and men had little economic alternative to working.

There are three answers to this question. The first is that, yes, the ghetto-poor culture would be transformed. A working matriarchy is very different from a non-working matriarchy. If poor women who work to feed themselves and their children prefer to stay unmarried—supporting their children without help from a stable working partner—that's their choice. At least they are out of the welfare culture; they will be able to participate in the larger working society with dignity.

The second answer, which naturally follows from the first, is that many working mothers will not want to make that choice. Certainly it's doubtful that they'll be willing to share their hard-earned paychecks with non-working men the way they might have been willing to share their welfare checks. Once work is the norm, and the subsidy of AFDC has been removed, the natural incentives toward the formation of two-parent families will reassert themselves. Why go crazy trying to raise a kid on $10,000 a year when you can marry another worker and live on $20,000 a year? It makes no sense. Soon enough ghetto women will be demanding and expecting that the men in their lives offer them stable economic support.

Finally, the next generation off welfare—men as well as women, even men growing up in single-mother homes—will be better prepared not only to find jobs but to get the skills that will let them find "good jobs." That's because they will have grown up in a home where work, not welfare, is the norm, where the rhythms and discipline of obligation pervade daily life. A growing body of evidence shows that one of the most important factors in determining success at school is whether a child comes from a working home. Simply put, if a mother has to set her alarm clock, she's likely to teach her children to set their alarm clocks as well.

Eventually, replacing welfare with work *can* be expected to transform the entire culture of poverty. It won't happen in one generation, necessarily, or even two. But it will happen. Underclass culture can't survive the end of welfare any more than feudal culture could survive the advent of capitalism.

What about mothers with very young children, two years and under? A destitute mother with a newborn infant presents the basic AFDC dilemma in its starkest form. Children need the most mothering in their earliest years. Yet more than half of American mothers with kids under three already work, most of them full-time.

One alternative is to allow temporary cash welfare—for, say; two years—when a mother has her first child. Once that time was up, young mothers would be offered only a WPA-style job and day care. The two-year limit would be non-renewable; mothers wouldn't be allowed to get more cash by having another baby. And a two-year free ride on welfare would be vastly different than the 18 years on welfare single mothers can now obtain with every birth. The economy of the ghetto, and the expectations of its residents, would change substantially. Potential single mothers would realize welfare wasn't going to sustain them for long; they'd probably know someone with a two-year-old who's run out of benefits.

But no free ride at all (except for in-kind nutritional assistance to avoid health problems) would clearly have stronger impact. Even a two-year dole might encourage some young women who would otherwise work or marry to have a baby first, get the check, and worry about working later. If we want to end the underclass, remember, the issue is not so much whether working or getting two years of cash will best help Betsy Smith, teenage high-school dropout, acquire the skills to get a good private sector job *after* she's become a single mother. It is whether the prospect of having to work will deter Betsy Smith from having an out-of-wedlock child in the first place—or, failing that, whether the sight of Betsy Smith trying to work and raise a child without a husband will discourage her younger sisters and neighbors from doing as she did. The way to make the true costs of bearing a child out of wedlock clear is to let them be felt when they are incurred—namely, at the child's birth. If would-be single mothers were faced with the prospect of immediately supporting themselves, most would choose a different and better course for their lives.

NO
Richard A. Cloward and Frances Fox Piven

PUNISHING THE POOR, AGAIN: THE FRAUD OF WORKFARE

During the presidential campaign, Bill Clinton repeatedly promised to "reform" the welfare system. Polls showed it was his most popular issue, and it continues to be a sure-fire applause-getter in speeches. But since the cheering stopped, Clinton has moved slowly. The next step will be the appointment of a commission and hearings. Nevertheless, the general direction Clinton intends to take is well known: Some job training, more workfare, new sanctions and an effort to cut women off the rolls after two years.

Such proposals reflect a rising tide of antiwelfare rhetoric, whose basic argument is that people receiving public assistance become trapped in a "cycle of dependency." Thus, Senator Daniel Patrick Moynihan grandiosely proclaims in the press that "just as unemployment was the defining issue of industrialism, dependency is becoming the defining issue of post-industrial society." Conservative political scientist Lawrence Mead warns that "dependency" signals "the end of the Western tradition?" The national press announces that dependency has reached epidemic proportions. According to these accounts, rising unemployment, declining wage levels and disappearing fringe benefits need not concern anyone. "The old issues were economic and structural," Mead says, and "the new ones are social and personal."

To cope with these new issues, the critics urge that women on welfare be put to work. Near-miraculous social and cultural transformations are predicted once welfare mothers are shifted into the labor market. Cohesion will be restored to family and community, crime and other aberrant behaviors will disappear and poverty will decline. Mickey Kaus, who advocates replacing welfare with a W.P.A.-style jobs program, invokes a grand historical parallel: "Underclass culture can't survive the end of welfare any more than feudal culture could survive the advent of capitalism." [W.P.A. is the Works Progress Administration, a public jobs program created during the Roosevelt administration.—Eds.]

But there is no economically and politically practical way to replace welfare with work at a time when the labor market is saturated with people looking for jobs. Unemployment averaged 4.5 percent in the 1950s, 4.7 percent in the 1960s, 6.1 percent in the 1970s and 7.2 percent in the 1980s, and job prospects look no better in the 1990s. The labor market is flooded with immigrants from Asia and Latin America, and growing numbers of women have taken jobs to shore up family income as wages decline. Confronted with an increasingly globalized economy, corporations are shedding workers or closing domestic plants and opening new ones in Third World countries with cheap labor. Meanwhile, defense industries are making huge workforce cuts.

Moreover, employers are increasingly offering "contingent work"—part-time, temporary and poorly paid. Some 30 million people—over a quarter of the U.S. labor force—are employed in such jobs. A substantial proportion of them would prefer permanent, full-time jobs but cannot find them. Contingent workers are six times more likely than full-time workers to receive the minimum wage, and they are much less likely to receive health and pension benefits.

Because most mothers who receive Aid to Families with Dependent Children [A.F.D.C.] are unskilled, they can command only the lowest wages and thus cannot adequately support their families, a problem that will grow worse as wages continue to decline. According to the Census Bureau, 14.4 million year-round, full-time workers 16 years of age or older (18 percent of the total) had annual earnings below the poverty level in 1990, up from 10.3 million (14.6 percent) in 1984 and 6.6 million (12.3 percent) in 1974. There is no reason to think that A.F.D.C. mothers can become "self-sufficient" when growing millions of currently employed workers cannot. In a study of the finances of welfare families, sociologists Christopher Jencks and Kathryn Edin found that "single mothers do not turn to welfare because they are pathologically dependent on handouts or unusually reluctant to work—they do so because they cannot get jobs that pay better than welfare."

Research on workfare programs bears this out. Sociologists Fred Block and John Noakes concluded that participants typically cannot find jobs that pay more than welfare. Reviewing the research in the field, the Center on Budget and Policy Priorities found that—highly publicized stories of individual successes notwithstanding—only a handful of people in work-fare programs achieved "a stable source of employment that provides enough income for a decent standard of living (at least above the poverty line) and job-related benefits that adequately cover medical needs." Still another general survey, this one sponsored by the Brookings Institution, reports that none of the programs succeed in raising earnings of welfare mothers more than $2,000 above grant levels. Political scientists John E. Schwarz and Thomas J. Volgy write in their book *The Forgotten Americans*, "No matter how much we may wish it otherwise, workfare cannot be an effective solution" because "low-wage employment riddles the economy." They note that in 1989 one in seven year-round full-time jobs, or 11 million, paid less than $11,500, which was roughly $2,000 below the official poverty line for a family of four.

The situation is actually much worse. When the poverty line was first calculated in the 1960s, the average family spent one-third of its income on food, and the poverty line was set at three times food costs, adjusted for family size.

But by 1990, food costs had dropped to one-sixth of the average family budget because the price of other components —such as housing and medical costs— had,inflated at far higher rates. If the 1991 official poverty line of $13,920 for a family of four had been recalculated to reflect changes in real costs, it would have been set at about 155 percent of the official rate, or $21,600. That is more than twice the $8,840 annual earnings of a full-time worker receiving the minimum wage of $4.25 per hour. . . .

Another reason to be skeptical about welfare-to-work programs is that, although they are promoted as economy measures, they would in fact be very expensive if implemented widely. Federal and state expenditures for A.F.D.C. now run about $20 billion, supplemented by another $10 billion in food stamp costs for welfare families. But workfare programs would cost tens of billions more. Administrative costs alone would overshadow any savings from successful job placements. And to this must be added the much larger costs of government-subsidized child care and health care —essential to mothers going off welfare, since the private market is curtailing such benefits for newly hired workers. Economist James Medoff estimates that the proportion of new hires who receive health benefits dropped from 23 percent to 15 percent during the past decade. Christopher Jencks estimates that A.F.D.C. mothers working at the minimum wage would have to be given "free medical care and at least $5,000 worth of other resources every year to supplement their wages," at a cost of up to $50 billion, a quixotic sum that Congress is unlikely to appropriate. Mickey Kaus offers a similar estimate of the cost of his recommendation for a mandatory jobs program

for the poor. Congress is certainly not unmindful of these costs, as it shows by its endless squabbling over whether health and day care benefits should be given to working recipients at all.

Given these constraints, the results of existing workfare programs are predictable enough. Studies show that a substantial proportion of welfare recipients who find jobs end up reapplying for welfare because they cannot survive on their earnings, even with welfare supplements, and because temporary child care and Medicaid supports run out, or because of periodic crises such as layoffs or illness in the family. Nevertheless, the charade goes on, as experts and politicians promise to put an end to welfare "dependency." None of it makes pragmatic sense.

* * *

Other professed goals of these work programs are equally irrational, such as the unsubstantiated assertions that putting welfare recipients to work would transform family structure, community life and the so-called "culture of poverty." Kaus insists that "replacing welfare with work can be expected to transform the entire culture of poverty," including family patterns, because "it's doubtful" that working women would "be willing to share their hard-earned paychecks with non-working men the way they might have been willing to share their welfare checks." Therefore, "the natural incentives toward the formation of two-parent families will reassert themselves." But Kaus presents no data to support the assumption that the source of a woman's income influences marriage or living arrangements. In our judgment, marriage rates might indeed increase if jobs paying adequate wages and benefits were available to men, as well as to women on welfare who choose to work, but that outcome seems entirely unlikely in view of current economic trends.

It is also doubtful that putting poor women to work would improve the care and socialization of children, as Kaus claims. "If a mother has to set her alarm clock, she's likely to teach her children to set their alarm clocks as well," he says, thus trivializing the real activities of most of these women. Many A.F.D.C. mothers get their children up every morning and, because of the dangers of the streets, escort them to school, walk them home and keep them in their apartments until the next morning. Forcing these overburdened women to work would add a market job to the already exhausting job of maintaining a home without sufficient funds or services while living in dangerous and disorganized neighborhoods.

Putting welfare recipients to work is advertised as the way to reverse the deterioration of community life. This is hardly a new idea. The minutes of a meeting of academics, intellectuals and administrators in New York City after Richard Nixon's 1968 presidential election reported a consensus that the rising welfare rolls accompanied by spreading urban riots and other manifestations of civil disorder proved that "the social fabric... is coming to pieces. It isn't just 'strained' and it isn't just 'frayed'; but like a sheet of rotten canvas, it is beginning to rip...." Converting A.F.D.C. to a work-fare system was the remedy; work would restore the social fabric.

More likely, removing women from their homes and communities would shred the social fabric even more. Putting mothers to work would deprive the poor community of its most stable element

—the women who, for example, have mounted campaigns to drive drug dealers from their housing projects and neighborhoods. Sally Hernandez-Piñero, chairwoman of the New York City Housing Authority, emphasized the important social role played by the approximately 65,000 women raising children alone in the New York City projects: "Anyone with even a nodding acquaintance with these women knows them for what they are, the sanity of the poor community, resourceful survivors of abandonment, slander and brutality.... In many poor communities, they are the only signatures on the social contract, the glue that keeps our communities from spinning out of control."

None of the critics convincingly explain why these women would contribute more to their communities by taking jobs flipping hamburgers. Nor do they explain why it would not be better public policy to shore up income supports (the real value of A.F.D.C. benefits has fallen by 43 percent since the early 1970s, and by 27 percent if food stamps are figured in) and social supports for women who are struggling to care for children under the junglelike conditions of urban poverty. Instead, the family and community work performed by these women—like the family and community work of women in general—is consistently ignored or devalued.

Feminists are not exactly rallying to the defense of their poorest sisters, perhaps because the issue of work provokes such strong feeling. Many welfare mothers do want to work, and they should have the chance, together with training and supportive benefits, such as day care and health care, as well as adequate wages and supplemental welfare payments. Under such conditions, many would take jobs, and coercion would be unnecessary. Realistically, however, such opportunities are not on the reform agenda. It is the charade of work that is on the agenda.

Despite workfare's record of failure, an aura of optimism still permeates the literature on welfare reform. Many experts are convinced that most welfare mothers can achieve self-sufficiency through work and that benign consequences for family and community will ensue. The key to eventual success, they say, is to find the proper mix of programs targeted at those who can best benefit from them. As theories and policies proliferate—none of them gaining ascendance for long, since none of them succeed in practice—the search goes on for new strategies, or a mix of strategies, that will produce the desired outcomes. As sociologist Sanford Schram points out, these initiatives serve "symbolic purposes at the expense of substantive benefits."

Politicians understand the value of this symbolism, however, and rush to divert voter discontent over rising unemployment and falling wage levels by focusing on "welfare reform," knowing that welfare mothers, a majority of whom are black and Hispanic, make convenient scapegoats. Welfare is thus defined as a major national domestic problem—bad for the country and bad for the poor. It drains public budgets and reduces work effort. Allowing poor mothers to opt out of paid work saps their initiative and induces disabling psychological and cultural patterns that entrench their incapacity for work all the more. Deepening poverty ostensibly follows. As Lawrence Mead puts it, the new inequality in the United States can be traced to the "nonworking poor."

Not only are better-off people encouraged to blame the poor for their own troubles but the rituals that degrade welfare recipients reaffirm the imperative of work at a time when wages are down, working conditions worse and jobs less secure. Kaus writes that while we cannot promise the poor who work that "they'll be rich, or even comfortably well-off" (and, he might have added, we cannot even promise them a living wage), "we can promise them *respect*" because they "would have the tangible honor society reserves for workers." The charade of work enforcement reform should thus be understood as a symbolic crusade directed at the working poor rather than at those on relief, and the moral conveyed is the shame of the dole and the virtue of labor, no matter the job and no matter the pay.

One thing seems clear: If Clinton and Congress actually adopt the proposed two-year cutoff of benefits in the current labor market, they will soon find themselves debating whether women unable to make it in the marketplace should be readmitted to the rolls. (During the 1992 presidential campaign, Clinton claimed that 17,000 Arkansas residents had been successfully moved off the A.F.D.C. and food stamp rolls under a state jobs program between 1989 and 1992, but the administrator of the program subsequently acknowledged that "many people returned to welfare during that period.") If they are not, the streets would soon fill with homeless women and children, and the venerable body of theory and historical research that attributes riots and political disorder to economic insecurity would once again be put to the test. It is hard to believe that national politicians will take that risk.

POSTSCRIPT

Should Welfare Recipients Be Put to Work?

In the midst of the Great Depression, Congress adopted the Social Security Act of 1935. Its major provision was the old age and survivors insurance scheme that is popularly called Social Security. A second feature was unemployment insurance, to assist workers during periods of temporary unemployment. Little remarked upon at the time was a provision designed to provide economic aid to widows and children, which has grown into the vast Aid to Families with Dependent Children (AFDC) system, the central feature of the federal welfare system.

AFDC has been praised, vilified, debated, amended, and augmented by food stamps, Medicare, and numerous other programs. The size and cost of these programs continue to grow, as does the number of Americans who are recipients of welfare assistance. In the six decades since the federal welfare system was first adopted, American productivity and prosperity have dramatically increased, but so have poverty and the provision of welfare programs by both the federal and state governments.

Mickey Kaus hopes that, just as the New Deal put people to work with the Works Progress Administration (WPA), his plan for a new WPA-style public works project can have the effect of replacing welfare with productive jobs for all able-bodied adults, resulting in the transformation of ghetto welfare culture into a working society. Like other critics of similar reforms, Richard Cloward and Francis Fox Piven believe that workfare will produce few full-time jobs, reduce the already low living standards of welfare recipients, and increase the cost to government.

The evolution of welfare policies is traced in Michael B. Katz, *The Undeserving Poor: From the War on Poverty to the War on Welfare* (Pantheon Books, 1989). Lawrence M. Mead, *The New Politics of Poverty* (Basic Books, 1992) presents a detailed criticism of the welfare system. Jonathan Kozol, in *Savage Inequalities: Children in America's Schools* (Harper Perennial, 1992), argues that the system fails because it does not deal with root causes, such as the inadequate education of poor children. John Kenneth Galbraith, in *The Culture of Contentment* (Houghton Mifflin, 1992), states that the plight of the poor is made worse by the increased use of cheap foreign labor by American companies. The periodical literature, already large, will grow as Congress debates reforms to the welfare system.

The opposing views are evidence that there are no easy answers to the hard questions raised by the movement to replace welfare with workfare. Can low-paying jobs provide a sufficient standard of living for millions of unskilled workers? Can enough jobs be created by private enterprise? Are we willing to undertake public projects to employ people dropped from the welfare rolls? How will we pay for child care for the single mothers who enter the job market? Our shared objectives of reducing poverty and welfare dependency do not lead to confident solutions.

ISSUE 15

Do We Need National Health Care Insurance?

YES: White House Domestic Policy Council, from *Health Security: The President's Report to the American People* (The White House, 1993)

NO: Irwin M. Stelzer, from "What Health-Care Crisis?" *Commentary* (February 1994)

ISSUE SUMMARY

YES: President Bill Clinton argues that the current health care system falls far short of providing universal and affordable coverage for all Americans and that a new system aimed at achieving this goal must be implemented.

NO: Irwin M. Stelzer, the director of Regulatory Policy Studies at the American Enterprise Institute, maintains that there is no crisis in the provision of health care in America and that radical changes will imperil the quality of medicine.

Many controversial issues were raised in the first two years of Bill Clinton's presidency, but none were more debated in and out of Congress than the president's proposal to establish a system of health care coverage for all Americans. By the time health care reform reached the floors of the Senate and House of Representatives, many bills had been drafted, and some of the president's proposals—health care alliances, universal coverage, and cost controls—had been altered or abandoned.

Those who favor far-reaching reform acknowledge that the current system in the United States provides outstanding health care for a majority of the people most of the time. Those who oppose sweeping reform concede that change is necessary to provide adequate coverage for those who do not now have it. Is it possible for the two sides to reconcile their differences?

Since World War II, more Nobel Prizes in physiology and medicine have been awarded to physicians and medical scientists working in the United States than in the rest of the world. It is widely acknowledged that the training and education of medical personnel in the United States is the best in the world. The latest medical technology is more widely available in the United States than anywhere else. It is no surprise that when wealthy people in other countries have a disease that is difficult to treat, they often seek treatment in the United States.

By contrast, it is estimated that more than 35 million Americans have no medical coverage and perhaps as many as another 100 million are underinsured. This is true despite the fact that roughly $900 billion a year is currently spent on health care in the United States. One-third of this amount is spent directly by the federal government. In 1993 the total expenditure for health care amounted to more than 14 percent of the gross national product, nearly 10 times the amount spent in the United States 40 years ago.

There are two overriding political issues involved in health care reform: coverage and cost. In 1965 the national government recognized and tried to remedy the problems of coverage and the availability of medical care by establishing Medicare, which provides some government-sponsored medical care for older people, and Medicaid, which provides some medical coverage for the poor. Nevertheless, the rising cost of private medical care increasingly puts it beyond the means of millions of Americans.

Although there is widespread conviction that something should be done, it is more difficult to decide what and how. Should the present mix of private payments, employer-sponsored medical programs, Medicaid, and Medicare be improved? Should public policy encourage the creation of health maintenance organizations so that administrative costs can be reduced? Should the federal government adopt universal health insurance for all employed persons, all citizens, or all persons?

Critics argue that medical costs in the United States are higher per capita than in other advanced countries but that too many people receive inadequate or no medical service. They point out that other industrial nations have some form of comprehensive national health insurance that prevents these problems. Opponents of a national scheme counter that experience indicates that a government bureaucracy would do a poor job of administering such a program, that it would deny individuals the right to choose their own physicians, and that additional costs would add to the national debt.

The government has at least three possible choices in confronting this issue. The first is to rely largely on the free market. This could be compatible with such reforms as requiring insurance companies to accept all potential buyers or providing tax credits for taxpayers and vouchers for poor people to make certain that everyone has the financial ability to obtain medical insurance. A second approach would require employers to provide medical coverage or contribute to a fund that would pay for coverage for those not otherwise insured. The most sweeping change in medical care would be brought about by the adoption of national health insurance, where the national government would be the single paying agent.

President Clinton's address to Congress advocating universal health care coverage marked the starting point for one of the most far-reaching examinations of social policy ever considered by Congress and the American people. Irwin M. Stelzer objects that the health care crisis is not real, that America's excellent system of health care would be imperiled by government interference, and that real corrections are possible within the current system.

YES

ADDRESS OF THE PRESIDENT TO THE JOINT SESSION OF CONGRESS, SEPTEMBER 22, 1993

If Americans are to have the courage to change in a difficult time, we must first be secure in our most basic needs. Tonight I want to talk to you about the most critical thing we can do to build that security. This health care system of ours is badly broken and it is time to fix it.

Despite the dedication of literally millions of talented health care professionals, our health care is too uncertain and too expensive, too bureaucratic and too wasteful. It has too much fraud and too much greed.

At long last, after decades of false starts, we must make this our most urgent priority, giving every American health security; health care that can never be taken away, health care that is always there. That is what we must do tonight.

On this journey, as on all others of true consequence, there will be rough spots in the road and honest disagreements about how we should proceed. After all, this is a complicated issue. But every successful journey is guided by fixed stars. And if we can agree on some basic values and principles we will reach this destination, and we will reach it together.

So tonight I want to talk to you about the principles that I believe must embody our efforts to reform America's health care system—security, simplicity, savings, choice, quality, and responsibility....

Now, we all know what's right. We're blessed with the best health care professionals on Earth, the finest health care institutions, the best medical research, the most sophisticated technology. My mother is a nurse. I grew up around hospitals. Doctors and nurses were the first professional people I ever knew or learned to look up to. They are what is right with this health care system. But we also know that we can no longer afford to continue to ignore what is wrong.

Millions of Americans are just a pink slip away from losing their health insurance, and one serious illness away from losing all their savings. Millions

From White House Domestic Policy Council, *Health Security: The President's Report to the American People* (The White House, 1993).

more are locked into the jobs they have now just because they or someone in their family has once been sick and they have what is called a preexisting condition. And on any given day, over 37 million Americans—most of them working people and their little children —have no health insurance at all.

And in spite of all this, our medical bills are growing at over twice the rate of inflation, and the United States spends over a third more of its income on health care than any other nation on Earth. And the gap is growing, causing many of our companies in global competition severe disadvantage. There is no excuse for this kind of system. We know other people have done better. We know people in our own country are doing better. We have no excuse. My fellow Americans, we must fix this system and it has to begin with congressional action.

I believe as strongly as I can say that we can reform the costliest and most wasteful system on the face of the Earth without enacting new broad-based taxes. I believe it because of the conversations I have had with thousands of health care professionals around the country; with people who are outside this city, but are inside experts on the way this system works and wastes money. . . .

Now, if I might, I would like to review the six principles I mentioned earlier and describe how we think we can best fulfill those principles.

First and most important, security. This principle speaks to the human misery, to the costs, to the anxiety we hear about every day—all of us—when people talk about their problems with the present system. Security means that those who do not now have health care coverage will have it; and for those who have it, it will

never be taken away. We must achieve that security as soon as possible.

Under our plan, every American would receive a health care security card that will guarantee a comprehensive package of benefits over the course of an entire lifetime, roughly comparable to the benefit package offered by most Fortune 500 companies. This health care security card will offer this package of benefits in a way that can never be taken away.

So let us agree on this: whatever else we disagree on, before this Congress finishes its work next year, you will pass and I will sign legislation to guarantee this security to every citizen of this country.

With this card, if you lose your job or you switch jobs, you're covered. If you leave your job to start a small business, you're covered. If you're an early retiree, you're covered. If someone in your family has, unfortunately, had an illness that qualifies as a preexisting condition, you're still covered. If you get sick or a member of your family gets sick, even if it's a life threatening illness, you're covered. And if an insurance company tries to drop you for any reason, you will still be covered, because that will be illegal.

This card will give comprehensive coverage. It will cover people for hospital care, doctor visits, emergency and lab services, diagnostic services like Pap smears and mammograms and cholesterol tests, substance abuse and mental health treatment.

And equally important, for both health care and economic reasons, this program for the first time would provide a broad range of preventive services including regular checkups and well-baby visits.

Now, it's just common sense. We know —any family doctor will tell you that people will stay healthier and long-term costs of the health system will be lower if we have comprehensive preventive services. You know how all of our mothers told us that an ounce of prevention was worth a pound of cure? Our mothers were right. And it's a lesson, like so many lessons from our mothers, that we have waited too long to live by. It is time to start doing it.

Health care security must also apply to older Americans. This is something I imagine all of us in this room feel very deeply about. The first thing I want to say about that is that we must maintain the Medicare program. It works to provide that kind of security. But this time and for the first time, I believe Medicare should provide coverage for the cost of prescription drugs.

Yes, it will cost some more in the beginning. But, again, any physician who deals with the elderly will tell you that there are thousands of elderly people in every state who are not poor enough to be on Medicaid, but just above that line and on Medicare, who desperately need medicine, who make decisions every week between medicine and food. Any doctor who deals with the elderly will tell you that there are many elderly people who don't get medicine, who get sicker and sicker and eventually go to the doctor and wind up spending more money and draining more money from the health care system than they would if they had regular treatment in the way that only adequate medicine can provide.

I also believe that over time, we should phase in long-term care for the disabled and the elderly on a comprehensive basis.

As we proceed with this health care reform, we cannot forget that the most rapidly growing percentage of Americans are those over 80. We cannot break faith with them. We have to do better by them.

The second principle is simplicity. Our health care system must be simpler for the patients and simpler for those who actually deliver health care—our doctors, our nurses, our other medical professionals. Today we have more than 1,500 insurers, with hundreds and hundreds of different forms. No other nation has a system like this. These forms are time consuming for health care providers, they're expensive for health care consumers, they're exasperating for anyone who's ever tried to sit down around a table and wade through them and figure them out.

The medical care industry is literally drowning in paperwork. In recent years, the number of administrators in our hospitals has grown by four times the rate that the number of doctors has grown. A hospital ought to be a house of healing, not a monument to paperwork and bureaucracy. . . .

Under our proposal there would be one standard insurance form—not hundreds of them. We will simplify also—and we must—the government's rules and regulations, because they are a big part of this problem. This is one of those cases where the physician should heal thyself. We have to reinvent the way we relate to the health care system, along with reinventing government. A doctor should not have to check with a bureaucrat in an office thousands of miles away before ordering a simple blood test. That's not right, and we can change it. And doctors, nurses and consumers shouldn't have to worry about the fine print. If we have this one simple form, there won't be any fine print. People will know what it means.

The third principle is savings. Reform must produce savings in this health care system. It has to. We're spending over 14 percent of our income on health care—Canada's at 10; nobody else is over nine. We're competing with all these people for the future. And the other major countries, they cover everybody and they cover them with services as generous as the best company policies here in this country.

Rampant medical inflation is eating away at our wages, our savings, our investment capital, our ability to create new jobs in the private sector and this public Treasury. You know the budget we just adopted had steep cuts in defense, a five-year freeze on the discretionary spending, so critical to reeducating America and investing in jobs and helping us to convert from a defense to a domestic economy. But we passed a budget which has Medicaid increases of between 16 and 11 percent a year over the next five years, and Medicare increases of between 11 and 9 percent in an environment where we assume inflation will be at 4 percent or less.

We cannot continue to do this. Our competitiveness, our whole economy, the integrity of the way the government works and, ultimately, our living standards depend upon our ability to achieve savings without harming the quality of health care.

Unless we do this, our workers will lose almost $600 in income each year by the end of the decade. Small businesses will continue to face skyrocketing premiums. And a full third of small businesses now covering their employees say they will be forced to drop their insurance. Large corporations will bear vivid disadvantages in global competition. And health care costs will devour more and more and more of our budget.

Pretty soon all of you or the people who succeed you will be showing up here, and writing out checks for health care and interest on the debt and worrying about whether we've got enough defense, and that will be it, unless we have the courage to achieve the savings that are plainly there before us. Every state and local government will continue to cut back on everything from education to law enforcement to pay more and more for the same health care.

These rising costs are a special nightmare for our small businesses—the engine of our entrepreneurship and our job creation in America today. Health care premiums for small businesses are 35 percent higher than those of large corporations today. And they will keep rising at double-digit rates unless we act.

So how will we achieve these savings? Rather than looking at price control, or looking away as the price spiral continues; rather than using the heavy hand of government to try to control what's happening, or continuing to ignore what's happening, we believe there is a third way to achieve these savings.

First, to give groups of consumers and small businesses the same market bargaining power that large corporations and large groups of public employees now have. We want to let market forces enable plans to compete. We want to force these plans to compete on the basis of price and quality, not simply to allow them to continue making money by turning people away who are sick or old or performing mountains of unnecessary procedures. But we also believe we should back this system up with limits on how much plans can raise their premiums year in and year out, forcing people, again, to continue to pay more for the same health care, without regard to inflation or the rising population needs.

We want to create what has been missing in this system for too long, and what every successful nation who has dealt with this problem has already had to do: to have a combination of private market forces and a sound public policy that will support that competition, but limit the rate at which prices can exceed the rate of inflation and population growth, if the competition doesn't work, especially in the early going.

The second thing I want to say is that unless everybody is covered—and this is a very important thing—unless everybody is covered, we will never be able to fully put the [brakes] on health care inflation. Why is that? Because when people don't have any health insurance, they still get health care, but they get it when it's too late, when it's too expensive, often from the most expensive place of all, the emergency room. Usually by the time they show up, their illnesses are more severe and their mortality rates are much higher in our hospitals than those who have insurance. So they cost us more.

And what else happens? Since they get the care but they don't pay, who does pay? All the rest of us. We pay in higher hospital bills and higher insurance premiums. This cost shifting is a major problem.

The third thing we can do to save money is simply by simplifying the system—what we've already discussed. Freeing the health care providers from these costly and unnecessary paperwork and administrative decisions will save tens of billions of dollars. We spend twice as much as any other major country does on paperwork. We spend at least a dime on the dollar more than any other major country. That is a stunning statistic. It is

something that every Republican and every Democrat ought to be able to say, we agree that we're going to squeeze this out. We cannot tolerate this. This has nothing to do with keeping people well or helping them when they're sick. We should invest the money in something else.

We also have to crack down on fraud and abuse in the system. That drains billions of dollars a year. It is a very large figure, according to every health care expert I've ever spoken with.

So I believe we can achieve large savings. And that large savings can be used to cover the unemployed uninsured, and will be used for people who realize those savings in the private sector to increase their ability to invest and grow, to hire new workers or to give their workers pay raises, many of them for the first time in years. . . .

People may disagree over the best way to fix this system. We may all disagree about how quickly we can do what—the thing that we have to do. But we cannot disagree that we can find tens of billions of dollars in savings in what is clearly the most costly and the most bureaucratic system in the entire world. And we have to do something about that, and we have to do it now.

The fourth principle is choice. Americans believe they ought to be able to choose their own health care plan and keep their own doctors. And I think all of us agree. Under any plan we pass, they ought to have that right. But today, under our broken health care system, in spite of the rhetoric of choice, the fact is that that power is slipping away for more and more Americans.

Of course, it is usually the employer; not the employee, who makes the initial choice of what health care plan the employee will be in. And if your employer offers only one plan, as nearly three-quarters of small or medium-sized firms do today, you're stuck with that plan, and the doctors that it covers.

We propose to give every American a choice among high-quality plans. You can stay with your current doctor; join a network of doctors and hospitals, or join a health maintenance organization. If you don't like your plan, every year you'll have the chance to choose a new one. The choice will be left to the American citizen, the worker—not the boss, and certainly not some government bureaucrat.

We also believe that doctors should have a choice as to what plans they practice in. Otherwise, citizens may have their own choices limited. We want to end the discrimination that is now growing against doctors, and to permit them to practice in several different plans. Choice is important for doctors, and it is absolutely critical for our consumers. We've got to have it in whatever plan we pass.

The fifth principle is quality. If we reformed everything else in health care, but failed to preserve and enhance the high quality of our medical care, we will have taken a step backward, not forward. Quality is something that we simply can't leave to chance. When you board an airplane, you feel better knowing that the plane had to meet standards designed to protect your safety. And we can't ask any less of our health care system.

Our proposal will create report cards on health plans, so that consumers can choose the highest quality health care providers and reward them with their business. At the same time, our plan will track quality indicators, so that doctors can make better and smarter choices of the kind of care they provide. We have evidence that more efficient delivery of health care doesn't decrease quality. In fact, it may enhance it.

Let me just give you one example of one commonly performed procedure, the coronary bypass operation. Pennsylvania discovered that patients who were charged $21,000 for this surgery received as good or better care as patients who were charged $84,000 for the same procedure in the same state. High prices simply don't always equal good quality.

Our plan will guarantee that high-quality information is available in even the most remote areas of this country so that we can have high-quality service, linking rural doctors, for example, with hospitals with high-tech urban medical centers. And our plan will ensure the quality of continuing progress on a whole range of issues by speeding the search on effective prevention and treatment measures for cancer; for AIDS, for Alzheimer's, for heart disease, and for other chronic diseases. We have to safeguard the finest medical research establishment in the entire world. And we will do that with this plan. Indeed, we will even make it better.

The sixth and final principle is responsibility. We need to restore a sense that we're all in this together and that we all have a responsibility to be a part of the solution. Responsibility has to start with those who profit from the current system. Responsibility means insurance companies should no longer be allowed to cast people aside when they get sick. It should apply to laboratories that submit fraudulent bills, to lawyers who abuse malpractice claims, to doctors who order unnecessary procedures. It means drug companies should no longer charge three times more for prescription drugs made in America here in the United States than they charge for the same drugs overseas.

In short, responsibility should apply to anybody who abuses this system and drives up the cost for honest, hard-working citizens and undermines confidence in the honest, gifted health care providers we have.

Responsibility also means changing some behaviors in this country that drive up our costs like crazy. And without changing it we'll never have the system we ought to have. We will never.

Let me just mention a few and start with the most important—the outrageous cost of violence in this country stem in large measure from the fact that this is the only country in the world where teenagers can rout the streets at random with semi-automatic weapons and be better armed than the police.

But let's not kid ourselves, it's not that simple. We also have higher rates of AIDS, of smoking and excessive drinking, of teen pregnancy, of low birthweight babies. And we have the third worst immunization rate of any nation in the western hemisphere. We have to change our ways if we ever really want to be healthy as a people and have an affordable health care system. And no one can deny that....

Now, these, my fellow Americans, are the principles on which I think we should base our efforts: security, simplicity, savings, choice, quality and responsibility. These are the guiding stars that we should follow on our journey toward health care reform.

Over the coming months, you'll be bombarded with information from all kinds of sources. There will be some who will stoutly disagree with what I have proposed—and with all other plans in the Congress, for that matter. And some of the arguments will be genuinely sincere and enlightening. Others may simply be scare tactics by those who are motivated by the self-interest they have in the waste the system now generates, because that waste is providing jobs, incomes and money for some people.

I ask you only to think of this when you hear all of these arguments: Ask yourself whether the cost of staying on this same course isn't greater than the cost of change. And ask yourself when you hear the arguments whether the arguments are in your interest or someone else's. This is something we have got to try to do together.

I want also to say to the representatives in Congress, you have a special duty to look beyond these arguments. I ask you instead to look into the eyes of the sick child who needs care; to think of the face of the woman who's been told not only that her condition is malignant, but not covered by her insurance. To look at the bottom lines of the businesses driven to bankruptcy by health care costs. To look at the "for sale" signs in front of the homes of families who have lost everything because of their health care costs....

I know we have differences of opinion, but we are here tonight in a spirit that is animated by the problems of those people, and by the sheer knowledge that if we can look into our heart, we will not be able to say that the greatest nation in the history of the world is powerless to confront this crisis.

Our history and our heritage tell us that we can meet this challenge. Everything about America's past tells us we will do it. So I say to you, let us write that new chapter in the American story. Let us guarantee every American comprehensive health benefits that can never be taken away.

NO

Irwin M. Stelzer

WHAT HEALTH-CARE CRISIS?

The idea that there is [a health-care] crisis stems, it would appear, from four sources. The first is the insecurity generated by the most recent recession. Most Americans' health insurance is linked to their jobs, with employers paying about 86 percent of the total cost: lose your job, lose your coverage; get a new job and you might not get coverage if you have a health problem. During a period of rising unemployment, enough Americans found this prospect sufficiently unsettling to create a constituency for changes in the way health-insurance coverage is maintained.

Then there is the concern over costs. Already claiming 14 percent of our gross national product—a figure high by international standards—health-care costs have also been rising. Many people have convinced themselves that unless something is done, health care will consume an ever-larger share of GNP [gross national product], leading in the end to the impoverishment of America.

Additional pressure for reform comes from the notion that *everyone*—no exceptions—should have health insurance as a matter of right. Since somewhere between 37 and 39 million Americans are now widely said to be without coverage, the system must be failing and it must be revamped to provide insurance for all.

A fourth contributor to the sense of crisis is the well-documented liberal bias of the major media. This factor helps to explain one of the great anomalies in the health-care debate: although 75 percent of Americans have been persuaded that there is a crisis (32 percent say the system "needs fundamental changes," and 47 percent that it "needs to be completely rebuilt"), 80 percent simultaneously report *themselves* as "very" or "somewhat" satisfied with the quality and cost of their own health care. "This contradiction," writes Fred Barnes in the premiere issue of *Forbes MediaCritic*, "can be attributed to the media-generated myths that have shaped America's view of its health-care system."...

* * *

Take the much-heralded 14-percent figure. The approximately $940 billion Americans spent on health care in 1993 did indeed represent a bit more than

14 percent of the nation's total output of goods and services. By what standard is that too much? Three are generally offered: other nations spend less; in the past we ourselves spent less; and the results we get do not justify the amount of money we put in.

But international comparisons—to begin with them—are notoriously flawed. First of all, we are the richest nation in the world, with more houses, cars, telephones, toilets, parks, and other amenities than most other nations can even imagine. As such, we cannot be expected to deploy increments of our rising incomes in the same way as do, say, the Japanese, 54 percent of whom in the average-income bracket still lack indoor toilet facilities (whereas only 1.8 percent of America's *poor* are without such facilities). If we prefer to devote a larger portion of our incomes to top-quality health care, what is wrong with that?

After all, we do not settle for the housing standards that prevail in poorer countries: we insist on central heating and air-conditioning, the latter now installed in nearly half of the homes of even those we classify as poor. Nor are tiny cars with mechanical clutches, common elsewhere, the stuff of which the American dream is made. Neither is spartan health care. Hence we afford ourselves the luxury of making much greater use than other countries do of expensive diagnostic techniques like CAT scans and ultrasound tests.

Another reason why international comparisons mean little is that they give no weight to differences in the quality of service. The *Congressional Quarterly* cites the fact that "Japan's government plays a much greater role in private health-care delivery than does the U.S. government" to explain how "Japan keeps its costs considerably lower than those of the United States." No mention of what Fred Barnes calls "Japanese... assembly-line treatment from doctors who see an average of 49 patients a day," and who perform gynecological examinations on scores of women assembled in a single nonprivate room, as physicians scramble to maintain incomes in the face of too-low per-capita reimbursements.

Such stringent government controls on physicians' fees do succeed in lowering the recorded cost of Japanese medical care. But because payment is based on patient visits, the doctor keeps the average length of each visit to five minutes, and the Japanese on average make twelve visits per year, or about three times as many as Americans, whose average visit length is fifteen to twenty minutes. These decreases in convenience for patients, and increases in patient time and travel costs, points out Patricia Danzon of the Wharton school, "are excluded from the national health accounts and from public visibility."

International cost comparisons also ignore queuing and other forms of rationing that reduce recorded costs by forcibly limiting the availability of the service. Like consumer goods in the old Soviet Union, medical services in many of the countries with which America's reformers invidiously compare the U.S. are cheap but hard to get.

Joseph White, a Brookings Institution researcher whose comparison of America's system with those of six other nations leads him to conclude that "America's health-care system must be reformed," nevertheless concedes that "Britain has restricted capacity severely and makes people wait much longer for services that Americans would consider necessary, than we would accept." Certainly, the British rule that patients over fifty-five are not eligible for kidney dialysis would not be acceptable here.

We further discover from White that Australia faces both availability restrictions and "spiraling costs," and that there are "stirrings of dissatisfaction" in France. On the other hand, he dismisses Canada's waiting lists as the result of "unexpected increases in demand... [rather] than... intentional constraints on capacity."

Here White shows no recognition that the shortages caused by government planning and operation are *often* "unintentional"—planners, immunized from the consequences of the shortages they create by preferential access to goods and services (did a Kremlin bureaucrat ever queue for anything?), rarely match demand and supply with any precision. And Canada's recent response to unbearable cost increases—a reduction in the services covered—passes without mention in White's analysis. Nor does he tell us what we learn from Patricia Danzon, who notes that Canadian physicians "work fewer hours as [government-mandated] expenditure ceilings are approached," thereby shifting the risks and costs of waiting for care to patients—and lowering the recorded cost of health care in Canada. This is not a trivial matter in a country in which 1.4 million people are waiting for medical service, and 45 percent of those queuing up for surgery say they are "in pain."

Japan, writes White, "has not yet experienced significant complaints about waiting lists." But that silence may well be due more to stoic acceptance of shortages than to their absence. As for Germany, it achieves its low costs by limiting malpractice suits; by eschewing extraordinary life-prolonging measures for those judged to be terminally ill; by buying fewer pieces of high-technology equipment than Americans typically use; and by price controls. Even so, costs are soaring and the German insurance funds are broke, despite premiums that come to 13 percent of payrolls.

* * *

Yet another reason why international comparisons are misleading is that they omit societal attitudes. A prominent British physician described to me how decisions are reached in that country about whether to expend resources in an effort to save a seriously damaged newborn, or to let nature take its course. A hospital staff conference, a quiet meeting with the parents, a decision. In America, in similar circumstances, draconian efforts would be made to prolong the child's life. So, too, at other stages of life, including extreme old age.

Indeed, it is the very success of these efforts that contributes to the high cost of health care: the dead are no burden to the system; survivors are. The high expenditures incurred thereby do not result from the greed of doctors (real earnings of American doctors have remained constant for the past fifteen years), or the inefficiency of hospitals, or the swollen profits of insurers, or the price-gouging of drug companies. Rather, they reflect a basic American value—mistaken in the view of certain health-policy experts but deeply held: damn the costs, save lives, and use expensive technologies whenever necessary....

High health-care costs in America also reflect another distinctive feature of our society—the social pathology of our underclass. None other than President Clinton pointed this out to an assembly of doctors at Johns Hopkins: "We'll never get the cost of health care down to where it is in other countries as long as we have higher rates of teen pregnancies and higher rates of low-birth-weight births and higher rates of AIDS, and, most important of all, higher rates of violence." And, he might have added, nothing in his own health-care plan addresses any of those problems.

Because other nations do not have as many crack babies, or bullet-riddled drug pushers, or members of urban gangs as we do, they spend less on health care. America's relatively high level of medical expenditures on these problems is no more due to faults in our health-care system than Alaska's relatively high expenditure on heating oil is due to inefficient furnaces. Nor would changing our health-care system help, as the following report in the pro-Clinton *New York Times* vividly suggests:

> In Washington, a sullen young woman named Margaret Williams was dragging her toddler into a medical van. He was more than a year behind on his vaccination shots.
> She had no job. She had no husband. She explained in disgust that she had no time to hassle with the social workers and the Medicaid forms that would have given her son free care.
> "They want you to run around, and do this or that for nothing," she said. In the meantime, her son had got rickets.

The costs Williams and her offspring will eventually impose on the health-care system will most likely prove significant. And no reform of the system itself will avoid that cost. Which means that the staggering health problems of the urban underclass provide no justification for a radical change in how we deliver health services. If anything, the opposite is true. Since it is a government-administered system—welfare—that is a major contributor to these problems, the case of Margaret Williams would seem to provide a compelling argument against turning the private health-care industry over to the kinds of bureaucracies that have established their incompetence in related fields.

Yet even if international comparisons were corrected to account for these factors, what would they tell us? America spends more per student on higher education than any other country in the world—$13,000 per year as against $6,000–$7,000 for 24 advanced-industrial nations. Do the academics who feel our per-capita health-care costs should be brought into line with those of other countries feel the same way about our outlays for higher education? If so, perhaps they would like to begin by capping academic salaries.

* * *

The second basis of comparison offered to support the contention that we are spending too much on health care is our own past. In 1960 we devoted 5 percent of GNP to health care; by 1993 we were up to the famous 14 percent. Yet we do not compare the price of a modern automobile—with automatic transmission, heating, air-conditioning, and stereo tape and CD decks, plus safety features including seat belts, air bags, ABS brakes, and crash-resistant design—with the price of a model-T Ford, and then complain about how much more the new car sells for. So why ignore quality changes in medical care? Indeed, ignoring such quality changes leads to a particularly serious misrepresentation of true costs where medical treatment is concerned.

Most people beyond the age of Washington's current crop of experts can remember when an operation to remove cataracts resulted in a hospital stay of two to four days and an even longer recuperative period at home. That surgery is now typically done on an outpatient basis. Again, as Dr. Ira Cohen, formerly chief of the Division of General Medicine at New York City's Beth Israel hospital, tells us, in the days when the electrocardiogram was the sole diagnostic tool, the victim of a heart attack could count on a four- to six-week hospital stay; now, improved diagnostic techniques and equipment replace guesswork with information about the extent of muscle damage and other problems, permitting the doctor to discharge the typical heart patient in a week or ten days. Or again, a gall-bladder laparoscopy costs roughly 20 percent more than surgical removal, but a hospital stay of perhaps a week is replaced by an outpatient procedure or an overnight stay, and three weeks off the job by about three to five days. Similarly with kidney-stone operations, where the widespread use of extracorporeal shock-wave lithotripsy has also been making surgery unnecessary, cutting the time in lost work to one-tenth of what it used to be.

Yet, astonishingly, the savings in lost wages nowhere appear in our accounting of trends in health-care costs. Nor do we have any way of measuring the savings in suffering and lost output that result from the higher medical outlays these new techniques often entail. If we did, we might find that health-care costs, properly measured, have not risen as much or as rapidly as the unadjusted data suggest.

Nor, so far as the future is concerned, can we credit the projections that bring us from 14 to 26 percent of GNP by 2030. Such projections all assume that recent trends in health-care prices and in the volume of services consumed will continue indefinitely. But this is unlikely. First, the health-care industry, circa 1994, is offering an unprecedented range of new products, from diagnostic tools to treatments. Like most new products, they will go through a cycle of rapid growth, followed by falling prices and costs as competition among suppliers emerges, consumers become more discriminating, and cost-saving production and application techniques are developed.

In addition, if faced with the costs of their decisions, consumers might adjust. Failure to acknowledge such elasticity of demand is what produced the forecasts that led President Carter to proclaim an "energy crisis." But instead of trebling to $100 per barrel, real oil prices have fallen by more than half, as consumers have learned to conserve and to use other, less expensive fuels.

* * *

So much, then, for the contentions that international comparisons and cost trends demonstrate that we spend too much on health care. What of the argument that our expenditures seem excessive when stacked up against results?

It is, of course, difficult to gauge just what "bang" we get for our health-care "buck." But the most commonly used standards are infant mortality and life expectancy, and by those America does badly: we seem to buy less life with more money than do other countries. For example, both Canada (10 percent) and Britain (6 percent) spend far less on health care than we do, but life expectancy at birth is higher, and infant mortality lower, in those countries.

Leave aside important questions about the comparability of these figures, and concentrate instead on the implicit assumption that these differences are attributable solely to differences in the efficiencies of the various health-care systems. To accept that hypothesis is to ignore all other influences—in the case of life expectancy, the fact that motor-vehicle deaths per 1,000 population are 28 percent higher in the United States than in Canada, and the fact that Americans consume 20 percent more cholesterol-laden beef and veal than do our neighbors to the north. Not to mention the effect on our longevity figures of the frighteningly high rate of homicide among young blacks.

As for infant mortality, Nicholas Eberstadt of the American Enterprise Institute shows conclusively that the low ranking of the U.S. is attributable to our higher illegitimacy rates (since unwed mothers of all races and in all income groups are more likely to give birth to low-weight babies). Add the disinclination of black women to avail themselves of prenatal care even when it is easily available and free, and the result is an infant-mortality rate that cannot be blamed on the structure of the health-care system.

In short, against the risks inherent in a radical transformation of that system, we cannot expect as probable benefits longer lives and increased infant-survival rates. Those goals *are* achievable, but only by major changes in the way Americans live—i.e., by driving, smoking, eating, and shooting less, and marrying more—and in a welfare system that, unlike our health-care system, has a proven record of failure. . . .

* * *

If there is no crisis in health-care costs, is there one in insurance coverage? Here we come to the second major statistic driving the health-care debate: at some point in 1991, the last year for which comprehensive data are available, 37 million people were without medical insurance. (This figure rose to 38.9 million in 1992, a year of relatively high unemployment, and one for which detailed data of the sort used below are not yet available.)

Note: these citizens are *not* denied health care, nor do they expire on the steps of hospitals because they cannot produce proof of insurance coverage. For hospital emergency rooms provide care to all comers. In fact, nonprofit hospitals, which constitute 88 percent of those in the U.S., cannot legally turn away any patient needing medical care, or unreasonably deny access to all the modern technology hospitals have available. And not just for the duration of the emergency: the hospital that sets a broken arm for an uninsured patient is obliged to see the treatment through. The care may not be luxurious, but neither is it casual. Per-capita health-care spending on the uninsured, pre-Medicare population is about 60 percent of per-capita expenditures on the insured population—a level sumptuous by the standards of other industrial countries.

Nonetheless, if the 37-million figure did mean what it is often taken to mean —that 15 percent (some estimates are as high as 17.4 percent) of our population lives with the unnerving and continual threat of being unable to pay for medical care—there would certainly be grounds for revising the way we provide medical services.

Fortunately, there is less of a problem here than meets the eye. Some of the uninsured are between jobs; some are students entering the labor market. Katherine Swartz, a specialist in health-care statistics at the Harvard University School of Public Health, points out that most of the uninsured are uninsured for only a short period of time. "Almost half of all uninsured spells end within six months and only about 15 percent of all uninsured spells last more than two years," she told *Congressional Quarterly*. The chronically-uninsured group in our society, then, numbers closer to 5.5 million than 37 million people.

And probably fewer than 5.5 million. For not all Americans without insurance find that condition imposed upon them. Only 1 percent of those under the age of sixty-five are uninsurable, according to the Employee Benefit Research Institute. More than half of the uninsured are members of families headed by full-time workers; 40 percent of the uninsured have incomes in excess of $20,000, and 10 percent have incomes in excess of $50,000; only 29 percent are below the poverty level. And those with incomes below $20,000 spend several times as much on entertainment, alcohol, and tobacco as they do on health care, which, says Nicholas Eberstadt, they seem "to treat... as an optional but dispensable luxury good." Furthermore, 37 percent of the uninsured are under the age of twenty-five, a generally healthy group—the University of Michigan's Catherine McLaughlin calls them "the young invincibles"—for whom health insurance is often not a cost-effective buy.

If we put all this together—the 15 percent of the uninsured without coverage for two years, plus some who are uninsured for a shorter time, minus those who choose to be uninsured—we come up with a figure of perhaps 3 percent of the population who—although able to obtain health care—cannot obtain affordable health insurance. The policy question thus becomes: should we perform radical surgery on our health-care system for the sake of that 3 percent? ...

* * *

We are left, finally, with a relatively simple set of choices. Everyone agrees that any scheme that would turn 14 percent of the economy over to what the *Economist* calls "a rickety apparatus of new bureaucracies" should be instituted only in response to a major breakdown in the private sector. The proponents of a radical overhaul claim that such a breakdown has occurred. But they are mistaken.

As we have seen, costs are tolerable, all things considered, and results are not unsatisfactory: as Senator Christopher Bond of Missouri observes, kings and sheikhs come here for treatment. And if we compare our private system with the Veterans Health Administration, which is already run by the government, the case against a lurch toward greater state control becomes even stronger. VA patients in need of such care as cardiac or orthopedic diagnosis often wait 60 to 90 days to see a specialist, and months more for surgery. And 55 percent of patients with routine problems wait three hours or longer to be examined for a few minutes by what former Congressman and VA attorney Robert Bauman describes as "an overworked doctor struggling with increasing numbers of patients and piles of government forms, regulations, controls, and policy directives." Is this the direction in which we want to go?

There are, to be sure, reforms that could and should be made within the context of our present system. In addition to subsidizing those who are involuntarily uninsured, the most important is to make coverage "portable," so that the temporary loss of a job does not deprive a worker of his insurance. Such tweaks to the system would certainly help.

POSTSCRIPT

Do We Need National Health Care Insurance?

Not everyone agrees that the American health care system is sick, and those who do are of different opinions as to what is wrong and what needs to be done to make it well. Should we leave the present system alone, provide medical assistance for the uninsured, mandate employer contributions, require universal coverage, cap the costs of drugs and medical procedures, eliminate private insurance, and substitute a single-payer scheme?

President Clinton kept his promise to promote health care reform, but he failed to win enactment of a national policy of universal coverage and cost containment. New expensive medical procedures and drugs will mean increased costs for those covered by health insurance. The issue will certainly be revived in Congress in the future and is likely to figure in future elections.

A series of articles in the *New York Times* are brought together in Erik Eckholm, ed., *Solving America's Health-Care Crisis* (Times Books, 1993), which examines the American system of providing medical care, insurance, rising costs, ethical questions, the health care systems of Canada, Germany, and Japan, and President Clinton's proposals for reform.

George C. Halvorson, in *Strong Medicine* (Random House, 1993), argues that what is wrong is that patients in the United States pay for procedures rather than outcomes. Halvorson believes that America does not need more government regulation, more money, or rationing, but to reward quality and efficiency.

Some people feel that the causes of poor health in the United States need to be reduced or eliminated. High mortality rates, persistent diseases, and learning disabilities are caused by poor nutrition, drug and alcohol abuse, and polluted air and water, according to Joseph D. Beasley, *The Betrayal of Health: The Impact of Nutrition, Environment, and Lifestyle on Illness in America* (Times Books, 1991).

Other critics believe that medical costs have gotten out of hand in part because expensive equipment and drugs tempt doctors and hospitals to prescribe unnecessary treatments and in part because modern medical technology can extend the life of a sick premature infant or a terminally ill person, but at costs that society simply cannot afford to pay. Given the finite limits that must be imposed on medical costs, how do we choose what we are—and are not—prepared to pay for?

ISSUE 16

Should Women Have a Right to Abortion?

YES: Ronald Dworkin, from *Life's Dominion: An Argument About Abortion, Euthanasia, and Freedom* (Alfred A. Knopf, 1993)

NO: Francis J. Beckwith, from "Pluralism, Tolerance, and Abortion Rights," in *Life and Learning: Proceedings of the Third University Faculty for Life Conference* (University Faculty for Life, 1993)

ISSUE SUMMARY

YES: Philosopher Ronald Dworkin argues that women have a right to control their own bodies, although states have an interest in reasonably regulating abortion.

NO: Philosopher Francis J. Beckwith maintains that pro-choice arguments are based on political and constitutional positions that cannot withstand logical and moral analysis.

Until 1973, the laws governing abortion were set by the states, most of which barred legal abortion except where pregnancy imperiled the life of the pregnant woman. In that year, the U.S. Supreme Court decided the controversial case of *Roe v. Wade.* The *Roe* decision acknowledged both a woman's "fundamental right" to terminate a pregnancy before fetal viability and the state's legitimate interest in protecting both the woman's health and the "potential life" of the fetus. It prohibited states from banning abortion to protect the fetus before the third trimester of a pregnancy, and it ruled that even during that final trimester, a woman could obtain an abortion if she could prove that her life or health would be endangered by carrying to term. (In a companion case to *Roe,* decided on the same day, the Court defined *health* broadly enough to include "all factors—physical, emotional, psychological, familial, and the woman's age—relevant to the well-being of the patient.") These holdings, together with the requirement that state regulation of abortion had to survive "strict scrutiny" and demonstrate a "compelling state interest," resulted in later decisions striking down mandatory 24-hour waiting periods, requirements that abortions be performed in hospitals, and so-called informed consent laws.

The Supreme Court did uphold state laws requiring parental notification and consent for minors (though it provided that minors could seek permission from a judge if they feared notifying their parents), as well as federal and state laws barring public funding for any abortion that is not necessary to save the woman's life. In 1989, in the case of *Webster v. Reproductive Health Services*, the Court went further, upholding provisions of a Missouri law that requires tests for viability on any fetus of more than 20 weeks gestation before performing an abortion and barring the use of public facilities or employees to perform an abortion that is not needed to save the pregnant woman's life.

The Supreme Court's 1992 decision in *Planned Parenthood of Southeastern Pennsylvania v. Robert P. Casey* was eagerly awaited, as it would determine how far the Supreme Court was prepared to go in constricting or overturning *Roe v. Wade*. As it turned out, neither side of the abortion issue was satisfied with the outcome. Four members of the Court were prepared to overturn *Roe* and give broad power to the states to restrict abortion as they choose. Two members of the Court wanted to return to the defense of abortion as originally set by *Roe*.

But three members of the Court sought what they perceived as a middle ground, although most advocates on the opposing sides would deny that such a middle ground exists. These justices were holding by the judicial rule of *stare decisis,* literally "to stand by things decided." The rule holds that long-settled constitutional interpretations on which people base their behavior should not be easily, if ever, overturned.

This had the effect of creating a five-member majority affirming *Roe*. Although the three justices in the middle opposed "undue burdens" imposed by states, such as spousal notification, they joined the four anti-abortion justices in upholding requirements for informed consent, mandatory waiting periods, and parental consent or notification for minors.

The division in the Court was so close that it could change the next time the Court considers the issue. This possibility was enhanced by the retirement in 1994 of justices Harry Blackmun and Byron White, who split on the abortion issue, and their replacement by new justices Ruth Bader Ginsburg and Stephen Breyer.

Although public opinion polls usually show a majority of Americans supporting both a right to abortion in some circumstances and certain constraints on its exercise in others, millions of Americans on both sides of the issue believe that this is a profoundly moral question that should not be decided by polls or elections. Both sides want a constitutional amendment enshrining their pro-choice or pro-life position, but there is no likelihood that such decisive action will ever be taken.

In the selections that follow, Ronald Dworkin, conceding the legitimacy of reasonable state regulation, believes that women must have the right to control their own bodies. Francis J. Beckwith defends the right to life and contends that none of the arguments supporting the right to abortion can withstand logical and moral analysis.

YES

Ronald Dworkin

ABORTION IN COURT

I [have] said that the difficult constitutional question in *Roe v. Wade* was not whether states are permitted under the Constitution to treat a fetus as a constitutional person. They plainly are not. I set out two other, much more difficult questions that our reformulation of the moral argument about abortion helps us to identify as the central issues in the constitutional debate. First, do women have a constitutional right of procreative autonomy—a right to control their own role in procreation unless the state has a compelling reason for denying them that control? Second, do states have this compelling reason not because a fetus is a person but because of a detached responsibility to protect the sanctity of human life considered as an intrinsic value?

Most of the lawyers who think *Roe v. Wade* was wrong have directed their arguments to the first of these questions. They say that women do not have a constitutionally protected right to procreative autonomy because no such right is mentioned in the text and because none of the "framers" of the Constitution intended women to have such a right. I have tried to show that these objections are misplaced because the constitutional provisions that command liberty and equality are abstract. The key legal question is whether the best interpretation of these abstract provisions, respecting the requirements of integrity I described, supports this right of procreative autonomy. If it does, then in the pertinent sense the Constitution *does* "mention" such a right, and those who created the Constitution *did* "intend" it.

The second question, too, is a matter of interpretation. On the best interpretation of the abstract provisions of the Bill of Rights, does government have the detached power to protect intrinsic values as well as the derivative power to protect particular people? Some people believe that government should not have this detached power at all, that government can properly act only to protect the rights or interests of particular people or creatures, not intrinsic values, which it must leave to individual conscience. (That was apparently the position of John Stuart Mill.) But this restricted view of the powers the United States Constitution allows government is ruled out by the constraints of integrity, because too much of American political practice assumes the contrary.

Neither cultural achievements nor animal species nor future human beings are creatures with rights or interests. But no one doubts that government may treat art and culture as having intrinsic value, or that government may act to protect the environment, endangered animal species, and the quality of life of future generations. Government may properly levy taxes that will be used to support museums, for example; it can forbid people to destroy their own buildings if it deems these to be of historical architectural value; it can prohibit manufacturing practices that threaten endangered species or injure future generations. Why should government not have the power to enforce a much more passionate conviction—that abortion is a desecration of the inherent value that attaches to every human life?

It is not true that an individual woman's decision to have an abortion affects only herself (or only herself and the fetus's father), for individual decisions inevitably affect shared collective values. Part of the sense of the sacred is a sense of taboo, and it is surely harder to maintain a taboo against abortion, and to raise one's children to respect it, in a community where others not only reject it but violate it openly, especially if they receive official financial or moral support.

So if, on the best understanding of the Constitution's abstract provisions, American states lack the power to forbid abortion, then this must be because of something specific about abortion or reproduction; it is not because states may not legislate to protect intrinsic values at all. I distinguished two issues—whether a woman has a right to procreative au-tonomy and whether states have a compelling interest in protecting the intrinsic value of human life. Our discussion has now brought them together as two sides of the same issue. Is there something special about procreation and abortion so that, though government may regulate people's behavior in other ways in order to protect intrinsic values, pregnant women have a right that government not forbid them to terminate their pregnancies?

The question so described lies at the intersection of two sometimes competing traditions, both of which are part of America's political heritage. The first is the tradition of personal freedom. The second assigns government responsibility for guarding the public moral space in which all citizens live. A good part of constitutional law consists in reconciling these two ideas. What is the appropriate balance in the case of abortion?

Both the majority and dissenting opinions in *Roe v. Wade* said that a state has an interest in "protecting human life." We have now assigned a particular sense to that ambiguous claim: it means that any political community has a legitimate concern in protecting the *sanctity* or *inviolability* of human life by requiring its members to acknowledge the intrinsic value of human life in their individual decisions. But this is still ambiguous. It might describe either of two goals, and the distinction between them is extremely important.

One is the goal of responsibility. A state might aim that its citizens treat decisions about abortion as matters of moral importance; that they recognize that fundamental intrinsic values are at stake in such decisions and decide reflectively, not out of immediate convenience but out of examined conviction. The second is the goal of conformity. A state might aim that its citizens obey rules and practices that the majority believes best express and protect the sanctity of life, that women abort, if ever, only in circumstances in which a majority thinks abortion appropriate or, at least, permissible.

These goals of responsibility and conformity are not only different but antagonistic. If we aim at responsibility, we must leave citizens free, in the end, to decide as they think right, because that is what moral responsibility entails. But if we aim at conformity, we demand instead that citizens act in a way that might be contrary to their own moral convictions; this discourages rather than encourages them to develop their own sense of when and why life is sacred.

The traditional way of understanding the abortion controversy, which we have now rejected, submerges the distinction between these two goals. If a fetus is a person, then of course the state's dominant goal must be to protect it, just as it protects all other people. And the state must therefore subordinate any interest it has in developing its citizens' sense of moral responsibility to its interest that they act on a specific moral conclusion: that killing people is wrong.

But when we shift the state's interest, as we have, to protecting an intrinsic value, then the opposition between the two goals moves into the foreground. The sanctity of life is a highly controversial, *contestable* value. It is controversial, for example, whether abortion or childbirth best serves the intrinsic value of life when a fetus is deformed, or when having a child would seriously depress a woman's chance to make something valuable of her own life. Does a state protect a contestable value best by encouraging people to accept it *as* contestable, understanding that they are responsible for deciding for themselves what it means? Or does the state protect a contestable value best by itself deciding, through the political process, which interpretation is the right one, and then forcing everyone to conform? The goal of responsibility justifies the first choice, the goal of conformity the second. A state cannot pursue both goals at the same time.

RESPONSIBILITY

I can think of no reason why government should not aim that its citizens treat decisions about human life and death as matters of serious moral importance. So in my view, the United States Constitution does allow state governments to pursue the goal of responsibility—but only in ways that respect the crucial difference between advancing that goal and wholly or partly coercing a final decision. May a state require a woman contemplating abortion to wait twenty-four hours before having the procedure? May it require that she be given information explaining the gravity of a decision to abort? May it require a pregnant teenage woman to consult with her parents, or with some other adult? Or a married woman to inform her husband, if she can? Must the government help to pay for abortion services for those too poor to pay themselves if it helps to pay for childbirth?

Since many constitutional lawyers think that the only issue in *Roe v. Wade* was whether states may treat a fetus as a person, they do not distinguish between the goals of coercion and responsibility; they have therefore assumed that if *Roe v. Wade* is right, and states may not coerce women by forbidding abortion altogether, it directly follows that states must include abortion in their medical aid programs and that they may not require that women delay abortion or consult with others or be given information. That explains why many lawyers thought that the Supreme Court's decisions in the years following *Roe*, which did allow states to discriminate in financial support and to regulate abortion in these various ways, amounted to a partial overruling or undermining of *Roe*. . . .

But when we understand *Roe* as I have suggested—as about inherent value and not about personhood—then we see that *Casey* [*Planned Parenthood of Southeastern Pennsylvania v. Casey* (1992)] dealt primarily with issues not resolved by *Roe*. It is perfectly consistent to insist that states have no power to impose on their citizens a particular view of how and why life is sacred, and yet also to insist that states do have the power to encourage their citizens to treat the question of abortion seriously. The joint opinion of Justices O'Connor, Kennedy, and Souter in *Casey* made that distinction clear: the three justices affirmed *Roe*'s rule that states may not prohibit abortion but nevertheless affirmed a state's legitimate interest in encouraging responsibility. "What is at stake is the woman's right to make the ultimate decision, not a right to be insulated from all others in doing so," they said, and therefore "states are free to enact laws to provide a reasonable framework for a woman to make a decision that has such profound and lasting meaning." A state may reasonably think, they added, that a woman considering abortion should at least be aware of arguments against it that others in the community believe important, so that "even in the earliest stages of pregnancy, the State may enact rules and regulations designed to encourage her to know that there are philosophic and social arguments of great weight that can be brought to bear in favor of continuing the pregnancy." . . .

COERCION

. . . Do the states of the United States have the power to decide for everyone that abortion insults the intrinsic value of human life and to prohibit it on that ground? In *Casey*, four justices said that they still aim to reverse *Roe* and declare that states do have that power. Are they right, as a matter of American constitutional law? Should any state or nation have that power, as a matter of justice and decent government?

As I said, government sometimes acts properly when it coerces people in order to protect certain intrinsic values: when it collects taxes to finance national museums or when it imposes conservation measures to protect endangered animal species, for example. Why is abortion different? Why can a state not forbid abortion on the same ground: that the majority of its citizens thinks that aborting a fetus, except, perhaps, when the mother's own life is at stake, is an intolerable insult to the inherent value of human life? There are two central and connected reasons why prohibiting abortion is a very different matter.

First, in the case of abortion, the effect of coercion on particular people— pregnant women—is far greater. Making abortion criminal may destroy a woman's life. Protecting art or historic buildings or endangered animal species or future generations is rarely as damaging to particular people, and might well be unconstitutional if it were. Second, our convictions about how and why human life has intrinsic importance, from which we draw our views about abortion, are much more fundamental to our overall moral personalities than our convictions about culture or about endangered species, even though these too concern intrinsic values. Our beliefs about human life are decisive in forming our opinions about *all* life-and-death matters—abortion, suicide, euthanasia, the death penalty, and conscientious objection to war. Indeed, their power is even greater than this, because our opinions about how and why our *own* lives have intrinsic value influence every major decision we make about how we live. Very few people's opinions about conserving the artifacts of a culture or saving endangered species are as foundational to their moral personality, as interwoven with the structural choices of their lives.

These interconnections are most evident in the lives of people who are religious in traditional ways. The connection between their faith and their opinions about abortion is not contingent but constitutive—the latter are shadows of religious beliefs about why human life itself is important, and these beliefs are at work in every aspect of their lives. Most people who are not religious also have general, instinctive convictions about whether, why, and how any human life has intrinsic value. No one can lead even a mildly reflective life without revealing such convictions, and they surface, for almost everyone, at the same critical moments in life—in opinions and decisions about children, death, and war, for example. An atheist may have convictions about the point or meaning of human life that are just as pervasive, just as foundational to his moral personality, as those of a devout Catholic, Jew, Muslim, Hindu, or Buddhist. An atheist's system

of beliefs may have, in the words of a famous Supreme Court opinion, "a place in the life of its possessor parallel to that filled by the orthodox belief in God." We may describe most people's beliefs about the inherent value of human life—beliefs deployed in their opinions about abortion —as *essentially* religious beliefs....

The Supreme Court, in denying the state the specific power to make contraception criminal, presupposed the more general principle of procreative autonomy I am defending. That is important, as I have said, because almost no one believes that the Court's contraception decisions should now be overruled. The law's integrity demands that the principles necessary to support an authoritative set of judicial decisions must be accepted in other contexts as well. It might seem an appealing political compromise to apply the principle of procreative autonomy to contraception, which almost no one now thinks states can forbid, but not to abortion, which powerful constituencies violently oppose. But the point of integrity— the point of law itself—is exactly to rule out political compromises of that kind. We must be one nation of principle: our Constitution must represent conviction, not the tactical strategies of justices eager to satisfy as many political constituencies as possible.

Integrity does not, of course, require that judges respect principles embedded in past decisions that they and others regard as *mistakes*. It permits the Supreme Court to declare, as it has several times in the past, that a given decision or string of decisions was in error, because the principles underlying it are inconsistent with more fundamental principles embedded in the Constitution's structure and history. The Court cannot declare everything in the past a mistake; that would destroy integrity under the pretext of serving it. It must exercise its power to disregard past decisions modestly, and it must exercise it in good faith. It cannot ignore principles underlying past decisions it purports to approve, decisions it would ratify if asked to do so, decisions almost no one, not even among the sternest critics of the Court's past performance, now disapproves of or regards as mistakes. The contraception cases fall into that category, and it would be both dangerous and offensive for the Court cynically to ignore the principles these cases presupposed in any decision it reaches about abortion.

So integrity demands general recognition of the principle of procreative autonomy, and therefore of the right of women to decide for themselves not only whether to conceive but whether to bear a child. If you remain in doubt—if you are not yet convinced that *Roe* was right on the most basic issues—then consider the possibility that in some states a majority of voters might come to think that it shows *disrespect* for the sanctity of life to continue a pregnancy in some circumstances-in cases of fetal deformity, for example. If a majority has the power to impose its own views about the sanctity of life on everyone, then the state could *require* someone to abort, even if that were against her own religious or ethical convictions, at least if abortion had become physically as safe as, for example, the vaccinations and inoculations we now expect our governments to require....

The *Casey* decision was important because it made plainer than ever before how central the abortion issue is to the very idea of freedom. Not just for America, but for any nation dedicated to liberty, the question of how far government may legitimately impose collective judgments about spiritual matters on individual citizens is absolutely crucial. It is hardly surprising that American law leaves women freer to follow their own conscience than do the laws of many other nations, for the Bill of Rights places more emphasis on individual liberty, especially in matters touching conscience and the sacred, than does any other constitution. *Roe v. Wade* is not yet wholly safe: if a single new justice is appointed who believes it should be overruled, it will fall. That would be a bleak day in American constitutional history, for it would mean that American citizens were no longer secure in their freedom to follow their own reflective convictions in the most personal, conscience-driven, and religious decisions many of them will ever make.

NO

Francis J. Beckwith

PLURALISM, TOLERANCE, AND ABORTION RIGHTS

Many people in the abortion-rights movement argue that their position is more tolerant than the pro-life position. After all, they reason, the abortion-rights movement is not forcing pro-life women to have abortion, but the pro-life movement *is* trying to deny all women the option to make a choice. Abortion-rights advocates use at least four arguments to articulate this position.

ARGUMENT FROM RELIGIOUS PLURALISM

It is sometimes argued that the question of when protectable human life begins is a religious question that one must answer for oneself. Justice Blackmun writes in *Roe v. Wade*, "We need not resolve the difficult question of when life begins. When those trained in the respective disciplines of medicine, philosophy, and theology are unable to arrive at any consensus, the judiciary, at this point in the development of man's knowledge, is not in a position to speculate." Hence, the state should not take one theory of life and force those who do not agree with that theory to subscribe to it. Blackmun writes in *Roe*, "In view of all this, we do not agree that, by adopting one theory of life, Texas may override the rights of the pregnant woman that are at stake." In his dissenting opinion in *Webster*, Justice Stevens goes even further than Blackmun: "The Missouri Legislature [which said that life begins at conception] may not inject its endorsement of a particular religious tradition in this debate, for 'the Establishment Clause does not allow public bodies to foment such disagreement.'" Thus for the pro-life advocate to propose that women should be forbidden from having abortions, on the basis that personhood begins at conception or at least sometime before birth, not only violates their right to privacy but also violates the separation of church and state. Such a separation is supposedly necessary to sustain tolerance in a pluralistic society....

There are several problems with this argument. First, it is self-refuting and question-begging. To claim, as Justices Blackmun and Stevens do, that the Court should not propose one theory of life over another, and that the decision

From Francis J. Beckwith, "Pluralism, Tolerance, and Abortion Rights," in *Life and Learning: Proceedings of the Third University Faculty for Life Conference* (University Faculty for Life, 1993), pp. 28–38. Notes omitted. This essay is an abridged version of a portion of chapter 5 of Francis J. Beckwith, *Politically Correct Death: Answering Arguments for Abortion Rights* (Baker Book House, 1993).

should be left up to each pregnant woman as to when protectable human life begins, is to propose a theory of life that hardly has a clear consensus in this country. Once one claims that certain individuals (pregnant women) have the right to bestow personhood on unborn humans, one implies that the bestowers are fully human. This is a theory of life held by a number of religious denominations and groups, whose amicus briefs Stevens oddly enough cites in a footnote in his *Webster* dissent. Moreover, what if a religious group arose that believed that personhood did not begin until the age of two and prior to that time parents could sacrifice their children to the devil? By forbidding child-killing after birth, the Court would be infringing upon the religious beliefs of this group, would it not? And in doing so, the Court would obviously be proposing one theory of life over another. Hence, in attempting not to propose one theory of life, Blackmun and Stevens in fact assume a particular theory of life, and by doing so clearly beg the question and show that their opinions cannot abide by their own standard of not proposing one theory of life.

Second, the fact that a particular theory of life is consistent with a religious view does not mean that it is exclusively religious or that it is in violation of the Establishment Clause of the Constitution. For example, many pro-life advocates argue for their position by emphasizing that there is non-theological support for their position, while many abortion-rights advocates, such as Mollenkott, argue that their position is theologically grounded in the Bible. Hence, the pro-life advocate could argue that the fact that a philosophically and scientifically plausible position is also found in religious literature, such as the Bible, does not make such a view

exclusively religious. If it did, our society would have to dispense with laws forbidding such crimes as murder and robbery simply because such actions are prohibited in the Hebrew-Christian Scriptures. Furthermore, some public policies, such as civil-rights legislation and elimination of nuclear testing—policies supported by many clergymen who find these policies in agreement with and supported by their doctrinal beliefs—would have to be abolished simply because they are believed by some to be supported by a particular religious theory of life. It is well-known that those who sought to abolish slavery in nineteenth-century America were unashamed to admit that their moral convictions were based almost exclusively on their Christian beliefs....

Third, this argument asks the pro-life movement to act as if its fundamental view of human life is incorrect and to accept the abortion-rights view of what constitutes both a just society and a correct view of human life. This asks too much of the pro-life movement, as philosopher George Mavrodes shows:

> Let us imagine a person who believes that Jews are human persons, and that the extermination of Jews is murder. Many of us will find that exercise fairly easy, because we are people of that sort ourselves. So we may as well take ourselves to be the people in question. And let us now go on to imagine that we live in a society in which the "termination" of Jews is an everyday routine procedure, a society in which public facilities are provided in every community for this operation, and one in which any citizen is free to identify and denounce Jews and to arrange for their arrest and termination. In that imaginary society, many of us will know people who have themselves participated in these procedures, many of us will drive

past the termination centers daily on our way to work, we can often see the smoke rising gently in the late afternoon sky, and so on. And now imagine that someone tells us that if we happen to believe that Jews are human beings then that's O.K., we needn't fear any coercion, nobody requires us to participate in the termination procedures ourselves. We need not work in the gas chamber, we don't have to denounce a Jew, and so on. We can simply mind our own business, walk quietly past the well-trimmed lawns, and (of course) pay our taxes.

Can we get some feel for what it would be like to live in that context?... And maybe we can then have some understanding of why they [the right-to-lifers] are unlikely to be satisfied by being told that they don't have to get an abortion themselves.

Since the abortion-rights advocate asks the pro-life advocate to act as if his fundamental view of human life is false, the pro-life advocate may legitimately view his adversary's position as a subtle and patronizing form of intolerance. When the "pro-choicer" rails at the pro-lifer, "Don't like abortion, don't have one," the pro-lifer hears, "Don't like murder, don't commit one" or "Don't like slavery, don't own a slave."

ARGUMENT FROM IMPOSING MORALITY

Some abortion-rights advocates argue that it is wrong for anyone to force his or her own view of what is morally right on someone else. They argue that pro-lifers, by attempting to forbid women from having abortions, are trying to force their morality on others. Aside from the fact that this argument makes the controversial assumption that all

morality is subjective and relative, there are at least three other problems with it.

First, it does not seem obvious that it is always wrong to demand that people behave in accordance with certain moral precepts. For instance, laws against drunk driving, murder, smoking crack, robbery, and child molestation all are intended to impose a particular moral perspective on the free moral agency of others. Such laws are instituted because the acts they are intended to limit often obstruct the free agency of other persons. For example, a person killed by a drunk driver is prevented from exercising his free agency. These laws seek to maintain a just and orderly society by limiting some free moral agency so that free moral agency is increased for a greater number. Therefore, a law forbidding abortion would unjustly impose a moral perspective upon another only if the act of abortion does not limit the free agency of another. That is to say, if the unborn entity is fully human, forbidding abortions would be just, since nearly every abortion limits the free agency of another (i.e., the unborn human).

Although it does not seriously damage their entire position, it is interesting to note that some abortion-rights advocates do not hesitate to impose their moral perspective on others when they call for the use of other people's tax dollars (many of whom do not approve of this use of funds) to help pay for the abortions of poor women.

Second, although he presents his position in the rhetoric of freedom, the abortion-rights advocate nevertheless imposes his perspective on others. All rights imply obligations on the part of others, and all obligations impose a moral perspective on others, to make them act in a certain way. Thus, the abortion-rights advocate, by saying that the pro-lifer is obligated not to interfere with the free choice of pregnant women to kill their unborn offspring, is imposing his moral perspective upon the pro-lifer who believes it is her duty to rescue the unborn because these beings are fully human and hence deserve, like all human beings, our society's protection. Therefore, every right, whether it is the right to life or the right to abortion, imposes some moral perspective on others to either act or not act in a certain way.

Third, it follows that the abortion-rights advocate begs the question. If the unborn are not fully human, the abortion-rights advocate is correct in saying that the pro-lifers are trying to force their morality onto women who want abortions. But if the unborn are fully human, a woman receiving an abortion is imposing her morality upon another. Therefore, unless the abortion-rights advocate assumes that the unborn are not fully human, his argument is not successful. Hence, the question of whose morality is being forced upon whom hinges on the status of the unborn.

ARGUMENT AGAINST A PUBLIC POLICY FORBIDDING ABORTION

There is another variation on the first argument from pluralism. Some people argue that it is not wise to make a public-policy decision in one direction when there is wide diversity of opinion within society. This argument can be outlined in the following way:

1. There can never be a just law requiring uniformity of behavior on any issue on which there is widespread disagreement.

2. There is widespread disagreement on the issue of forbidding abortion on demand.
3. Therefore, any law that forbids abortion on demand is unjust.

One way to show that this argument is wrong is to show that premise 1 is false. There are several reasons to believe that it is. First, if premise 1 is true, then the abortion-rights advocate must admit that the United States Supreme Court decision, *Roe v. Wade*, is an unjust decision, since the Court ruled that the states, whose statutes prior to the ruling disagreed on the abortion issue, must behave uniformly in accordance with the Court's decision. If, however, the abortion-rights advocate denies that *Roe* was an unjust decision, then he is conceding that it is false that "there can never be a just law requiring uniformity of behavior on any issue on which there is widespread disagreement." Second, if premise 1 is true, then the abolition of slavery was unjust because there was widespread disagreement of opinion among Americans in the nineteenth century. Yet nobody would say that slavery should have remained as an institution. Third, if premise 1 is true, then much of civil-rights legislation, about which there was much disagreement, would be unjust. Fourth, if premise 1 is true, then a favorite abortion-rights public policy proposal is also unjust. Some abortion-rights advocates believe that the federal and/or state government should use the tax dollars of the American people to fund the abortions of poor women. Large numbers of Americans, however, some of whom support abortion rights, do not want their tax dollars used in this way. And fifth, if premise 1 is true, then laws forbidding pro-life advocates from preventing their unborn neighbors from being aborted would be unjust. One cannot say that there is not widespread disagreement concerning this issue. But these are the very laws which the abortion-rights advocate supports. Hence, this argument is self-refuting, since by legislating the "pro-choice" perspective the government is "requiring uniformity of behavior on an issue on which there is widespread disagreement." That is to say, the abortion-rights advocate is forcing the pro-lifer to act as if she were a pro-choicer. By making "no law," the government is implicitly affirming the view that the unborn are not fully human, which is hardly a neutral position.

Another way to show that this argument is not successful is to challenge the second premise and show that there is not widespread disagreement on the question of whether abortion on demand should be forbidden. Recent polls have shown that a great majority of Americans, although supporting a woman's right to an abortion in the rare "hard cases" (such as rape, incest, and severe fetal deformity), do not support abortion on demand, the abortion-rights position that asserts that abortion should remain legal during the entire nine months of pregnancy for any reason the woman deems fit. According to one poll, taken by *The Boston Globe* and WBZ Broadcasting, the vast majority of Americans would ban abortions in the following circumstances: "a woman is a minor" (50%), "wrong time in life to have a child" (82%), "fetus not of the desired sex" (93%), "woman cannot afford a child" (75%), "as a means of birth control" (89%), "pregnancy would cause too much emotional strain" (64%), "father unwilling to help raise the child" (83%), "father absent" (81%), "mother wants abortion/father wants baby" (72%), "father wants abor-

tion/mother wants baby" (75%). This is why the journalist who reported this poll concluded that "most Americans would ban the vast majority of abortions performed in this country.... While 78 percent of the nation would keep abortion legal in limited circumstances, according to the poll, *those circumstances account for a tiny percentage of the reasons*" (emphasis added). Therefore, the second premise in this argument is wrong. There is not "widespread disagreement on the issue of forbidding abortion on demand."

ARGUMENT FROM "COMPULSORY" PREGNANCY

Some abortion-rights advocates, wanting to get a rhetorical edge in public debate, refer to pro-life legislation as "tantamount to advocating compulsory pregnancy." This is not really an argument in a technical sense, since it has only a conclusion and contains no premises to support the conclusion. It is merely an assertion that begs the question, since it assumes the non-personhood of the unborn—the point under question. To cite an example, a man who murdered his wife and children would be begging the question as to the personhood of his victims if he referred to the laws that forbid murder as tantamount to advocating *compulsory marriage* and *compulsory fatherhood.* Can you imagine a father or a mother arguing that he or she is not obligated to obey child-support laws because they are "tantamount to advocating *compulsory parenthood*"? A rapist could argue on the same grounds and conclude that laws against rape are "tantamount to advocating *compulsory chastity*." And the slave owner, the pro-choicer of the mid-nineteenth-century political scene, could easily conclude that Lincoln's Emancipation Proclamation, since it robbed him of slave ownership, was "tantamount to advocating compulsory government-mandated relinquishing of private property."

In sum, a law that forbids the brutal victimizing of another person is inherently a just law, whether the victim is an unborn child, an adult woman, a youngster, or an African-American. Hence, the real question is whether the unborn are fully human, not whether pro-life legislation advocates "compulsory pregnancy."

POSTSCRIPT

Should Women Have a Right to Abortion?

Few issues in modern American society arouse anything like the moral passion and political fervor of the issue of abortion. Should women have the right to choose whether or not to carry a pregnancy to term, or should the "right to life" bar voluntary abortion? While pro-choicers focus on the pregnant woman and speak of the "fetus," pro-lifers emphasize the "unborn child."

Pro-lifers ask: Do abortions cause pain to fetuses? Do women become psychologically scarred by abortion? Does legalized abortion produce insensitivity to human life? Pro-choicers in turn ask: What harm is done to an unmarried teenage girl in bearing a baby? Who will raise and care for all the unwanted children? Will not prohibition produce, as it always has, countless unsafe back-alley abortions?

Public opinion appears to change depending upon the language used when the question is put. There are also substantive shifts of opinion depending in part on whether the pregnant woman simply exercises a preference not to have a child, suffers economic hardship, is a minor, was raped, or was a victim of incest.

Heated discussion of the abortion issue continues: it is a part of many election campaigns at all levels of government, including the 1992 presidential election; Congress continues to consider both the Freedom of Choice Act, which would permit abortions, and a constitutional amendment that would forbid abortions; debate continues over restrictions on the sale of RU-486, an abortion-inducing drug that is available in Europe but banned in the United States.

Dozens of books have dealt with these issues since *Roe v. Wade* in 1973. Robert M. Baird and Stuart E. Rosenbaum, eds., *The Ethics of Abortion: Pro-Life vs. Pro-Choice*, rev. ed. (Prometheus Books, 1993), contains a wide variety of views, including those of Robert H. Bork, Ronald Dworkin, Anna Quindlen, and Richard Selzer. An unbiased history of abortion as an American political issue can be found in Barbara Hinkson Craig and David M. O'Brien, *Abortion and American Politics* (Chatham House Publishers, 1993).

Books that purport to establish a common ground include: Elizabeth Mensch and Alan Freeman, *The Politics of Virtue: Is Abortion Debatable?* (Duke University Press, 1993); Lawrence Tribe, *Abortion: The Clash of Absolutes* (W. W. Norton, 1990); and Roger Rosenblatt, *Life Itself: Abortion in the American Mind* (Random House, 1992).

In 1992 the Democratic and Republican platforms took diametrically opposite positions on abortion. The Democrats endorsed the *Roe* decision, called for publicly funded abortions for those unable to pay, and backed the Freedom of Choice Act, then pending in Congress, a bill that would write into statute the principles of *Roe v. Wade* and—according to interpretations of some supporters and opponents—that might even strike down many of the abortion-related restrictions that the Court had already allowed under *Roe*, such as mandatory parental notification. If this position seemed extreme to many, so did that of the Republicans, which called for a "human life" amendment to the Constitution banning abortion and for congressional legislation extending the protection of "life" in the Fourteenth Amendment to that of "unborn children." The Republican platform contained no language that would provide for exceptions, either for rape, incest, or even the life of the woman, though both President George Bush and Vice President Dan Quayle endorsed exceptions in all three cases; most pro-lifers do agree that cases where the woman's life is endangered are special.

ISSUE 17

Does the Religious Right Threaten American Freedoms?

YES: David Cantor, from *The Religious Right: The Assault on Tolerance and Pluralism in America* (Anti-Defamation League, 1994)

NO: Dick Armey, from "Freedom's Choir: Social and Economic Conservatives Are Singing the Same Song," *Policy Review* (Winter 1994)

ISSUE SUMMARY

YES: Anti-Defamation League analyst David Cantor warns that the "religious right" seeks to disregard pluralism, dissent, and tolerance, and to impose its moral views on American society.

NO: Republican U.S. representative Dick Armey (Texas) believes that personal virtue and traditional values are promoted by cultural and religious conservatives who oppose having values imposed upon them.

The United States has more members (in excess of 130 million) of more churches (340,000) than any other country in the world. More than 95 percent of all Americans profess a belief in God. Recently, the growth of so-called cult religions and the increasing visibility of born-again Christians remind us that religion remains a powerful force in American society.

Because religious tolerance was a compelling issue when the United States was founded, the first clauses of the First Amendment to the Constitution deal with the relationship between the nation and religion. The Supreme Court now interprets these clauses to be binding upon the states as well as the national government.

The actual words are: "Congress shall make no law respecting an establishment of religion, or prohibiting the free exercise thereof." For the most part, the "free exercise" clause does not pose many constitutional controversies. The "establishment" clause does.

For the past 40 years, the U.S. Supreme Court has been examining and resolving church-state controversies. Sometimes it has appeared as if the Supreme Court supports the view of those who invoke Thomas Jefferson's famous metaphor about the necessary "wall of separation" between church and state. This appears to be the case in what has proven to be the most controversial church-state issue: the right of children and teachers to start their school day with a prayer.

In the case of *Engel v. Vitale* (1962), a 22-word prayer, recited daily in a number of public schools throughout the state of New York, became the center of a national controversy:

Almighty God, we acknowledge our dependence upon Thee, and we beg Thy blessings upon us, our parents, our teachers, and our country.

This prayer, composed by the New York State Board of Regents (the governing body of the school system), was intended to be nondenominational. It was also voluntary, at least in the sense that the children were not required to recite it and could leave the room when it was recited. Nevertheless, the Court declared it unconstitutional, and in subsequent cases it also outlawed Bible reading and reciting the Lord's Prayer.

Other Supreme Court decisions have defended the right of the state to accommodate differing religious views. The Court has upheld a state's reimbursement of parents for the cost of sending their children to church-related schools on public buses, the loan of state-owned textbooks to parochial school students, and grants to church colleges for the construction of religiously neutral facilities. Public acknowledgment of religion is supported by such longstanding practices as having chaplains in the armed forces, tax exemptions for churches, and the motto "In God We Trust" on coins.

The Supreme Court has sought to define the constitutional boundaries of state support of religion by forbidding religious instruction in a public school class but permitting "release time" programs, which allow a student to be absent from public school in order to attend a religious class elsewhere. In 1990 the Supreme Court upheld the right of religious clubs to meet in public schools under the same conditions as other voluntary student organizations.

Those who advocate an impenetrable wall of separation would forbid direct or indirect aid to religious bodies or religious causes. They oppose the efforts of the so-called religious right to impose on all Americans their moral values regarding religious practice, sexual behavior, artistic or other expression, and public policy. They believe that these moral zealots constitute a small but militant minority who have won political power in groups ranging from local school boards to state Republican organizations. This position is elaborated by David Cantor on behalf of the Anti-Defamation League.

The religious right probably consists of some (but far from all) Protestant evangelicals and fundamentalists, a smaller proportion of strict Catholics, and a very small number of Orthodox Jews. Together with other cultural conservatives, they fear that the greatest danger to American democracy is the decline of personal and family values, and the best remedy is the teaching of these values in the schools and churches and their adoption in public policy. This view is amplified by Representative Dick Armey.

YES

David Cantor

THE RELIGIOUS RIGHT:
THE ASSAULT ON TOLERANCE
AND PLURALISM IN AMERICA

INTRODUCTION

It is easy to see that it is particularly important in democratic times to make spiritual conceptions prevail, but it is far from easy, to say what those who govern democratic peoples should do to make them prevail.

... when it comes to state religions, I have always thought that, though they may perhaps sometimes momentarily serve the interests of political power, they are always sooner or later fatal for the church.

—Alexis de Tocqueville
Democracy in America, 1835

"Spiritual conceptions" have flourished in this country since the first Pilgrims dropped anchor off Provincetown in 1620. Though the theocratic plans of these New England dissidents barely survived a generation, "the first nation to disestablish religion remains a marvel of religiosity," as Garry Wills has written. Tocqueville knew well, like Jefferson and Madison before and Justice Hugo Black after him, that coerced religion corrupts the coercers and the religion. "European Christianity," the great historian wrote, "has allowed itself to be intimately united with the powers of this world. Now that these powers are falling, it is as if it were buried under their ruins."

During the past 15 years, an exclusionist religious movement in this country has attempted to restore what it perceives as the ruins of a Christian nation by seeking more closely to unite its version of Christianity with state power. Ironically, the groups and activists that have come to be known as the "religious right" crusade both rhetorically and in their policy aims against the very protection—the separation of church and state—that has secured the vitality of religion throughout American history.

This crusade has proceeded in the 1990s through grassroots campaigns to "return faith to our public schools," subsidize private religious education, roll back civil rights protections, oppose all abortions, and ensure that "pro-family Christians" gain control of the Republican Party. National groups with many thousands of members have spurred these efforts, inciting the movement with grim cadences of warfare. "This is really the most significant battle of the age-old conflict between good and evil, between the forces of God and forces against God," strategist Paul Weyrich has maintained. Christian Coalition leader Pat Robertson warns his followers to "expect confrontations that will be not only unpleasant but at times physically bloody." He asserts: "Just like what Nazi Germany did to the News, so liberal America is now doing to the evangelical Christians. It's the same thing."

Thus embattled, groups and activists have ratcheted up their rhetoric. Leading figures denounce church/state separation as "religious cleansing," "a socialist myth," "a lie of the left," "not a wall but a coffin." The day after delivering the benediction at the 1984 Republican convention, Rev. W. A. Criswell told CBS: "There is no such thing as separation of church and state. It is merely a figment in the imagination of infidels."

Similarly, political targets are often dispatched with virulence and paranoia: opponents are not merely wrong, they are "the enemy" and "Satanic." Feminists "kill their children, practice witchcraft and become lesbians." Abortion is the " 'Final Solution' . . . just like Hitler, it calls for the planned, state-sponsored EXTERMINATION of an entire class of innocent citizens. . . ." Public education is "a socialist, anti-God system of education." Gays and lesbians comprise the "most pernicious evil today." A former Congressman speaks of "the homosexual blitzkrieg" and maintains: "Unlike the French, who wept in the streets of Paris as the Germans marched by, we don't even know we've been conquered."

The hysteria of this language excites resentment on all sides and degrades or disallows reasonable discourse. It reflects as well a basic rejection of a society that includes dissent and pluralism—the modern democratic state. The political agenda of the religious right movement is, in turn, an attempt to legislate this rejection. Flimflam histories contending that the original "Christian" United States has been undone by a small, powerful anti-Christian elite provide bogus intellectual support and further poison public goodwill. As with other revisionist efforts, this religious right assault on history is a vehicle for anger and scapegoating: here, pluralism itself is scapegoated, and the religious right's crowded pandemonium comprises essentially any agency or figure associated with pluralism, including non-religious right evangelicals.

Unsurprisingly, this bitter push to replace the wall of separation with a citadel of Christianity—while suggesting that those who defend the wall are "enemies of God"—has been abetted, sometimes at the highest levels, by figures who have expressed conspiratorial, anti-Jewish, and extremist sentiments. On numerous other occasions, movement leaders have demonstrated a disturbing insensitivity to Jews and Jewish concerns. This apparent commonplace of life in the city on a hill, which has only one neighborhood, calls to mind Saul Bellow's warning: "Everybody knows there is no fineness or accuracy of suppression. If you hold down one thing, you hold down the adjoining."

Free Exercise

Yet those who object to the religious right movement too often engage the intolerance and stereotyping they purport to decry. Anti-Christian bigotry may be exaggerated by Pat Robertson and others, but it is not merely a figment in the imagination of evangelicals. The disdain of H. L. Mencken, who called fundamentalists "yokels," "half-wits," and "gaping primates," unfortunately lingers in the popular imagination. As Yale law professor Stephen Carter has suggested recently, critics err when they imply that the religious right poses a concern because of its religiosity rather than its platform. The problems raised by the movement are secular. "We must be able," states Carter, "to distinguish a critique of the content of a belief from a critique of its source."

The extensive political training and school curricula scrutiny encouraged by religious right groups, for instance, is frequently viewed by critics as a threat to, rather than an exercise of, good citizenship—and a prod for opponents to do likewise. Yet few such concerns regarding church-state separation were sounded when Christians organized on behalf of civil rights or the nuclear freeze (though others complained, of course). This is plainly inconsistent and illiberal.

Like anyone else, evangelical Christians have the right to organize, to run for office, to lobby, to boycott, to demonstrate, to attempt to implement their views. More than that, a healthy democracy encourages and depends on their doing so; it depends, that is, on a jumble of voices in the public square. Throughout American history, religion—largely a vigorous, splintery Protestantism—has been at the center of social movements: abolition, temperance, civil rights, opposition to war, abortion. Similarly, contemporary religious right activism has grown out of a widely shared sense of cultural breakdown—buttressed by reams of grievous statistics about crime, health, families— that seems to have exhausted the remedial policies of secular governance.

Religion has served democracy at such junctures precisely because, separated from the state, it exerts a moral authority that challenges the power of the state. As Carter writes, "A religion is, at its heart, a way of denying the authority of the rest of the world." Moreover, it keeps secularists and pluralists honest by asking how pluralism, which entails moral pluralism, is something other than a friendly face of nihilism. Sociologist James Davison Hunter quotes a satirical anti-abortion advocate in regard to this problem of ethical relativism: "Personally, I'm opposed to the bombing of abortion clinics, but I don't want to impose my mortality on anyone else."

The religious right goes wrong, however, because it would respond to the problem of moral authority by asking the state to mandate values—a state upon which it means to impose its own religious identity. Rather than compete for the spiritual allegiance of citizens— a competition that has fostered both religion and liberty—conservative evangelicals would command it. Their public policies ultimately attack the source of their own strength, and of the country's.

THE "RELIGIOUS RIGHT": A DEFINITION

The groups and activists described in these pages dislike the designation "religious right"—a promiscuous media concoction that has sometimes lent itself to caricature and derogation. Religious conservatives usually prefer a less sectarian tag, like the irenic "pro-family movement," or the fuzzy "people of faith." Most Americans consider themselves "pro-family" and claim religious faith, however, and the phrase "religious right" is fair when it is specific: in this report it refers to an array of politically conservative religious groups and individuals who are attempting to influence public policy based on a shared cultural philosophy that is antagonistic to pluralism and church/state separation. The movement consists mainly of Protestants, most of them evangelical or fundamentalist, a far smaller number of Catholics, and a smattering of Jews.

Some stereotype-busting is in order. The majority of evangelicals and fundamentalists—roughly 30 million Americans—are not affiliated with religious right groups. Billy Graham, most notably, has not made common cause with the movement, and such leading evangelical figures as Crystal Cathedral televangelist Robert Schuller and former Surgeon General C. Everett Koop have maintained a congenial distance. Additionally, while religious right activists are almost exclusively members of the Republican Party, many evangelicals are Democrats. These include Jimmy Carter, to name a famous example, most born-again African-Americans, and a small constellation of evangelical activists that may be dubbed the "religious left." A number of socially conservative Catholics also tend to vote Democratic.

For these reasons, while religious right voter registration efforts and shifting affiliations have added millions of white evangelicals to GOP rolls since 1979, the popular characterization of devout Christians as diehard Republicans is distorted. According to 1992 Gallup surveys, while 41 percent of Republicans identified themselves as "born again," the proportion was nearly the same for Democrats—39 percent. Similarly, 79 percent of Republicans claim to be church members, as do 71 percent of Democrats. Further, 65 percent of Republicans and 63 percent of Democrats agree that religion is "very important" in their lives.[1]

Catholic and Jewish Groups

Along with the modest if growing number of Catholic figures and far fewer Jews actively involved with the religious right movement, several politically conservative Jewish and Catholic groups concur with many of the movement's legislative goals. These organizations have sided with their largely Protestant counterparts on such issues as federal aid to private schools, civil rights, and abortion. These ideological affinities have largely played out on paper and in Washington in response to particular cases and bills—through the filing of briefs and through congressional testimony. Ongoing alliances between Jewish and evangelical groups are negligible, and between Catholic and evangelical groups relatively few, although some Catholic and religious right activists (notably the Christian Coalition, the Free Congress Foundation, and the Catholic Campaign for America) have sought more thoroughgoing relations.

ADL [the Anti-Defamation League] strongly opposes the encroachment on church/state separation underlying the policy aims of some Catholic and Jewish conservative organizations. However, given the as yet limited public interaction between Catholic and evangelical organizations,[2] and the virtual absence of interaction between Jewish and evangelical groups, and given differences in strategy, rhetoric, and impact, the Catholic and Jewish groups will not be considered in this report.

THE RELIGIOUS RIGHT IN THE 1990s

"The Christian community got it backwards in the 1980s. We tried to change Washington when we should have been focusing on the states. The real battles of concern to Christians are in neighborhoods, school boards, city councils and state legislatures."

—Ralph Reed
March 14, 1990 *The Washington Post*

"In the nineties, the Religious Right is going to be composed of a host of independent, locally sponsored and funded organizations that work in unison."

—Tim LaHaye
December 15, 1989 *Christianity Today*

The Movement's Main Features
The first of the two most significant features of the religious right movement in the 1990s has been the role of local affiliates in implementing the movement's agenda. The 1990 aim—to push the program up through the grassroots—has become 1994's reality. The national offices of the movement's major organizations provide resources, strategy, and political training, often by means of weekend civic activism courses in local churches—viz., the Christian Coalition's leadership schools or Focus on the Family's Community Impact Seminars.

These sessions, though often premised on distorted and sectarian notions of the Constitution and American history, have equipped activists with an estimable nuts-and-bolts political knowhow and dedication. The sessions spawn or strengthen politically active local chapters of national groups, as well

as independent community efforts that draw on the resources of many of the national groups.

The second significant feature of the contemporary religious right is unity. Local networks reflect the shared agenda and close working relations of groups on a national level. Jodie Robbins, a former assistant to Christian Coalition executive director Ralph Reed, has said, "Pat Robertson is in constant contact with Beverly LaHaye, with Jim Dobson, with Don Wildmon, and a lot of the national abortion groups. So it's really hand in hand."

National leaders speak at each other's conferences, appear on each other's broadcasts, contribute to each other's publications, and make common cause with respect to major policy issues—ranging from disallowing gays and lesbians in the military to campaign strategizing....

CONCLUSION

In the spring of 1994, the religious right appears to be thriving. Major groups have reported substantial growth during the past year—some claim to have doubled or even tripled their size.[3] While a number of these claims are viewed skeptically by critics, the movement's electoral, legal, and legislative efforts proceed with greater ambition than ever, spurred by the possibilities of the November elections and apparently favorable national trends regarding school prayer and other issues.

In a March mailing, for instance, the Christian Coalition announced plans to disseminate a 1994 Election Year Congressional Scorecard to all of "America's 40 million Christian voters." A new legal funding pool for religious liberty cases, the Alliance Defense Fund, has been formed with support from Pat Robertson, James Dobson, Donald Wildmon, and other conservative evangelical leaders. Additionally, lawyers from Robertson's and Wildmon's legal outfits have represented a Mississippi public high school principal fired in November for allowing student prayers to be broadcast over the school's intercom (the principal has since been reinstated). The efforts of these organizations are part of a larger public flurry: thousands rallied in support of the administrator, and in Mississippi and at least nine other states legislation has been enacted or introduced calling for a return of some form of government-sponsored prayer in public schools.

Electioneering and school prayer hardly encompass religious right activism, of course: cultural disagreements play out with growing intensity in local skirmishes over familiar issues—civil rights for gays and lesbians, abortion, school choice, school curricula. The coming year looks to be a period of heightened activity, and the movement's leaders are heady with recent gains and the promise of more.[4]

Success

Why is the religious right flourishing now? Why has it flourished? Several reasons may be suggested.

First, America *is* religious. Almost all Americans, as the religious right correctly reminds us, believe in God. No other nation in the industrialized world believes as widely. Ninety-four percent of our citizens profess faith in God, 90 percent say they pray, 80 percent say the Bible is the inspired word of God. As opposed to indicating a new trend, these figures reflect a constant feature in the nation's history: the religious impulse of Americans.

Moreover, the country is widely perceived as undergoing a crisis of values, and such times of uncertainty excite religious feeling. The particular concerns of the religious right reflect worries in the broader culture. Movement leaders have recognized more clearly than their opponents that issues like educating children or civil rights protection for gays and lesbians have a powerful resonance for most Americans. As these leaders have argued, such concerns are not merely political; they engage conceptions of ultimate moral truth. Conflict over the issues, sociologist James Davison Hunter contends, is "inevitably expressed as a clash over national life itself ... a struggle over national identity—*over the meaning of America,* who we have been in the past, who we are now, and perhaps most important, who we, as a nation, will aspire to become...."

Periods of cultural dislocation also arouse nostalgia. Romantic pangs for a lost, purer age have been a defining feature of American rhetoric and thought since the country's founding. From James Fenimore Cooper's Leatherstocking lamentations over the young nation's lost innocence in the 1820s to the "Take America Back" jingoism of contemporary politicians, the idea of a romanticized, dateless past has pervaded American secular and religious imaginations. This nostalgia traces in part to the Puritans and their jeremiads—sermons of castigation that invoked biblical ages as an incentive to (and promise of) future spiritual improvement.

Today, many religious conservatives have taken refuge in the notion of a "Christian nation"—an Edenic era when America was peacefully and uniformly Christian. This evangelical romanticism serves a two-fold purpose. It offers hope:

a better if unspecified past may yet be resurrected, and the country saved. And because, according to the myth, that past was ruined by godless forces, Christian nostalgia also justifies a sense of victimization and provides scapegoats.

Lastly, its commitment to local Republican politics has clearly revitalized and shaped the religious right. By virtue of this commitment, the movement has achieved national importance. With no clear popular champion or presidential frontrunner, and some policy differences among leading figures, the Party currently lacks an ideological center of gravity. Religious right voters, growing numbers of whom have earned places in Party structures, seem poised to provide it. For this reason, the attendance of Republican mandarins at religious right gatherings is by now a commonplace.[5]

The Problem of Success
The very reasons for the religious right's ascendancy suggest the perils of the movement. Its religious thought has always supported one side of various partisan political issues, with the result that a "Christian" imprimatur is stamped on conservative Republican policies. The assignment of a single doctrinally orthodox position to varied issues of governance—a "Christian" health care plan or a "Christian" balanced budget amendment—trivializes religious convictions.

Moreover, a vigorous religious witness cannot be supported by romanticized, revised history. American history is, in important part, the history of a remarkably vital Christianity. But beneath a broadly Protestant, nationalist canopy —further unfurled during this century to include Catholics and Jews (and, recently, Muslims)—this faith has been usually expressed in vigorous contention.

America's democratic vistas have comprised fertile soil for spiritual innovation; they have bloomed with new doctrines and eschatologies, new religions and denominations and branches and sects. "In this country that refused an established church," notes Leon Wieseltier, "churches are ceaselessly established." Indeed, the United States is home to more churches per capita than any other country in the world, a fact that underscores the vitality, disagreement, and freedom—religious and secular—that American Constitutional democracy has engendered.

This "practice of difference," so to speak, is likely the surest measurement of a society's freedom. Yet nothing more aptly characterizes the religious right movement than its hostility to difference, both within its own faith tradition and outside of it. American history is a continuing correction of mistakes, of improvement through moral crises that involve a clash between apparently nonnegotiable interests. A free country is disputatious and always partly dissatisfied. Consensus—as Henry Louis Gates notes —is "hammered out": it is clangorous and colliding. The religious right, in its attempt to unite its sectarian religious witness with the force of law, strives to supersede the most democratic form of discourse: the argument. The movement's disdain for consensus instead assumes the superiority of coercion to persuasion.

This coercive impulse is nourished by social upheaval. Pluralism, dissent, and tolerance are slightly valued during such times, and for this reason the sense of decline has been an enemy of liberty. Religious right groups and activists, suffused with a sense of the nation's moral decay, would jettison the shared life the First Amendment both makes possible and demands in favor of a nation that cannot exist freely and, on these shores, never did. Inevitably, their rejection of a shared life is expressed as a rejection of those with whom they would have to share. Charged with feelings of besiegement—reflected in phony histories and fevered rhetoric—their rejection easily slides into paranoia and scapegoating. It should not be surprising that the movement traffics with bigots and conspiracists, or that some activists and leaders themselves engage in bigotry and conspiracy-mongering.

Tocqueville Redux

One misfortune of the religious right's enterprise is that by opposing pluralism in response to the ills of a pluralistic society, conservative evangelicals will only lessen a needed voice—their own. Throughout American history, religion has been the single greatest agent for social amelioration and against state encroachment. Religious ideas should flourish "in democratic times," as Tocqueville stated, and the present time—argumentative, beset by crises, confused by a blare of new and old voices—is especially democratic.

But Tocqueville noted as well that state religions "are always sooner or later fatal for the church." Establishment compromises religious authority, as the history of Europe demonstrates; this same history is a long chronicle of compromises ended in dying churches, or wrought in bloodshed—a chronicle that has not ended in Northern Ireland, or Bosnia. So James Madison wrote that in the United States church and state were separated to "keep forever from these shores the ceaseless strife that has soaked the soil of Europe in blood for centuries." Tocqueville understood what the religious right does not: religion is strengthened, not weakened, by the separation of church and state. It is weakened, not

strengthened, by their union. Our society of proliferating faiths and creeds and dogmas, of open embrace, may be legitimately criticized: the moral and tangible ills of a free state worsen for lack of religious address. But a better democracy can not be fashioned by steamrolling our First Amendment mechanism for consensus—the very mechanism that allows a religious right. The genius of the Constitution is that it strikes equally for liberty and belief. The religious right's attack degrades both.

NOTES

1. Recent studies demonstrate that white voters who say they attend church regularly are likely to be Republicans. This is particularly true among members of predominantly evangelical denominations —the Southern Baptist Convention, the Assemblies of God, the Church of the Nazarene, among others —as opposed to those in the diminishing mainline congregations, including Episcopalians, Presbyterians, and Methodists.

2. Although this interaction has on occasion been substantial, as between the Archdiocese of New York and the Christian Coalition during New York's 1993 school board elections. Additionally, in early May 1994 the Archdiocese of Philadelphia planned to distribute 300,000 Christian Coalition voter guides pertaining to Pennsylvania's gubernatorial primary candidates.

3. Some examples: in a March mailing the Christian Coalition claimed "more than 900,000 members," at least a 100 percent increase since September 1993. Similarly, Donald Wildmon's American Family Association, in a March newspaper advertisement, reported the support of "more than 1,500,000 families," an unlikely 300 percent gain since the summer of 1993. Citizens for Excellence in Education also claims a roughly 50 percent rise in local chapters during the past year.

4. More militant anti-abortion leaders do not share the sanguine mood. In response to the Supreme Court's January 1994 decision allowing racketeering statutes to be used against abortion protesters (NOW v. Scheidler), Operation Rescue founder Randall Terry stated, "The Supreme Court has told civil protest to go to hell." Terry added: "This is a vulgar betrayal of over 200 years of tolerance towards protest and civil disobedience." Veteran anti-abortion organizer Joseph Scheidler, respondent in the Court's recent case, told the Los

Angeles Times, "Personally, I don't think violence works. I'm not one of the ladies in pink, I'm not a wimp. But I'm not with the arson and bomb squad either. Guys I've worked with for years and shared my views are saying, 'Wait a minute, maybe it's time to get a little more forceful.' I used to be able to sit around a table and without any prevarication at all say these were non-violent people. I can't anymore. I'm somewhat surprised at how many are saying we have to go ahead with this Holy War."

5. It may also be noted some religious right (and secular right) leaders claim that the election of Bill Clinton significantly boosted their groups.

NO

Dick Armey

FREEDOM'S CHOIR: SOCIAL AND ECONOMIC CONSERVATIVES ARE SINGING THE SAME SONG

RISE OF RELIGIOUS CONSERVATIVES

The first thing that needs to be understood about today's cultural conservatives, which I rather loosely identify with the religious right, is that they are entirely a defensive movement. It's not as if Pat Robertson and his compatriots were brainstorming one afternoon and suddenly hit upon the idea of infiltrating the government and using its power for their own ends.

Rather, millions of evangelicals and orthodox Catholics in the 1970s felt their way of life to be under subtle but determined attack by federal policies. They organized politically, after decades of shunning politics, not to impose their beliefs on others, but because the federal government was imposing its values on them.

Specifically, many leading cultural conservatives point to the threat of government regulation of private schools as the catalyzing event. Paul Weyrich writes:

> What caused the movement to surface was the federal government's moves against Christian schools. This absolutely shattered the Christian community's notion that Christians could isolate themselves inside their own institutions and teach what they pleased. The realization that they could not then linked them to the long-held conservative view that government is too powerful and intrusive, and this linkage is what made the evangelicals active.

Richard Viguerie, who observed the movement from its inception, points in particular to a proposed IRS ruling in 1978 that would have saddled all-private schools with the burden of proving that they were not founded to evade antidiscrimination laws—a ruling that would have put federal authorities in the position of denying Christian schools their tax exempt status on dubious grounds. Ralph Reed Jr., the executive director of the Christian Coalition, agrees. "The spark that ignited the pro-family movement was the fear of increased government regulation of church schools."

From Dick Armey, "Freedom's Choir: Social and Economic Conservatives Are Singing the Same Song," *Policy Review*, no. 67 (Winter 1994). Copyright © 1994 by The Heritage Foundation. Reprinted by permission.

Other issues were crucial as well. Phyllis Schlafly was mainly occupied with national security issues until she was confronted with the proposed Equal Rights Amendment in 1972. Faced with the prospect that overreaching federal courts would use the loosely worded amendment to justify unprecedented intrusions into private affairs, possibly even moving against the Catholic Church for harboring an all-male clergy, she organized hundreds of thousands of new political activists.

And even the enemies of the cultural conservative movement recognize the crucial importance of the Supreme Court's *Roe v. Wade* abortion decision. "*Roe* was a powerful stimulus to the right-to-life movement," the editors of the *New Republic* wrote in 1989, "which in turn was a cornerstone of the New Right, which is still a powerful political force today."

Nothing provoked more justified fear among devout believers than the sudden realization in the 1970s that an appointed, nine-member court could—with no accountability—impose its views on abortion, pornography, public prayer, education, and even sexuality on every community in the country.

Someone once quipped that "America is a country with a population as religious as India's ruled by a political elite as secular as Sweden's." Devout believers in middle America have certainly long believed that to be true, and they warily tolerated it. But once it became clear that an arbitrary federal authority could strike down the considered laws of 50 state legislatures on a whim, extend its control to religious institutions, and use amendments to the Constitution to engineer social revolutions, very little seemed safe. The cultural conservatives'

"diabolical" agenda was, and is, simply to neutralize the government's influence on disputed moral questions, and then to minimize the government's power to ensure it would not threaten their way of life in the future.

DEFENDING FAMILY RIGHTS

To be sure, the ACLU [American Civil Liberties Union] and other groups delight in finding some religious right field organizer who takes a more expansive view of cultural conservative goals. Occasionally, some religious right leaders have made intemperate remarks. But we can best judge the intentions of the movement by the issues it has actually pursued in the national arena. Far from being the right-wing Savonarolas of ACLU executive director Ira Glasser's imagination, their goals have been remarkably modest.

Take the debate over funding for the National Endowment for the Arts (NEA), an important issue because it served more than any other to feed the Left's fantasies of martyrdom at the hands of cultural fanatics. The NEA, a government board which doles out $170 million in arts funding, found itself in a maelstrom in 1989 when it chose to fund an absurd work of art by the artist Andres Serrano. Mr. Serrano used NEA money to take a crucifix, suspend it in a jar of human urine, and photograph it. Naturally, Christians and members of other faiths across the country were outraged—but at what? Not especially at Mr. Serrano, but at the federal government for using their money to subsidize him.

Although the Left cried censorship, I defy anyone to find a moment in the debate when cultural conservatives questioned Mr. Serrano's right to produce his "art." They simply argued that the taxpayers should not finance it. It was as if the art community believed censorship was having someone try to deny an artist a federal check.

I argued that if we were really opposed to censorship, we ought to close down the NEA entirely and avoid having an unelected government board deciding what constitutes art and what does not—a position which earned me the praise of such religious right leaders as Mississippi's Reverend Donald Wildmon.

Notice that the religious right did not argue that the federal government should reverse itself and fund Christian art, only that it remain neutral, neither encouraging nor discouraging particular works. That didn't stop the avant garde left from calling religious conservatives "cultural ayatollahs."

On another telling issue, a couple of years earlier, Congress was debating a child care bill that had been drafted, more or less, by Marion Wright Edelman of the Children's Defense Fund. The bill would have set up a new federal bureaucracy of Great Society proportions to funnel money to child-care centers—but only federally regulated child-care centers. That meant only large, secular child-care institutions. If a child-care center was in a church basement, it might still get money, but only after it put tarps over any crosses or other religious ornaments evident on the walls.

Conservatives, led by The Eagle Forum and Concerned Women for America, strenuously opposed the plan as "anti-family." It was not that they objected to people placing their children in daycare, something that was clearly a matter of individual choice. The problem was that the government would in effect be encouraging only one type of child-rearing arrangement—working parents

who put their children in large child-care centers. At the same time, it would force all families, including so-called traditional families that made huge sacrifices to raise their children in their own homes, to foot the bill.

They proposed instead a neutral alternative. Rather than give the money to the child-care centers, why not give it directly to parents and allow them to spend it as they saw fit? That way, the parents could use the money to alleviate the costs of whatever child-rearing arrangements they chose—whether that was raising their children in the home with a stay-at-home parent, placing them in daycare, or placing their children in an informal child-care setting, such as in the care of a relative or neighbor. There was never an attempt by the cultural conservatives to use federal power to encourage an "Ozzie and Harriet"–style family arrangement, as Representative Pat Schroeder derisively puts it. They simply asked that the government remain even-handed and allow free people to decide their family styles themselves, without the decision being unduly influenced by Washington.

What about all the school textbook cases, which earned the cultural conservatives the epithet of "book burners" by the civil libertarians? Every once in a while politically active Christians are charged with trying to have certain textbooks removed from school shelves, or have creationism taught alongside evolution, or insist that sex education be based on abstinence. Their opponents revel in these cases, since such issues allow them to portray cultural conservatives in the worst, most anti-intellectual, know-nothing light. But with rare, localized exceptions, the religious right in these cases was defending the communities' right of self-determination against encroachments from distant government authorities. In the old issue of prayer in the classroom, for example, individual communities chose to pray in public, as they had for as long as anyone could remember. Federal court orders said they could not.

In other misunderstood cases, the rights of parents themselves were threatened. For weeks this fall, in one example, voters in Northern Virginia were carpet-bombed with political ads charging that a Republican candidate wanted to have the *Wizard of Oz* taken out of a school curriculum. The charge was not true. In fact, the candidate had simply given legal advice to some parents who, for religious reasons, did not want their children reading books containing good witches. These parents didn't want the book taken off the shelves; they merely wanted school authorities to refrain from forcing their children to read it.

RESISTING THE GAY AGENDA

Finally, let's examine gays in the military.... While many military retirees opposed the policy on the grounds of military effectiveness—a position anyone interested in preserving freedom could endorse—the cultural conservatives were mainly concerned that the government would be casting an aura of legitimacy on the gay lifestyle, and thus take sides on an issue that was being hotly debated in the society at large.

As the cultural conservatives see it, society as a whole is still unsure of how we should respond as individuals to our gay citizens. Certainly the public is becoming more tolerant of gays, but it is not clear where this will lead. Some believe that homosexuality is normal and

healthy and should be treated as such. Others believe it is a moral abomination and should be discouraged. Still others, the majority in my opinion, decline to pass judgment on gays as individuals but shrink from endorsing their lifestyle. If the federal government were to abruptly change a long-standing tradition and allow gays in the armed forces, it would throw its enormous moral authority behind the first view, possibly preventing a different, more appropriate, social consensus from developing.

Indeed, the so-called "anti-gay" agenda of religious conservatives is geared toward nothing more than preserving people's freedom to decide for themselves how to respond to gays. Colorado recently earned itself the enmity of half of Hollywood when it passed a proposition denying gays special privileges under law. In practice, the Colorado proposition means that if a person believes homosexuality is normal, he is free to act accordingly. But if he believes that it is immoral or unhealthy and doesn't want his children exposed to it, he cannot be forced to rent his spare bedroom to a practicing homosexual couple. (Significantly, when a group tried to persuade Oregon voters to adopt a broader proposition, one which would actually declare in law that homosexuality was wrong, the voters rejected it, and the group has since rightly confined itself to working for "no special privileges.")

We are still left to deal with the difficult issue of abortion, however. Many who have followed this reasoning so far will still consider abortion as Exhibit A in their contention that the cultural conservatives mean to interfere with individual freedom. But that depends on what one means by "individual." If we accept the idea that the fetus is a human being, then the cultural conservatives' campaign against abortion is actually waged in the defense of freedom—an individual's freedom to live. Even an extreme libertarian accepts an absolute obligation for the government to protect its people from unjust aggression by others. Assuming that an unborn child is in fact a person—as I firmly believe it is—there can be no problem, and certainly no philosophical inconsistency, in supporting the government's duty to defend it.

William F. Buckley Jr., I thought, put the issue quite well. When one of the guests on "Firing Line" asked him how he could advocate "getting the government off our backs" at the same time he desired the government to "reach into our homes" and restrict abortion, he replied: "Why, for the same reason the government can 'reach into my home' and tell me I can't have a slave in the closet." In each case, it is merely defending a basic human right. Whatever differences individuals within the party have on abortion, they have nothing to do with different philosophies about the role of government and everything to do with different philosophies of humanity itself.

A CULTURAL FREE MARKET

It is certainly true that on the most prominent cultural issues—the values displayed in art, family arrangements, attitudes towards homosexuals—cultural conservatives have pronounced personal views. What is striking, however, is that they rarely look to the government, certainly not the federal government, to enforce their views, let alone to impose them on others. Their political program, properly understood, is nothing more

than to neutralize the government's influence on disputed value questions and minimize the government's power in order to prevent it from attempting to exert any such influence in the future. They want the government to allow people to decide these issues by themselves.

Allow people to decide these issues by themselves.... The cultural conservatives —as judged by their actual political program—implicitly believe in a kind of cultural free market in which free people, regulated through largely noncoercive means, may arrive at the best possible solution to the social questions that currently divide us.

As they see it, if the federal government were not subsidizing bigoted anti-Christian art, that art would be rejected by the public and consigned to a limited counterculture audience. Without federal subsidies of family disintegration— either in the form of welfare programs that have destroyed our inner cities and child-care programs geared solely to the institutionalization of children—the traditional family would flourish as it has in generations past. And without President Clinton using the enormous federal bureaucracy to express his personal view of homosexuality, a social consensus on the subject would naturally evolve —one that neither persecutes homosexuals nor accepts their lifestyle as normal, happy and healthy. Fervent proselytizers though they may be in their private life, the cultural conservatives' political program is aimed solely at minimizing the government's role in these issues.

Cultural conservatives fear the power of the modern state for precisely the reason that [Friedrich von] Hayek, the patron saint of modern market economics, outlined 50 years ago in *The Road to Serfdom*. They know that with its enormous control of economic resources—the power to tax, to fund programs, to regulate vast types of activities—the state can slowly but determinedly spread its control over their culture and erode their way of life.

LEADING VIRTUOUS LIVES

Anyone who has spent much time around flesh-and-blood cultural conservatives—say, your average Southern Baptist family in Texas, for example—knows that they have utmost confidence that, as long as the central government does not take sides on disputed value questions, people are most likely to live virtuous lives, as they understand them. If the only weapon being used in the so-called "culture war" is the entirely peaceful one of persuasion by words and deeds, they believe they will win it. Only when coercive power is employed by a distant, central authority will they lose. Their idea of the world is of a hard-working, God-fearing America that would be doing just fine were it not for government policies that erode traditional values. I think this view is a fair description of our country's plight, but whatever the objective reality, it is clear that the cultural conservatives believe this is the case. They thus neither seek nor desire to capture the government themselves and use it to impose their views on others. They simply want it to get out of the way.

POSTSCRIPT

Does the Religious Right Threaten American Freedoms?

We can separate church and state, but we cannot keep religion out of politics. Deeply held religious views color attitudes on such deeply divisive issues as abortion, pornography, the civil rights of homosexuals, population control, hate speech, race relations, the moral conduct of public officials, school prayer, federal aid to church schools, the welfare state, and capital punishment.

The political history of the United States attests to the important roles that different religious views have played in shaping public policy on slavery and abolitionism, women's suffrage, Prohibition and its repeal, the civil rights movement, the cold war against the Soviet Union, the Vietnam War, and the efforts to restrict or ban nuclear weapons. Mark A. Noll, ed., *Religion and American Politics* (Oxford University Press, 1990) contains essays by leading scholars examining the impact of religion on American public life throughout the nation's history.

The "religious right" may be identified as those groups locally seeking public school prayer and other policies sympathetic to organized religion and nationally working for the election of a pro-family values, anti-abortion president. A sympathetic treatment of many of these issues is in William J. Bennett, *The De-Valuing of America: The Fight for Our Culture and Our Children* (Summit Books, 1992). A liberal analysis of church-state relations in the recent past is in Garry Wills, *Under God: Religion and American Politics* (Simon & Schuster, 1990).

Some of the most outspoken leaders of the new Christian right in the recent past have been Jerry Falwell and the Moral Majority, Pat Robertson and the Christian Coalition, and Phyllis Schlafly and the Eagle Forum. A comprehensive and balanced presentation of the views of these and other Christian conservatives can be found in Michael Lienesch, *Redeeming America: Piety and Politics in the New Christian Right* (University of North Carolina Press, 1993). The more extreme views of white supremacist groups committed to a religious position known as Christian Identity is examined in Michael Barkun, *Religion and the Racist Right: The Origins of the Christian Identity Movement* (University of North Carolina Press, 1994).

Kenneth D. Wald, *Religion and Politics in the United States,* 2d ed. (Congressional Quarterly Press, 1992) is a balanced treatment of the political impact of religious beliefs, institutions, and practices.

PART 4

America and the World

What is the role of the United States in world affairs? From what premise—realism or idealism—should American foreign policy proceed? What place in the world does America now occupy, and in what direction is it heading? American government does not operate in isolation from the world community, and the issues in this section are crucial ones indeed.

- Must America Be the World Leader?

- Should the United States Pursue Economic Competitiveness?

- Should the United States Put More Restrictions on Immigration?

- Is America Declining?

ISSUE 18

Must America Be the World Leader?

YES: Richard M. Nixon, from *Beyond Peace* (Random House, 1994)

NO: Jonathan Clarke, from "The Conceptual Poverty of U.S. Foreign Policy," *The Atlantic Monthly* (September 1993)

ISSUE SUMMARY

YES: The late president Richard M. Nixon argues that America is the only responsible power with the experience and vision to lead the world.

NO: Writer Jonathan Clarke says that the United States must break away from "neo–cold war orthodoxy" and stop trying to play the world's policeman.

Beginning in 1989, the Soviet empire began to collapse. One by one, the grim satellite regimes of Eastern Europe—Poland, Hungary, East Germany, Czechoslovakia, Bulgaria, Albania, Romania—were overthrown in what was called the "velvet revolution" because of its relative lack of bloodshed. By the time Russia declared its independence in 1991, the Soviet Union was no more.

The cold war was already waning when the Soviet Union entered its last years, but the death of Soviet communism meant that the cold war could never make a comeback. As Secretary of State Warren Christopher has observed, the Soviet Union was the "reference point" of American foreign policy in the cold war era. The fear of Soviet expansion of communism dominated the minds of American policymakers. But by the end of 1991, all that was over.

American policymakers are still groping to understand the implications of this fact. As one commentator put it, "It's like a lost limb—we reach to scratch it, but it's just not there anymore." The metaphor is inexact. The Soviet Union was more like a tumor than an arm or a leg. But it did provide a familiar mark —or blob—on the world landscape, and in that sense it helped the United States set its compass. The picture today is more confused: we do not have the neat "bipolar world," as it used to be called, with the West confronting the Soviet bloc, but a vastly more complicated arena of individual states making individual decisions, sometimes coalescing, more often going their own ways. It is a more uncertain world than it was during the cold war. How should the United States guide its foreign policy in such a world? What are the options and the possibilities? What of the old ways should be retained, and what should be discarded? How do we make sense out of this new world?

In 1922 Walter Lippmann, the great journalist-philosopher, first introduced the term *stereotype* into the language of social science. "Stereotypes," wrote

Lippmann, are the "pictures in our heads," the simple models or "fictions" we use to represent the complex world in which we live. Lippmann is often misunderstood as condemning stereotypes. Actually, he insisted that we cannot do without them. "For the real environment is altogether too big, too complex, and too fleeting for direct acquaintance. We are not equipped to deal with so much subtlety, so much variety, so many permutations and combinations." We use these models just as we use road maps; like maps, they are schematic representations of reality. Stereotypes, Lippmann concluded, are bad only when they become complete fictions, when they do not fit the facts, when they mislead us rather than guide us.

The following arguments proceed from two very different models of what the world is like today. Richard Nixon sees it as a forest, once dominated by a handful of mighty oaks, which has undergone a fire. The only large tree left undamaged is the United States. All the rest are either saplings or creepers. Whether we like it or not, then, we must undertake the main burden of world leadership; we cannot rely on the UN or any other international body for leadership. And at times we must be willing to undertake unilateral military actions when it is in our interest to do so. A contrasting model (Lippmann would say stereotype) is provided by Jonathan Clarke. For him, though he does not use the metaphor, the world is more like a rank jungle, with new species of plants and animals constantly appearing and old ones disappearing. The United States must learn to live with this bewildering variety of flora and fauna, and it must do so with modesty and subtlety. It is not a mighty oak but one tree among many, and it does not have any need or reason to dominate. Perhaps one of these models will be seen to have fit the facts of our time, to have been the right one for policymakers in the 1990s. But which?

YES

Richard M. Nixon

AMERICA MUST LEAD

Leaders of small countries at times have a clearer understanding of how the world works than do leaders of major countries, who are burdened with the day-to-day responsibilities of world leadership. During a conversation I had in 1967 with one such leader, Singapore's Lee Kwan Yew, he likened the world to a forest. "There are great trees, there are saplings, and there are creepers," he said. "The great trees are Russia, China, Western Europe, the United States, and Japan. Of the other nations, some are saplings that have the potential of becoming great trees, but the great majority are creepers, which, because of lack of resources or lack of leadership, will never be great trees."

Since he made that statement twenty-seven years ago at the height of the Cold War, a political forest fire has swept over the world. Although Russia, China, Japan, Western Europe, and the United States are still the only giant trees in the forest, the fire has dramatically changed them and the world around them. Communism has collapsed in the Soviet Union. One hundred million people in Eastern Europe have been liberated from communist domination. China is no longer an enemy of the United States and is using capitalist tools to achieve communist goals. Japan has become an economic superpower. Western Europe, no longer united by the threat from the East, is searching for a new rationale for NATO, a new relationship with the newly liberated nations of Eastern Europe and the former Soviet Union, and a new momentum toward economic unity. After bearing the burden of free-world leadership for forty-eight years, the American people, as indicated by the 1992 presidential election, want to devote their attention and their resources to their problems at home rather than those abroad.

Profound disagreement exists about the role the United States should play in the era beyond peace. A number of arguments against a continued American leadership role in the world have wide appeal:

- Because of the downfall of the Soviet Union, there is no need for American global leadership.
- Since the United States carried the major burden of the Cold War, other nations should lead now.

From Richard M. Nixon, *Beyond Peace* (Random House, 1994). Copyright © 1994 by Richard M. Nixon. Reprinted by permission of Random House, Inc.

- Even assuming that we are the only ones who can lead, we should give priority to our pressing domestic problems.
- The United States, with huge budget deficits and trade imbalances, can no longer afford to lead.
- Because of our massive problems at home, the United States is not worthy to lead.

All of these statements are wrong.

Only the United States has the combination of military, economic, and political power a nation must have to take the lead in defending and extending freedom and in deterring and resisting aggression. Germany and Japan may have the economic clout but they lack the military muscle. China and Russia have the potential military might, but they lack the economic power. None has sufficient standing with all the world's great powers, none has the record of half a century of leadership. As the only great power without a history of imperialistic claims on neighboring countries, we also have something all these countries lack: the credibility to act as an honest broker.

The popular idea that the United Nations can play a larger role in resolving international conflicts is illusory. During the last forty-eight years, the U.N. has debated, passed resolutions on, and contemplated intervention in scores of conflicts in every part of the world. But it has acted militarily on only two occasions: when the Soviet Union boycotted the Security Council vote during the Korean War, and when President Bush enlisted the U.N. to support our efforts to defeat Iraqi aggression during the Persian Gulf War. As former U.S. Ambassador to the U.N. Jeane Kirkpatrick has observed, "Multilateral decision making is complicated and inconclusive. U.N. operations —in Bosnia or in Somalia or wherever— are characteristically ineffective."

Those who have led their peoples through the ultimate crisis of war understand better than anyone else that no leader can permit his country's interests to be held hostage to the whims of an international body. Winston Churchill was one such leader. I vividly remember my last meeting with him in 1958. I had gone to London to represent the United States at the dedication of the chapel at St. Paul's Cathedral honoring the American dead in World War II. I called on him at his home, where he was recovering from a stroke....

I found that while Churchill had lost his power and some of his energy, he had lost none of his unique understanding of how the world worked. After a limp handshake, he ordered a glass of brandy. The effect when he drank it was like lighting a match to dry twigs. Our discussion ranged far and wide, from developments in the Soviet Union to a minidispute between Ghana and Guinea. When I asked him about the U.N., he said that he had supported it from the beginning and believed it had a significant role to play. But he added, "Under no circumstances can a major nation submit an issue affecting its vital interests to the U.N. or any other collective body for decision."

The concept of "assertive multilateralism" being advanced by some U.N. supporters can only be described as naïve diplomatic gobbledygook. A collective body cannot be effective unless it has leadership. As de Gaulle told André Malraux shortly before his death, "Parliaments can paralyze policy. They cannot initiate it." Even a collective body as closely knit as NATO was not able to be "assertive" in Bosnia. Can anyone seriously suggest that a collective body such as the U.N., one third of whose members have populations smaller than that of the state of Arkansas and half of which are not stable democracies, could be "assertive"?

This does not mean that the United Nations should be thrown on the scrap heap of history. It does mean that without leadership from the world's strongest nation, the U.N. will not act. We should enlist U.N. support for our policies but not put the U.N. in charge of them. The suggestion that the United States should put American troops under a U.N. command to give collective security a chance to work is completely unacceptable. To serve as President means accepting ultimate responsibility for the lives of troops put in harm's way. It would be not only unwise but immoral for him to deliver the lives of American soldiers into the hands of an international bureaucrat selected by the United Nations. . . .

In the 1992 presidential campaign, a sign in the Clinton campaign office read, "It's the economy, stupid." That was good politics but poor statesmanship. There is a world of difference between campaigning and governing. We cannot have a strong domestic policy unless we have a strong foreign policy. We cannot be at peace in a world at war, and we cannot have a healthy economy in a sick world economy.

Since the end of World War II, the United States has been the world's most powerful symbol of political and economic freedom. The Cold War was not merely a conflict between two opposing armies. It was a conflict over two opposing ideologies. We triumphed because we were rich economically and strong militarily, but we were rich and strong precisely because of our dedication to the ideas of freedom. The values of political and economic freedom that have guided our country since the days of the American Revolution are the moral imperatives that impel us to play a leading role in the world.

Those who doubt our worthiness to lead should look at our record over the past forty-eight years. We have helped our enemies as well as our friends to recover from the devastation of World War II. We returned Okinawa to Japan and integrated both Japan and Germany into the community of Western nations. We have provided over $1 trillion in foreign aid to nations in the developing world. Since the end of the Cold War, we have returned Subic Naval Base to the Philippines; launched aid programs to Eastern Europe and the former Soviet Union; continued to protect South Korea and Japan; freed Kuwait and protected Saudi Arabia and other Gulf states from Iraqi aggression; safeguarded Israel's security; assisted anticommunist forces in Angola, Cambodia, and Afghanistan; supported peaceful democratic revolutions in the Philippines, in Latin America, and in South Korea; and been generous in our humanitarian aid to Somalia and other countries suffering man-made or natural disasters. Our record has not been perfect, but no other nation in history can match it. It is a record of benevolent leadership and of advancing not only our selfish interests but the values of political and economic freedom.

As we enter the twenty-first century, we must adopt a clear-headed policy based on practical idealism and enlightened realism. For the first time in fifty years, we have the power to set a course for the next century so that all, not just some, nations can experience the victory of freedom over tyranny in the world.

Over the past few years, foreign policy observers have made the following points in articles and commentaries:

- The democratic revolution in Russia and its political and free-market reforms are irreversible.
- European political and economic integration will eliminate the need for a continued U.S. role in NATO.
- The disappearance of the Soviet threat in the Far East means the end of geopolitical competition and conflict in East Asia.
- The U.S.–led victory in the Persian Gulf War ensured the stability of the Middle East and Western access to Middle Eastern oil.

All of these statements are false.

When the reactionary left's coup against Mikhail Gorbachev failed in August 1991, a half-century of superpower conflict ended. Yet Russia remains vulnerable to extreme nationalists and reactionaries intent on reversing free-market and democratic reforms. The European Community has stalled in its effort to achieve economic and political integration, and Europe is falling victim again to parochialism. Asia is threatened with conflict based on competing interests and traditional rivalries. The Persian Gulf remains a tinderbox that could catch fire at any moment.

We have not achieved perfect peace, which philosophers have been writing about for centuries and which Immanuel Kant described as "perpetual peace." This idea has always had enormous appeal. But it will never be achieved, except at diplomatic think tanks and in

the grave. During my last meeting with Leonid Brezhnev in the Crimea in 1974, I jotted down this note on a pad of paper: "Peace is like a delicate plant. It has to be constantly tended and nurtured if it is to survive. If we neglect it, it will wither and die."

After the collapse of communism in the Cold War and the defeat of aggression in the Persian Gulf War, many observers concluded that we were witnessing the beginning of a new world order. They were wrong. The Cold War divided the world, but peace did not unite it. Instead of order, we find disorder in many areas of the world. The United States and the Soviet Union have kept the lid on potential small wars, but since World War II there have been one hundred and fifty of them. Eight million more people have been killed in those small wars than lost their lives in World War I. Most of those wars would have occurred had there been no superpower conflict. Since the end of the Cold War, the threat of small wars has substantially increased. Today, seventy-seven conflicts, based on tribal, national, ethnic, or religious hatreds, are being fought, and ruthless dictators such as Saddam Hussein...and Muammar Qaddafi are poised to attack their neighbors.

During the Cold War, the leaders of the United States and the Soviet Union knew that they had the power to destroy each other and the rest of the world. This sharply reduced the possibility of global nuclear war. Pariah nations such as North Korea and Iraq, which are now trying to join the nuclear club, would not have these restraints. Consequently, the danger of a nuclear war is greater now than during the Cold War. Stopping nuclear proliferation therefore must be a top priority for all of the major nuclear powers—Russia, China, the United States, Great Britain, and France.

All of these issues—the former Soviet Union, the future of Europe, the rivalry in East Asia, the stability of the Persian Gulf, and avoiding nuclear anarchy—represent strategic priorities for the United States. None of them can be resolved without a commitment of American world leadership. We cannot react to every emergency call like an international 911 operator. But we *must* respond to those that affect our vital interests in the world....

No one would question that our vital interests were involved in World War I, World War II, and the Cold War. But American Presidents invariably clothed our interests in idealistic rhetoric. World War I was not simply a war to defend our interests against imperial Germany's aggression. It was a "war to end war" and to make the world safe for democracy. World War II was not just a war to defend U.S. interests against Nazi and Japanese aggression. It was a war to extend four great freedoms to all people. The Cold War was not just a war to defend our interests against aggressive communism. It was a war to defend and extend freedom and democracy in the world. No war more seriously involved our vital interests than the Persian Gulf War. But even then, the practical objective of defending our access to oil resources was coupled with the idealistic goal of preserving the independence of Kuwait and advancing the cause of democracy.

As realists, we do not want to become involved in foreign ventures unless our interests are threatened. As idealists, we insist that what is right for us must also be right for others. Bill Safire properly observed, "America will not defend with its lives what it cannot defend with its conscience."

Enlargement is a tricky word. In photography, a negative can be enlarged to a three-by-five snapshot or a wall-size mural. Based on the record so far, the [Clinton] administration is aiming for wallet-size. Some officials clearly believe that the United States overextended itself during the Cold War, particularly in Vietnam, one of its major battles. They tend to resist American involvement, except in humanitarian activities that have overwhelming public support. They have yet to face up to the fact that it will at times be necessary to use American power and influence to defend and extend freedom in places thousands of miles away if we are to preserve it at home. It is a role that will require global vision and big plays from this President and every successive one in the era beyond peace.

In his Inaugural Address, John F. Kennedy vowed "to pay any price, bear any burden, meet any hardship, support any friend, oppose any foe, in order to assure the survival and the success of liberty." Even during the Cold War, such a policy was praiseworthy but unrealistic. Then, as now, world peace was threatened by several enemies of liberty. We cannot afford to fight them all at once. Since the Cold War, the choices about how and when to fight for peace and freedom have become even more complex.

We must begin by asking ourselves what kind of world we want, now that we have peace. Ideally, all nations should have free economic systems, free political systems, and an unfailing commitment to social justice and human rights. But the world is not a blank canvas on which we can paint our vision. We must take its myriad realities into account as we seek to realize our goals. The United States cannot become involved in every nation or region where our ideals have not been achieved. We favor extending peace and freedom—but extending peace without compromising our interests or principles, and extending freedom without risking peace. If peace is our only goal, then the victory of freedom may be imperiled. If freedom is our only goal, then peace will be imperiled. It is the burden of being the only superpower that there are things we do not wish to do that we must do, and it is the burden of being a responsible superpower that there are things we wish to do that we cannot do.

In a world without a dominant enemy, we must consider each situation on its merits. Will our involvement be consistent with our values? Will it serve our interests? Will it serve the interests of our friends? Will it serve the interests of those directly involved? During the Cold War, the answer to each of these questions, where our efforts to oppose communist expansionism and Soviet aggression were concerned, was yes. The answer to each question should also be yes regarding our efforts to help bring about the victory of freedom in the former Soviet Union. No other single factor will have a greater political impact on the world in the century to come than whether political and economic freedom take root and thrive in Russia and the other former communist nations. Today's generation of American leaders will be judged primarily by whether they did everything possible to bring about this outcome. If they fail, the cost that their successors will have to pay will be unimaginably high.

NO
Jonathan Clarke

THE CONCEPTUAL POVERTY OF
U.S. FOREIGN POLICY

THE NEO–COLD WAR ORTHODOXY

[President] Clinton's foreign-policy team needs a fresh source of energy. To date it has failed to deliver any of the "bold new thinking" of which [Secretary of State Warren] Christopher improbably spoke at the time of his nomination. (Quite to the contrary, in perhaps the most decisive action thus far of his tenure as Secretary of State, Christopher moved swiftly to silence the one senior State Department official, Under Secretary of State for Political Affairs Peter Tarnoff, who dared to speak, albeit tentatively and off the record, of the need to close the gap between U.S. foreign-policy aspirations and resources.) Instead, what has emerged is a defensive rehash of warmed-over ideas adding up to what might be called "neo–Cold War orthodoxy" or "sole-remaining-super-power syndrome."

The central contention of this traditionalist school is that, a few ritual genuflections in the direction of new thinking aside, it is business as usual. The United States must remain "activist" in foreign policy and prepared to intervene in any of the world's problems. To this end it must retain a large military and, in the words of Secretary of Defense Les Aspin, the readiness to "fight every day." Advocates of reform who suggest that in today's much improved security environment there is less need for American interventionism, or that military solutions are less applicable to contemporary problems, are stigmatized as isolationists or 1930s-style appeasers.

Proponents of this no-change approach have hardly been prolific writers or speakers about the fundamentals underlying their ideas, but the evidence at hand indicates that their views draw on four main theses:

- The end of the Cold War has not reduced the level of international threat. New dangers have replaced the old ones.
- The collapse of the Soviet-American superpower bipolarity has made the world a more unstable and complex place.
- Only the United States has the power to solve the problems of the world.

From Jonathan Clarke, "The Conceptual Poverty of U.S. Foreign Policy," *The Atlantic Monthly* (September 1993). Copyright © 1993 by Jonathan Clarke. Reprinted by permission.

- The United States has a unique moral responsibility to protect humanitarian values.

These assumptions freeze U.S. foreign policy in a Cold War time warp. If they are accepted and followed, the United States will remain the world's policeman, military spending will remain high, the peace dividend will be meager, and U.S. diplomacy will too readily reach for military solutions....

A DISCRETIONARY JUNGLE

The first thesis asserts that despite the cessation of the Soviet threat, the United States still faces a hostile world. CIA Director James Woolsey has won the accolade of a cartoon in *The Economist* for his vivid image of the world as a "jungle filled with a bewildering variety of poisonous snakes." In the same vein Chester A. Crocker, a former assistant secretary of state, has written that "historic changes since 1989 have profoundly destabilized the previously existing order without replacing it with any recognizable or legitimate system. New vacuums are setting off new conflicts. Old problems are being solved, begetting new ones."

Before going on to look at these new problems, recall the ultimate threat that hung over the United States every day of the Cold War: total national annihilation through the doctrine of "mutual assured destruction." Now that this threat is, in the words of Senators Sam Nunn and Richard Lugar, "at an all time low," it requires a major effort of imagination to recollect that twenty-four months ago nuclear submarines roamed the ocean depths, strategic bombers were on twenty-four-hour-alert active duty, and hardened silos were on active main-

tenance, all to prevent the destruction of the United States in a thermonuclear holocaust.

The secondary threat from the Soviet Union during the Cold War was global opposition to American interests and values. This took the form of both armed aggression and clandestine subversion. In effect the Soviets were standing on the other side of the school yard saying, "We repudiate all that America stands for. We represent a better system, a better way of organizing society. Follow us —or else." In the face of this across-the-board challenge, the Cold War arms buildup and the containment policy were an inevitable and logical reaction.

What are the new threats to which the foreign-policy establishment has been drawing our attention so urgently? Nuclear proliferation, anti-democratic movements, Islamic fundamentalism, narcotics, ethnic tumult, international terrorism: these are real problems, real dangers, and should not be underestimated.

Close analysis, however, shows that they share an interesting element: not one carries with it the immediate physical threat of annihilation of the United States which was present every second of the Cold War. There is a discretionary quality about them. A direct Soviet attack on Germany or South Korea would have activated the treaty-defined obligation of a U.S. military response. Today we can pick and choose. The "principals committee" (consisting of the President's top national-security advisers) can discuss options for weeks, while the Secretary of State can embark on a week-long tour of European capitals to seek allied support. The leisurely six months of unopposed buildup between Desert Shield (August of 1990) and Desert Storm (January of 1991) makes the point. This is not to deny the reality of the new threats; it is simply to note that they are of a different quality. Today's threats do not present a *systemic* challenge to American interests. The very existence of Soviet communism was predicated on global opposition to the United States; today's world holds no such enemy. The attempts of Charles Krauthammer and other syndicated columnists to construct a new Comintern out of Iranian-inspired Islamic fundamentalism, or of the Harvard professor Samuel Huntington and other academics to detect a new source of global conflict in a form of Bismarckian *Kulturkampf* [conflict between civil government and religious authorities] between "the West and the rest," collapse under the weight of their internal contradictions.

To be sure, today's threats are not entirely toothless. The introduction of nuclear weapons to the Korean peninsula, for example, provoking as it might a copycat reaction in Japan and Indonesia, would be of great concern. But this is very different from the situation that prevailed during the Cold War. We now have no adversary who possesses the ballistic missiles, massed armor, and industrial base of the Warsaw Pact countries. The challenge to American interests is tangential or by extension. Today's discretionary problems simply do not carry the same weight as yesterday's. life-threatening dangers. To argue that they do undermines the credibility of the traditionalists as architects of U.S. foreign policy for the next century.

In terms of the threat to the United States itself or its allies, the world environment is far more benign today than it was formerly. Contrary to Christopher's assertions, America's foreign-policy agenda is very far from "overflowing with crises and potential disasters."

The United States does not face the rise of a dominant, hegemonic power. There is therefore much less threat-based need for the United States to become actively involved in regional conflicts. Management of these can safely be delegated to nations nearer the action, with the United States playing a supporting role.

BELGRADE IS NOT MUNICH

The second thesis concerns the concept of stability or order in a bipolar world and a multipolar one. Implicit in it is a remarkable reinterpretation of history. Foreign-policy experts from the Cold War era, even including such a forward-thinking writer as the former Secretary of Defense James Schlesinger, would have us believe that the Cold War was a period of "unique disciplines" inasmuch as each side recognized the constraints implicit in the other's capacity for massive retaliation.

The theory goes that during this period the superpowers contented themselves with playing, through surrogates, a bloodless and painless version of the "great game" by a mutually agreed set of Marquis of Queensberry rules that imposed limits on the potential spread of conflict. The theorists now argue that the dissolution of the fear of nuclear holocaust "has made the world safe for conventional war," and that such a war, for example in the Balkans or the Caucasus, could ignite conflict across a continent.

This analysis calls upon us to indulge in collective amnesia about the Cold War. Unfortunately, the facts cannot be forgotten so readily. The list is long and unappetizing. The Soviet Union really did try to blockade Berlin and draw Greece behind the Iron Curtain; children really did hide under their desks during the Cuban missile crisis; Soviet tanks really did roll into Prague, Budapest, and Kabul; on Soviet orders, refugees really were shot and allowed to bleed to death under the Berlin Wall; dictatorships in Cuba, Ethiopia, Angola, and Mozambique really did rise on the backs of Soviet-equipped and -trained security services; state sponsors of anti-American terrorism really were fêted in Moscow; the Soviet Union really did bankroll the Communist parties of Western Europe and Latin America. None of this was a dream. To combat all this, the West really did live on the nuclear high wire. And as for conventional war during the Cold War, the history books burgeon with the records of major conflagrations: Vietnam, Biafra, Chad, the Iran-Iraq war, successive Arab-Israel wars, the India-Pakistan war, Nicaragua, El Salvador, the Indonesian confrontation, the Chinese annexation of Tibet, the ethnic massacres in Sri Lanka, the Turkish invasion of Cyprus.

The hard reality is that the Cold War was a period of sustained global instability, not one of blissful Soviet-American condominium between consenting adult partners. At the global level a change of vast significance has since taken place. The threat of nuclear self-destruction no longer hangs over the world. The disappearance of this threat has removed a huge source of instability. What people find confusing, however, is that at the sub-global or local level the world gives the appearance of being wildly unstable. Across the map more red lights seem to be blinking in such hitherto unfamiliar places as Bosnia, Armenia, Georgia, Abkhazia, Tajikistan, South Ossetia, and the Trans-Dniester Republic, among other trouble spots.

Adherents of the neo–Cold War orthodoxy misinterpret these developments as well, regarding them as denoting a more anarchic world. They seek to present these conflicts as outgrowths of a new chaos that will be deepened if Washington adopts what President Bush called a "passive and aloof" policy. In fact, though their names are exotic, these conflicts are not different in intensity from many others that have disfigured this century and, it is certain, will continue into the next. The end of the Cold War has not ended history. Rather, the breakup of the Soviet empire has stranded many population groups on the wrong side of borders that themselves emerged from the breakup in 1917–1918 of the earlier Hohenzollern, Romanoff, Hapsburg, and Ottoman empires. Sometimes border adjustment will take place without bloodshed (for example, the fusion of East and West Germany and the divorce between the Czech Republic and Slovakia), but, as often as not, conflicts will occur as people attempt to right perceived wrongs or assert ancient irredentist claims. . . .

THE SOLE-REMAINING-SUPERPOWER SYNDROME

The third and fourth theses—that only the United States has the power to solve the world's problems, and that the United States has a unique moral responsibility to protect humanitarian values —both derive from the sole-remaining-superpower syndrome. Underlying both is the thought that, as George Bush said, "there is no one else." National Security Adviser Anthony Lake has spoken in a similar vein of the United States' "monopoly on power."

This outlook has resulted in an important conceptual error in our status quo foreign policy. It assumes that the mere identification of problems is enough to trigger American involvement. While paying lip service to the view that the United States cannot be the world's policeman, it blithely calls for the United States to prevent Europe from dissolving into "chaos," to offer security guarantees to Ukraine, to interpose American forces in any possible conflict between China and Japan, and to guard the Golan Heights—to name a diverse list of actual or potential commitments that were under discussion in the first six months of this year [1993].

This approach is thorny with difficulties. The most important of these is the implicit assumption that some form of U.S. intervention, most often military, is the best or indeed a viable route toward a solution of the problem under consideration. During the Cold War, when the challenges faced by the United States or its allies were often of a military nature, recourse to arms was often necessary. The Soviets would not have left Afghanistan had not the United States armed the *mujahideen*. Grenada and the Caribbean generally would not be the sleepy, democratic backwater it is today if the United States had not intervened to throw out Bernard Coard and his Communist bully boys.

The world has, however, moved on. Even if for argument's sake one concedes that the United States has vital interests in every corner of the globe, today's problems are still far less susceptible to military solutions than the earlier ones were. The reason for the lack of consensus on Bosnia was not that the U.S. military could not do the job of repelling Serbian aggression but that this was only part of the job. We wanted also to persuade Serbs, Croats, and Muslims to live side by side in peace. For this purpose high-level bombing seems as inappropriate across the Atlantic as it would be in Los Angeles in mediating the feuds of the Bloods and the Crips.

American policy analysts who suffer from the sole-remaining-superpower syndrome are not alone in placing too high a value on military might. Brian Urquhart, the former UN undersecretary-general for special political affairs, advocated in *The New York Review of Books* the creation of a UN force to be globally deployed with rules of engagement that, unlike today's, would allow the UN troops to shoot before they were shot at. This sounds fine; it is always tempting to imagine that the man with the badge and the gun can sort things out. The scheme might even have worked in the set-piece confrontations of the Cold War, but the "internal security" character of today's problems—even those, such as Bosnia or Nagorno-Karabakh, that have a pseudo-international format but are in all essentials civil wars—makes the U.S.–marshal approach much less promising. Changing the color of the helmets or relabeling the approach as "assertive multilateralism" will not render the application of military power to civilian problems any more successful. After all, we do not argue that a firepower deficit is what keeps us from solving the problems of our inner cities.

A further example of the inapplicability of the military option may be found in connection with Islamic fundamentalism. Even if one accepts the fanciful proposition that Iranian-driven fundamentalism is the new problematic "ism" of the post–Cold War era, it is extremely doubtful that U.S. military intervention can provide any sort of solution. The West has a dismal track record in understanding Islam. Ill-considered Western support for the repressive policies of Shah Reza Pahlavi is in part responsible for the anti-Western virulence of today's regime in Tehran. A policy that offers more of the same in, say, Egypt or Saudi Arabia is courting disaster—all the more so if it risks delivering enormous stocks of state-of-the-art military equipment into the hands of fanatics....

MORE WILL THAN WALLET

A further problem with the status quo approach is that the sole-remaining-superpower syndrome betrays a curiously old-fashioned mindset deriving from the 1950s, when the United States produced more than 40 percent of world GDP. With the U.S. share now about 20 percent, one does not need to be a believer in Paul Kennedy's theory of "imperial overstretch" to see that the American comparative advantage is not at all what it was. The European Community, for example, now has a larger economy than the United States does. Of course, in the strictly military sphere the United States remains pre-eminent. In a stand-up fight, if the enemy does us the favor of running across an open field and up a hill into our artillery, as in Pickett's charge on the third day at Gettysburg, the United States is more than a match for anyone. But one theme of post–Cold War analysis is that stand-up fights will be few and far between. The radio-controlled land mine and the sniper's rifle will be the weapons of choice. Talk of a monopoly of power fails to take account of something Clinton himself has said: "The currency of national strength in this new era will be denominated not only in ships and tanks and planes, but in diplomas and patents and paychecks."

To accept responsibility for all the world's problems is to ignore the necessity for economic trade-offs. Foreign policy can no longer be formulated in a resource vacuum. In his inaugural address in 1989 President Bush said that America had "more will than wallet." Four years and a trillion dollars of additional debt later, the time has come to align policy aspirations with resource realities....

WHY MORALITY IS NOT ENOUGH

The fourth thesis in support of the status quo has to do with morality. This appears under many guises, such as humanitarian relief, resistance to genocide, human rights, and support for democracy. It includes new rationales for international activism, such as the ideas of UN Secretary-General Boutros Boutros-Ghali on limited sovereignty, which would facilitate outside intervention in the previously sacrosanct area of domestic affairs.

These ideas have great appeal in the United States, where the proposition that America has a special moral duty to right the wrongs of the world has been a resonant theme ever since Woodrow Wilson, in introducing his Fourteen Points to govern the Armistice settlement of the First World War, consciously repudiated the traditional but, in his view, amoral European and American practices of balance-of-power politics and pursuit of national interest. Whereas John Adams could write in 1783, "There is a Ballance of Power in Europe. Nature has formed it. Practice and Habit have confirmed it, and it must exist forever," and John Quincy Adams in his famous July 4, 1821, address could say of America that "She goes not abroad in search of monsters to destroy," Wilson took the

United States into the Great War not to restore the equilibrium of Europe but to "vindicate the principles of peace and justice."

The loss of the Soviet Union as the leitmotif of American interventionism has brought morality to prominence as proponents of the Cold War orthodoxy seek to resist change. The issue for the Clinton Administration is not whether morality belongs in the foreign-policy realm but the practical choices that derive from its presence there. This is not going to be an easy circle to square. Previous Administrations have tried and come up short. Jeane Kirkpatrick's ingenious but specious distinction between different sorts of dictatorships—"ours," who are "authoritarian," and "theirs," who are "totalitarian"—comes to mind.

Alas, unless morality is anchored in some coherent concept of national interest, it is likely to prove an erratic compass. The reasons are familiar: Morality is indivisible. It does not apply selectively. If it is right to support democracy in the former Soviet republics, then it must be wrong to neglect encroachments on it in Algeria and Peru. If we demand that Hong Kong accept Vietnamese boat people, we ourselves must do the same for Haitian ones. If it was our duty to provide succor to Somalia, we should do likewise for Sudan.

Morality demands total commitment. Half measures are not allowed. If we are called upon to counter genocide in Bosnia, we must deliver, even if that means ground troops, casualties, and tremendous expenditures. Morality is also timeless. If on moral grounds Warren Christopher rejects the concept of Muslim safe havens in Bosnia one week, he cannot credibly or logically withdraw his objection a month later.

Advocates of placing morality at the center of foreign policy dismiss these issues as irrelevant to anything except a "petty consistency." They assert that, in the manner of a hospital emergency room, it is possible to perform triage on international problems and come up with a list of priorities. This, of course, goes to the crux of the question, Where do morality and practicality meet? Morality, as a long-standing motivator in U.S. foreign policy, will necessarily point the way to areas where American values and public opinion demand activity. This is as it should be. But two things are clear:

First, triage can take place only on the basis of American national interest. If the civil war in Bosnia attracts our interest while that in Angola does not, this cannot be because killing is less morally repugnant in Africa than in Europe. It must be because the United States has a greater national-interest stake in Bosnia than in Angola. Of course, this dilutes the moral message. It is well to bear in mind Churchill's words: "The Sermon on the Mount is the last word in Christian ethics.... Still, it is not on those terms that Ministers assume their responsibilities of guiding states."

Second, as discussed above in connection with military intervention, even if morality appears to make an overwhelming case for activism, it must still be balanced by considerations of effectiveness. Where is the morality if U.S. arms supplied to the Bosnian Muslims do no more than, in the words of the British Foreign Secretary, Douglas Hurd, "greatly increase the killing and the length of the war"? How are American values enhanced if, in support of human rights, trade sanctions are applied against China which bring political liberalization to a halt, snuff out the fledgling democratic movement in Hong Kong, and ultimately strengthen the Communist old guard's grip on power?

THE LIMITS OF FORCE

The central error the traditionalists make is to try to freeze in place the traditional politico-military approach to international problem-solving. According to this approach, although political means come first, military force is never far behind. For the reasons given above, the passing of the Cold War has rendered this thinking obsolete. The United States will be making a critical mistake if, as [U.S. ambassador to the UN Madeleine] Albright is urging, it gives this old approach a new lease on life under UN auspices.

The major consequence of the persistence of this thinking will be to saddle the United States with continued excessive military costs. Although the defense establishment would have us believe that costs have been cut to the bone and that, in the words of Admiral Frank Kelso, the chief of naval operations, the military is "on the ragged edge of readiness," the reality is otherwise. Despite promised reductions in spending,the military budget will still consume more than $1.3 *trillion* over the next five years, and a further $150 billion will go for intelligence. It will take until 1998, nearly ten years

after the Berlin Wall came down, before spending in terms of constant dollars returns to the levels of the late 1950s and mid-1970s. This is more than 150 percent of the combined expenditures of all the other members of NATO; in 1991 the United States spent $850 more per capita on defense than Japan. Our NATO allies are more than matching the U.S. defense reductions. Something is out of balance here....

* * *

Before his inauguration in 1913, President-elect Woodrow Wilson told his friends, "It would be an irony of fate if my administration had to deal chiefly with foreign affairs." There is little doubt that President Clinton would echo this sentiment. But as Bosnia, Somalia, and Russia show, there is no escape. To enable him to bring stability and consistency to this aspect of his job, the President needs a new strategic model. At present he is receiving backward-looking advice that, because it fails to take account of the dramatic changes in the world and the deterioration of domestic finances, opens a gap between rhetoric and performance. This damages American credibility. The nation is entitled to something better. The President should have the courage of his convictions and demand the real changes that he was elected to bring about.

POSTSCRIPT

Must America Be the World Leader?

Nixon shoots a few barbs at the Clinton administration for what he perceives as its weakness in foreign policy. Clearly, candidate Clinton placed his greatest emphasis on domestic affairs: the economy, health care, crime, and welfare. President Clinton, however, has been forced to confront a troubled world, from the Balkans and Somalia to Haiti and Cuba. It is still unclear which of the two approaches, Nixon's or Clarke's, he is more likely to favor. Although Clinton authorized an invasion of Haiti in September 1994 to restore democracy to the nation (which was averted at the last minute when a peaceful agreement was reached), on the whole, Clinton's caution in matters of foreign policy seems more in line with the cautious view of Clarke.

David Remnick's *Lenin's Tomb: The Last Days of the Soviet Empire* (Random House, 1993) is an exciting account of the collapse of a regime that terrified the world but lasted less than 75 years. Leading policymakers in American administrations from John F. Kennedy to George Bush have contributed informed essays to Edward K. Hamilton, ed., *America's Global Interests: A New Agenda* (W. W. Norton, 1989). George Kennan, architect of America's cold war "containment" policy, has offered his own views about what to do after the cold war. See "After the Cold War," *The New York Times Magazine* (1989). See also James Schlesinger, "Quest for a Post–Cold War Foreign Policy," *Foreign Affairs* (Special Edition, "America and the World 1992/93").

America today seems a long way away from the time when President Kennedy could proclaim this country ready to "pay any price, bear any burden, meet any hardship, support any friend, oppose any foe to assure the survival and the success of liberty." It was a cocky statement from a cocky young president, and there are few American policymakers of any political view who would embrace it today. Nixon calls it "unrealistic," and Clarke would probably use stronger adjectives. Still, the survival and success of liberty in the world is a worthy goal for a great nation to promote. The question seems to come down to the price and burden necessary to achieve it.

ISSUE 19

Should the United States Pursue Economic Competitiveness?

YES: Lester Thurow, from *Head to Head: The Coming Economic Battle Among Japan, Europe, and America* (William Morrow, 1992)

NO: Paul Krugman, from "Competitiveness: A Dangerous Obsession," *Foreign Affairs* (March/April 1994)

ISSUE SUMMARY

YES: Economist Lester Thurow believes that the future of American prosperity depends upon its ability to redirect its economy to compete more successfully in international markets.

NO: Economist Paul Krugman believes that an obsession with international competitiveness is not necessary for, and may be damaging to, increased economic well-being.

Can America compete? It seems an odd question to ask about the most productive nation in world history. For many years after the end of World War II, it has, with approximately seven percent of the world's population, produced nearly one-half of the dollar value of goods and services. American exports dominated many world markets.

In recent decades, other countries, most conspicuously the defeated countries of Germany and Japan, have become major economic powers. Today the world's most productive economies are those of the United States, Japan, and the European Community, which includes Germany and the other nations of Western Europe. Rising new industrial powers have succeeded in penetrating American markets to an unparalleled extent.

This is not to say that American exports do not remain significant. In the mass entertainment arts of motion picture, television, and popular music, the United States is dominant. Despite the rivalry of foreign corporations and countries, America still leads in computer hardware and software sales, drug development, and aircraft production. But many American industries have declined and some have disappeared. All of the television sets and many other consumer electronic goods sold in the United States are made abroad. More than one-fourth of the new automobiles are imported, or made by Japanese companies in the United States, including many cars with American nameplates. Much of the clothing Americans buy is made in the smaller but growing economies of Asia. Some major motion picture studios, several large supermarket chains, and valuable real estate properties (including Rockefeller Center in New York City) are owned by foreign corporations.

As a result of buying more and selling less abroad, the United States, long accustomed to being the world's leading creditor nation, has become the greatest debtor nation. Interest payment on our national debt consumes about fifteen cents of every dollar the government spends. This presently amounts to $300 billion a year that could otherwise be spent to improve society and stimulate production, or to lower taxes and increase purchasing power.

Indebtedness is not a new American phenomenon. When the first U.S. government took office after the Constitution was ratified, Revolutionary War debts had not been paid. In 1790, the national debt was $75 million, more than fifteen times the government's annual revenue. Alexander Hamilton, the nation's first secretary of the Treasury, wrote: "A national debt, if it is not excessive, will be a national blessing." Today's immense debt is less than four times the government's annual revenue. Is it excessive? Does it take too much federal revenue from other purposes and reduce investment in productivity and jobs? Does it make foreign investors prosperous at the expense of Americans? Or is it a blessing? Does borrowed money pay for research, product development, and new employment? Does it raise our standard of living?

Asking if America can compete may not be the right question. Many poor nations compete in international trade because they are low-wage countries with low standards of living. To remain competitive with the growth in productivity in rich countries, poor countries allow their wages and living standards to decline. That is a price America is unwilling to pay.

Critics of competitiveness believe that is a price we are paying. Although the U.S. has created 35 million new jobs in the past two decades, compared with only 8 million in Western Europe, many are low-paying and unskilled jobs, widening the gap between the lowest-paid and highest-paid workers. Of the world's major economies, only the United States has seen real wages fall in the last decade.

Must the United States do whatever is necessary in order to remain economically competitive with other industrial nations? Massachusetts Institute of Technology economist Lester Thurow argues that America must become more competitive in order to maintain and improve its high standard of living, and this will require the adoption of policies and strategies that are consistent with our history and traditions.

Economist Paul Krugman, a colleague of Thurow's at MIT, disagrees. He argues that America can be economically successful without being internationally competitive. He believes that thinking in terms of competitiveness risks wasteful government spending, protectionism, trade wars, and the adoption of undesirable economic policies.

YES   Lester Thurow

HEAD TO HEAD

From everyone's perspective, replacing a military confrontation with an economic contest is a step forward. No one gets killed; vast resources don't have to be devoted to negative-sum activities. The winner builds the world's best products and enjoys the world's highest standard of living. The loser gets to buy some of those best products—but not as many as the winner. Relative to the military confrontations of the past century, both the winners and the losers are winners in the economic game ahead. Being aggressively invaded by well-made Japanese or German products from firms that intend to conquer American markets is not at all equivalent to the threat of a military invasion from the Soviet Union or mainland China. Nor does it hark back to the German and Japanese military invasions of World War II.

Quite the contrary, the competition revolves around the following questions: Who can make the best products? Who expands their standards of living most rapidly? Who has the best-educated and best-skilled work force in the world? Who Is the world's leader in investment—plant and equipment, research and development (R&D), infrastructure? Who organizes best? Whose institutions—government, education, business—are world leaders in efficiency? To be forced by one's economic competitors to do all of these things is a good thing—not a bad thing.

Military competitions are ultimately wasteful. Resources must be devoted to activities that at best (unused), do not contribute to future human welfare, and at worst (used), are destructive to human welfare. Economic competitions are exactly the opposite. Governments are forced to focus on how they can most efficiently make life better for their citizens. "Economic warfare" is not at all equivalent to "military warfare" despite the use of the word *warfare* in both terms. If the world can reduce its spending on armaments, there is a peace dividend to be had in both the developed and the underdeveloped world.

From an American perspective, it is also important to remember that being just one of a number of wealthy countries in a wealthy world is far better than being the only wealthy country in a poor world—even if Americans are sometimes envious of those newly wealthy neighbors, and even if those newly wealthy neighbors sometimes force Americans to rethink how they live.

In the economic contest that lies ahead, the world is not divided into friend and foe. The game is simultaneously competitive and cooperative. One can remain friends and allies, yet still want to win.

THE TWENTY-FIRST CENTURY

The nineteenth century is remembered as the century of Great Britain. It was the dominant economic power. The twentieth century will be remembered as the century of the United States. It was, and is, the dominant economic power. In terms of the calendar, the twenty-first century has not yet quite begun, but a future economic historian looking backward will date the end of the twentieth century slightly early. Just as the fall of the Berlin Wall in November of 1989 marked the end of the old contest between capitalism and communism, so the integration of the European Common Market, on Jan. 1, 1993, will mark the beginning of a new economic contest in a new century at the start of the third millennium. At that moment, for the first time in more than a century, the United States will become the second largest economy in the world. This reality will become the symbol for the start of the competition that determines who will own the twenty-first century....

* * *

It is the official American position that it does not need to worry about the national strategies of other countries. Foreign national strategies simply won't work. But this is a belief that looks increasingly untenable if one looks at the industries that have been lost, such as robots, or industries under threat, such as aircraft manufacturing. It also confronts a world of man-made comparative advantage where the brainpower industries of the future will exist in those places where institutions organize to capture them.

The rest of the world is not cheating when it employs national strategies. That is just the way those nations play economic football. Americans can respond in one of three ways:

1. True believers in the American way can argue that we Americans have got it right and that the Germans and the Japanese have got it wrong. In the end their national strategies will hurt them more than they help. Keep the faith!
2. The agnostics can argue for changing American laws to permit American firms to get together if they wish. Try a few experiments with national industrial policies. Let a thousand flowers bloom!
3. The converts (heretics?) can argue for an aggressive American effort to counter foreign national strategies with American strategies. Fight fire with fire!

Bench marking reveals a variety of foreign models. The Japanese Ministry of International Trade and Industry (MITI) orchestrates the development of a game plan in Japan. In Germany the large industrial banks, among them, the Deutsche Bank, are the conductors of the economic orchestra. Government-owned firms play a key role in France. But none of these foreign systems could easily be grafted onto the U.S. system. America is going to have to find a uniquely American way to develop a game plan.

The nature of the problems are neatly encapsulated in America's experience with amorphous metals—metals made by rapidly quenching alloys of iron, boron, and silicon to give them a glasslike consistency that has exceptional electrical and magnetic properties. Amorphous metals were developed by Allied-Signal, a New Jersey–based firm, in the early 1970s. Much of the market for the products it makes is in Japan. If Japanese engineers had used amorphous metals, they would have saved one billion dollars per year in electricity costs alone. But Japanese officials intervened to delay patent approval for eleven years, which left very little time to use the products before the original patents expired. Japanese companies were also persuaded not to use amorphous metals until the American patents expired. As the end of the patents approached (1993), MITI announced a catch-up program involving thirty-four Japanese companies in an effort to learn how to make amorphous metals themselves so that no time would be lost when the patents expired. What should have been a market of over one hundred million dollars per year has never been a market of more than a few million.

What should Americans do when other nations target an industry where they have a technical lead? Screams and protests do very little good. After intensive negotiations with the American trade representative, the Japanese agreed to buy thirty-two thousand amorphous-metal transformers (0.5 percent of the market) before the patents run out in 1993—essentially nothing. Allied-Signal has been accused by security analysts of having spent too much money on research and development. If it cannot make its R&D pay off by selling its products, it should do no R&D. On one level, the stock-market analysts are right. If products cannot be sold, they should not have been invented.

To be successful, American firms have to be able to build dominant market shares when they have technological leadership. If this is prohibited by foreign industrial policies, others will effectively compete in the U.S. market when they have technical superiority, but American firms will not be able to compete effectively in foreign markets when Americans have technological superiority.

The key difference between the United States and the rest of the industrial world is not the existence of protection. About 25 percent of all U.S. imports, double the amount of two decades ago, are now affected by nontariff trade barriers. International businessmen see Japan as the world's most unfair trading nation, but they see the United States as the third most unfair after Korea and Japan. The European Community has published a book listing hundreds of American violations of free trade.

If industrial policies are defined as trade protection, American industrial policies are as extensive as those in either Germany or Japan. But as the Japanese say, it is a "loser-driven" industrial policy —the product of random political lobbying power to gain protection for dying industries. The rest of the world's industrial policies involve strategic thinking and are "winner-driven." The Japanese protect amorphous metals; the Americans protect low-tech steel. While Americans are afraid to use the term *industrial policy*, the Europeans are proudly designing pan-European industrial policies.

The results show. Although a big decline in the value of the dollar succeeded in reducing the Japanese–U.S.

trade deficit, the high-tech, high-wage part of the trade deficit is expanding. America is increasingly depending upon low-wage, low-tech commodity exports to balance its trading accounts. Any country can be competitive as a low-wage country. Any country can reduce its wage level by reducing the value of its currency. The issue is not balancing trading accounts but being competitive while paying high wages.

At some point Washington will have to come to grips with foreign industrial policies. What does one do when other nations target an industry? ...

In 1989 and 1990 the Bush administration was engaged in an internal intellectual debate revolving around high-definition television (HDTV): Should the Defense Department subsidize research on HDTV? Sadly, the debate remained an abstract ideological debate about the merits of government interference in the market rather than a real debate over whether HDTV was the place to jump back into consumer electronics, and if so, how? The ideological crusaders in the White House, a troika composed of John Sununu, Richard Darman and Michael Boskin, beat the advocates of government research subsidies in the Commerce and Defense departments, but it is also clear that their victory was temporary. The issue will continue to reappear.

It is of course possible to argue that the American system is uniquely unsuited to formulating strategic policies. [An] article by Pietro S. Nivola in the *Brookings Review* provides a good example of the argument. In outline, the argument is as follows:

1. America has a "closet industrial policy" hidden in its Defense Department.

2. Target industries in the rest of the world haven't earned high or even normal rates of return.

    a. Scholars argue over whether Japanese industrial policies have helped or hurt.

3. Industry-led industrial policies could become self-serving to the firms that participated.

    a. It is hard to figure out "who is us" when American firms manufacture abroad and foreign firms manufacture in the United States.

    b. Lemon socialism* might result.

4. Americans would not be very good in defensive "tit-for-tat" industrial policies, since American government institutions aren't very flexible.

    a. Random interventions aren't always bad.

Because of our own incompetence, we may be able to do nothing better than do nothing. No one can prove with complete certainty that this argument is wrong. But what we do know for certain is that the American system as it is now formulated isn't working. That is what falling real wages, stagnant productivity growth, and a growing high-wage trade deficit mean. America may try something new, and it may fail, but nothing will have been lost—the old ways aren't working anyway.

In the real world of the twenty-first century, defensive industrial policies are unavoidable. To have any chance, America's corporations at least need a defensive strategic-trade policy in the United States. Such a policy is not designed to help American corporations

*[Thurow's term for industrial policy.—Eds.]

(there is the problem of who is us), it is simply part of a general strategic-growth policy designed to help the American people. Public investments made to gain sustainable advantages should be limited to investments that will stay in America, such as investments in skills or domestic infrastructure.

Beyond such home investments, the search for strategic advantage abroad now revolves around process R&D investments. In Japan, MITI has shifted from the foreign-exchange and capital-allocations strategies of earlier decades to a strategy of pushing key technologies. The Europeans have set up an alphabet soup of cooperative R&D projects— Esprit, Jessi, Eureka—designed to do the same for European firms. While the details differ as to how it is done on the other sides of the Atlantic and Pacific oceans, the basic organizational structures are similar.

As George Lodge, a Harvard Business School professor, has described in detail in his... book, *Perestroika for America*, strategies are industry-led when groups of companies, not government civil servants, propose the technologies that should be pushed. Governments never provide more than 50 percent of the total funding. If companies don't think that projects are worth risking some of their own money, the projects simply aren't done. Companies have to put together consortia, so that the government is not subsidizing a special favorite. More than one company has to think that the technology is important. In Europe the consortia have to come from more than one country. In the United States they could be required to come from more than one region. The idea is to magnify private funds with public funds, not to publicly finance research and development. The

projects must have finite lifetimes with clearly stated objectives. No project is publicly funded forever. The purpose of a project must never be to advance knowledge for the sake of advancing knowledge. Other institutions, such as the National Science Foundation, have that task. The bureaucracy that makes the funding decisions can be very small, since business firms are making the basic go–no-go decisions when they decide whether they are willing to risk their own money.

Economic analysis shows that there are gains to be made with strategic trade policies, especially in industries with increasing returns, and this advantage will get bigger in a world of man-made comparative advantage and trading blocks. If government aid drives technology faster, everyone is a winner in the long run. More funds go into important areas that will raise long-run living standards, and no region of the world is going to be able to keep any key technology secret for more than a short period of time. A twenty-first-century civilian R&D race for supremacy among the economic superpowers is far better than the twentieth-century military R&D race for supremacy among the military superpowers.

Ideally, a new GATT [General Agreement on Tariffs and Trade] for quasi trading blocks would limit government aid to R&D subsidies. But in a world without clearly defined rules that determine what governments can permissibly do to aid their strategic industries, America's game plan has to go beyond an R&D policy. Like American companies that advertise they will not knowingly be undersold, the United States should announce that it will duplicate any policies put in place in the rest of the world. Foreign industrial policies in wealthy countries will be matched dollar for dollar. Any subsidy going to Airbus Industries in Europe will be matched by an equivalent subsidy to the American airframe-manufacturing industry. Any delay in permitting an American telecommunication device to be used abroad, such as the delays Motorola experienced in Japan with its cellular telephones, will be matched with delays for advanced Japanese equipment in the United States. Americans are no longer in a position to force the rest of the world to play the economic game by its rules, but Americans can play the game by their rules. If they want to play hardball, we'll play hardball. . . .

AN EMPIRICAL EXPERIMENT

A decade ago it was possible to argue that instead of experimenting with strategic-growth policies to stimulate investments (physical and human), business groups, and national strategic planning, America could solve its problems by moving to a more vigorous form of traditional Anglo-Saxon capitalism. Both Mrs. Thatcher in Great Britain and Mr. Reagan in the United States were elected on such platforms. Both advocated a return to "ancient virtues"—that is, they emphasized the role of the individual in economic performance, the stress on the Anglo-Saxon *I*. Government enterprises were privatized in Great Britain. American personal income taxes were dramatically lowered. Both experiments are now more than a decade old. Neither succeeded.

In the United Kingdom unemployment is higher than it was when Mrs. Thatcher came into office (7.3 percent versus 5.8 percent), and the UK continues its slow drift down the list of the world's richest countries. In the United States productivity growth was negative in the two years before Reagan took office and in the two years after he left office. What was a small trade surplus became a large trade deficit.

Empirical experimentation revealed that a return to ancient Anglo-Saxon virtues is not the answer.

BOTTOM-LINE BENCH MARKING

Japan and Germany, the countries that are outperforming America in international trade, do not have less government or more motivated individuals. They are countries noted for their careful organization of teams—teams that involve workers and managers, teams that involve suppliers and customers, teams that involve government and business.

There is nothing antithetical in American history, culture, or traditions to teamwork. Teams were important in America's history—wagon trains conquered the West, men working together on the assembly line in American industry conquered the world, a successful national strategy and a lot of teamwork put an American on the moon first (and thus far, last). But American mythology extols only the individual—the Lone Ranger or Rambo. In America, halls of fame exist for almost every conceivable activity, but nowhere do Americans raise monuments in praise of teamwork. Only national mythology stands between Americans and the construction of successful economic teams. To say this is not, however, to say that change is easy. History is littered with the wrecks of countries whose mythologies were more important than reality.

NO

Paul Krugman

COMPETITIVENESS: A DANGEROUS OBSESSION

THE HYPOTHESIS IS WRONG

In June 1993, Jacques Delors made a special presentation to the leaders of the nations of the European Community [EC], meeting in Copenhagen, on the growing problem of European unemployment. Economists who study the European situation were curious to see what Delors, president of the EC Commission, would say. Most of them share more or less the same diagnosis of the European problem: the taxes and regulations imposed by Europe's elaborate welfare states have made employers reluctant to create new jobs, while the relatively generous level of unemployment benefits has made workers unwilling to accept the kinds of low-wage jobs that help keep unemployment comparatively low in the United States. The monetary difficulties associated with preserving the European Monetary System [EMS] in the face of the costs of German reunification have reinforced this structural problem.

It is a persuasive diagnosis, but a politically explosive one, and everyone wanted to see how Delors would handle it. Would he dare tell European leaders that their efforts to pursue economic justice have produced unemployment as an unintended by-product? Would he admit that the EMS could be sustained only at the cost of a recession and face the implications of that admission for European monetary union?

Guess what? Delors didn't confront the problems of either the welfare state or the EMS. He explained that the root cause of European unemployment was a lack of competitiveness with the United States and Japan and that the solution was a program of investment in infrastructure and high technology.

It was a disappointing evasion, but not a surprising one. After all, the rhetoric of competitiveness—the view that, in the words of President Clinton, each nation is "like a big corporation competing in the global marketplace" —has become pervasive among opinion leaders throughout the world. People who believe themselves to be sophisticated about the subject take it for granted that the economic problem facing any modern nation is essentially one of competing on world markets—that the United States and Japan are competitors in the same sense that Coca-Cola competes with Pepsi—and are unaware that anyone might seriously question that proposition. Every few months a new best-seller warns the American public of the dire consequences of losing the "race" for the 21st century.[1] A whole industry of councils on competitiveness, "geo-economists" and managed trade theorists has sprung up in Washington. Many of these people, having diagnosed America's economic problems in much the same terms as Delors did Europe's, are now in the highest reaches of the Clinton administration formulating economic and trade policy for the United States. So Delors was using a language that was not only convenient but comfortable for him and a wide audience on both sides of the Atlantic.

Unfortunately, his diagnosis was deeply misleading as a guide to what ails Europe, and similar diagnoses in the United States are equally misleading. The idea that a country's economic fortunes are largely determined by its success on world markets is a hypothesis, not a necessary truth; and as a practical, empirical matter, that hypothesis is flatly wrong. That is, it is simply not the case that the world's leading nations are to any important degree in economic competition with each other, or that any of their major economic problems can be attributed to failures to compete on world markets. The growing obsession in most advanced nations with international competitiveness should be seen, not as a well-founded concern, but as a view held in the face of overwhelming contrary evidence. And yet it is clearly a view that people very much want to hold—a desire to believe that is reflected in a remarkable tendency of those who preach the doctrine of

competitiveness to support their case with careless, flawed arithmetic.

This article makes three points. First, it argues that concerns about competitiveness are, as an empirical matter, almost completely unfounded. Second, it tries to explain why defining the economic problem as one of international competition is nonetheless so attractive to so many people. Finally, it argues that the obsession with competitiveness is not only wrong but dangerous, skewing domestic policies and threatening the international economic system. This last issue is, of course, the most consequential from the standpoint of public policy. Thinking in terms of competitiveness leads, directly and indirectly, to bad economic policies on a wide range of issues, domestic and foreign, whether it be in health care or trade.

MINDLESS COMPETITION

Most people who use the term "competitiveness" do so without a second thought. It seems obvious to them that the analogy between a country and a corporation is reasonable and that to ask whether the United States is competitive in the world market is no different in principle from asking whether General Motors is competitive in the North American minivan market.

In fact, however, trying to define the competitiveness of a nation is much more problematic than defining that of a corporation. The bottom line for a corporation is literally its bottom line: if a corporation cannot afford to pay its workers, suppliers, and bondholders, it will go out of business. So when we say that a corporation is uncompetitive, we mean that its market position is unsustainable—that unless it improves its performance, it will cease to exist. Countries, on the other hand, do not go out of business. They may be happy or unhappy with their economic performance, but they have no well-defined bottom line. As a result, the concept of national competitiveness is elusive.

One might suppose, naively, that the bottom line of a national economy is simply its trade balance, that competitiveness can be measured by the ability of a country to sell more abroad than it buys. But in both theory and practice a trade surplus may be a sign of national weakness, a deficit a sign of strength. For example, Mexico was forced to run huge trade surpluses in the 1980s in order to pay the interest on its foreign debt since international investors refused to lend it any more money; it began to run large trade deficits after 1990 as foreign investors recovered confidence and began to pour in new funds. Would anyone want to describe Mexico as a highly competitive nation during the debt crisis era or describe what has happened since 1990 as a loss in competitiveness?

Most writers who worry about the issue at all have therefore tried to define competitiveness as the combination of favorable trade performance and something else. In particular, the most popular definition of competitiveness nowadays runs along the lines of the one given in Council of Economic Advisors Chairman Laura D'Andrea Tyson's *Who's Bashing Whom?:* competitiveness is "our ability to produce goods and services that meet the test of international competition while our citizens enjoy a standard of living that is both rising and sustainable." This sounds reasonable. If you think about it, however, and test your thoughts against the facts, you will find out that there is much less to this definition than meets the eye.

Consider, for a moment, what the definition would mean for an economy that conducted very little international trade, like the United States in the 1950s. For such an economy, the ability to balance its trade is mostly a matter of getting the exchange rate right. But because trade is such a small factor in the economy, the level of the exchange rate is a minor influence on the standard of living. So in an economy with very little international trade, the growth in living standards—and thus "competitiveness" according to Tyson's definition—would be determined almost entirely by domestic factors, primarily the rate of productivity growth. That's domestic productivity growth, period —not productivity growth relative to other countries. In other words, for an economy with very little international trade, "competitiveness" would turn out to be a funny way of saying "productivity" and would have nothing to do with international competition.

But surely this changes when trade becomes more important, as indeed it has for all major economies? It certainly could change. Suppose that a country finds that although its productivity is steadily rising, it can succeed in exporting only if it repeatedly devalues its currency, selling its exports ever more cheaply on world markets. Then its standard of living, which depends on its purchasing power over imports as well as domestically produced goods, might actually decline. In the jargon of economists, domestic growth might be outweighed by deteriorating terms of trade.[2] So "competitiveness" could turn out really to be about international competition after all....

Moreover, countries do not compete with each other the way corporations do. Coke and Pepsi are almost purely rivals: only a negligible fraction of Coca-Cola's sales go to Pepsi workers, only a negligible fraction of the goods Coca-Cola workers buy are Pepsi products. So if Pepsi is successful, it tends to be at Coke's expense. But the major industrial countries, while they sell products that compete with each other, area also each other's main export markets and each other's main suppliers of useful imports. If the European economy does well, it need not be at U.S. expense; indeed, if anything a successful European economy is likely to help the U.S. economy by proving it with larger markets and selling it goods of superior quality at lower prices.

International trade, then, is not a zero-sum game. When productivity rises in Japan, the main result is a rise in Japanese real wages; American or European wages are in principle at least as likely to rise as to fall, and in practice seem to be virtually unaffected.

It would be possible to belabor the point, but the moral is clear: while competitive problems could arise in principle, as a practical, empirical matter the major nations of the world are not to any significant degree in economic competition with each other. Of course, there is always a rivalry for status and power—countries that grow faster will see their political rank rise. So it is always interesting to *compare* countries. But asserting that Japanese growth diminishes U.S. status is very different from saying that it reduces the U.S. standard of living—and it is the latter that the rhetoric of competitiveness asserts.

One can, of course, take the position that words mean what we want them to mean, that all are free, if they wish, to use the term "competitiveness" as a poetic way of saying productivity, without actually implying that international competition has anything to do with it. But few writers on competitiveness would accept this view. They believe that the facts tell a very different story, that we live, as Lester Thurow put it in his best-selling book, *Head to Head*, in a world of "win-lose" competition between the leading economies....

THE THRILL OF COMPETITION

The competitive metaphor—the image of countries competing with each other in world markets in the same way that corporations do—derives much of its attractiveness from its seeming comprehensibility. Tell a group of businessmen that a country is like a corporation writ large, and you give them the comfort of feeling that they already understand the basics. Try to tell them about economic concepts like comparative advantage, and you are asking them to learn something new. It should not be surprising if many prefer a doctrine that offers the gain of apparent sophistication without the pain of hard thinking. The rhetoric of competitiveness has become so widespread, however, for three deeper reasons.

First, competitive images are exciting, and thrills sell tickets. The subtitle of Lester Thurow's huge best-seller, *Head to Head*, is "The Coming Economic Battle among Japan, Europe, and America"; the jacket proclaims that "the decisive war of the century has begun... and America may already have decided to lose." Suppose that the subtitle had described the real situation: "The coming struggle in which each big economy will succeed or fail based on its own efforts, pretty much independently of how well the others do." Would Thurow have sold a tenth as many books?

Second, the idea that U.S. economic difficulties hinge crucially on our failures in international competition somewhat paradoxically makes those difficulties seem easier to solve. The productivity of the average American worker is determined by a complex array of factors, most of them unreachable by any likely government policy. So if you accept the reality that our "competitive" problem is really a domestic productivity problem pure and simple, you are unlikely to be optimistic about any dramatic turnaround. But if you can convince yourself that the problem is really one of failures in international competition —that imports are pushing workers out of high-wage jobs, or subsidized foreign competition is driving the United States out of the high value-added sectors— then the answers to economic malaise may seem to you to involve simple things like subsidizing high technology and being tough on Japan.

Finally, many of the world's leaders have found the competitive metaphor extremely useful as a political device. The rhetoric of competitiveness turns out to provide a good way either to justify hard choices or to avoid them. The example of Delors in Copenhagen shows the usefulness of competitive metaphors as an evasion. Delors had to say something at the EC summit; yet to say anything that addressed the real roots of European unemployment would have involved huge political risks. By turning the discussion to essentially irrelevant but plausible-sounding questions of competitiveness, he bought himself some time to come up with a better answer (which to some extent he provided in December's white paper on the European economy—a paper that still, however, retained "competitiveness" in its title).

By contrast, the well-received presentation of Bill Clinton's initial economic program in February 1993 showed the usefulness of competitive rhetoric as a motivation for tough policies. Clinton proposed a set of painful spending cuts and tax increases to reduce the Federal deficit. Why? The real reasons for cutting the deficit are disappointingly undramatic: the deficit siphons off funds that might otherwise have been productively invested, and thereby exerts a steady if small drag on U.S. economic growth. But Clinton was able instead to offer a stirring patriotic appeal, calling on the nation to act now in order to make the economy competitive in the global market—with the implication that dire economic consequences would follow if the United States does not.

Many people who know that "competitiveness" is a largely meaningless concept have been willing to indulge competitive rhetoric precisely because they believe they can harness it in the service of good policies. An overblown fear of the Soviet Union was used in the 1950s to justify the building of the interstate highway system and the expansion of math and science education. Cannot the unjustified fears about foreign competition similarly be turned to good, used to justify serious efforts to reduce the budget deficit, rebuild infrastructure, and so on?

A few years ago this was a reasonable hope. At this point, however, the obsession with competitiveness has reached the point where it has already begun dangerously to distort economic policies.

THE DANGERS OF OBSESSION

Thinking and speaking in terms of competitiveness poses three real dangers. First, it could result in the wasteful spending of government money supposedly to enhance U.S. competitiveness. Second, it could lead to protectionism and trade wars. Finally, and most important, it could result in bad public policy on a spectrum of important issues.

During the 1950s, fear of the Soviet Union induced the U.S. government to spend money on useful things like highways and science education. It also, however, led to considerable spending on more doubtful items like bomb shelters. The most obvious if least worrisome danger of the growing obsession with competitiveness is that it might lead to a similar misallocation of resources. To take an example, recent guidelines for government research funding have stressed the importance of supporting research that can improve U.S. international competitiveness. This exerts at least some bias toward inventions that can help manufacturing firms, which generally compete on international markets, rather than service producers, which generally do not. Yet most of our employment and value-added is now in services, and lagging productivity in services rather than manufactures has been the single most important factor in the stagnation of U.S. living standards.

A much more serious risk is that the obsession with competitiveness will lead to trade conflict, perhaps even to a world trade war. Most of those who have preached the doctrine of competitiveness have not been old-fashioned protectionists. They want their countries to win the global trade game, not drop out. But what if, despite its best efforts, a country does not seem to be winning, or lacks confidence that it can? Then the competitive diagnosis inevitably suggests that to close the borders is better than to risk having foreigners take away high-wage jobs and high-value sectors. At the very least, the focus on the supposedly competitive nature of international economic relations greases the rails for those who want confrontational if not frankly protectionist policies.

We can already see this process at work, in both the United States and Europe. In the United States, it was remarkable how quickly the sophisticated interventionist arguments advanced by Laura Tyson in her published work gave way to the simple-minded claim by U.S. Trade Representative Mickey Kantor that Japan's bilateral trade surplus was costing the United States millions of jobs. And the trade rhetoric of President Clinton, who stresses the supposed creation of high-wage jobs rather than the gains from specialization, left his administration in a weak position when it tried to argue with the claims of NAFTA foes that competition from cheap Mexican labor will destroy the U.S. manufacturing base.

Perhaps the most serious risk from the obsession with competitiveness, however, is its subtle indirect effect on the quality of economic discussion and policymaking. If top government officials are strongly committed to a particular economic doctrine, their commitment inevitably sets the tone for policymaking on all issues, even those which may seem to have nothing to do with that doctrine. And if an economic doctrine is flatly, completely and demonstrably wrong, the insistence that discussion adhere to that doctrine inevitably blurs the focus and diminishes the quality of policy discussion across a broad range of issues, including some that are very far from trade policy per se.

Consider, for example, the issue of health care reform, undoubtedly the most important economic initiative of the Clinton administration, almost surely an order of magnitude more important to U.S. living standards than anything that might be done about trade policy (unless the United States provokes a full-blown trade war). Since health care is an issue with few direct international linkages, one might have expected it to be largely insulated from any distortions of policy resulting from misguided concerns about competitiveness.

But the administration placed the development of the health care plan in the hands of Ira Magaziner [an influential figure in the Clinton administration]. Magaziner's prior writings and consulting on economic policy focused almost entirely on the issue of international competition, his views on which may be summarized by the title of his 1990 book, *The Silent War*. His appointment reflected many factors, of course, not least his long personal friendship with the first couple. Still, it was not irrelevant that in an administration committed to the ideology of competitiveness Magaziner, who has consistently recommended that national industrial policies be based on the corporate strategy concepts he learned during his years at the Boston Consulting Group, was regarded as an economic policy expert.

We might also note the unusual process by which the health care reform was developed. In spite of the huge size of the task force, recognized experts in the health care field were almost completely absent, notably though not exclusively economists specializing in health care, including economists with impeccable liberal credentials like Henry Aaron of the Brookings Institution. Again, this may have reflected a number of factors, but it is probably not irrelevant that anyone who, like Magaziner, is strongly committed to the ideology of competitiveness is bound to have found professional economists notably unsympathetic in the past—and to be unwilling to deal with them on any other issues.

To make a harsh but not entirely unjustified analogy, a government wedded to the ideology of competitiveness is as unlikely to make good economic policy as a government committed to creationism is to make good science policy, even in areas that have no direct relationship to the theory of evolution.

ADVISERS WITH NO CLOTHES

If the obsession with competitiveness is as misguided and damaging as this article claims, why aren't more voices saying so? The answer is, a mixture of hope and fear.

On the side of hope, many sensible people have imagined that they can appropriate the rhetoric of competitiveness on behalf of desirable economic policies. Suppose that you believe that the United States needs to raise its savings rate and improve its educational system in order to raise its productivity. Even if you know that the benefits of higher productivity have nothing to do with international competition, why not describe this as a policy to enhance competitiveness if you think that it can widen your audience? It's tempting to pander to popular prejudices on behalf of a good cause, and I have myself succumbed to that temptation.

As for fear, it takes either a very courageous or very reckless economist to say publicly that a doctrine that many, perhaps most, of the world's opinion leaders have embraced is flatly wrong. The insult is all the greater when many of those men and women think that by using the rhetoric of competitiveness they are demonstrating their sophistication about economics. This article may influence people, but it will not make many friends.

Unfortunately, those economists who have hoped to appropriate the rhetoric of competitiveness for good economic policies have instead had their own credibility appropriated on behalf of bad ideas. And somebody has to point out when the emperor's intellectual wardrobe isn't all he thinks it is.

So let's start telling the truth: competitiveness is a meaningless word when applied to national economies. And the obsession with competitiveness is both wrong and dangerous.

NOTES

1. See, for just a few examples, Laura D'Andrea Tyson, *Who's Bashing Whom: Trade Conflict in High-Technology Industries*, Washington: Institute for International Economics, 1992; Lester C. Thurow, *Head to Head: The Coming Economic Battle among Japan, Europe, and America*, New York: Morrow, 1992; Ira C. Magaziner and Robert B. Reich, *Minding America's Business: The Decline and Rise of the American Economy*, New York: Vintage Books, 1983; Ira C. Magaziner and Mark Patinkin, *The Silent War: Inside the Global Business Battles Shaping America's Future*, New York: Vintage Books, 1990; Edward N. Luttwak, *The Endangered American Dream: How to Stop the United States from Becoming a Third World Country and How to Win the Geo-economic Struggle for Industrial Supremacy*, New York: Simon and Schuster, 1993; Kevin P. Phillips, *Staying on Top: The Business Case for a National Industrial Strategy*, New York: Random House, 1984; Clyde V. Prestowitz, Jr., *Trading Places: How We Allowed Japan to Take the Lead*, New York: Basic Books, 1988; William S. Dietrich, *In the Shadow of the Rising Sun: The Political Roots of American Economic Decline*, University Park: Pennsylvania State University Press, 1991; Jeffrey E. Garten, *A Cold Peace: America, Japan, Germany, and the Struggle for Supremacy*, New York: Times Books, 1992; and Wayne Sandholtz et al., *The Highest Stakes: The Economic Foundations of the Next Security System*, Berkeley Roundtable on the International Economy (BRIE), Oxford University Press, 1992.

2. An example may be helpful here. Suppose that a country spends 20 percent of its income on imports, and that the prices of its imports are set not in domestic but in foreign currency. Then if the country is forced to devalue its currency—reduce its value in foreign currency—by 10 percent, this will raise the price of 20 percent of the country's spending basket by 10 percent, thus raising the overall price index by 2 percent. Even if domestic *output* has not changed, the country's real *income* will therefore have fallen by 2 percent. If the country must repeatedly devalue in the face of competitive pressure, growth in real income will persistently lag behind growth in real output.

It's important to notice, however, that the size of this lag depends not only on the amount of devaluation but on the share of imports in spending. A 10 percent devaluation of the dollar against the yen does not reduce U.S. real income by 10 percent —in fact, it reduces U.S. real income by only about 0.2 percent because only about 2 percent of U.S. income is spent on goods produced in Japan.

POSTSCRIPT

Should the United States Pursue Economic Competitiveness?

In recent years, the per capita gross domestic product (GDP) growth in Japan averaged more than two-and-a-half times that of the United States; growth in West Germany before unification with East Germany was nearly twice that of the United States. At present growth rates, both countries could have a larger per capita GDP than the United States in only a few years. Part of the explanation is that the rate of industrial and economic investment in Japan is twice as much as in the United States and one-third higher in the European Community. China has the fastest-growing economy in the world, and the newly industrialized economies of South Korea, Taiwan, Hong Kong, and Singapore are also rapidly expanding. Although the level of U.S. productivity remains the highest, its rate of growth lags behind all of these countries.

The decline of America's economic power has been dramatic. Financier Felix Rohatyn has observed that "in just twenty-five years we have gone from the American century to the American crisis." If America has been less competitive than some other industrial nations in recent decades, it is in part attributable to the fact that for nearly a half-century the United States expended a vast proportion of its wealth, talent, and resources on military armaments, while other democratic nations have concentrated their wealth, talent, and resources on the production of machines for industry and goods for consumers. The disintegration of the Soviet Union has meant that the U.S. can cut back sharply on the development and stockpiling of weapons of war, although there are those who debate the nature of those cuts.

Some reasons why other nations have had faster growing economies have to do with contrasting lifestyles and social values. These differences are examined in David Halberstam, *The Reckoning* (William Morrow, 1986). If America has been less successful in competing in Japan than Japan has been in the United States, the fault may not be cultural differences or trade restrictions. J. Jeffrey Morgan, *Cracking the Japanese Market: Strategies for Success in the New Global Economy* (Free Press, 1991), believes that the failure is due to apathy and ignorance. Tom Jackson, *The Next Battleground: Japan, America, and the New European Market* (Houghton Mifflin, 1993), believes that both the United States and Japan must compete for influence in Europe, which is emerging as the world's largest market.

It is difficult to calculate which country's workers work harder, but it is easy to determine which work longer. South Koreans average a 55-hour work week, Taiwanese 48, and Japanese 41, compared with 37 for Americans. This does not take into account the fact that Japanese workers have half the American rate of absenteeism and typically take only about half of their allotted vacation time. In a recent international survey regarding what matters most, Americans ranked work eighth, behind the education of children, a satisfactory love life, and other values, while Japanese ranked work second, after good health. It is probable that if Americans worked longer and harder at lower wages, the United States would be more competitive. This is an option most Americans would reject.

Critics of competitiveness believe that we should not make the nation more productive at the cost of a lower standard of living for most Americans. Both the advocates and critics of international economic competitiveness agree that increased productivity will occur if we adopt policies that raise educational achievement, reduce welfare dependency and make all able-bodied people productive, and stimulate savings and investments. The question remains whether or not these ends can be achieved with or without competing economically with other nations.

ISSUE 20

Should the United States Put More Restrictions on Immigration?

YES: Daniel James, from "Close the Borders to All Newcomers," *Insight* (November 22, 1993)

NO: Stephen Moore, from "Give Us Your Best, Your Brightest," *Insight* (November 22, 1993)

ISSUE SUMMARY

YES: Daniel James, an advisor to Carrying Capacity Network in Washington, D.C., wants a moratorium on immigration, which, he claims, is taking away jobs from American workers, threatening the environment, and breaking up American culture.

NO: Economist Stephen Moore insists that immigrants have created more jobs than they have taken away and have greatly enriched the economy and culture.

In 1949 a delegation of Native Americans went to Washington to tell lawmakers about the plight of America's original occupants. After meeting with Vice President Alben Barkley, the delegation got up to leave. But one old Sioux chief stayed a moment longer to deliver a parting word to the vice president. "Young fellow," he said, "let me give you a little advice. Be careful with your immigration laws. We were careless with ours."

Today, many Americans—sons and daughters of earlier immigrants— would probably second the chief's words. Legal immigration is now about a million per year (sometimes it is higher), and with illegal immigrants the total is probably much more. In terms of numbers, immigration is now almost comparable to the level it reached during the early years of this century, when millions of immigrants arrived from southern and eastern Europe. A majority of the new immigrants, however, do not come from Europe. The largest percentages come from Mexico, the Philippines, Korea, and the Caribbean, while European immigration has shrunk to about 10 percent. Much of the reason for this shift has to do with changes made in U.S. immigration laws during the 1960s. Decades earlier, in the 1920s, America narrowed its gates to people from certain regions of the world by imposing quotas designed to preserve the balance of races in America. But in 1965 a series of amendments to the Immigration and Nationality Act put all the world's peoples on an equal footing in terms of immigration. The result, wrote journalist Theodore H. White, was "a stampede, almost an invasion" of non-European immigrants.

The new immigrants come to the United States to flee tyranny and terrorism, to escape war, to join relatives already here. Above all, they come because America is an island of affluence in a global sea of poverty; here they have the potential to earn many times what they could hope to earn in their native countries. The question, hotly debated in every format from state and national legislatures to radio talk shows, comes down to this: what will these millions of new immigrants do to this country—or for it?

Much of the debate has to do with bread-and-butter issues. Will the new immigrants take away jobs from American workers? Or do they fill jobs that American workers do not want anyway, helping to stimulate the economy? Another aspect of the debate concerns health care and the environment. Will immigrants contribute to toxic waste, smog, and urban crowding? Will they bring new diseases, or bring back old ones formerly conquered? Yet these same fears were voiced at the turn of this century when Americans worried about "hordes of immigrants" from southern and eastern Europe. Finally, there is the cultural issue. Will the new immigrants add healthy new strains to U.S. cultural inheritance, broadening and revitalizing it? Or will they produce so much cultural diversity as to destroy America's cultural unity?

All of these issues are touched upon in the debate that follows, though the disputants put their greatest emphasis on the economic issue. Writer Daniel James worries that recent immigration has already thrown more than 2 million Americans out of work, adding immeasurably to America's economic woes. James speaks for many Americans, particularly those living in border states like California and Arizona, who worry about what James calls the "tidal wave" of immigration. Several border states have already sued the federal government, claiming that immigration is draining their resources. Researcher Stephen Moore, however, insists that "immigrants don't just take jobs, they create jobs," and he provides examples to back his contention.

YES

Daniel James

CLOSE THE BORDERS TO
ALL NEWCOMERS

Strip the rhetoric from the evolving immigration debate and the bottom line becomes crystal clear: We may desire more and more immigrants, but can we afford so many of them? In his recently published memoirs, *Around the Cragged Hill*, George F. Kennan, perhaps [America's] most eminent statesman, goes to the heart of the matter:

> "We are already, for better or for worse, very much a polyglot country; and nothing of that is now to be changed. What I have in mind here are sheer numbers. There *is* such a thing as overcrowding. It has its psychic effects as well as its physical ones. There *are* limits to what the environment can stand."

The sheer numbers are indeed mind-boggling:

- 10.5 million immigrants, including those arriving illegally, entered the U.S. in the 1980s. That topped the previous record of 8.8 million who came here from 1901 to 1910.
- 15 to 18 million more newcomers, both legal and illegal, are projected to reach America in the 1990s, assuming our present immigration policy remains unchanged. Already, the number arriving in this decade is greater than for the same period in the previous decade. And there were nearly 1.2 million immigrants in 1992, 20 percent more than in 1991.
- 30 million immigrants—perhaps as many as 36 million—are expected to arrive in the first two decades of the next century, according to demographic projections and extrapolation of 1991–92 Census Bureau data.

The last two projections indicate that between 45 million and 54 million people—almost equal to the population of Great Britain—will be entering the U.S. in little more than a generation.

Add the 20 million immigrants who arrived from 1965 to 1990, and the grand total who will have entered the U.S. in just over a half-century (1965–2020) will be 65 million to 74 million.

There is no precedent for these numbers anywhere in the world. They constitute the biggest wave of immigration ever to a single country. Called the "fourth wave" of immigration to the U.S., it is really a tidal wave.

Yet the numbers are conservative. Unforeseeable trends in countries that generate immigrants could swell the tidal wave even higher than projected. It is likely, for example, that the demise of Cuba's communist dictatorship would send a flood of refugees to Miami comparable to the 125,000 *Marielitos* who inundated it in 1980.

Mexico is an even bigger concern. In the 1980s, it sent the U.S. nearly 4 million immigrants, more than the total for all of Asia. Two great "push" factors will drive ever more of them northward: high population growth—Mexico's present 90 million inhabitants will become 110 million by 2000—and unemployment/underemployment levels of 40 to 50 percent.

The North American Free Trade Agreement [NAFTA] ... may generate a temporary upsurge in illegal border crossings. It would draw more Mexicans to the relatively affluent north and make entering the U.S. affordable. Meanwhile, an expected rise in imports of cheaper U.S. corn would bankrupt Mexico's peasant class, the *campesinos,* and drive them to seek work stateside. Only years from now would NAFTA create enough jobs to keep Mexicans at home.

The cost to U.S. taxpayers of accepting endless numbers of immigrants is intolerable. We learn from a new study, "The Costs of Immigration," by economist Donald Huddle, that the net 1992 public assistance cost of the 19.3 million immigrants who have settled here since 1970 was $42.5 billion, after subtracting $20.2 billion they paid in taxes.

Huddle examined costs in 22 categories of federal, state and local assistance available to immigrants, including a package of 10 county welfare and health services. The largest net costs for immigrants in 1992 were $16 billion for education (primary, secondary and bilingual), $10.6 billion for health and welfare services and $8.5 billion for Medicaid.

Criminal justice and corrections costs for immigrants were found by Huddle to total more than $2 billion in 1992. The social price was greater: A disproportionately large number of illegals were in prison for committing felonies. In California, they made up 11 percent of all inmates.

Huddle also found that immigrants in 1992 displaced—probably forever—2.07 million American workers. This should answer the oft-debated question: Do immigrants take jobs away from Americans?

It is true that American workers frequently turn down tasks that immigrants willingly perform, such as picking fruit and vegetables under inhumane conditions or making garments in urban sweatshops. But that hardly explains the virtual elimination of blacks from jobs in entire industries. In Los Angeles, unionized blacks have been displaced by nonunion Hispanics in janitorial services, and in Washington, D.C., by Latino immigrants in hotels and restaurants.

The puzzling question is: Why does the U.S. continue to import competition for American workers at a time of high unemployment? The Labor Department reports that 8.5 million Americans, about 6.7 percent of our work force, are unemployed. Our two principal minorities suffer most from joblessness—12.6 percent of blacks and 9.7 percent of Latinos—and they are the most vulnerable to displacement.

Immigration costs will rise further in this decade, Huddle forecasts. He projects that from 1993 to 2002, 11.1 million legal and illegal immigrants will be added to the 19.3 million post-1970 immigrants already here, for a total of 30.4 million. Their net cost to taxpayers during the next decade would come to $668.5 billion, which is larger than the $496 billion of the national deficit that President Clinton and Congress have pledged to erase over five years.

Indeed, the savings from reducing immigration could be applied to cutting the deficit considerably, with less pain to the taxpayer than paring public services and raising taxes, as the administration proposes. Alternatively, Huddle suggests, such savings could be used to finance investment tax credits to create and maintain 4.1 million private sector jobs, or 1.4 million public works and service jobs, throughout the decade.

Impossible to quantify, but perhaps more devastating in the long run, is the cost of excessive immigration to the environment. As more and more people are added to our population—already excessive at 260 million—the greater the environmental degradation will be. The immigrants will contribute to increasing energy use, toxic waste, smog and urban crowding, all of which affect our mental and emotional health as well as the ecosystem.

Our population is increasing by 3 million a year, a rate faster than that of any other advanced country. California provides an example of what can happen to a nearly ideal environment when it is overwhelmed by too many people. Since 1980, its population has zoomed from 23.7 million to more than 31 million, an increase of almost one-third. As a consequence, Los Angeles and its once pristine bay are all but hopelessly polluted, and San Diego and Orange counties are fast becoming sad miniatures of Los Angeles.

Equally alarming is the impetus that uncontrolled immigration provides to separatism and its obverse, multiculturism. Those living in areas where there are many other immigrants, such as Los Angeles and Texas's Rio Grande Valley, see no need to learn English and so live in virtual isolation from the general population. As long as these barrios are constantly replenished with newcomers from Mexico—virtually a stone's throw away—their inhabitants will feel less and less need or desire to assimilate. This process encourages a kind of natural separatism that could lead to political separatism.

Richard Estrada, a journalist and scholar, sees an ominous parallel with Quebec: "If Francophone Quebec can bring the Canadian confederation to the brink of disintegration even though France lies an ocean away, should there not at least arise a certain reflectiveness about our Southwest, which lies contiguous to an overpopulated Third World nation?"

A growing number of Americans of all classes and ethnic groups share these concerns about immigration and favor reducing it. For at least two decades, a majority of Americans have expressed in various polls their desire to stop or reduce immigration. In January 1992, a Gallup Poll found that 64 percent of registered voters would vote for a presidential candidate who favored tougher laws on immigration. In December, the Latino National Political Survey discovered that Hispanics overwhelmingly believed there is too much immigration.

* * *

Even politicians who previously shunned immigration as a taboo subject are jumping onto the immigration reform bandwagon. From President Clinton, a Democrat, to California's Gov. Pete Wilson, a Republican, most are clamoring to curb illegal immigration. We can hope that they soon will understand that the main problem, as the public generally has perceived, is legal immigration.

Serious though illegal immigration is, *legal* immigration poses a much graver problem. We receive more than three times as many legal immigrants, including refugees, as illegal ones. Their numbers are projected to grow exponentially, because under the 1990 Immigration Act they are permitted to bring in an endless procession of family members. In 1992, for example, family-related immigrants totaled 594,000, or 49 percent of the 1.2 million immigrants who entered the U.S. that year.

Legal immigrants account for almost three-quarters of the total costs calculated by the Huddle study. Thus, of the $668.5 billion projected net cost to taxpayers for all immigrants from 1993 to 2002, legal immigrants would account for $482 billion. Illegal aliens would cost $186.4 billion.

The most effective way to curb illegal immigration is to declare a moratorium on *all* immigration. Why? If the U.S. clamps down on illegals but permits legal immigration to continue uncontrolled, that tells the world we are not serious about solving either problem, for it is easier to reduce or halt the legal flow than to hunt down those who arrive undercover. To do so would require a mere stroke of the pen and wouldn't cost taxpayers extra—Congress could just reform the Immigration Act of 1990, which is directly responsible for the 40 percent increase to immigration. That would send the unequivocal message to anyone who plans to enter the U.S. that we cannot afford to receive them—at least for the time being.

The message would ring loud and clear to would-be illegal immigrants that we mean business. It must be backed up, however, by a whole range of law enforcement measures that are now on the books but are ignored or not used effectively. In addition, to smoke out illegals and also eliminate the racket in fraudulent documents, Congress should approve a universal ID, much like the health security card that President Clinton displayed when he presented his health plan.

The ID cards would identify those who are legally in the U.S. and entitled to work and receive benefits. Local and state authorities should be directed to share information on illegals with the Immigration and Naturalization Service to aid in apprehending them; at present, authorities deny such information to the INS, in effect protecting illegals.

Instead of sending the National Guard to patrol the border as advocated by some lawmakers. it would be more effective to give the Border Patrol sufficient personnel to do its job. At least 2,000 new agents should be added to the current force of about 4,000, as well as equipment such as better night sensors and new vehicles. The Customs Service will also require additional personnel, particularly if NAFTA is put into effect and vehicular traffic from Mexico increases as expected.

A vital component of any program to curb immigration must be the cooperation of the Mexican government. The White House should take advantage of our cordial relations with Mexico and our growing economic clout to request that our southern neighbor cease its traditional (though unwritten) policy of regarding the U.S. as a safety valve.

A U.S. moratorium on immigration would yield highly positive gains by allowing the 20 million immigrants now within our borders time to assimilate into the mainstream. It would remove the pressure of new millions crowding into inner-city barrios and encourage existing inhabitants to break out of them. This would mitigate the danger of separatism, counter multiculturalist trends, defuse interethnic tensions and reduce crime and violence.

If this prescription sounds like a pipe dream, let us recall that restrictive legislation in 1924 cut immigration to a trickle, allowing enough time for the masses of immigrants the U.S. had then to overcome the obstacles to assimilation. That literally saved America. For when the Japanese struck at Pearl Harbor in 1941 and the U.S. was confronted by their military might plus that of Ger-many, which already had conquered Europe and had just invaded the Soviet Union, our nation stood united against them. Sadly, one doubts whether today's America, torn by an identity crisis spawned by divisive forces, would be capable of meeting a similar threat.

The United States is headed for a crisis of incalculable magnitude if mass immigration continues unchecked. The argument of those who favor an open border is that immigrants have always contributed to our society, and so they have. But we no longer can afford the world's "huddled masses" when our own are so often homeless and jobless. If we permit immigration to continue uncontrolled, it will explode in a full-blown crisis that will extend beyond the vociferous separatism/multiculturalism debate to engulf us in a violent civil conflict.

America is under siege. It is threatened from without by international terrorism and from within by centrifugal forces that already have revealed their capacity for destruction in bloody riots from Los Angeles to Miami, from Washington to Manhattan.

NO

Stephen Moore

GIVE US YOUR BEST, YOUR BRIGHTEST

For many Americans, the word "immigration" immediately conjures up an image of poor Mexicans scrambling across the border near San Diego to find minimum-wage work and perhaps collect government benefits. Recent public opinion polls confirm that the attitude of the American public toward immigration is highly unfavorable. Central Americans are perceived as welfare abusers who stubbornly refuse to learn English, Haitians are seen as AIDS carriers, Russian Jews are considered to be mafiosi, and Asians are seen as international terrorists. The media reinforce these stereotypes by battering the public with negative depictions of immigrants.

The conception of immigrants as tired, poor, huddled masses seems permanently sketched into the mind of the public, just as the words are sketched irrevocably at the feet of the Statue of Liberty. But the Emma Lazarus poem simply does not describe the hundreds of thousands of people who are building new lives here in the 1990s. It would be more appropriate if the words at the base of the statue read: "Give us your best, your brightest, your most energetic and talented." Why? Because in large part those are the people who come to the United States each year.

Before we start slamming shut the golden door, it might be worthwhile to find out who the newcomers are and how they truly affect our lives.

Anyone who believes that immigrants are a drain on the U.S. economy has never visited the Silicon Valley in California. Here and in other corridors of high-tech entrepreneurship, immigrants are literally the lifeblood of many of the nation's most prosperous industries. In virtually every field in which the United States asserted global leadership in the 1980s—industries such as computer design and softwear, pharmaceuticals, bioengineering, electronics, superconductivity, robotics and aerospace engineering—one finds immigrants. In many ways these high-growth industries are the modern version of the American melting pot in action.

Consider Intel Corp. With profits of $1.1 billion in 1992, it is one of the most prolific and fast-expanding companies in the United States, employing tens of thousands of American workers. It is constantly developing exciting, cutting-edge technologies that will define the computer industry in the 21st century.

And it is doing all of this largely with the talents of America's newest immigrants. Three members of Intel's top management, including Chief Executive Officer Andrew S. Grove, from Hungary, are immigrants. Some of its most successful and revolutionary computer technologies were pioneered by immigrants, such as the 8080 microprocessor (an expanded-power computer chip), invented by a Japanese, and polysilicon FET gates (the basic unit of memory storage on modern computer chips), invented by an Italian. Dick Ward, manager of employee information systems at Intel, says: "Our whole business is predicated on inventing the next generation of computer technologies. The engine that drives that quest is brainpower. And here at Intel, much of that brainpower comes from immigrants."

Or consider Du Pont-Merck Pharmaceutical Co., an $800 million-a-year health care products company based in Wilmington, Del., which reports that immigrants are responsible for many of its most promising new product innovations. For example, losartan, an anti-hypertensive drug, was developed by a team of scientists that included two Chinese and a Lithuanian. Joseph Mollica, Chief Executive Officer of Du Pont-Merck, says that bringing together such diverse talent "lets you look at problems and opportunities from a slightly different point of view."

Intel and Du Pont-Merck are not alone in relying on immigrants. Robert Kelley Jr., president of SO/CAL/TEN, an association of nearly 200 high-tech California companies, insists: "Without the influx of Asians in the 1980s, we would not have had the entrepreneurial explosion we've seen in California." David N. K. Wang, vice president for worldwide business operations at Applied Materials Inc., a computer-technology company in California, adds that because of immigration, "Silicon Valley is one of the most international business centers in the world."

Take away the immigrants, and you take away the talent base that makes such centers operate. Indeed, it is frightening to think what would happen to America's global competitiveness if the immigrants stopped coming. Even scarier is the more realistic prospect that U.S. policymakers will enact laws to prevent them from coming.

New research has begun to quantify the contributions of immigrants to American industry. The highly respected National Research Council reported in 1988 that "a large fraction of the technological output of the United States [is] dependent upon foreign talent and that such dependency is growing." Noting that well over half of all scientists graduating with doctorate degrees from American universities and one in three engineers working in the United States are immigrants, the report states emphatically: "It is clear ... that these foreign-born engineers enrich our culture and make substantial contributions to the U.S. economic well-being and competitiveness."

The United States' competitive edge over the Japanese, Germans, Koreans and much of Europe is linked closely to its continued ability to attract and retain highly talented workers from other countries. A 1990 study by the national Science Foundation says, "Very significant, positive aspects arise from the presence of foreign-born engineers in our society."

For example, superconductivity, a technology that is expected to spawn hundreds of vital new commercial applications in the next century, was discovered by a physicist at the University of Houston, Paul C. W. Chu. He was born in China and came to the U.S. in 1972. His brilliance and inventiveness have made him a top contender for a Nobel Prize.

Of course, if Chu does win a Nobel, he will join a long list of winners who were immigrants in America. In the 20th century, between 20 percent and 50 percent of the Nobel Prize winners, depending on the discipline involved, have been immigrants to the United States. Today there are more Russian Nobel Prize winners living in the U.S. than there are living in Russia.

Public opinion polls consistently reveal that a major worry is that immigrants take jobs from American workers. The fear is understandable but misplaced. Immigrants don't just take jobs, they create jobs. One way is by starting new businesses. Today, America's immigrants, even those who come with relatively low skill levels, are highly entrepreneurial.

Take Koreans, for example. According to sociologists Alendro Portes and Ruben Rumbaut, "In Los Angeles, the propensity for self-employment is three times greater for Koreans than among the population as a whole. Grocery stores, restaurants, gas stations, liquor stores and real estate offices are typical Korean businesses." Cubans also are prodigious creators of new businesses. The number of Cuban-owned businesses in Miami has expanded from 919 in 1967 to 8,000 in 1976 to 28,000 in 1990. On Jefferson Boulevard in Dallas, more than 800 businesses operate, three-quarters of them owned by first- and second-generation Hispanic immigrants. Just 10 years ago, before the influx of Mexicans and other Central Americans, the neighborhood was in

decay, with many vacant storefronts displaying "for sale" signs in the windows. Today it is a thriving ethnic neighborhood.

To be sure, few immigrant-owned businesses mature into an Intel. In fact, many fail completely. Like most new businesses in America, most immigrant establishments are small and only marginally profitable. The average immigrant business employs two to four workers and records roughly $200,000 in annual sales. However, such small businesses, as President Clinton often correctly emphasizes, are a significant source of jobs.

It should not be too surprising that immigrants are far more likely than average U.S. citizens to take business risks. After all, uprooting oneself, traveling to a foreign culture and making it requires more than the usual amount of courage, ambition, resourcefulness and even bravado. Indeed, this is part of the self-selection process that makes immigrants so particularly desirable. Immigrants are not just people—they are a very special group of people. By coming, they impart productive energies on the rest of us.

This is not just romanticism. It is well-grounded in fact. Countless studies have documented that immigrants to the United States tend to be more skilled, more highly educated and wealthier than the average citizen of their native countries.

Thomas Sowell, an economist and senior fellow at the Hoover Institution in Stanford, Calif., reports in his seminal study on immigration, "Ethnic America," that black immigrants from the West Indies have far higher skill levels than their countrymen at home. He also finds that the income levels of West Indies immigrants are higher than those of

West Indies natives, American blacks and native-born white Americans.

Surprisingly, even illegal immigrants are not the poverty-stricken and least skilled from their native countries. Surveys of undocumented immigrants from Mexico to the United States show that only about 5 percent were unemployed in Mexico, whereas the average unemployment rate there was about three times that level, and that a relatively high percentage of them worked in white-collar jobs in Mexico. In addition, surveys have found that illiteracy among undocumented Mexicans in the U.S. is about 10 percent, whereas illiteracy in Mexico is about 22 percent.

Perhaps the greatest asset of immigrants is their children, who tend to be remarkably successful in the U.S. Recently, the city of Boston reported that an incredible 13 of the 17 valedictorians in its public high schools were foreign-born—from China, Vietnam, Portugal, El Salvador, France, Italy, Jamaica and the former Czechoslovakia. Many could not speak a word of English when they arrived. Public high schools in Washington, Chicago and Los Angeles also report remarkably disproportionate numbers of immigrant children at the top of the class. Similarly, Westinghouse reports that over the past 12 years, about one-third of its prestigious National Science Talent Search winners have been Asians. Out of this group might emerge America's next Albert Einstein, who himself was an immigrant.

So one hidden cost of restricting immigration is the loss of immigrants' talented and motivated children.

In the past century, America has admitted roughly 50 million immigrants. This has been one of the largest migrations in the history of the world. Despite this infusion of people—no, because of it —the United States became by the middle of the 20th century the wealthiest nation in the world. Real wages in America have grown more than eightfold over this period. The U.S. economy employed less than 40 million people in 1900; today it employs nearly 120 million people. The U.S. job machine had not the slightest problem expanding and absorbing the 8 million legal immigrants who came to this country in the 1980s. Eighteen million jobs were created.

But what about those frightening headlines? "Immigration Bankrupting Nation." "Immigrants Displacing U.S. Workers." "Foreigners Lured to U.S. by Welfare."

Here are the facts. The 1990s census reveals that roughly 6 percent of native-born Americans are on public assistance, versus 7 percent of the foreign-born, with less than 5 percent of illegal immigrants collecting welfare. Not much reason for alarm. Because immigrants tend to come to the United States when they are young and working, over their lifetimes they each pay about $20,000 more in taxes than they use in services, according to economist Julian Simon of the University of Maryland. With 1 million immigrants per year, the nation gains about $20 billion more than cost. Rather than fiscal burdens, immigrants are huge bargains.

Nor do immigrants harm the U.S. labor market. A comprehensive 1989 study by the U.S. Department of Labor concluded: "Neither U.S. workers nor most minority workers appear to be adversely affected by immigration—especially during periods of economic expansion." In the 1980s, the top 10 immigrant-receiving states —including California, Florida, Massachusetts and Texas—recorded rates of unemployment 2 percentage points below the U.S. average, according to the

Alexis de Tocqueville Institution in Arlington, Va. So where's the job displacement?

We are now witnessing in America what might be described as the return of the nativists. They are selling fear and bigotry. But if any of their allegations against immigrants are accurate, then America could not have emerged as the economic superpower it is today.

In fact, most Americans do accept that immigration in the past has contributed greatly to the nation's economic growth. But they are not so sanguine in their assessment of present and future immigrants. It is strangely inconsistent that Americans believe that so long-standing and crucial a benefit is now a source of cultural and economic demise.

Shortly before his death, Winston Churchill wrote, "The empires of the future are the empires of the mind." America is confronted with one of the most awesome opportunities in world history to build those empires by attracting highly skilled, highly educated and entrepreneurial people from all over the globe. The Andrew Groves and the Paul Chus of the world do not want to go to Japan, Israel, Germany, France or Canada. Almost universally they want to come to the United States. We can be selective. By expanding immigration but orienting our admission policies toward gaining the best and the brightest, America would enjoy a significant comparative advantage over its geopolitical rivals.

By pursuing a liberal and strategic policy on immigration, America can ensure that the 21st century, like the 20th, will be the American century.

POSTSCRIPT

Should the United States Put More Restrictions on Immigration?

James's proposal for dealing with what he views as the immigration crisis is a radical one: a moratorium on immigration coupled with a national I.D. card for certifying legal status. When the latter proposal was first brought up in Congress in the early 1980s, there were cries of "gestapo." As for the moratorium, that was done once before, in 1924, for eastern and southern European immigration, and it was later called racist. James argues that the breathing spell it afforded helped in the assimilation of Italian, Jewish, and Slavic immigrants. Assuming that is true, a few questions remain: Did the assimilation justify the restriction? Is assimilation necessarily desirable?

Ronald Takyaki, *Strangers from a Different Shore: A History of Asian Americans* (Little, Brown, 1989) is a noted history of Asian immigrants that describes the racism that they faced. Stanley Lieberson and Mary C. Waters, in *From Many Strands* (Russell Sage Foundation, 1988), show that ethnic groups from European origins are assimilating, marrying outside their groups, and losing their ethnic identities. Two major works debate whether or not immigrants, on average, economically benefit America: George Borjas, *Friends or Strangers* (Basic Books, 1990), says that they do not, and Julian L. Simon, *The Economic Consequences of Immigration* (Basil Blackwell, 1989), insists that they do. Wilton S. Dillion, *The Cultural Drama: Modern Identities and Social Ferment* (Smithsonian Institution, 1974) is a collection of essays exploring the tension between cultural diversity and American identity. Lawrence Auster, in *The Path to National Suicide: An Essay on Immigration and Multiculturalism* (American Immigration Control Foundation, 1990), argues that more Third World immigration will undermine America's cultural unity. See also Peter Brimelow, "Time to Rethink Immigration?" *National Review* (June 22, 1992). Disagreeing with this viewpoint are Ben Wattenberg and Karl Zinmeister, "The Case for More Immigration," *Commentary* (April 1990), and Francis Fukuyama, "Immigrants and Family Values," *Commentary* (May 1993).

The recent waves of immigration have apparently overwhelmed the federal Immigration and Naturalization Service (INS). From September 11 to 15, 1994, the *New York Times* ran a series of investigatory articles on corruption, incompetence, and lack of morale in INS offices throughout the country. Among its findings: "Telephones go unanswered, mail goes unopened, and immigrants stand in day-long lines that often lead them to surly, untrained workers who cannot answer their questions." Though the INS is a Justice Department bureau, even Attorney General Janet Reno has trouble getting through by phone!

As the *New York Times* reported in the last one of the five articles ("Insider's View of the I.N.S.: 'Cold, Rude and Insensitive,'" by Deborah Sontag with Stephen Engleberg, September 15, 1994): "The agency expends most of its effort serving more than four million people from around the world who each year make simple and perfectly legal requests for benefits, from working papers to citizenship. Every one of these clients pays a fee, generating $575 million this year [1994], or a third of the agency's budget. Yet immigration officials acknowledge that the agency often fails to provide them with humane, efficient service.... 'We're a monopoly, yet we make people suffer,' said Phil Waters, the acting director of the agency's San Francisco office. 'It's crazy. People are paying good money to get service from the Government, and we're not giving it.'"

The article further observed that, in part, the difficulties at the INS grow out of its twofold mission, which is sometimes viewed by outsiders as in conflict: "On the one hand, the agency polices the borders and airports, arrests criminals and expels illegal immigrants. On the other, it provides services to an overwhelming majority who travel or already live here legally."

Clearly, immigration poses many questions to be resolved, but like most of the issues debated in this book, there is little consensus about how immigration should be handled.

ISSUE 21

Is America Declining?

YES: Edward N. Luttwak, from "Is America on the Way Down? Yes," *Commentary* (March 1992)

NO: Robert L. Bartley, from "Is America on the Way Down? No," *Commentary* (March 1992)

ISSUE SUMMARY

YES: Foreign policy strategist Edward N. Luttwak contends that Japan and Europe will soon be richer than the United States because of the failure of America's economic policies and social programs.

NO: *Wall Street Journal* editor Robert L. Bartley asserts that America is, and will remain, the wealthiest country and that it will continue to play the role of world leader.

After World War II the United States emerged as the most powerful nation in the world. In part this was because of the cumulative economic costs of two world wars for Germany, Great Britain, Japan, and the Soviet Union. America escaped the physical devastation that these nations suffered, and its economy boomed during and after World War II. With its unequalled prosperity and power, the United States assumed international leadership in armaments, investments, and aid.

Changing circumstances have raised serious questions regarding that leadership role: *Is it necessary?* Many Americans believe that, with the dissolution of the Soviet Union, sharp cuts in America's military forces and commitments abroad are possible. *Can we afford it?* America is no longer clearly the world's most prosperous nation. Between 1980 and 1992, its national debt more than quadrupled, from $900 billion to more than $4 trillion. America must make hard choices, and when unemployment is high and the economic future not promising, domestic needs are likely to receive the highest priority.

Even though public opinion polls show some pessimism, it is difficult for Americans to accept the view that this nation's power and influence will not endure. Yet historians have always noted the rise and fall of great powers, as has contemporary historian Paul Kennedy in his widely acclaimed and much debated book *The Rise and Fall of the Great Powers* (Random House, 1987). Kennedy summarized his thesis thusly: "The historical record suggests that there is a very clear connection *in the long run* between an individual Great Power's economic rise and fall and its growth and decline as an important military power (or world empire)." Nations must spend to create the armies and navies that protect their wealth and security; but if they spend too much, they weaken their economic competitiveness. "Imperial overstretch" is Kennedy's term for the tendency of great powers to commit too much wealth to overseas commitments and too little to domestic economic growth.

Kennedy identified the loss of power with the decline of economic competitiveness. In his account, the most powerful nations in the last five centuries —successively, Spain, the Netherlands, France, and England—were unable or unwilling to tax themselves sufficiently to pay for their armed forces and empires, and the United States now finds itself in a comparable position. The greater the power of a state, the greater the expenditure that must be made to support it.

There is an almost instinctive American rejection of any theory that even suggests that historical forces determine our fates independent of our wills. Public rhetoric expresses a conviction that there is little that Americans cannot achieve, if they will it and work to achieve it. The qualities that made it possible for earlier American generations to settle a subcontinent and make it prosper—idealism, dedication to a common purpose, a willingness to sacrifice for significant long-range goals—can enable this generation to keep America prosperous and powerful into the future.

A further objection is that Kennedy's generalizations confuse different cases. After all, the United States has not created an international empire similar to those established by Spain, France, or England. To be sure, the United States, by virtue of its military and economic power, has exercised leadership; but that is very different from direct domination. American support for the United Nations, economic aid to rebuild war-torn Europe, and mutual security acts with the noncommunist nations of Europe and Asia have been the acts of an ally, not a conqueror.

The collapse of the Soviet Union and its communist allies appears to leave the United States as the only superpower, rebutting predictions of America's decline. However, if the measure of power is now economic and not military, Japan and a newly united Europe emerge as formidable challengers to American dominance and leadership.

The issue of decline cuts across ideological lines. In the following selections, two conservatives, Edward N. Luttwak and Robert L. Bartley, reach opposite conclusions based on their interpretations of America's role in the post–cold war era.

YES   Edward N. Luttwak

IS AMERICA ON THE WAY DOWN?

When will the United States become a third-world country? One estimate would place the date as close as the year 2020. A more optimistic projection might add another ten or fifteen years. Either way, if present trends simply continue, all but a small minority of Americans will be impoverished soon enough, left to yearn hopelessly for the lost golden age of American prosperity.

Nor can American decline remain only economic. The arts and sciences cannot flower and grow without the prosperity that pays for universities, research centers, libraries, museums, the theater, orchestras, ballet companies. It was the ample earnings of Italian traders and bankers that fed the scholars, painters, sculptors, architects, and poets who gave us the Renaissance. When Italy was by-passed by the new flows of oceangoing trade, its impoverished merchants and bankrupt financiers could no longer commission artists or keep scholars at their work, so that economic decline was followed in short order by the bleak downfall of Italian art and scholarship.

Finally, democracy too must become fragile once better hopes are worn away by bitter disappointment. What Americans have in common are their shared beliefs, above all in equality of opportunity in the pursuit of affluence. It would be too much to expect that democratic governance would long survive the impoverishment of all Americans except for a small privileged minority of inheritors, agents of foreign interests, and assorted financial manipulators.

When Buenos Aires was still a leading world metropolis, when the people of Argentina still enjoyed their famous steak-at-every-meal abundance that lasted into the 1950's, they would never have believed that their future would be a 40-year slide into poverty. Equally, the citizens of the U.S., still today by far the richest country in the world, steadfastly refuse to recognize what future is in store for them unless they can alter the course they are now on. Yet the simplest numbers confirm the slide, and suggest the chilling forecast.

From Edward N. Luttwak, "Is America on the Way Down? Yes," *Commentary* (March 1992). Copyright © 1992 by The American Jewish Committee. Reprinted by permission of *Commentary* and the author. All rights reserved. Notes omitted.

* * *

In 1970, Americans were two-and-a-half times as productive as the Japanese, and twice as productive as the citizens of the European Community on average. By 1980, the pattern of decline had already set in. The United States was still well ahead of the European Community and Japan, but its edge has been cut in half in a mere ten years, while West Germany had actually overtaken it.

At that point, in 1980, a simple straight-line projection of the sort that professional economists deplore as much too simplistic would have suggested that in one more decade the United States would be overtaken by the richer Europeans and by Japan. And that is exactly what happened.

This being a 20-year trend and not just a brief downturn, it is perfectly reasonable to calculate what the future numbers would be if the United States were to remain on its present path. Already in the year 2000, Japan's gross national product per person would be twice that of America, while the richer European countries would have a 50-percent edge over the United States. Ten years after that, Japan would be more than three times as productive per person as the United States, and the richer European countries would be almost twice as productive per person as the United States.

Finally in 2020, when the children of today's middle-aged Americans will themselves be middle-aged, the richest Europeans would be more than twice as productive, while the gap between Japanese and Americans at 5-to-1 would be just about the same as the 1980 gap between Americans and Brazilians. At that point, the United States would

definitely have become a third-world country—at least by Japanese standards. Certainly Americans would no longer be in the same class as West Europeans....

* * *

There is no doubt that to project the future by simply extending the past is a procedure truly simplistic, because unexpected changes can always outweigh continuities. But so far, at least, the path seems straight enough—and straight downhill. It is also true that international comparisons can easily be distorted by abrupt exchange-rate fluctuations: one reason Switzerland reached the astounding gross national product of $30,270 per person in 1989 was that the Swiss franc happened to be very high during that year. Moreover, all fluctuations aside, exchange rates routinely deform comparisons because they reflect only the *international* supply and demand for capital, goods, and services denominated in any particular currency (as well as speculation and central-bank manipulations), and not the much greater amount of purely domestic transactions. Hence currencies can be greatly overvalued or undervalued as compared to their purchasing power at home.

Because the United States has chosen to open its markets to imports to a much greater extent than most other countries, let alone famously import-phobic Japan and Korea, the great outflow of dollars reduces the exchange rate far below the dollar's purchasing power at home. If we rely on a measure based on purchasing-power parities, we find that the United States scores much higher in international comparisons. Yet while purchasing-power values can depict living standards more or less realistically, it is only comparisons based on straight exchange rates that determine the "who-does-what-to-whom" of the international economy—including the little matter of which parties can buy attractive pieces of other (open-door) economies, and which parties can only sell them off. And that, of course, can make the enjoyment of even splendid living standards somewhat ephemeral.

Finally, if we switch to the purchasing-power plus gross-domestic-product criterion, we find that although the United States is still ahead, the trend is just as unfavorable as it is with other measures, and the pattern of relative decline just as evident.

To be sure, both the gross national product and the gross domestic product are indeed gross measures: a car accident increases both of them by the amount of ambulance, hospital, and bodyshop bills, while a healthy drop in cigarette smoking reduces them as sales and excise taxes go down. Nor can any international comparison be free of all sorts of distortions, large and small, no matter what criterion is employed, if only because the different consumption preferences prevalent in different countries are hard to equate. And yet, after all possible objections and all proper reservations are listed, it cannot finally be denied that the totality of all the relevant numbers contains irrefutable evidence that the American economy has long been in severe decline by world standards—and still is.

* * *

Many observers would reach the same verdict without need of any numbers. Follow a traveler from Tokyo to New York—though it would be much the same if he came from Zurich, Amsterdam, or Singapore. After leaving his taxi at Tokyo's downtown City Air Terminal —a perfectly ordinary Tokyo taxi and therefore shiny clean, in perfect condition, its neatly dressed driver in white gloves—our traveler will find himself aboard an equally spotless airport bus in five minutes flat, with his baggage already checked in, boarding card issued, and passport stamped by the seemingly effortless teamwork of quick, careful porters who refuse tips, airline clerks who can actually use computers at computer speed, passport officers who act as if it were their job to expedite travel, and bus crews who sell tickets, load baggage, and courteously help the encumbered while strictly keeping to departure schedules timed to the exact minute.

Then, after an hour's bus ride over the crowded expressway to the gleaming halls of Tokyo's Narita international airport, and after the long trans-Pacific flight, when our traveler finally arrives, he will be confronted by sights and sounds that would not be out of place in Lagos or Bombay. He has landed at New York's John F. Kennedy airport.

Instead of the elegance of Narita, or Frankfurt, or Amsterdam, or Singapore, arriving travelers at one of the several JFK terminals that belong to near-bankrupt airlines will find themselves walking down dingy corridors in need of paint, over frayed carpets, often struggling up and down narrow stairways alongside out-of-order escalators. Those are JFK's substitutes for the constantly updated facilities of first-world airports. The rough, cheap remodeling of sadly outdated buildings with naked plywood and unfinished gypsum board proclaims the shortage of long-term money to build with, of invested capital. Equally, the frayed carpets, those defective escalators, and the pervasive minor dirt reveal how day-to-day money is being saved:

by deferred maintenance—the most perfect sign of third-world conditions, the instantly recognizable background of South Asian, African, and Latin American street scenes, with their potholed streets, dilapidated buildings, crudely painted signs, and decrepit buses.

If the sheer lack of capital to provide proper facilities is the first third-world trait, the second is undoubtedly the lack of skill and diligence in the labor force. This phenomenon will be brutally obvious as soon as our traveler arrives in the customs hall, where baggage is contemptuously thrown off the incoming belts in full view of the hapless passengers. By then he will be too exhausted to complain: after a long flight, he is likely to have waited for hours to have his passport examined.

In due course, if our traveler transfers to a domestic flight, he may well encounter airline porters already paid to place suitcases on conveyor belts who nevertheless ask for tips in brusque undertones, just as in Nairobi or Karachi, sometimes hinting that the baggage might not arrive safely if no money changes hands. And he will in all probability then be trapped in slow lines while imminent flight departures are called out, waiting to be checked in by untrained clerks who tap on computer keyboards very slowly, with one finger.

Here, then, is the final trait typical of the third world—the chronic disorganization of perfectly routine procedures.

If our traveler is headed for a Manhattan hotel, he can choose between a dirty, battered, and possibly unsafe bus, or a dirtier and more battered taxi, usually driven by an unkempt lout who resembles his counterparts in Islamabad or Kinshasa rather than in London or Tokyo, where licensing requirements are strict

and dress codes are enforced. At that point, a first-time visitor may still believe that both airport and taxi are glaring exceptions to the America he had always imagined—clean, modern, efficient. If so, he will immediately be disillusioned by the jolting drive over potholed highways and crumbling bridges, through miles of slums or miserable public housing.

Not as colorful as in Jakarta or Madras, the passing scene will still amaze those who come from the many European and even Asian cities where slums are now reduced to isolated survivals in remote parts of town (New York tour guides report a growing demand for the thrills of the South Bronx from European tourists quite uninterested in its pleasant greenery or the zoo, but eager to see open-air drug dealing at street corners, and the rows of burned-out buildings). After this unsettling encounter with an America already in full third-world conditions, an affluent tourist will next reach the luxurious glitter of a Manhattan hotel, but even there beggars may be standing near the door, just as in New Delhi or Lima.

* * *

It seems only yesterday that the professional optimists among us were still pointing to the continued American dominance of the world's entertainment, biotechnology, and aviation industries to reassure us that all was well, in spite of the virtual extinction of the U.S. consumer-electronics industry, the steady retreat of the auto industry, the drastic decline of the steel industry, and the widespread collapse of the machine-tool industry, still very much the foundation of all other industries.

Since then, Columbia Pictures has been sold to Sony, which had already purchased CBS Records in a previous transaction; the multimedia industry leader MCA has been sold off to Matsushita; Time-Warner, which includes HBO, has been partly sold to Toshiba and C. Itoh for $1 billion; and other notable names now belong to French and Italian interests. Word has it that it is only a matter of time before the remaining entertainment giants will go on the block in full or in part. Even hugely successful Disney, long the toast of Wall Street, chose to sell off the ownership of the hugely profitable Disneylands in France and Japan to local investors, in a typical exercise of capitalism-without-capital in the New American style.

Thus, Michael Jackson records may still sell by the millions all over the world, and American films may continue to dominate the global market, but the profits and the resulting opportunity for further capital accumulation now accrue to foreign owners.

Then there is the biotechnology industry, the *locus classicus* of the dynamic creativity and bold entrepreneurship that are supposed to compensate for all the other weaknesses of the American economy. The names of both buyers and sellers are far more obscure than in the Hollywood pairings, and the deals are much smaller (e.g., Chugai's $100 million purchase of Gen-Probe), but the great sell-off is under way just the same.

The pattern is by now well established. Americans still do most of the inventing, but because they cannot find capital at home to build the required facilities, they sell out to Japanese and European companies, receiving millions in license fees for products whose sales can eventually earn billions. Unfortunately, it is only those millions—and not the billions that will be earned mainly by foreign companies—

that can be taxed to pay for basic research as well as all other government expenditures. As it is, the United States spent $5 billion on biotechnology research in 1990 as compared with only $1.7 billion for Japan, and less for Europe, but it is the Japanese and Europeans who are prospering, in great part by selling products originally developed in the U.S., mostly at the taxpayers' expense....

* * *

When a farmer is reduced to selling off his broad acres rather than only his crops, his ultimate fate is not in doubt. Of course the analogy should be false because instead of a waning stock of acres, there is the unending flow of new technology that comes from the constantly celebrated creativity of our pluralist, multi-ethnic, undisciplined but ever-dynamic society.

Note, however, the small print that accompanied the dramatic announcement of the very latest example of that famous creativity. As soon as the suitably Korean-born chief developer of digital High-Definition (HD) TV revealed that the suitably small company he works for had totally overtaken the Japanese giants and their merely analog HD-TV, the company's owner, General Instrument, let it be known that it would not even try to raise the capital needed to produce and market the new invention, preferring to license production to established TV manufacturers, i.e., the Japanese TV giants.

In a manner literally pathetic, for pathos is the emotion evoked in the spectators to an inevitable downfall, a company spokesman hopefully speculated that if 20 million HD-TV sets were sold annually, its royalties at $10 per set could amount to as much as $200 million a year, a nice bit of change as they say—but truly mere change as compared to the $20–25 *billion* that the actual producers would earn each year, largely, no doubt, by exports to the United States.

But that is by now standard operating procedure, given our bootless capitalism-without-capital. It was Ampex, a U.S. company, which first developed the video-recorder technology that was then licensed for mere change to Matsushita, Sony, and the rest of those vigorous exporters—though of course their VCR export earnings did come back to the United States, through the purchase of CBS Records, Columbia Pictures, and MCA.

It is all very well to speak of the "globalization of industry" and to deride concerns for the nationality of production in an era of "transnational manufacturing," but when Taiwan acquires 40 percent of Douglas, or Japan's consortium has 20 percent of the next Boeing airliner, they assume no such responsibility for funding future U.S. aviation research, or Medicare for that matter—and the future earnings from those efforts will accrue to their balance of payments, and not ours.

* * *

What is happening to the U.S. aviation industry in particular exposes the embarrassingly wide gap between the realities of what I have labeled geoeconomics, and the free-trade-plus-globalization fantasy that remains unchallenged dogma for so many Americans, not least in the Bush White House.

To begin with, the American aviation industry's only significant foreign competitor is the European consortium Airbus Industrie, which has been very successful of late even against Boeing, by selling its government-subsidized aircraft with the aid of government-subsidized loans at low interest. Similarly, Taiwan Aerospace is a government-guaranteed company, no more exposed to the vagaries of the free market than the Vatican; as such, it will always be able to count on government subsidies to underbid Douglas subcontractors, thereby taking over specialized manufactures conducive to its own planned growth into an independent maker of civilian airliners.

The wider meaning of such narrowly-aimed industrial subsidies and "national technology programs" is plain enough. Just as past generations were put in uniform to be marched off in pursuit of geopolitical schemes of territorial conquest, today's taxpayers in Europe and elsewhere have been persuaded to subsidize geo-economic schemes of industrial conquest. The free-trade true believers smile at such foolish generosity, and invite us to enjoy the resulting subsidy of our own consumption. Thus they safeguard the interests of the citizen-as-consumer, while ignoring the interests of the citizen-as-producer, but of the two roles it is only the latter that comports with the satisfactions of achievement and the dignity of employment. Moreover, the benefits of subsidized consumption that displaces our own production can only last so long as we still have acreage, famous buildings, golf courses, industries, and new technologies to sell off.

As for globalization, while 40 percent of Douglas can freely be bought by Taiwan, or 40 percent of Boeing could be bought by Japan at any time, a U.S. buyer would have rather greater chances of being allowed to acquire 40 percent of the Sistine Chapel than 40 percent of Mitsubishi Industries.

It is this flat refusal of reciprocity that justifies concerns over the scope of Japanese direct investment in U.S. manufacturing and research companies —far more consequential acquisitions than Rockefeller Center or any number of golf courses. At the last count, total European direct investment in the U.S. was still very much larger, at $262 billion, than Japan's $69.7 billion. But it is not racism that accounts for the widespread concern over the latter and not the former, as even well-informed Japanese sincerely believe. Almost all European countries positively encourage almost all U.S. acquisitions and almost all forms of U.S. investment, while in Japan, as in Korea, only the likes of soft-drink bottling plants can be established or acquired without hindrance.

For free-trade-plus-globalization true believers, this entire discussion of foreign investment in the U.S., and of the barriers to U.S. investment in Japan and Korea, misses the point entirely. Foreign investment, they ceaselessly point out, brings jobs, thereby neatly offsetting the consequence of their other article of faith: import-caused unemployment. Equally, U.S. investment abroad exports jobs, and if other countries are foolish enough to keep it out, the loss of optimal earnings for capital is compensated by the retention of employment within the United States. Both claims are perfectly valid, but to leave it at that, as many do, ignores the wider implications of foreign investment on both sides.

In the first place, when U.S. auto production, for example, is displaced by the output of foreign-owned "transplants," the complete employment pyramid of technical designers, development engineers, stylists, corporate managers, and sundry ancillary professionals is decapi-

tated, leaving only the base of assembly-line workers with a few junior-executive positions thrown in.

And this is precisely the object of the geo-economic competition that is increasingly dominating the main arena of world affairs, now that geopolitics is being provincialized to the unfortunate lands where armed conflict is still plausible, if not actually under way. The goal of geo-economics is not to accumulate gold, as in mercantilism, for it is not kings in need of coin to pay their regiments who are the protagonists, but rather corporate executives and their bureaucratic allies. Their aim is not territorial security or territorial expansion but its geo-economic equivalent: the conquest of the more desirable roles in the world economy.

Thus geo-economics is the very appropriate expression of meritocratic ambitions projected onto the world scene, just as geopolitics once expressed quintessentially aristocratic ambitions. Transplants do replace some of the jobs lost to imports, but what jobs? Are they the jobs that we would want for our children?

* * *

None of this is to say that Japanese corporate expansionism, or foreign interests in general, are responsible for the woes of the American economy. Decades of unilateral market access have undoubtedly weakened American businesses and contributed to their decapitalization. But it would obviously be foolish to blame foreigners for our own policies, and our own delusions. I do not recall any commandos from Japan's Ministry of International Trade and Industry (MITI) descending on Washington to impose unreciprocated Japanese access to American markets and American technology. Nor can Toyota or Hyundai be blamed if the U.S. government simply fails to insist on reciprocity, trusting instead in the gentle conduct of interminable negotiations that yield insignificant results.

Certainly neither our European competitors nor the Japanese can be blamed for the long list of self-inflicted wounds that have been engendering the third-worldization of America.

They did not arrange the regulatory and business-culture changes that brought the mores and urgencies of Las Vegas to Wall Street and corporate boardrooms across the land, to subordinate both future growth and current employment to immediate payoffs for well-placed principals.

They had no say in the most original invention of American statecraft: representation without taxation to extract "entitlements" galore, so that savings, already scant, have been absorbed in Treasury paper, instead of modern factories or updated infrastructure.

They did not seize control of our classrooms, to discredit the discipline and absolute standards that are the prerequisites of all education, nor lately appoint the "multiculturalism" inspectors who equate arithmetic with racism, and who annex the study of history to group therapy.

Nor did foreigners devise our spectacularly antisocial "social" programs, by now most nefariously entangled in both racial politics and the crudest racism. There are very few Afro-Swedes, yet because Sweden is very generous to unmarried mothers, such mothers account for 50.9 percent of all births, as opposed to 25.7 percent in the less generous United States, and only 1 percent in notably ungenerous Japan, where 99 percent of all children are still compelled to grow up with both fathers and mothers. That,

no doubt, is yet another of those exotic Japanese practices devised by the sinister MITI—certainly nothing enhances a country's competitive position more than a population properly brought up in stable families.

The list is by no means complete. The many new perversions of the administration of justice could add an entire list of their own, from ruinous product-liability awards against the manufacturers of 50-year-old machinery for one-year-old accidents, to the abandonment of the loitering laws, which leaves policemen powerless against urban predators. But even the few dysfunctions listed above would have been sufficient to propel our rapid slide into third-world conditions, complete with an entire generation of children as doomed as the street waifs of Rio de Janeiro. The newborn son of a long-gone teenage father and fifteen-year-old mother, with a grandmother in her thirties and a great-grandmother in her forties—all of them unmarried, uneducated, and unemployed—has become a rather common American type, destined from birth to roam the streets in between episodes of casual labor, crime, addiction, and imprisonment.

A search for the deeper sources of all the blatantly obvious diseases of American society would take us very far —though it might be said in passing that Anglo-Saxon style individualism could only be successful so long as there was still enough Calvinism to go around. But at least the immediate causes of our third-worldization are simply economic, a matter of capital and labor. And while the inadequate diligence of our labor force obviously has no simple cause, the immediate reason for our disastrous shortage of capital is plain enough.

Americans have little to invest because they save so little.

Obviously, it is possible to invest without saving, if others lend the necessary money. And of course the United States has borrowed hugely in recent years, and also absorbed a vast amount of foreign investment. Yet given the size of the American economy, even the huge inflow of money from abroad could not possibly remedy the disastrous difference between our rate of savings and those of our competitors.

*   *   *

In any case, the relentless erosion of the entire economic base of American society is revealed by undisputed statistics that have none of the flaws of international comparisons. During the last 20 years —half a working lifetime—American "non-farm, non-supervisory" employees actually earned slightly less, year by year. As a matter of fact, by 1990 their real earnings (corrected for inflation) had regressed to the 1965 level. Will they regress further—perhaps to the 1960 level by 1995, and then to the 1955 level by the year 2000? It seems distinctly possible. Given the lack of invested capital, it is only with ever-cheaper labor that we can compete internationally. Therein lies our own path to Bangladesh.

Who are these poor unfortunates whose real earnings have been declining since 1965? Are they perhaps some small and peculiar minority? Not so. In November 1990, the last month for which those statistics are complete, they numbered 74,888,000, or just over 81 percent of all non-farm employees— that is, more than eight out of ten of all Americans who are not self-employed, from corporate executives earning hundreds or even thousands of dollars per hour, to those working at the minimum wage.

Far from being a minority whose fate cannot affect the base of American society, then, they *are* the base of American society, the vast majority of the labor force of manufacturing, mining, construction, transport, utility, wholesale and retail trade, finance, insurance, real estate, all other service enterprises, and government employees.

How can the entire structure of American affluence and advancement from luxurious living to scientific laboratories *not* decline when the vast majority of all working Americans are earning less and less? And how can the U.S. not slide toward third-world conditions if this absolute decline continues while in both Western Europe and East Asia real earnings continue to increase?

Inevitably, the most telling comparison is with Japan. In 1970, Japanese manufacturing employees earned only just over a quarter (or more precisely 27 percent) as much as their American counterparts. In 1988, they earned 7 percent more. If the trend were to continue straight on both sides, in 18 more years American earnings would be reduced to less than a quarter (23 percent) of the Japanese level, almost the same proportion as now obtains between Brazilian and American hourly wages in manufacturing.

It stands to reason that by then the United States would become Japan's Brazil, an amusing, sometimes unsettling country of vast expanses with a cheerful but impoverished third-world population. The casual banter that nowadays greets errors of blatant incompetence in American offices, factories, and shops, the patient silence evoked even by acts of willful negligence and aggressive apathy; the learned ability to ignore unkempt urban vagrants and all their importunings; and generally our increasing acceptance of breakdowns, delays, and all forms of physical decay—all this shows that we are indeed adapting to our fate, by acquiring the necessary third-world traits of fatalistic detachment. But they, of course, ensure that the slide will continue.

NO

Robert L. Bartley

IS AMERICA ON THE WAY DOWN?

To the ordinary, everyday sense of mankind, America has not declined, it has prevailed. Its foe of two generations has collapsed and now even seeks to adopt American institutions of democracy and market economics.

Though to people who use their eyes and ears it is obvious that American influence in the world is on the rise, we have not been able to put the notion of decline behind us. For a segment of American opinion refuses to use its eyes and ears. Instead, proponents of decline confuse themselves with statistics they do not understand, or in some cases willingly distort. They invoke jingoism by turning international trade into some kind of combat, instead of a series of mutually beneficial arrangements among consenting adults.

The notion of decline has recently been a fad of the Left, in alliance with a coterie of nonideological special interests. It is instructive to remember, though, that as the 1980's opened decline was a theme of the Right. Conservatives, notably but far from solely Jean-François Revel, warned that the West was falling behind in the military competition with the Soviet Sparta. It found itself manipulated by Soviet campaigns like the one that stopped the neutron bomb. The United States, the natural leader of the alliance, was wracked by inflation and stagnant productivity at home, preoccupied with hostages held by a primitive cleric, and unable even to fly six helicopters across the desert.

In those days, conservatives worried that the West lacked the will to use its superior economic resources even to defend itself. They can take heart that their warnings were heeded, that free peoples found the will to resist, that fear of Communist arms did not stunt them into self-doubt and inaction. But American will is now being tested in a more subtle way by the theme of decline, another recipe for confusion and self-destruction. If America generally falls prey to this delusion, it may throw away its birthright as the hub of a new and progressive world civilization.

On the Right, the notion of decline faded as Ronald Reagan filled the military spare-parts bins, frankly labeled the Soviet Union an "evil empire," invaded Grenada, bombed Libya, revived the option of missile defense. The diplomatic turning point was 1983, when the West withstood a determined Soviet campaign, including street demonstrations and the suspension of arms negotiations, to stop the deployment of Pershing missiles in Europe. At the same time, the United States was curbing its inflation with Paul Volcker's monetary policy and reviving economic growth with Ronald Reagan's tax cuts. Seven years of uninterrupted economic expansion did wonders for military preparedness, diplomatic creativity, and public morale. The economic revival that started in the United States and quickly spread to Europe proved the final undoing of the totalitarian challenge.

The containment policy the West had patiently pursued for two generations predicted that under steady pressure the Soviet empire would mellow or crack. Then it happened at a stroke. In 1989 the Berlin Wall was breached, and by 1991 the Communist remnants proved themselves inept even at coup-making. Meanwhile, an American-led attack decimated the world's fourth-largest army in six weeks of combat and at the cost of 148 Americans lost in action. The world's new military balance was clear, leaving only the mysteries of why President Bush stopped short of Baghdad and how the hysterical Cassandras who had predicted a desert debacle managed to retain their *bona fides* as military experts.

Nor is American predominance merely or even primarily a matter of military power. American ideals of democratic pluralism and market economics were spreading not only in the former Soviet Union but throughout South America, Eastern Europe, and even Africa. America remains the favored destination of the world's refugees and immigrants. Its university system (despite the political-correctness plague) is unparalleled: it graduates many foreign nationals in science and engineering, of course, but many of them choose to stay in the U.S.

For all the accomplishments of the industrious Japanese, America still dominates scientific innovation. Many transnational corporations, even if based in Germany or Switzerland, locate their research divisions in New Jersey or North Carolina. Japanese auto companies open design labs in Los Angeles. Above all, the U.S. utterly dominates the single capstone technology of our era, which in every language is called "software."

* * *

Whatever the momentary economic ups and downs, too, the plain fact is that the United States is the wealthiest society in the history of mankind. Or at least this is plain to the economically literate, who understand that no meaningful comparison can be based on momentary exchange rates among different national currencies. In translating among currencies to make international comparisons, the only meaningful basis is purchasing-power parity (PPP), the exchange rate at which two currencies would each buy the same basket of goods. The Organization for Economic Cooperation and Development spends endless hours of tedious calculation to churn out PPP rates precisely for the purpose of facilitating such comparisons.

Under the current regime of floating exchange rates, currencies can vary widely from their purchasing-power parity. This distorts comparisons and above all trends—for temporary and reversible variations in exchange rates are likely to swamp any changes in underlying fundamentals. As recently as 1985, the dollar was well over its PPP rate, exaggerating the American standard of living. In later years, the dollar has been below PPP, making America look less wealthy than it actually is.

So current comparisons built on current exchange rates show America falling behind, but properly adjusting the comparisons to PPP makes the picture entirely different. *The Economist Book of Vital World Statistics*, for example, found that at 1988 figures and exchange rates, the United States ranked only ninth in the world in gross domestic product per capita—behind Switzerland, Japan, and the Scandinavian countries. But it also reported that at PPP exchange rates, the American standard of living was far above other advanced nations. With the U.S. at 100, Canada rated 92.5 and Switzerland 87.0. Then came the Scandinavian nations and some small countries, including Kuwait. West Germany rated tenth at 78.6, and Japan twelfth at 71.5. Other developed nations trailed.

In short, the American standard of living is substantially above that of Japan and most of Europe.

This is confirmed by physical measures. American automobile ownership, for example, is one car for every 1.8 persons. Iceland has two people for each car, while Canada, New Zealand, and West Germany have 2.2. France has 2.5, the United Kingdom 2.8, and Japan 4.2. Similarly, there are 1.2 Americans per television set, compared to 1.7 Japanese and 2.4 Germans. The United States is also one of the world's great undeveloped countries, with 26.3 persons per square mile, compared to 102.1 in France, 233.8 in the United Kingdom, 246.1 in West Germany, 324.5 in Japan, and 395.8 in the Netherlands. While I have no figures handy, the American standard of living is most evident of all in housing; the Japanese measure apartment sizes in tatami mats.

As for the recent trends, the American economy led the world out of the economic crisis of the late 1970's by staging so remarkable a boom between 1983 and 1990 that it is now hard to remember such bywords as "stagflation" or "malaise" or "Euro-pessimism." In this expansion, the U.S. economy grew by 31 percent after adjustment for inflation, about equivalent to building 1982 West Germany from scratch. Real disposable income per capita rose by 18 percent. Productivity resumed growth after stagnating in the 1970's, and in fact surged in manufacturing. Manufacturing output grew faster than GNP, and exports leapt by more than 92 percent. More than eighteen million new jobs were created, even while the *Fortune* 500 companies pared their payrolls. Tax revenues kept pace with GNP growth and, since this was supposedly a decade of greed, it should be noted that charitable giving grew at 5.1 percent a year, compared with 3.5 percent a year over the previous 25 years.

Again, a remarkable leap in living standards is confirmed by physical measures. In 1980, hard as it may be to remember, only 1 percent of American households owned a videocassette recorder. By 1989, the figure was more than 58 percent. For all practical purposes, every video rental shop in the nation was started during the seven fat years. In 1980, cable-television systems reached 15 percent of American households, mostly in remote areas with difficult reception. At the end of the decade, half of all homes were wired. In 1981, when the Apple II was a hackers' toy, a little over two million personal computers were in use in the whole country. That year, IBM introduced its first PC, and Apple followed with the Macintosh in 1984. By 1988, the two million PC's had exploded to 45 million. Of this number, roughly half were in homes.

* * *

The most remarkable feature of the 1980's, though, was economic globalization. The 24-hour trading markets were stitched together; dollars circled the world at electronic speed. Rock-and-roll invaded Prague and Moscow, and Japanese auto companies built plants in Tennessee (Nissan), Ohio (Honda), and Kentucky (Toyota). "Interdependence" became the new byword, though one inadequate to describe the evolution of the world economy into an organic whole.

As the U.S. economy led the world out of the doldrums of 1982, the world voted with its money. In 1979, foreigners invested $38.7 billion in the United States; in 1980 this number was $58.1 billion. But investment inflows soared to $83.0 billion in 1981, $93.7 billion in 1982, $130.0 billion in 1985, and $229.8 billion in 1987. With the Volcker monetary policy and the Reagan tax cuts, America was where the world's investors saw the most promising return. And demand in America created the export markets that led Europe out of its pessimism.

A great source of the confusion about the American economy, and a great source of the current poor-mouthing, is that the United States has still not come to terms with its integration into the world economy. Thus America's sages gazed on the developments sketched above and decided the sky was falling. In sending their money here those perfidious foreigners expected to get paid back. Indeed, the whole reason they were sending their money here was that they anticipated a higher return here than they could get at home. Their eagerness to invest in America instead of at home was turning us into—shame!—a debtor nation. And, of course, the American

purchases that stimulated the European revival were reflected in—horrors!—a trade deficit.

In 1976 an official U.S. government advisory committee studying the international statistics suggested that

> the words "surplus" and "deficit" be avoided insofar as possible.... These words are frequently taken to mean that the developments are "good" or "bad" respectively. Since that interpretation is often incorrect, the terms may be widely misunderstood and used in lieu of analysis.

Following the committee's recommendations, the Commerce Department stopped publishing most of what had up to then been a plethora of different "balances"—the current accounts balance, the basic balance, the net liquidity balance, the official settlements balance. Because the bureaucrats thought they had to publish something, they kept the merchandise trade balance, which has been used in lieu of analysis ever since.

What the advisory committee understood, and what cannot be emphasized too much, is that international statistics are an accounting identity; they will balance tautologically, by definition. After all, for every buyer there has to be a seller. The various trade balances are only different stopping places in a great circle of transactions. Except for zero, there is no bottom line.

The most constructive way to look at the international accounts is to divide them into three parts, which must by definition net out to zero. The two big halves are, first, trade in goods and services, and, second, investment. These are essentially two sides of the same coin; normally a trade deficit is financed by an investment surplus, or inflow.

And a trade surplus will accompany investment outflows. The third part of the international accounts is called "official financing"; if trade and investment do not offset each other, the central banks have to step in and act as balance wheel—this can represent a problem if, as happened with U.S. accounts in the mid 1970's, there are simultaneous outflows of trade and investment.

In the normal investment-trade seesaw, though, a zero trade balance is not normal or even desirable. The U.S. ran a trade deficit for nearly all of its first 100 years, and generated trade surpluses under the Smoot-Hawley Tariff in the midst of the Great Depression. Normally, a rapidly growing economy will demand more of the world's supply of real resources and run a trade deficit. It will also provide attractive investment opportunities and attract capital inflows. In a healthy world, the two will offset each other, for periods of perhaps a century.

Yet somehow we have come to measure our nationhood by the one statistic of the trade balance. The real mystery is why we even collect it; if we kept similar statistics for Manhattan island, Park Avenue would lie awake at night worrying about its trade deficit. We have even come to view trade as some kind of nationalistic competition. Winning, apparently, is selling more to the rest of the world than we buy from it. Leaving aside the fact that this is ultimately impossible, why? If we could do it, what would we do with the proceeds, bury them in Fort Knox?

* * *

... [F]ar from sinking into decline, America is now at the center of one of the great, exciting moments in mankind's economic history. A second industrial revolution is remaking world society. Not since the industrial revolution itself has technological advance been so breathtaking, or more pregnant with changes in the way mankind lives and thinks of itself.

More breathtaking now, probably, than even then. James Watt's steam engine pales beside what our generation has already seen: the splitting of the atom, the decoding of the gene, and the invention of the transistor and the computers it spawned. These are not only magnificent leaps of the technological imagination, they are potential precursors of currently unimaginable economic advance. Atomic power, unless cold fusion turns out to be real after all, has perhaps not realized what we once thought of as its potential. The first fruits of biotechnology are just now entering the markets. But already the transistor and the rest are changing the world.

Indeed, we live every day with the electronic revolution. As the first industrial revolution changed an agricultural economy into an industrial economy, a second industrial revolution is changing an industrial economy into a service economy. More specifically, into an information economy, in which the predominant activity is collecting, processing, and communicating information. We are headed toward a world in which everyone on the globe is in instant communication with everyone else.

It is this web of instant communication that has stitched the world into increasing interdependence. In fact, throughout this century the world economy has been more interdependent than anyone realized: the Great Depression, for example, was preeminently a world event, and its origins lay in disturbances in the international economy. But with today's 24 hour financial markets and transnational corporations, economic interdependence is hard to miss.

The same web of instant communication is responsible for the political developments that have rocked our age. Orwell, in his *Nineteen Eighty-Four*, saw information technology as an instrument of Big Brother. We are now seeing clearly that it is quite the opposite. The onslaught of the information age played a key role in liberating Eastern Europe and in spreading democratic currents through the Soviet Union and the developing world. The totalitarians have found they cannot control a people in touch with the outside. In Albert Wohlstetter's phrase, *the fax shall make you free.* Big Brother can of course build a society without computers, but that society will not be able to compete in the modern world, as China seems to be learning after Tiananmen Square.

The precision weapons demonstrated with such effect in the Gulf War are also an aspect of information technology. They promise to make combat once again the province of professional warrior against professional warrior; no longer need philosophers talk about "mutual assured destruction"—the targeting of women and children with nuclear missiles. Once we fully understand this, it will redound to the benefit of civilians everywhere.

Naturally our time and our nation have their problems. Americans should take education more seriously, instead of subordinating it to goals like racial balance and asbestos removal. Our legal system should let police enforce the law against vagrants, and should stop inflicting a parasitic tort-bar industry upon us. Our political system is so frozen it seems unable to address these everyday problems.

More broadly, there is such a thing as being too liberated, having too many options. We are still learning to live with our new freedoms. The onslaught of modernity has not been good for institutions such as the family. We are overly susceptible to fads—health scares, for example—and for that matter the fad of declinism.

* * *

For all these problems, what mostly needs to be explained is not what is wrong with America, but how so much of our articulate elite can so completely mistake reality. A great part of the answer is that progress is unsettling, as rapid change always is. Looking back over history, indeed, we see that ages of economic advance have often been ages of pessimism.

In particular, history's all-time champion economic pessimist, Thomas Malthus, published his first essay on population in 1798; this was 29 years after James Watt's first patent in connection with the steam engine. The first industrial revolution, in other words, was the venue for Malthus's gloomy theorizing. He was explaining why economic progress was impossible just as mankind was taking the greatest economic leap in history.

Not surprisingly, the Malthus paradox attracted the attention of Joseph A. Schumpeter, our century's greatest economic historian and one of its greatest economists. One chapter in his massive *History of Economic Analysis* relates how ancient societies were worried about overpopulation, but after about 1600 this changed completely. The prevailing attitude was that "increasing population was the most important symptom of wealth; it was the chief cause of wealth; it was wealth itself."

"It is quite a problem to explain why the opposite attitude," Schumpeter wrote, "should have asserted itself among economists from the middle of the 18th century on. Why was it that economists took fright at a scarecrow?" Malthusian pessimism did not develop despite the progress of the industrial revolution, Schumpeter concluded. It developed because of the progress.

Long-run progress, Schumpeter pointed out, causes short-run problems, and

in the industrial revolution of the last decades of the 18th century, these short-run vicissitudes grew more serious than they had been before, precisely because the pace of economic development quickened.

This is not to say that the short-run problems were imaginary. In the short run, technological advance destroyed agricultural jobs faster than it created manufacturing jobs, especially since guilds and the like created bottlenecks. A type of mass unemployment arose that had been unknown in the Middle Ages, and with it urban slums, gin mills, and great social debates over the Poor Laws. Malthus's pessimism was echoed a few decades later by Dickens. But we now know that during the lives of both men mankind was rapidly building wealth.

If, then, we are currently experiencing a second industrial revolution, it is not surprising to hear such Malthusian themes as overpopulation and the exhaustion of resources echoing through our public discourse. From the primitive technology of a wooden sailing ship, the earth's forces look overwhelming. Now that we have the technological prowess to put men on the moon, the earth looks like a fragile flower, puny beside our own powers.

The rapid change of the second industrial revolution, moreover, upsets established institutions and established elites. As instant information and instant markets erode the power of governments, so too they erode the power of corporate chieftains and labor bosses. We can now all watch the poor chairman of Exxon writhing over an oil spill in Alaska. Many chief executives find themselves displaced, albeit with golden parachutes: half of *Fortune*'s top 500 corporations in 1980 were gone from the list in 1990. Under the force of industrial competition and information on wages and working conditions, labor unions find their private-sector membership declining.

So too with intellectual elites, who find their skills fading in relevance and their positions endangered. Perhaps political correctness in the academy is best seen as a brand of Luddism. And surely much of our articulate class feels threatened in a deeply personal way by the notion that a historic corner was turned under a simple-minded movie actor.

This mixture of neurosis, special pleading, ideological hostility, ignorance, and confusion is obviously a phenomenon to be reckoned with. Indeed, even an unbridled optimist has to admit that there is after all one way America actually could decline. To wit, if this neurotic pessimism becomes a self-realizing prophecy.

* * *

This would be a historic tragedy, for the confluence of the second industrial revolution and the collapse of totalitarianism presents the human race with an unparalleled opportunity. The decade of the 1990's is not a time for pessimism, but a time for large thoughts and large ambitions. The tide in the affairs of men is running, and we must take the current when it serves. The brightest hope for mankind today is that the breaching of the Berlin Wall on November 9, 1989 marked the end of a beastly era that started with the assassination of Archduke Francis Ferdinand in Sarajevo on June 28, 1914.

The consciousness of everyone alive today was forged in an abnormal era, a century of world war, revolution, and totalitarianism. While mankind has always suffered wars and other miseries, our century ranks with the most wretched in history. Technology turned battle from a contest of knights into an assault on whole civilian populations. A Great Depression sank the world economy. With the rise of Hitler and Stalin, the human soul was under siege. World War II dissolved into a worldwide confrontation between the West and Communism.

At issue was the nature of man—a cog in the great dialectical machine of history, or an autonomous individual capable of free will and self-government? If reform succeeds in Russia, or even survives, all this will be history. We will have a new era to define.

The skyline of Paris is dominated by the great monument to an earlier and less gruesome era. The Eiffel Tower was erected for the Paris Exposition of 1889 to celebrate the scientific and engineering prowess of *La Belle Epoque*. *La Belle Epoque*, of course is typically associated with *fin de siècle* Paris, the Paris of Toulouse-Lautrec. It was an age of extraordinary flowering of the arts, when Manet, Degas, and Monet fought the battles that led to the *Salon des Refusés*. It was also an age of extraordinary science, with the likes of Louis Pasteur and Madame Curie. Most of all, it was an age of faith in human progress. Even the dour Emile Zola invoked "a century of science and democracy."

The hub of this civilization was Great Britain. With the Corn Laws it practiced free trade *unilaterally*, to the benefit of its own consumers and the advancement of underdeveloped nations. With the Royal Navy it protected freedom of the seas (and suppressed the slave trade). With the pound sterling, it was the anchor of an exceptionally efficient international monetary mechanism known as the gold standard. Goods, labor, and capital moved freely to their most productive uses throughout an integrated economy spanning two continents and more.

The biggest beneficiary of this system was the United States of America. Open immigration peopled its lands. Open markets in Europe took its grain, at the expense of agricultural interests in Europe and especially England. Despite these sales, its hunger for capital goods was such that it ran trade deficits year after year, but this mattered little because of consistent investment inflows. For, most important of all, the London financial markets mobilized the capital of the civilization as a whole for the prodigious and exciting task of developing the North American continent.

* * *

Today we are in a position to build a new version of the institutions of the *Belle Epoque* and rekindle its spirit. We can hope, too, to avoid another Sarajevo, for the technology of the second industrial revolution is less threatening than that of the first. The Eiffel Tower was the product of a master engineer, in its way a monument to central planning. The smelting of steel and the building of railroads were enterprises that demanded central planning and the mobilization of massive capital. Napoleon had demonstrated how to conscript whole societies for war, and in the ensuing century the experience of mankind taught it efficient logistics and bureaucratic order. The very advance of science led philosophers like Marx to think of "laws of history." In 1914 this technology, combined of course with the recurrent follies of mankind, marched the world into war.

Ever since, we have been struggling to tame the impact of technology and the mindset it engenders. As the assembly line turned men into interchangeable cogs, the centralized, bureaucratic state became a breeding ground of totalitarianism. But the technology of the second industrial revolution empowers the governed rather than the governors. In its constant churning today's technology has a dark side to be conquered, but its bright side offers the hope of a liberating era.

Certainly technology is not everything. Its opportunities must be exploited by the human spirit. Our dilemma is that all of us living in the 1990's have been taught from the cradle not to believe in dreams. We are cynical about politicians, and they

live down to our expectations. Instead of a century of science and democracy we have Andy Warhol proclaiming that everyone will be famous for fifteen minutes. Instead of Toulouse-Lautrec we have Robert Mapplethorpe.

And instead of the promise of world cooperation led by the United States, we have the gloomy apostles of decline, alarmed because goods and capital move across lines someone drew on maps, trying to manufacture conflict out of the peaceful and mutually beneficial intercourse among peoples.

The last time the will of the West was tested, it rose to the challenge. In particular, the American electorate understood that the threat was Soviet Communism, not the military-industrial complex. With the more subtle test of a litany of decline coming out of Cambridge, Detroit, and Washington, there will again be confusion and apparent close calls, but in the end the delusion will not sell. Indeed, given any sort of intellectual and political leadership to frame the challenge, the American nation will rise to the rich opportunity before it.

POSTSCRIPT

Is America Declining?

The publication of Paul Kennedy's *The Rise and Fall of the Great Powers* (Random House, 1987) provided the historical framework for national soul-searching regarding America's future role in the world. Despite the disagreement between Luttwak and Bartley over whether or not the United States is declining, there is no doubt that other nations have been growing and will likely continue to grow in productivity, military power, and international influence.

Pessimism regarding America's chances of remaining the world's most prosperous and most powerful nation is sometimes tempered with hope. Walter Russell Mead urges cutbacks in American commitments in *Mortal Splendor: The American Empire in Transition* (Houghton Mifflin, 1987). Like Kennedy, Mead traces parallels with past empires and concludes that decline is inevitable, but Mead maintains that America can shape its postimperial future.

Steven Schlosstein, in *The End of the American Century* (Congdon & Weed, 1989), concludes that the United States has declined economically because it has become inferior to Japanese society with respect to the quality of education, the stability of family life, the balance between personal and collective welfare, and other social and economic factors.

Pessimism regarding America's power and influence in the post–cold war world is rejected by analysts who believe that the nation has the ability and the will to continue to play a leading role under changing conditions. This is the position of Joseph S. Nye, Jr., *Bound to Lead: The Changing Nature of American Power* (Basic Books, 1990). Nye argues that only the United States possesses great resources of land, population, military power, economic capacity, scientific discovery, and technology.

Kennedy's decline thesis is also rejected by Richard McKenzie, "The Decline of America: Myth or Fate?" *Society* (November/December 1989), and Owen Harries, "The Rise of American Decline," *Commentary* (May 1988). For Norman Podhoretz, the issue is not overstretching or overspending but national will. In *The Present Danger* (Simon & Schuster, 1980), he poses the question, "Do we have the will to reverse the decline of American power?"

Whatever our conclusions, the debate prompted by the theory of decline compels us to examine the nature and consequences of American values and goals in relation to the rest of the world.

CONTRIBUTORS
TO THIS VOLUME

EDITORS

GEORGE McKENNA is a professor of political science and the chair of the Department of Political Science at City College, City University of New York, where he has been teaching since 1963. He received a B.A. from the University of Chicago in 1959, an M.A. from the University of Massachusetts in 1962, and a Ph.D. from Fordham University in 1967. He has written numerous articles in the fields of American government and political theory, and his publications include *American Populism* (Putnam, 1974) and *American Politics: Ideals and Realities* (McGraw-Hill, 1976). He is the coeditor, with Kurt Finsterbusch, of The Dushkin Publishing Group's *Taking Sides: Clashing Views on Controversial Social Issues,* now in its eighth edition, and he is the author of the textbook *The Drama of Democracy: American Government and Politics,* 2d ed. (The Dushkin Publishing Group, 1994).

STANLEY FEINGOLD was born in New York City in 1926. He attended high school in the city and received his bachelor's degree from the City College of New York. He received his graduate education at Columbia University and taught political science at City College. From 1970 to 1974, he was given a special appointment as Visiting Professor of Politics at the University of Leeds, England. At present he is a professor at Westchester Community College, a unit of the State University of New York.

STAFF

Mimi Egan   Publisher
Brenda S. Filley   Production Manager
Libra Ann Cusack   Typesetting Supervisor
Juliana Arbo   Typesetter
Lara Johnson   Graphics
Diane Barker   Proofreader
David Brackley   Copy Editor
David Dean   Administrative Editor
Richard Tietjen   Systems Manager

AUTHORS

HERBERT E. ALEXANDER is the director of the Citizens Research Foundation in Los Angeles, California, and a professor of political science at the University of Southern California, Los Angeles.

DICK ARMEY, congressman (R) from Texas, 26th District (1985–present; term ends 1995), is the ranking Republican member of the Joint Economic Committee. He is also a member of the Education and Labor Committee and on the Banking, Finance, and Urban Affairs Committee. He received a B.A. from Jamestown College, an M.A. from the University of North Dakota, and a Ph.D. in economics from the University of Oklahoma. Before running for Congress, he was the chairman of the economics department at the University of North Texas.

ROBERT L. BARTLEY, a recipient of the 1980 Pulitzer Prize for editorial writing, is the editor and vice president of the *Wall Street Journal*, with primary responsibility for the editorial page. He is a member of the Council on Foreign Relations and the American Political Science Association, and he holds honorary doctor of laws degrees from Macalester College and Babson College.

FRANCIS J. BECKWITH is a lecturer in philosophy at the University of Nevada, Las Vegas, as well as a senior research fellow of the Nevada Policy Research Institute and a professor at large for Simon Greenleaf University. His research interests focus on areas of ethics, philosophy of religion, social philosophy, comparative religion, and bioethics, and he is on the North American editorial board of the journal *Ethics and Medicine*. His publications include *The Abortion Controversy: A Reader* (Jones & Bartlett, 1994).

JEFFREY M. BERRY is a professor of political science at Tufts University in Medford, Massachusetts. He is the author of *Feeding Hungry People* (Rutgers University Press, 1984) and *The Interest Group Society*, 2d ed. (Scott Foresman, 1989), and he is the coauthor, with Kent E. Portney and Ken Thomson, of *The Rebirth of Urban Democracy* (Brookings Institution, 1993).

CARL T. BOGUS is a contributor to *The American Prospect*.

ROBERT H. BORK is the John M. Olin Scholar in Legal Studies at the American Enterprise Institute in Washington, D.C., a privately funded public policy research organization. He is also a former U.S. Court of Appeals judge for the District of Columbia Circuit.

DAVID CANTOR is a member of the research department for the Anti-Defamation League in New York City.

ROBERT B. CHARLES is a litigation attorney for the international law firm of Well, Gotshal, and Manges in Washington, D.C. He received a B.A. from Dartmouth College in 1982, with highest distinction in government, an M.A. in politics, philosophy, and economics from Oxford University in 1984, and a J.D. from Columbia University Law School in 1987. He is a member of the Council on Foreign Relations, the New York Bar Association, the Connecticut Bar Association, and the Maine Bar Association. He has published a number of articles on constitutional law and politics.

JONATHAN CLARKE, a writer, was a member of the British Diplomatic Service from 1973 to 1992.

RICHARD A. CLOWARD is a professor in the School of Social Work at Columbia University in New York City.

RONALD DWORKIN is a professor of law at New York University in New York City and a University Professor of Jurisprudence at Oxford University in Oxford, England.

TERRY EASTLAND is the editor of Forbes's *MediaCritic* and a fellow of the Ethics and Public Policy Center in Washington, D.C.

THOMAS BYRNE EDSALL is a political reporter for the *Washington Post*. He is the author of *Chain Reaction: The Impact of Race, Rights, and Taxes on American Politics* (W. W. Norton, 1991).

STANLEY FISH is the chair of the Department of English and a professor in the School of Law at Duke University in Durham, North Carolina. Considered to be a pioneering literary theorist, he is the author of more than 75 publications, including *Doing What Comes Naturally: Change, Rhetoric, and the Practice of Theory in Legal and Literary Studies* (Duke University Press, 1989). He has held academic appointments at the University of California, Berkeley; the University of Southern California, Los Angeles; and Columbia University.

LOIS G. FORER (d. 1994) served as the judge of a trial court of general jurisdiction in Philadelphia, Pennsylvania. She received the American Bar Association's 1985 Silver Gavel Award, and she is the author of five books.

DANIEL JAMES is an advisor to Carrying Capacity Network in Washington, D.C., an organization that focuses on issues pertaining to the carrying capacity of the Earth, including immigration, population, and the environment. He is the author of *Illegal Immigration—An Unfolding Crisis* (University Press of America, 1991).

MICKEY KAUS is the editor of *New Republic* magazine.

CHARLES R. KESLER is an associate professor of government and the director of the Henry Salvatori Center at Claremont McKenna College in Claremont, California. He has written extensively on American constitutionalism and American political thought, and he is the co-editor, with William F. Buckley, Jr., of *Keeping the Tablets: Modern American Conservative Thought* (Harper & Row, 1987). He received an A.B. in social studies and a Ph.D. in government from Harvard University.

PAUL KRUGMAN is a professor of economics at the Massachusetts Institute of Technology in Cambridge, Massachusetts. His publications include *The Age of Diminished Expectations: U.S. Economic Policy in the 1990s* (MIT Press, 1990).

CHARLES R. LAWRENCE III is a professor in the School of Law at Georgetown University in Washington, D.C.

MARTIN A. LEE is a cofounder of Fairness and Accuracy in Reporting (FAIR) in New York City, an organization that encourages pluralism in media and promotes free speech and a free press for U.S. citizens. He is also the publisher of FAIR's journal *Extra!*

ROBERT W. LEE is a contributing editor for *The New American* and the author of *The United Nations Conspiracy* (Western Islands, 1981).

LEONARD W. LEVY was the Andrew W. Mellon All-Claremont Professor of

Humanities and the chair of the Graduate Faculty of History at the Claremont Graduate School until his retirement in 1990. His publications include *The Origins of the Fifth Amendment* (Macmillan, 1969), for which he won the 1969 Pulitzer Prize in history, and *Blasphemy! Freedom of Expression and Religion* (Alfred A. Knopf, 1993).

EDWARD N. LUTTWAK holds the Arleigh Burke Chair in Strategy at the Center for Strategic and International Studies in Washington, D.C.

H. JOACHIM MAITRE is a professor of journalism and of international relations at Boston University in Boston, Massachusetts, and the director of Boston University's Center for Defense Journalism.

STEPHEN MOORE is an economist with the Cato Institute in Washington, D.C., a public policy research foundation.

RICHARD M. NIXON (1913–1994) was the 37th president of the United States, serving from 1969 to 1974. His publications include *Nineteen Ninety-Nine: The Global Challenges We Face in the Next Decade* (Simon & Schuster, 1988).

FRANCES FOX PIVEN is the Distinguished Professor in the Graduate School and University Center at the City University of New York in New York City.

DANIEL D. POLSBY is the Kirkland and Ellis Professor of Law at Northwestern University in Evanston, Illinois. He has also held academic positions at Cornell University, the University of Michigan, and the University of Southern California. He has published numerous articles on a number of subjects related to law, including employment law, voting rights,

broadcast regulation, and weapons policy.

SAMUEL L. POPKIN is a professor of political science at the University of California, San Diego. He has been an active participant in and an academic analyst of presidential elections for over 20 years, most recently serving as a consultant to the Clinton campaign in 1992, for which he worked on polling and strategy.

DONALD L. ROBINSON is a professor of government at Smith College in Northampton, Massachusetts.

NORMAN SOLOMON is a media critic whose news analyses and articles have been published in numerous magazines and newspapers. His publications include *Killing Our Own: The Disaster of America's Experience With Atomic Radiation* (Delacorte Press, 1982), coauthored with Harvey Wasserman.

SHELBY STEELE is an associate professor of English at San Jose State University in San Jose, California.

IRWIN M. STELZER studies economic and regulatory policy issues as the director of Regulatory Policy Studies at the American Enterprise Institute in Washington, D.C., a privately funded public policy research organization. The U.S. economic and political columnist for London's *Sunday Times*, the *Boston Herald*, and Australia's *Courier Mail*, he has written and lectured on economic and policy developments in the United States and Britain, particularly as they relate to privatization and competition policy.

MATTHEW L. STEPHENS is a pastor of the Ninth Street United Methodist Church in Covington, Kentucky, and a chaplain at Ohio's Lebanon Correctional

Institute. He is also the chair of the National Interreligious Task Force on Criminal Justice, an organization of the National Council of Churches of Christ.

NADINE STROSSEN is a professor in the School of Law at New York University in New York City and a general counsel for the American Civil Liberties Union.

LESTER THUROW is a professor in the Sloan School of Management at the Massachusetts Institute of Technology in Cambridge, Massachusetts. He received M.A. degrees from Balliol College and Harvard University in 1960 and 1964, respectively, and he received a Ph.D. from Harvard University in 1964. He is the author of *Poverty and Discrimination* (Brookings Institution, 1969), for which he won the David A. Wells Prize from Harvard University, and of *Generating Inequality: The Distributional Mechanisms of the Economy* (Basic Books, 1975).

MARTIN TOLCHIN is a Washington, D.C., correspondent for the *New York Times*.

SUSAN TOLCHIN is a professor of public administration at George Washington University in Washington, D.C.

GIL TROY is the author of *See How They Ran: The Changing Role of the Presidential Candidate* (Free Press, 1991).

FRED WERTHEIMER is the president of Common Cause in Washington, D.C., a citizen's lobbying organization. He is the author of numerous law review articles on campaign finance reform and a series of Common Cause investigative studies on the role of money in American politics. He is a graduate of the University of Michigan and of Harvard Law School.

GEORGE WILL is a *Newsweek* columnist, an ABC News commentator, and the author of several books.

JAMES WOOTTON is the president of Safe Streets Alliance in Washington, D.C.

INDEX